THE RISE OF THE MODERN YIDDISH THEATER

JEWS IN EASTERN EUROPE

Jeffrey Veidlinger
Mikhail Krutikov
Geneviève Zubrzycki

Editors

THE RISE OF THE MODERN YIDDISH THEATER

Alyssa Quint

Indiana University Press

This book is a publication of

Indiana University Press
Office of Scholarly Publishing
Herman B Wells Library 350
1320 East 10th Street
Bloomington, Indiana 47405 USA

iupress.indiana.edu

 The paper used in this publication meets the minimum requirements of the American National Standard for Information Sciences—Permanence of Paper for Printed Library Materials, ANSI Z39.48-1992.

Manufactured in the United States of America

Cataloging information is available from the Library of Congress.

ISBN 978-0-253-03861-6 (cloth)
ISBN 978-0-253-03862-3 (ebook)

1 2 3 4 5 23 22 21 20 19

לכּבֿוד די אַמאָליקע:
Loretta and Morris Gordon (z"l)
Jean and Issie Quint (z"l)

און לכּבֿוד די צוקונפֿטיקע:
Oliver, Julia, and Eve

Contents

Acknowledgments

During the many years I spent writing this book (or thought about writing it), I benefited from the encouragement and good company of many colleagues, friends, and members of my family. I am sincerely grateful for the wisdom and guidance of mentors Ruth Wisse, Jay Harris, Marcus Moseley, and David Roskies. Your valuable scholarship inspired this work. The manuscript evolved into its present form, in part, from stimulating conversation with friends and colleagues. Together we discussed the challenges of seeing the Yiddish theater as embedded in a larger cultural and historical context. For these conversations, and for the many moments of insight and friendship they have shown me, I thank Marion Aptroot, Jeremy Dauber, Elissa Bemporad, Debra Caplan, Glenn Dynner, Stef Halpern, Joshua Karlip, Barbara Kirshenblatt-Gimblett, Rebecca Kobrin, Cecile Kuznitz, Tony Michaels, David Mazower, Ken Moss, Roberta Newman, Eddy Portnoy, Jeffrey Shandler, Vasili Schedrin, Michael Steinlauf, Miryem Trinh, Jeffrey Veidlinger, Jenna Weissman Joselit, and Steve Zipperstein. Thank you to Jonathan Brent and the YIVO Institute for their support while I completed the final stages of this book. For their expertise and willingness to help me prepare the book for press, I owe a debt of gratitude to my YIVO colleagues including Fruma Mohrer, Gunnar Berg, Mila Sholokhova, Alex Weiser, Leo Greenbaum, Ettie Goldvasser, Chava Lapin, Marek Web, Vital Zajka, Ben Kaplan, and Sarah Ponichtera. And to Faina Burko and Yaakov Sklar for help with my Russian translations. Thanks to Harriet Yassky and Noam Green for their editorial work on my manuscript and to Alexander Kotik in Moscow for tracking down many of the Russian-language reviews I mention in this book. Thank you to Dee Mortensen, Paige Rasmussen, Rachel Erin Rosolina, and Carol McGillivray at Indiana University Press for your help in preparing my manuscript for press.

While writing this book, I have benefited from the financial and institutional support of the Memorial Foundation, Harvard University's Center for Jewish Studies, the Center for Advanced Judaic Studies at the University of Pennsylvania, and the YIVO Institute for Jewish Research. I am extremely grateful for this support.

For reading drafts of some or all of this book with enormous patience, generosity, and intelligence, I thank my friends Joel Berkowitz, Shelly Eversley, ChaeRan Freeze, Barbara Henry, Glenn Kurtz, Jessica Lang, Olga Litvak, Jeffrey Veidlinger, and Misha Krutikov.

To my parents, Sylvia and Ted Quint, who have forever showered me with love; to my in-laws, Terry and Aron Steinman, for their loving support and babysitting hours; to my sisters, Jody, Shoshana, and Mia; and my sisters- and brothers-in-law, Deb, Marissa, John, Jonathan, Adam, Adam, and Rob: thank you for your curiosity in my work, and thank you for supporting it when it was the farthest thing from the object of your curiosity. Thank you for watching the kids and, at other times, providing me with irresistible distraction. On that note, most especially, my thanks is owed my children, Oliver, Julia, and Eve, who keep me entranced with all they say and do. And thank you Daniel Steinman, my best editor of all and the love of my life.

Note on Transliteration

Most of the sources for this study are in Yiddish, Russian, and, to a lesser extent, Hebrew, French, and German, so I have had to transliterate the names of people and titles of works. I have transliterated Yiddish according to the guidelines of the YIVO Institute except when a name has currency in English that deviates from these guidelines. Many of the people mentioned in this book used different names in different languages (Abram in Russian, Avrom in Yiddish, and even Abraham in English). In most cases, I go with the spellings preferred by the *YIVO Encyclopedia of Jews in Eastern Europe*. For Russian, I have generally followed the Library of Congress rules without diacritical marks. For Hebrew, I have also followed the Library of Congress rules and avoided diacritics. Unless otherwise indicated, all translations are my own.

THE RISE OF THE MODERN YIDDISH THEATER

The Social Life of Jewish Theater in the Russian Empire

An Introduction

In the eighth of his *Eight Octavo Notebooks*, Franz Kafka (1883–1924), a perhaps unlikely enthusiast of Yiddish theater, recorded the memories of a Yiddish actor named Isaac Loewy. When they met, Loewy was part of a small professional Yiddish theater troupe from Poland that performed in Prague. According to Kafka's transcription of their conversation, Loewy reports that when he was a young boy, his Hasidic parents considered the theater "*treyf*" (literally, unkosher)—"for Gentiles and sinners." Nonetheless, he explained, he was so drawn to theater that he would regularly attend non-Jewish performances in Warsaw's Grand Theater. Before visiting the theater, Loewy would "buy a collar and a pair of cuffs for every performance" in order to blend in with the audience only to "throw them into the Vistula" on his way home. Later, Loewy discovered theater in the Yiddish language: "That completely transformed me. Even before the play began, I felt quite different from the way I felt among 'them' [i.e., the Gentiles]. Above all, there were no gentlemen in evening dress, no ladies in low-cut gowns, no Polish, no Russian, only Jews of every kind, in caftans, in suits, women and girls dressed in the Western way. And everyone talked loudly and carelessly in our mother tongue, nobody particularly noticed me in my long caftan, and I did not need to be ashamed at all."[1]

That night, which took place sometime in the early 1900s, Loewy took in a show by one of roughly ten impresarios who had risen rapidly in the wake of the first Yiddish-language theater staged in 1876 for Russian audiences by its first successful theater producer and playwright, Avrom Goldfaden (born Goldenfaden, 1840–1908). It was Goldfaden's works that Loewy would come to know best. After being the first to stage commercially viable Yiddish-language theater in Romania in 1876, Goldfaden was also the first to successfully negotiate the legal protection of Yiddish performance with the Russian government in 1878. Goldfaden's oeuvre was the most performed work throughout the Yiddish theater's cultural ascendancy. Beyond the productions of his operettas that Goldfaden insisted on personally overseeing, his plays were also rapidly disseminated in manuscript copies as well as in published editions that began publication in 1886; they were even transmitted orally from actor to actor. Loewy himself would come to act in productions of Goldfaden's operettas. We know about these productions, in part, from Kafka's diaries. Kafka avidly attended the Yiddish theater performances and believed they put him in touch with a form of Judaism that he insisted was more authentic than any he had so far encountered.[2]

It is not Kafka's experience of Yiddish theater, however, in which I am interested; it is Loewy's. And Loewy's cultural encounter with Yiddish theater is significantly different from that of Kafka. Loewy, for instance, did not crave authenticity; rather, he sought out performance. As he describes it, Loewy experienced his first evening of Yiddish theater as the shock of the familiar. As he recounted to Kafka, he had already known Jewish performance, albeit sacred performance. "Only at [the Holiday of] Purim was there theater," he recounts, "for then, Cousin Chaskel stuck a big black beard on top of his little blond goatee, put his caftan on back to front and played the part of a jolly Jewish peddler—I could not turn my little childish eyes away from him."[3] As a teenager, Loewy came to know the Italian opera company that performed in Warsaw's Grand Theater: "I heard from Israel Feldscher's boy that there was really such thing as a theater where people really acted and sang and dressed up, every night not only on Purim, and that there was such theater even in Warsaw and that his father had several times taken him to it."[4] Loewy would take in such operas as Giuseppe Verdi's *Aida* and Giacomo Meyerbeer's *Les Huguenots*. Yiddish theater, however, constituted an event in Loewy's eyes that was separate and apart from both of these. In the Yiddish theater, Loewy experienced the intimacy of his native language and clothing blended with the unfamiliar social setting of comingling Jewish men and women in a secular theater house. Against these features, the combination of which he never would have imagined or predicted, Loewy felt unburdened. For one thing, he did not need to alter his appearance; absent is the self-consciousness he had felt among non-Jewish theatergoers. Loewy casually reveals that, on attending performances at the Grand Theater, he adjusted his appearance and dismantled these adjustments as he left, indicating a practice of subtle chameleonism. As much as non-Jewish performances attracted Loewy, he never fantasized about participating in them, putting aside whether that was even a possibility. For Loewy, only the Yiddish theater offered him the opportunity to become an actor and, on a more abstract level, to experience a heightened state of being himself.

Loewy's experience introduces the encounter at the center of this book: the influence of Goldfaden's theater on the lives actually lived by its first actors and, to a lesser extent, the reciprocal influence of these lives on his theater. I concentrate on the modern Yiddish theater's first years from 1876 to 1883, with Goldfaden's theatrical works at the core of a broader inquiry into the social life of Jewish theater in imperial Russia. Hence, my lens on Goldfaden is doubled. Through a study of Goldfaden's libretti and a consideration of the lives of the early members of his troupes, I trace the interconnectedness between culture in the narrow sense of artistic production and culture in the broader sense of social structures, societal divisions, private and public spheres, and self-presentation and self-understanding. I focus on the experiences of Russian Jewish actors, male and female, in the early period of the modern Yiddish theater in light of the Yiddish theater's growing presence in their lives. In this regard, I explore two discrete levels of performance: episodes of (1) social performances that are reflected and even promoted in the (2) scripted performances that Goldfaden staged in theaters. How did the men and women who played on its stage absorb the theater into their lives? Also how is Goldfaden's deep engagement with his actors reflected in his compositions (libretti)? Bound closely to the ideas of identity and social performance, the Yiddish theater illuminates an array of intangibles—strategies of social adaptation, for example—that played out in the lives of the actors. I suggest that the theater reflected a language of performance beyond the stage itself. With "Jewish theater," then, I highlight both onstage and offstage structures of self-conscious performance and the "social life" of my title applies to the circulation of these cultural practices among its actors.

The Yiddish Theater: A Neglected Literature and Orphaned History

The Yiddish Literary versus Goldfaden's Theater

Notwithstanding the importance of performance in the field of modern Jewish history, the story of the rise of the Yiddish theater under the tutelage of Goldfaden, a preeminent figure of the Russian Jewish Enlightenment-cum-Russian theater entrepreneur has never found its place in the cultural record of Yiddish culture. A genealogy of the deep prejudices that have informed the scholarship on Goldfaden and the Yiddish theater may be traced to 1888, when S. N. Rabinovitch (1859–1916), known by his nom de plume, Sholem Aleichem, undertook to impose artistic standards on modern Yiddish literature. Still a budding Yiddish novelist, Sholem Aleichem deemed himself the arbiter of popular taste and, to this end, published the first edition of *Folksbibliotek*, an annual compendium of exemplary works of modern literary Yiddish. Also in 1888 he published an essay, "The Judgment of Shomer" (*Shomers mishpet*) that attacked Nahum Shaikevitsh (1849–1905), widely known by his acronym Shomer, and his pulpy Yiddish novels and romances. *Folksbibliotek* and *Shomers mishpet* were twin efforts at cultural gatekeeping and at cultivating a reader who could distinguish between literary and commercial fare. In his later work, Sholem Aleichem called Shaikevitsh to task for poisoning the tastes of the modern Yiddish-reading public with knock-offs of European potboilers or stories about crooked counts and damsels in distress, none of whom reflect the Jewish experience. A good Yiddish literary work, unlike those of Shaikevitsh, must adhere to the structures of highbrow European literature, Sholem Aleichem insisted in his essay, but must depict a "Jewish" conflict and a "Jewish" resolution.[5] In the first pages of his essay, Sholem Aleichem supplied his reader with the names of the four authors whom he argued were the finest that the eastern European Jewish vernacular had generated to date. Alongside three novelists, Sholem Yankev Abramovitsh (1835–1917), Yitskhak Yoel Linetski (1839–1915), and I. M. Dik (1807/14–1893), who in their works "carried [Yiddish] over from the language of the Bible translation . . . into a living literature," Sholem Aleichem listed Avraham Goldfaden (1840–1908):

> These four giants, these great individuals, forged a new language and breathed the European spirit into our old jargon [Yiddish]. And masses of new readers sprung up! The public took up Yiddish with enthusiasm, with all the passion of the Jewish people. There was barely a Jewish home in which people were not clutching their sides with laughter reading Linetski's *Dos poylishe yingl* (The Polish Lad), published in the first Yiddish newspaper *Kol-mevaser* . . . did not sing the immortal sweet songs of Goldfaden; did not ingest, declaim, and perform by heart the wonderful scenes from Abramovitsh's *Di takse*.[6]

Sholem Aleichem both explicated and took delight in the efflorescence of a refined and high-minded literature that depicted its Jewish subject matter with requisite realism and moral restraint and managed to satisfy the appetites of the Russian Empire's almost one million Yiddish readers.[7]

When he wrote *The Trial of Shomer*, Sholem Aleichem did not yet understand that he and his peers had not yet made their presence known to most Yiddish readers even as their prestige grew among a segment of mostly city-dwelling Jewish intellectuals.[8] Yes, the Yiddish works he describes existed and saw publication. But these novels and plays, including his own works, did not find the commercial audience in the 1870s and 1880s that he had assumed was well in place, given the millions of Yiddish readers who lived in the empire. By 1888, for instance, *The Herald* (*Kol Mevasser*, 1862–1872), the Yiddish-language periodical in which Linetski's anti-Hasidic satire *The Polish Lad* was serialized, had collapsed for lack of subscribers. Its editor, Alexander Zederbaum (1816–1893), had succeeded in attracting literary talent but, as its mere 250 subscribers show, the newspaper failed to reach a wide base of readers. Similarly, Abramovitsh's *The Tax*, a drama about the meat and candle tax levied on the residents of a shtetl by a corrupt Jewish council, was read by a tiny readership of like-minded reformers.

But *The Trial of Shomer* also reflects Sholem Aleichem's willful denial of a prestigious literary figure who had achieved the popularity he coveted: Goldfaden. Sholem Aleichem's admiration of Goldfaden's "songs" can only be a deliberate whitewash of his achievements. Sholem Aleichem knowingly ignored, for instance, Goldfaden's fourteen acclaimed operettas for which he had negotiated a publishing contract with the Warsaw-based publisher Boymritter and Gonshor a year earlier. Far more important, Goldfaden had staged these Yiddish operettas in big-city opera houses for Russian audiences since 1876. He staged his works repeatedly before audiences that, unlike Sholem Aleichem's phantom readers, were real and numerous: theatergoers who bought tickets and wrote reviews. Goldfaden's name was known within and beyond Russian Jewish society as the empire's most prolific composer of Yiddish operettas. In fact, at the time, Goldfaden's public profile was greater than that of any modern Yiddish writer including Sholem Aleichem, a virtual unknown beyond a small coterie of Russian Jewish writers. But even in 1888, by which time Goldfaden had profoundly changed the landscape of Russian Jewish culture, Sholem Aleichem does not deem it necessary to even mention his theatrical works. Goldfaden's Yiddish theater is the elephant in the room, lurking in the shadows of Shomer.[9]

Sholem Aleichem's treatment of Goldfaden was part of a pattern of passive aggressiveness toward Goldfaden's theater assumed by Goldfaden's colleagues and "friends."[10] They conceded his national stature but begrudged him his commercial success and, even more, bitterly resented his embrace of Jewish caricature on the stage. Memoirist Sh. Tsitron recalls hearing Y. L. Peretz complain to Goldfaden that his work suggests that the Jewish people are undeserving of a proper literature. Evoking Sholem Aleichem's "Jewish" ingredient, Peretz could go only as far as to give Goldfaden a backhanded compliment: "Had I talent like yours I would build on much more serious aspects of Jewish life."[11] While it had little effect on Goldfaden's success as an impresario, his peers' low opinion of him poisoned how Goldfaden saw himself and his work—something that is reflected in the copious if unfinished memoirs he began to write in the late 1880s.

The contemporary reception of Goldfaden and his own attitude toward his career, in turn, shaped the perspective of critics and historians. One can trace a line from Sholem Aleichem's willful neglect of all but Goldfaden's songs and poetry in 1888 to the attitude assumed by the Yiddish literary critic Shmuel Niger writing in 1926. Between these points one might contemplate Goldfaden's multiple memoirs of self-loathing and Peretz's negative pronouncements of Yiddish theater (from the 1890s to 1910s).[12] The year 1926, the fiftieth anniversary of Goldfaden's first Yiddish theatrical performances, was marked by an issue of the prestigious literary journal *Literarishe bleter*.[13] But the tributes are half-hearted at best. Niger, doyen of Yiddish literary criticism, pronounced on Goldfaden's oeuvre thus: "Avraham Goldfaden . . . occupies an important place in the history of the Yiddish theatre. He is the creator of today's Yiddish stage, especially of the operetta and melodrama and even with his literary and dramatic work he claims this place more so than he might lay claim to the history of Yiddish literature. He has not, as far as we know, written even one dramatic work that has a real literary-artistic value—even his best texts make sense only when the floodlights of the stage fall upon them."[14]

To the critic Y. Schipper, Goldfaden was a "transitional figure" whose work reflected the primitive performance of Yiddish tavern entertainers.[15] Although sympathetic to Goldfaden's work, the Soviet theater critic Shakhne Epstein echoed Schipper's judgment, if only unintentionally. Distressed that Goldfaden "was never before taken seriously as an artist," Epstein credited a Goldfaden revival (*banayung*) for the development of a theater "emancipated" from its reliance on "the literati" since his theater drew on the "power" of movement and improvisation.[16] Perhaps the tribute of Polish Jewish modernist director and playwright Michał Weichert (1890–1967), however, summarizes most succinctly the state of Goldfaden's legacy, which has remained more or less without revision and unquestioned until recently.[17] Weichert is also dismissive of Goldfaden's written work. He believed that Goldfaden's enduring achievement is "the awakening of the theatrical impulse . . . the inclination toward happiness and play" that animates Yiddish theater.[18] In an effort to cast Yiddish theater as avant-garde, Weichert, among other twentieth-century critics, depicted his theater as an example of primitive folk art. An obvious indication of how far scholars have wandered from historical reality is their depiction of the figure of Goldfaden—notorious during his lifetime for his refined self-presentation and even haughtiness—as a primitive and, elsewhere, a *badkhn*, an uneducated wedding jester.[19]

Yiddish Theater, Commercial and Middle Class

Yiddish critics' dismissive treatment of Goldfaden's work also resulted in the orphaned historical state of Goldfaden's theater, which has received little in the way of contextualization or analysis. Instead of an examination of his work and its historical significance, Goldfaden has grown into a figurehead, "the father of the Yiddish theater," that attracted the energy of apologists and Marxist historians interested in consolidating a lineage of Jewish folk performance. Otherwise, the research on Goldfaden consists of documents meticulously gathered and published with annotations that call out for broader discussion. The analytical scholarship positions Goldfaden exclusively in relation to "the folk" as source and audience of the Yiddish theater.[20] Goldfaden's most immediate audience, however—those that took in the performance of his own professional troupes (and not the amateur troupes that transmitted his works to shtetl residents)—was urban and middle class. This is, perhaps, the most important historical argument of my book, for this inaccuracy alone has generated a host of unresolved discrepancies and mischaracterizations of Goldfaden's person and career that have been duplicated by subsequent historians. Not only has it discouraged analysis of his literary output, but also it has prevented an understanding of his theater's engagement with the Russian middle class for which he composed and staged his operettas. Finally, the close identification of Goldfaden as the father of the institution of Yiddish theater, and a discussion of the theater as his single-handed achievement, has also diverted attention away from the lives of the actors and audience who best reflect the social and cultural consequences of Goldfaden's enterprise.

A precise record of Goldfaden's theater troupe from 1876 to 1883 and an analysis of his work enrich appreciation of the nineteenth-century Russian Jewish commercial audience that eluded Sholem Aleichem. Who paid to enjoy Yiddish culture in late nineteenth-century Russia and why? How did these consumers—and not, say, the publication of the *Folksbibliotek*—drive the growth of Yiddish culture? Literary historian Dan Miron has shown that a narrow swath of educated, multilingual Yiddish writers (Sholem Aleichem among them) spoke in one voice in designating the Yiddish language as debased and the literature they themselves generated as intended for reading only by the semiliterate masses.[21] But in fact, these writers—who failed to tap into a critical mass of their intended readership—constituted much of each other's audience. They created a rarefied hothouse for the incubation of "Yidishe literatur" or "Jewish/Yiddish literature," so called because it projected the values most in keeping with an unofficial ideological vision of the Jewish people. In contrast, the audience of the Yiddish theater contained multitudes. Its viewers were varied in their ethnic and religious backgrounds and in their levels of education and the languages they spoke. In their wake they left a paper trail that evidences their engagement with the theater they viewed—among them, theater notices and reviews published at the time of the performances and copious memoirs penned over decades. Mirroring the discomfort with the Yiddish theater felt by the crafters of the Jewish literary canon, Miron argues that the only worthy Yiddish theater of this era resides in the innate performativity of this rarefied Jewish/Yiddish literature. I want to challenge this assertion with a focus on the literature or libretti of Goldfaden's operettas while paying special attention to the social currency they absorbed and, in turn, quickly accumulated on the stage. I view the libretti of Goldfaden's work not as aesthetic works of genius of little significant context but as socially situated and socially determined—texts that grew from among their producers, actors, and audiences.

My attempt at reconstructing an impression of Yiddish theater's audience, urban and mostly urbane, brings into focus the consumers of the Yiddish theater that we know something about already from previous scholarship. Most of those who took in performances by Goldfaden's troupe had already known the inside of a Russian theater hall. In general, attendance at the theater assumed a central place in the lives of city-dwelling Jews whose numbers climbed throughout the nineteenth century.[22] Michael Steinlauf writes, for instance, that "the Warsaw Jewish plutocracy had become fixtures in the front rows of the State Theaters (*Teatr Rzadowe*), while in the upper balcony (the so-called *paradyz*), Yiddish-speaking Jews in traditional dress were a common sight."[23] And as Jeffrey Veidlinger observes of memoirs penned by Jews in late imperial Russia, "Almost everyone imagined themselves on the stage when itinerant theaters came to town."[24] Yiddish actors who first took in theater as audience members, like Loewy, provide a sense of what it was like to attend the theater during this era. And while Yiddish theater invited some Jewish theatergoers to become theater actors, it invited virtually all its visitors to assimilate performance into their lives.[25]

While little effort has been made to consider the Yiddish theater in its Russian context, it was of a piece with a nineteenth-century Russian performing arts scene that was variegated culturally and linguistically. Decades before the arrival of Yiddish theater, Odessa's opera culture was so passionately embraced by the city's multiethnic population that it formed claques that "usually pitted the Italians and Greeks against the Jews."[26] Yiddish theater benefited immediately from the wide-ranging tastes of non-Jewish Russian theatergoers, which had long included a diet of works in foreign languages as well as the performance of ethnicity on the stage. Considered by many of Goldfaden's colleagues to be ugly, ethnic elements of his theatrical productions played to the expectations of Russia's theater audiences. The government had long regulated what images of Jews were permitted on Russian public stages. Moreover, among the subsidized theaters that operated with Russian state support were Italian opera companies because of Italian cultural primacy and German theater troupes for the sizable and influential German ethnic population that lived in the empire.[27] The latter was particularly important to Yiddish theater in that its venues and audiences were most receptive to Yiddish shows. In his discussion "Ital'yanshchina" about the rise and fall of Italian opera's privilege in imperial Russia, Richard Tarushkin points out that the French opera challenged the dominance of Italian opera in the late 1860s.[28] This is consistent with Goldfaden's mention of composers like Jacques Offenbach (1819–1880), Fromenthal Halévy (1799–1862), Giacomo Meyerbeer (1791–1864), and Alexandre Charles Lecocq (1832–1918) as influential or as sources of important borrowings.[29]

By the late 1870s, a push for indigenous Slavic culture on the Russian stage competed with the enduring presence of imported Western opera and operetta consumed in the original languages and in translation. Goldfaden's works do not register significant Russian musical influence per se. His fluency with Western opera, however, reflects the popularity it enjoyed in Russian opera houses. It was likely that the new focus on Slavic musical motifs by Russian composers inspired Goldfaden to elevate Jewish folk music and integrate it in his operettas. Goldfaden's controversial comic operettas, however, as well as his historical dramas, accounted for only some of the Jewish-themed works on the Russian stage. Russian audiences were comfortable seeing the depiction of Jewish people on their stage in other languages, and Jewish themes drew more Jews to the theater.[30] It is unclear if in Europe, generally, or in Russia, specifically, there was any causal relationship between Jewish themes on the stage and their disproportionate theater attendance, and yet both are true. As Russian historian Richard Stites writes about Russia, "Jews, despite stringent restrictions of Orthodox Judaism and its

Hasidic variant, made their way to the stalls and boxes from Poltava to Romny to Odessa, even though some comedies were slated with anti-Semitic remarks or even centered on an anti-Jewish theme."[31]

The Yiddish theater was one of a growing number of commercial theaters making inroads in the provinces of the Russian Empire while the Imperial Theatres Directorate continued to exert control on the theater performed in Russia, especially in St. Petersburg and Moscow.[32] Its troupes pursued relatively newer Jewish settlements in cities like Kiev, Kharkhov, and Nikolaev and reflected the growing presence of Russia's business elite as investors in cultural life as well as its growing middle class as audience members.[33] Newspaper notices and reviews in non-Jewish Russian newspapers alongside news about the movement of Goldfaden's troupe (often to cities still restricted to Jewish residence or beyond the Pale of Settlement) illustrate that Yiddish theater commanded diverse audiences during its early years.[34] Ironically, the Yiddish theater was shut down by tsarist edict in 1883, when only months before the monopoly of the Imperial Theatres Directorate had been permanently dismantled and private and commercial theater companies had begun enjoying unprecedented freedom.[35]

Methodology and Sources: Approaching Literature and Jewish History

This book is a history of the first years of the Yiddish theater (1876–1883), and it focuses on the life of Goldfaden as exemplary and illuminating of the lives—especially the *mentalités*—of his actors and their shared milieu. This book is neither a literary biography of Goldfaden nor a dedicated treatment of his works. I focus on a brief window of seven years, during which time the modern Yiddish theater decisively coalesced as the product of Goldfaden's carefully crafted public persona and entrepreneurial savvy. Emphasis on performance shifts the lens from pure literary biography to microhistory's thick description of a brief period; it moves away from a concern with ideology to a concern with *mentalités*, in this case, attitudes shared by the modern Yiddish theater's first participants. Finally, it moves away from attention paid to schematic history with broadly applied explanatory power and moves toward the elaboration of revealing idiosyncratic details and local and anecdotal questions captured in source texts.[36] To this end, portraits of the theater's players are anchored in the world beyond the stage, mostly but not exclusively in the lives of Goldfaden and the actors who self-consciously refashioned themselves in Goldfaden's image. I link their behavior to people who adopted strategies of social performance in their daily lives quite apart from the theater. Thus, I deploy a doubled conception of performance that weds the orbit of theatrical performance with the orbit of social performance. The lives of the first actors of the Yiddish theater, men like Yisroel Grodner

(1848–1887), Sigmund Mogulesco (1858–1914), and Avrom Fishzon (1843–1922), illustrate the reciprocal relationship between their evolution as actors on the stage and their embrace of the celebrity and sophistication they thought to be necessary ingredients of their lives off the stage. In this regard, historian Nina Warnke's fascinating study of American Yiddish theater claques (from the 1890s through the World War I era) is an important precedent to my work.[37] Documented aspects of the actors' offstage lives apply to a broader population of Jews whose small-scale improvisations were part of their adaptation to the more secular social and cultural patterns of city life. As Naomi Seidman wrote recently in her book *The Marriage Plot*, "It is now clear to most critics that no single 'secularism' exists (including the Jewish world), despite the universalist claims and aspirations of some varieties of secularism." Seidman argues persuasively that "the abandonment of Jewish practice invites cultural rather than philosophical analysis, drawing our attention to new patterns of (ambivalent, paradoxical, and partial)" behavior.[38] In step with this idea are the memoirs of the actors that repeatedly describe clothing and facial hair (signifiers of Jewish practice) and make no mention of any articles or disquisition on the Haskala.[39]

The Yiddish theater's brands of performance and entrepreneurism registers only faintly in records of the eastern European Jewish experience, which reflects the inclination to privilege ideas when studying the lives of intellectuals. In fact, we know this formative era best, for instance, through the lives of the Russian Jewish intelligentsia and their ideological commitments.[40] For example, Shmuel Feiner's important article, "The Pseudo-Enlightenment and the Question of Jewish Modernization," serves as both predecessor and foil to my book. In it, Feiner highlights incidents of Jews comporting themselves as moderns even though they lacked a philosophical claim to such conduct. Those who possessed the philosophical framework—who spoke in the name of reform—believed its ideology alone to be a way to an authentic modern Jewish self. Feiner acknowledges that, "pseudo-Enlightenment" was a negative coinage loaded with the anxiety felt by ideologues who feared the corruption of the intellectual life of the Jewish people: "The fact is that the term [pseudo-Enlightenment] itself did not correctly define the historical phenomenon to which it referred, and if it is not ascribed to *maskilic* rhetoric it can be misleading."[41] For Feiner, there is a discrete historical phenomenon that exists outside the anxious viewpoint of the maskilim but he stops short of reaching beyond the blinkered view and limited vocabulary of his subjects. Steven Zipperstein, in *The Jews of Odessa*, likewise comments thoughtfully on questions of culture that lay beyond the purview of literary or intellectual orbits:

> The city's intellectuals, though often ill at ease with what they considered to be the materialistic tenor of the city, frequently found themselves and their work profoundly affected by it and by what they believed to be its up-to-the-minute trends, which they felt they could ignore only at the risk of losing touch with

> important new developments. . . . The images that Odessa provided them and many others—most importantly, perhaps, the image of a society almost haphazardly embracing aspects of modernity without systematically evaluating it—gave them a unique and, in the minds of some, also a profoundly disturbing perspective on modern Jewish society.[42]

What place did the "up-to-the-minute trends" play in the lives of Jews of late imperial Russia? Often lacking a textual center of gravity, social performance resists documentation but claims a vital place in an array of forms in the world of the theater and beyond. The discovery and deployment of new forms of social capital, "the ability to assert and deploy one's personality and self-regard"[43] that the historian Eli Lederhendler believes eastern European Jewish immigrants found in America, relate to examples of social performance in Goldfaden's world.[44]

In contrast to the suspicion and dismissal of social performance that register in the works and lives of his contemporaries, Goldfaden's person and theatrical works reflect his strong consciousness of performance. Goldfaden was cut from the same fabric as his Jewish intellectual peers who convened in Odessa and Warsaw and on the pages of a number of highbrow Hebrew and Yiddish journals. Educated in Jewish texts, Goldfaden began his career with the respect of some of the most rigorous Jewish thinkers of his day. While some of his peers ardently embraced Zionism after the pogroms of 1881 and 1882, Goldfaden was among many who continued believing in the eventual emancipation of Russia's Jews. His operettas suggest that he was part of the cohort of Jewish leaders whose commitment to the social reform of the Jews was matched only by worry over assimilation and the fragility of Jewish national solidarity. His deployment of performance was hardly at odds with a steady Russian Jewish identity. Some of Goldfaden's libretti frame the performance of identity as a national act that promotes harmony and stability among Jews and enables their good work for themselves as well as for non-Jews.[45] Two of his most important libretti urge Jewish audiences away from intramural ideological purity. While Goldfaden hardly speaks in one voice about performance—he is, in turns, suspicious of performance but also encouraging of its utility—his model characters are social chameleons who bridge divides by changing their costume or even their religious affiliation. Goldfaden invites fellow Jews to perform the identity that works best for them in the context in which they find themselves. While membership to the Jewish People is by blood alone, intramural divisions are fungible.

More than his politics, however, Goldfaden's own nimble "performance," both on and off the stage, unlocks fascinating and, for the most part, previously unexamined dimensions of his milieu that have little to do with ideology. Goldfaden was a pioneer of self-promotion. Before the staging of his shows, placards imprinted with his image were posted on city streets. His exquisitely groomed facial hair and wire-rimmed glasses became a familiar public imprimatur.

Goldfaden enjoyed a relatively high profile as Russia's foremost Yiddish impresario but he was hardly alone in his dandyish behavior. Jews arriving in Russia's cities from surrounding shtetls and villages worked through unprecedented dilemmas of self-presentation. Goldfaden's preoccupation with self-fashioning only exemplifies the self-fashioning that was a vital part both of the actors' rise and, to varying degrees, the lives of many Jews moving from provincial towns to the empire's growing cities. Here, I track how Goldfaden and his contemporaries executed these changes by way of imitation ("*nokhmakhn*" in Yiddish) and performance.[46] While economic factors were at play in encouraging the preoccupation with appearance and fashion, self-fashioning was hardly the result of embourgeoisement alone. Goldfaden, for instance, was broke when he staged the founding performances of his theater, but he did so, as he describes with relish, in an impeccably tailored suit including top hat, tails, and white gloves.

Goldfaden's Memoirs

The Rise of the Modern Yiddish Theater rereads Goldfaden's libretti and traces the continual movement of attitudes between the aesthetic sphere of his works and the larger culture sphere in which it was embedded. How do Goldfaden's libretti register nuances of the theater's social context and even beyond? Stephen Greenblatt's idea of "the circulation of social energy" offers a critical road map for this project. "Through its representational means," he writes, "social energy" is always circulating between "the mode of theater" and the "society out of which that theater has been differentiated."[47] Likewise, I present Goldfaden's libretti alongside resonant "elements of the society" that I have reconstructed from contemporary texts like newspaper accounts and memoirs. For me, the pleasure of reading resides in the connections among texts that, in this case, illuminate the ways in which Goldfaden's libretti—dismissed by some as cheap knockoffs of European operettas—register the nuances of their Jewish cultural world.

Another set of core source texts at the basis of the story of the rise of the modern Yiddish theater is memoiristic. The questions I raise about Goldfaden's libretti speak directly to the characteristics of the rise of the Yiddish actor, a central topic of my book. I ask, for instance, "What impact of the newly created Yiddish theater can we discern in the conduct, the self-presentation, and self-understanding of its first actors?" I am, thus, interested in culture as defined by David Biale in his multivolume edited work on Jewish culture: "What people do, what people say about what they do and, finally, how they understand both of these activities."[48] In terms specific to my study, what people wore (for instance, did they wear long caftans or short jackets?) and how they conducted themselves (for instance, did they call themselves by their Jewish names or did they adopt Russian ones?) are abiding topics of discussion. My reliance on memoirs, however, makes it so the latter two of Biale's three categories—what people said about what they did and how they understood these activities—take on particular prominence.

I rely on memoir and biographical literature as a historical source and, thus, vociferously dismiss suspicions among some historians that autobiographical works are failed sources of objective truth.[49] My project is framed by Goldfaden's autobiographical writings in which his defensiveness about his theatrical activity and his bitterness toward his colleagues distort his memory of the theater's rise. Still, even parts of Goldfaden's memoirs, alongside the memoirs penned by actors and serialized in the Russian and Yiddish press—and even recollections gathered by oral interview and published by theater historian Zalmen Zylbercweig in his *Encyclopedia of Yiddish Theater*—represent a rich trove of untapped historical information. In particular, memoirs by Avrom Fishzon, Bina Abramovitsh (b. 1865), Jacob Adler (1855–1926), Isaac Librescu (1850–1930), China Braginska (b. 1874), Dovid Kessler (1860–1920), Nahum Shaikevitsh (1849–1905), Bertha Kalich (1874–1939), and Hersh Amasia (b. 1864), I glean the soft tissue of their milieu, information regarding class and *mentalité* that are of particular interest to me.[50] I am persuaded, as the historian Louise Knight argues in her essay "Sibling Rivalry: History and Memoir," that, if read with common sense and against the grain of "the intentional self-presentation" of their authors, memoirs can, in fact, be a reliable historical source.[51] To this end, I consider how the recollections of memoirists align with the evidence other sources provide. I dismiss Goldfaden's self-aggrandizing claims about being the only cultivator of Yiddish theater in his day, for instance, but closely consider his detailed documentation of his clothing and appearance that he wore when stepping on to the modest stage of Shimon Mark's tavern in Iași.[52] Biographies and memoirs are embedded with traces of the behavior and *mentalité* of a class of actors whose converging life trajectories began from a diversity of points along wide and variously intersecting socioeconomic and ideological spectrums. My book, then, provides a historical framework for my rediscovery of the actors' lives as they have been documented—often with relish and charm—by themselves in memoirs, by biographers, and most notably by the self-appointed biographer extraordinaire of the Yiddish theater, Zalmen Zylbercweig, in his legendary six-volume encyclopedia. Rather than presenting a life as a linear set of class, economic, or ideological commitments, the category of social performance emphasizes a subject's social experimentation, the vagaries of human whim, and the many accommodations that compromised beliefs and consistency. What did Jews of this place and era think about in presenting themselves to others? In the case of the players included in the following pages, self-fashioning is a vehicle of self-realization and self-advancement rather than a corruption of moral or ideological values. Like Loewy, many of the actors who played in the theater and, presumably, most of the theater's audience would not self-consciously craft and understand their adaptation to modernity according to the dictates of an article or book. They fashioned their identity in relation to those around them, parsing their sameness and difference with impermanence and adjusting their appearance and conduct either to communicate an identity or to camouflage it—to please their family or to test new social circles and fresh experiences. Loewy's sartorial adjustments before entering Warsaw's Grand Theater reflect his need for performance that transcended Jewish law as they reflect his abiding desire to return to the law's limits after the show. Narrative by narrative, the *mentalités* of the first modern Yiddish theater actors materialize. Many of these narratives are penned by those who initially took in Yiddish theater as consumers and, with time, became actors themselves; in this way, we are privy to the thoughts of the audience, albeit a self-selected group, like Loewy, whose passion for the theater would urge him to join a troupe. Their lives as consumers and then as participants—according to their own words—expand upon the particulars of the culture that the theater generated, a culture that encouraged the performance of one's self on and off the stage as a form of self-realization rather than as thoughtless mimicry (cf., Miron and Feiner). These cultural elements defy the quantification of a social historian or the categories of the intellectual historian. But they also defy, in the most satisfying way, the categories of our current cultural-historical record of the Jewish experience in late imperial Russia. The actors' impressions of their lives in the theater and society, intimate and quirky, unlock dimensions of Russian Jewish life that have been left in the shadow of ideology, religion, and politics by the scholarship that has made us most familiar with this time period. While they hardly speak in one voice, these memoirs offer insight into life trajectories driven by talent, curiosity, and entrepreneurship.

Chapter Outline

This book offers a series of close readings of a selection of Goldfaden's operettas and an attempt to capture their social and historical reverberations in memoiristic literature penned by actors and from actor biographies. Among the operettas I examine are Goldfaden's pastoral *Shulamis*, set in ancient Israel; his controversial comic operettas like *The Two Kuni-Lemls*; and works like *The Grandmother and the Granddaughter* and *The Sorceress* that transcend strict generic categories. Rather than lingering on Goldfaden's grotesque depiction of fanatical and infantile Jewish men or vituperative females that made these works notorious, I try instead to call attention to the complexities of language and social behavior contained in these operettas and to tease out relationships between the works and their first performers. In so doing, I try to unlock the lives of the first actors in Romania and in the Russian Empire during this brief window when the theater was permitted. Instead of returning to the characteristics of these plays that have unsettled the most vociferous of their critics, I focus on their multiple and even contradictory ideological strands, their open-ended meaning, and the way they privilege strategies of social conduct over ideological purity. I challenge Goldfaden's version of his life and the theater that was distorted so heavily by his defensiveness toward his peers and his gripes with actors.

Chapter 1, "Goldfaden, Elite," treats Goldfaden's historical significance as a pioneer of middle-class Russian Jewish culture and eschews the prevailing idea of Goldfaden as a producer of folk culture.[53] It introduces scholarly precision to his cultural contribution and rereads and integrates the sources that had been so carefully collected by previous historians. Drawing on memoirs, his own and those of his peers, I consider how Goldfaden, the son of a modest and pious clockmaker, rose to a lofty social class and then into a celebrity of noble bearing and manner. Goldfaden was a product of his immersion in a seminary that was devoted to Russian and Jewish culture as well as the cultivation of refinement in its students. In the eyes of his peers and in the public eye when he reached it, Goldfaden attached this air of refinement to Yiddish culture. Scholars have misunderstood Goldfaden, in part, because of the very peculiar and complicated state of his memoirs: while he intended to write with gushing praise about his most celebrated years as a successful impresario in Russia, in fact Goldfaden only managed to complete memoiristic and autobiographical pieces about his childhood and first years in Romania. In general, his life-writing is marked by defensiveness and self-deprecation that distort his accomplishment.

"The Rise of the Yiddish Actor" (chap. 2) charts the phenomenal rise of the Yiddish actor in Goldfaden's image, alongside a reading of his operetta *The Sorceress*. In *The Sorceress*, Hotsmakh, a *badkhn* (or wedding jester) and peddler, plays the role of the traditional male hero alongside the operetta's more conventional young hero, Marcus. Although he is a character that had become a subject of vitriol on the part of the Jewish intelligentsia for the way he cheats his customers, Hotsmakh emerges as the decoder or hermeneutic of the false post-sacred world of its assimilated bourgeois Jewish residents. The characters Hotsmakh and Marcus also comment on the rise of the Yiddish actor and the way in which a new version of community formed around the Yiddish theater.

Chapter 3, "The Rise of the Yiddish Theater Audience," argues that the fictional character of the Hasid underwent a radical shift of meaning on Goldfaden's public stage from one only representing Hasidic Jews to one with which modern Jewish audience members identified. Moreover, it explores Goldfaden's perspective on the problem of Jewish visibility and the complicated relationship between traditional clothing and the Jew. *The Two Kuni-Lemls*, a Yiddish *Measure for Measure*, in which the modern and educated Max disguises himself as a Hasid, echoes with the contentious debates over Jewish clothing in the Russian Empire and Jewish stereotypes on the Yiddish stage.

Chapter 4, "The Rise of the Yiddish Playwright," explores Goldfaden's historical operetta *Doctor Almasada and the Jews of Palermo* and focuses on the character of Alonso. Alonso appears to be the devoted Christian apprentice of the honorable and Jewish Doctor Almasada who is also in love with Almasada's daughter, Miriam. Later in the operetta, Alonso reveals himself to be Jewish and explains that he pretended to be a Christian in order to circulate among Christians and to practice Doctor Almasada's lifesaving medicine among them. This chapter looks at a number of Jewish-Christian narratives that claimed the Yiddish stage during this period alongside the remarkable number of Yiddish playwrights who were also baptized Christians, including Osip Lerner, Jacob Gordin, Moyshe Horowitz, and Benedict Ben-Tsiyon.

"The Rise of the Female Yiddish Actress" is explored in chapter 5. Although women were among the first Yiddish actors, the troupes as they first developed under Goldfaden and his competitors cultivated an elaborate culture of cross-dressing male actors to make up for the small number of female actors. Goldfaden's early works expressed hostility to women and an accompanying desire to protect the all-male multigendered Yiddish stage—even as Goldfaden knew that the acquisition of female actors was the surest way for the Yiddish theater to attain equal footing with other national theaters. I discuss the intricate culture of playing Jewish women that evolved among the male actors (including dress and manner) and touch on the actors' relationship to the female characters they inhabited. Goldfaden's composition of his most enduring operetta, *Shulamis, Or the Daughter of Jerusalem*, reveals a fuller acceptance of female actors as well as an acknowledgment of their distinct voice in modern Jewish cultural life. This chapter analyzes the break *Shulamis* represents in this way but also depicts its enduring misogynistic elements in her character. Drawing on surviving sources about the first female Yiddish players on the Yiddish stage, I offer a comprehensive discussion of this important topic.

Chapter 6, "The Ban, Cultural Momentum, and the Modern Yiddish Theater," tells the history of the ban on Yiddish theater that was circulated in September 1883, a date that marks the end of the Yiddish theater's first era. It also charts the cultural high point of the Yiddish theater, moments when Goldfaden's theater is recognized on the Russian theatrical landscape and the momentum accumulated before the ban was put in place. Finally, it tracks the transition of Goldfaden from an elite purveyor of city culture to one whose work proliferated throughout the Pale of Settlement in a way that is more in line with the depiction of his person and works by twentieth-century scholars.

Notes

1. Quoted in Franz Kafka's unfinished record of actor Isaac Loewy's life story, "Concerning the Jewish Theater," in *Dearest Father: Stories and Other Writings*, trans. Ernst Kaiser and Eithne Wilkins (New York: Schocken, 1954), 129–135.

2. On Kafka and his strong preoccupation with the Yiddish stage, see Evelyn Torton Beck, *Kafka and the Yiddish Theater: Its Impact on His Work* (Madison: University of Wisconsin, 1971). For a persuasive reexamination of the impact of the Yiddish theater on Kafka's imagination, see Ernst Pawel, *The Nightmare of Reason: A Life of Franz Kafka* (New York: Farrar, Straus and Giroux, 1992), especially 239–249.

3. Kafka, *Dearest Father*, 129.

4. Ibid., 130.

5. Justin Cammy, "Judging *The Judgment of Shomer*," in *Arguing the Modern Jewish Canon*, ed. Justin Cammy, Dara Horn, Rachel Rubinstein, and Alyssa Quint (Cambridge, MA: Harvard University Press, 2008), 93. Sholem Aleichem's efforts to differentiate Jewish and European literary characteristics recur throughout the life of Yiddish literature and bleed into other realms like highbrow versus lowbrow and parochialism versus deparochialism. For a thoughtful discussion of these intersecting issues, see chapter 3 of Kenneth B. Moss, *Jewish Renaissance in the Russian Revolution* (Cambridge, MA: Harvard University Press, 2009).

6. Quoted from Cammy, "Judging *The Judgment of Shomer*," 132.

7. Dovid Fishman, *The Rise of Modern Yiddish Culture* (Pittsburgh, PA: University of Pittsburgh Press, 2005). See Gennady Estraikh's thoughtful parsing of the census numbers of the empire's Yiddish speakers: Gennady Estraikh, "On the Acculturation of Yiddish Speakers in Late Imperial Russia," *La Rassegna Mensile di Israel, terza serie, Il mondo yiddish: saggi* 62, no. 1/2 (July-August 1996): 217–228.

8. Alyssa Quint, "'Yiddish Literature for the Masses?' A Reconsideration of Who Read What in Jewish Eastern Europe," *AJS Review* 29, no. 1 (April 2005): 61–89; Nathan Cohen, "The Yiddish Press and Yiddish Literature: A Fertile But Complex Relationship," *Modern Judaism* 28, no. 2 (May 2008): 149–172.

9. Sholem Aleichem's whitewash of Goldfaden's greatest literary and theatrical achievements in favor of his nationalist songs is partly explained by the jealousy he had of Goldfaden and Shomer's celebrity. Sholem Aleichem's late novel *Wandering Stars* [*Blonzhende shtern*], an unflattering roman à clef about Goldfaden, depicts him as an exploitative impresario. Strangely, the novel also adopts the names of Goldfaden's most famous characters like Hotsmakh for his own characters. In other words, as a roman à clef, its subjects are quite transparent. It was first published in serial form simultaneously in the New York *Morning Newspaper* (*Morgn zhurnal*) and Warsaw's *Today* (*Haynt*) beginning only months after Goldfaden died in 1909. Chone Shmeruk, *Sholem Aleichem: madrikh le-khayav ve-leyetzirotav* [Sholem Aleichem: A Guide to His Life and Work] (Tel-Aviv: Publication of the Porter Institute for Poetics and Semiotics, 1980), 66. For a treatment of Sholem Aleichem's own mediocre career in Yiddish theater, see Alisa Solomon, *Wonder of Wonders: A Cultural History of Fiddler on the Roof* (New York: Metropolitan Books, 2015), chap. 1.

10. For more examples of critical jabs taken by colleagues, see Osip Lerner's introduction to his Yiddish translation of *Uriel Acosta* (1885) and Dovid Apateyker, *Ha-nevel* (1881). Both are included in "Notistn," *Hundert Yor Goldfaden*, ed. J. Shatsky (New York: YIVO Institute for Jewish Research, 1940), 372–373.

11. Sh. L. Tsitron, *Dray literarishe doyres: zikhroynes vegn yidishe shrifshteler* [*Three Literary Generations*] (Vilna: Sh. Shreberk, 1920).

12. See Michael Steinlauf's brilliant article, "Y.L. Peretz's Fear of Purim," *Jewish Social Studies* 1, no. 3 (Spring 1995): 44–65, which is a defense of the Yiddish theater as it had evolved until Peretz's attempt at literary theater. Steinlauf rebukes Peretz for not recognizing the

theater as an expression of folk culture, something he purported to support. It is unlikely that Goldfaden—at least during the period from 1876 to 1883—would have been comfortable with calling his theater folksy. He aimed for conservative bourgeois culture.

13. See the entire issue of *Literarishe bleter* 49 (1926). There is also a preoccupation of origins by Yiddish theater historians and what event constitutes the first moment of the theater's life. See, for instance, Zalmen Zilbercweig, "Iz dos yidishe teater gegrindet in berdichev, yasi, oder gor in konstantinopl?" *Literarishe bleter* 49 (1926): 149.

14. Shmuel Niger, "Di lider fun avrom goldfadn: tsu goldfadn's yuvilium," *Tsukunkft* 3 (1926): 150. Niger was an admirer of Goldfaden's poetry.

15. Y. Schipper, "Der uftu fun avrom goldfadn," *Literarishe bleter* 95 (1926): 133–134.

16. Shakhne Epstein, "Der veg funem nayem teater: vegn moris shvarts' uffirung fun goldfadn's 'Di tsvey kuni-lemls," *Frayhayt*, February 9, 1924, 6.

17. Popular reassessments of Goldfaden grow more sympathetic with time. See Avrom Reyzen, "Avrom Goldfaden—folks-dikhter un grinder fun nayem yidishn teater," *Forverts*, June 30, 1940, 5. This and other reassessments from 1940, a year that saw tributes in honor of the hundredth anniversary of Goldfaden's birthday, are collected in Sholem Perlmutter's unprocessed collection at YIVO, RG 289, Box 129.

18. Michał Weichert, "Avrom goldfadn's teatrale misye," *Literarishe bleter* 95 (1926): 134–135; *Trupe tansentsap* (Tel-Aviv: Menorah, 1966). For more on Weichert's fascinating life in the Yiddish theater, his experiences during the war in Warsaw, and his career as a critic, see Zalmen Zylbercweig's *Leksikon fun yidishn teater*, 6 vols. (New York: Elisheva, 1931–1970): III, 344–345 and his memoirs. *Zikhroynes* (Tel-Aviv: Menorah, 1960–1970).

19. The Soviet critic M. Litvakov wrote the following: "Avrom Goldfaden was the last of the disappearing genial Jewish *badkhonim*, wedding jesters, Purim jesters; in him lived the intuitive strength of the people's comedian."

20. Bilov and Veletnistki delve most seriously into the origins of Goldfaden's theater while Uri Nusinov and Yehezkel Dobrushin afforded most value to Goldfaden's work as artistic products. Uri Nusinov, for instance, argues for the organic quality of Goldfaden's works by pointing out interesting parallels between his poems and dramatic works; Yekhezkel Dobrushin analyzes Goldfaden's dramaturgical principles. See "Sotsiale figurn in a Goldfadns ershte verk: materialn tsu der kharakteristik fun a. goldfadns shafn," *Tsaytshrift* 1 (Minsk: 1926): 87–103; and "Goldfadns dramturgye," *Di dramaturgye fun di klasiker* (Moscow: 1948): 6–52.

21. Dan Miron, *A Traveler Disguised* (New York: Schocken, 1970).

22. See discussion of the Russian Jews' attendance of the Russian theater in Jeffrey Veidlinger, *Jewish Public Culture in the Late Russia Empire* (Bloomington: Indiana University Press, 2009).

23. Michael Steinlauf, "Cul-de-Sac: The 'Inner Life of Jews' on the Fin-de-Siècle Polish Stage," in *Culture Front: Representing Jews in Eastern Europe*, ed. Benjamin Nathans and Gabriella Safran (Philadelphia: University of Pennsylvania Press, 2008), 119–120.

24. Veidlinger, *Jewish Public Culture*, xvi. See also the references to theater attendance by Jews in Freeze and Harris, ChaeRan Y. Freeze and Jay M. Harris, eds., *Everyday Jewish Life in Imperial Russia: Select Documents, 1772–1914* (Waltham: Brandeis University Press, 2013).

25. See Paul Du Quenoy, *Stage Fright: Politics and the Performing Arts in Late Imperial Russia* (University Park: Pennsylvania State University Press, 2009); and Richard Stites, *Serfdom, Society, and the Arts in Imperial Russia* (New Haven, CT: Yale University Press, 2008). See the essays in *Between Tsar and People: Educated Society and the Quest for Public Identity in Late Imperial Russia*, ed. Edith W. Clowes, Samuel D. Kassow, and James L. West

(Princeton, NJ: Princeton University Press, 1991) that explore "the ways in which cultural production formulated and shaped public consciousness," the "sociocultural codes embedded in various cultural artifacts," "and the kinds of public responses to these codes" (12). For further reading on this topic in the context of late imperial Russia, see Iurii Lotman's seminal article on the Decembrists, eighteenth-century Russian noblemen turned revolutionaries, "The Decembrist in Daily Life (Everyday Behavior as a Historical-Psychological Category)," *The Semiotics of Russian Cultural History* (1985): 95–149.

26. Stites, *Serfdom, Society, and the Arts in Imperial Russia*, 254.

27. This is well attested to in the Russian press of this time. Gerald Seaman, "Nineteenth Century Italian Opera as seen in the Contemporary Russian Press," *New Zealand Slavonic Journal* (1994): 145. Also see Serhii Plokhy, *Unmaking Imperial Russia* (Toronto: University of Toronto Press, 2005).

28. Richard Tarushkin, *Defining Russia Musically* (Princeton, NJ: Princeton University Press, 1997), 208–209.

29. Ronald Robboy's discussion of Goldfaden's musical compositions in *Avrom Goldfaden's Shulamis: A Critical Edition* (forthcoming).

30. Jewish-themed works also include Anton Rubinstein's *The Maccabees*. See chapter 4 of this book on the Jewish-themed historical operettas and operas as a context for Goldfaden's own historical operetta. See Veidlinger's discussion of Russian Jewish-themed works as a draw for Jewish audiences, *Jewish Public Culture*, 174. Also see Steinlauf, "Cul-de-Sec: The 'Inner Life of Jews' on the Fin-de-Siècle Polish Stage," in *Culture Front: Representing Jews in Eastern Europe*, eds. Benjamin Nathans and Gabriella Safran (Philadelphia, University of Pennsylvania Press, 2008): 119–144.

31. Stites, *Serfdom, Society, and the Arts in Imperial Russia*, 278.

32. See Murray Frame's article, "'Freedom of the Theatres': The Abolition of the Russian Imperial Theatre Monopoly," *The Slavonic and East European Review* 83, no. 2 (April 2005): 254–289; and Edith Clowes, "The Moscow Art Theater," in *Between Tsar and People: Educated Society and the Quest for Public Identity in Late Imperial Russia*, ed. Edith W. Clowes, Samuel D. Kassow, and James L. West (Princeton, NJ: Princeton University Press, 1991), 274.

33. See, for instance, Natan M. Meir, *Kiev Jewish Metropolis: A History, 1859–1914* (Bloomington: Indiana University Press, 2010). See page 3 for a description of Kiev's residents.

34. Evgeni Binevich's comprehensive bibliography is an important key to my study. See E. Binevich, *Istoriia evreiskogo teatra v rossii. 1876–1883. Annoturoviannaia bibliografia* (Moscow: n.p., 1997).

35. For the freedom granted to commercial theater in 1883, see "'Freedom of the Theatres': The Abolition of the Russian Imperial Theatre Monopoly," *The Slavonic and East European Review* 83, no. 2 (April 2005): 254–289. On the ban imposed on the Yiddish theater, see John Klier, "'Exit, Pursued by a Bear': Russian Administrators and Ban on Yiddish Theatre in Imperial Russia," in *Yiddish Theatre: New Approaches* (Oxford: The Littman Library of Jewish Civilization, 2003), 159–174. See my challenge of some of Klier's conclusion in chapter 6.

36. See Robert Darnton's introduction and conclusion in *The Great Cat Massacre and Other Episodes in French Cultural History* (New York: Vintage Books, 1985). On microhistory, see also Jill Lepore, "Historians Who Love Too Much: Reflections on Microhistory and Biography," *The Journal of American History* 88, no. 1 (2001): 129–144; Nancy Stieber, "Microhistory of the Modern City: Urban Space, Its Use and Representation," *Journal of the Society of Architectural Historians* 58, no. 3 (1999): 382–391; and Barbara Kirshenblatt-Gimblett, "The Corporeal Turn," *The Jewish Quarterly Review* (Summer 2005): 447–461.

37. Warnke demonstrates that the fans—or *patriotn* as they were called—inhabited a social sphere in which they practiced an intense devotion to an actor who they adulated, protected, and after which they modeled themselves. As Boaz Young, a former patriot and actor explained, "For the amateur actor, the professional actor was a God and teacher; he imitates his speech, his make-up, and his gait on stage." Quoted in Nina Warnke, "*Patriotn* and Their Stars: Male Youth Culture in the Galleries of the New York Yiddish Theatre," in *Inventing the Modern Yiddish Stage*, ed. J. Berkowitz and B. Henry (Detroit: Wayne State University Press, 2012), 161–183.

38. See Naomi Seidman, *The Marriage Plot: or, How Jews Fell in Love with Love, and with Literature* (Stanford, CA: Stanford University Press, 2016), Kindle edition, "Introduction."

39. In the questions I raise and the social and cultural arenas I examine, I am indebted to the works of Steve Zipperstein, *The Jews of Odessa: A Cultural History, 1794–1881* (Stanford, CA: Stanford University Press, 1986); and Benjamin Nathans, *Beyond the Pale: The Jewish Encounter with Late Imperial Russia* (Berkeley: University of California Press, 2002). See also Kenneth Moss's review of historiography, "At Home in Late Imperial Russian Modernity—Except When They Weren't: New Histories of Russian and East European Jews, 1881–1914," *The Journal of Modern History* 84 (June 2012): 401–452.

40. The scholarly treatment of nineteenth- and twentieth-century Russian Jewish fiction focuses on literary output and intellectual development and not the social reverberations of these texts. For some of the finest examples of such studies, see Marcus Moseley, *Being for Myself Alone: Origins of Jewish Autobiography* (Stanford, CA: Stanford University Press, 2006); Olga Litvak, *Conscription and the Search for Modern Russian Jewry* (Bloomington: Indiana University Press, 2006); and Kenneth Moss, *Jewish Renaissance and the Russian Revolution* (Cambridge: Harvard University Press, 2009).

41. Shmuel Feiner, "The Pseudo-Enlightenment and the Question of Jewish Modernization," *Jewish Social Studies*, New Series, 3, no. 1 (Autumn 1996): 62–88.

42. Zipperstein, *The Jews of Odessa*, 153.

43. Eli Lederhendler, *Jewish Immigrants and American Capitalism 1880–1920* (Cambridge, MA: Cambridge University Press, 2009), xix.

44. See Meir, *Kiev*, 31–36. Eugene Avrutin, *Jews and the Imperial State: Identification Politics in Tsarist Russia* (Ithaca, NY: Cornell University Press, 2010). See Benjamin Nathans's discussion of "social fictions" in *Beyond the Pale*. See also Eli Lederhendler, "Guides for the Perplexed: Sex, Manners and Mores for the Yiddish Reader in America," in *Jewish Responses to Modernity: New Voices in America and Eastern Europe* (New York: New York University Press, 1994), 140–148; and Iris Parush, *Reading Jewish Women: Marginality and Modernization in Nineteenth-Century Eastern European Jewish Society*, trans. Saadya Sternberg (Lebanon, NH: Brandeis University Press, 2004).

45. This dovetails well with the work of Brian Horowitz who recognizes nationalism—not as grassroots—but as stemming from the highly acculturated elite. This idea is already apparent in Goldfaden's epic poem "Dos pintele yid."

46. Works on social performance include Erving Goffman, *The Presentation of Self in Everyday Life* (New York: Anchor Books, 1959).

47. Stephen Greenblatt, *Shakespearean Negotiations: The Circulation of Social Energy in Renaissance England* (Berkeley: University of California Press, 1988), 14; and Stephen Greenblatt, *Renaissance Self-Fashioning from More to Shakespeare* (Chicago: University of Chicago Press, 1980, 2005), 179.

48. David Biale, ed. *Cultures of the Jews: A New History* (New York: Schocken Books, 2002). See also Paula Fass, "Cultural History/Social History: Some Reflections on a Continuing Dialogue," *Journal of Social History* 37, no. 1, Special Issue (Autumn 2003): 39–46.

49. It is unclear whether or not scholars like Marcus Moseley, who mapped the world of nineteenth-century Jewish autobiography so beautifully, would even consider these memoirs as qualifying as the fictionalized Jewish autobiographical tradition. See his book, *Being for Myself Alone*.

50. A list of memoirs, almost all of them barely read or referenced by previous historians, is listed separately in the bibliography. Most were serialized in Yiddish periodical literature between 1890 and 1920 and they constitute the earliest personal records of participants in the theater's first chapter. Joel Berkowitz supplies a thorough list of actors' memoirs that were published in book form, "Introduction," *Yiddish Theatre*, 13n22 in and beyond this period.

51. Louise W. Knight, "Essay: Sibling Rivalry: History and Memoir," *The Women's Review of Books* 24, no. 4 (July-August 2007): 12–14. See also Glenn Dynner, "The Hasidic Tale as a Historical Source: Historiography and Methodology," *Religion Compass* 3, no. 4 (2009): 655–675.

52. The historian Robert Darnton writes, "If culture is idiomatic it is retrievable. And if enough of its texts have survived, it can be excavated. . . . We can stop seeing how documents 'reflect' their social surroundings, because they were imbedded in a symbolic world that was social and cultural at the same time." Darnton, *The Great Cat Massacre*, 260.

53. This chapter is influenced considerably by a number of articles in *Between Tsar and People: Educated Society and the Quest for Public Identity in Late Imperial Russia*, ed. Edith W. Clowes, Samuel D. Kassow, and James L. West (Princeton, NJ: Princeton University Press, 1991).

1 Goldfaden, Elite (1876–1883)

Introduction

In 1875 Avrom Goldfaden was comfortably ensconced in the best room at the Black Eagle, one of the most fashionable hotels in Czernovitz, then a city in the Austro-Hungarian Empire (now Chernivtsi, Ukraine). Goldfaden would travel to Iași a year later and establish Yiddish theater, but even before this trip he had grown into a writer of considerable reputation with three published books of poetry.[1] He certainly acted the part. Granted, his fame only extended to a circumscribed constellation of Hebrew and Yiddish poets and other members of the East European Jewish intelligentsia—a group of hundreds, maybe thousands. His Yiddish songs, sung by Jewish singers in taverns, amplified this celebrity. Goldfaden luxuriated in the attention he commanded, attracting admirers who sought him out for a polite exchange of ideas or to bask in the warm glow of his relative renown. One such admirer was the Hebrew poet David Yeshayahu Zilberbusch (1854–1936), just shy of twenty, who had recently made his way from the pious pews of the study house to experiment with modern ideas and Hebrew verse. In his memoirs, Zilberbusch recounts how ill-prepared he felt for the visit—but not out of a sense of intellectual inferiority. Instead, the young man, schooled in the Bible and the Talmud, worried about lapses of etiquette. Zilberbusch had seldom been in the company of such a refined man as Goldfaden. As he tells it, he was nervous, still "innocent to the correct way one receives visitors." Goldfaden's aura was grand. Zilberbusch recalls:

> He had a large sitting room, with an alcove for a bed and wash-basin, the doorway was hung with blue velvet drapes. A thick carpet covered the floor. There was a sofa, a polished dark wood table, with leather-upholstered chairs around it. In a corner, near a window, stood a piano and a writing desk.
>
> When I arrived at about eleven o'clock he had, I think, been sitting at the desk. He was wearing a gray dressing gown with blue stripes at the collar, and embroidered velvet slippers. On his nose, highly polished, gold-framed glasses. . . . What impressed me were the golden frames and the expansive style of living of a Jewish author.[2]

Never mind that, as most biographers rightly point out, Goldfaden had declared bankruptcy two years earlier in Odessa and left the Russian Empire for Lemberg (Lviv, Ukraine) for fear of debtor's prison, only to start a Yiddish newspaper that failed. But Goldfaden's precarious financial situation did not figure in the conversation with Zilberbusch. Instead, Zilberbusch raised what he thought to be the burning question of their day, that of "Haskala," of bringing the Enlightenment to their benighted Jewish brethren of Russia. Remarkably, Goldfaden was dismissive of this idea and casually explained to the budding intellectual, "I get what I need from my little Jew," with both the language and air more evocative of a Polish nobleman than someone invested in the enfranchisement of his fellow Jews.[3] Thus Goldfaden allowed Zilberbusch to approach him, but only to demonstrate how unapproachable he was. This would be Goldfaden's way. His mystique was evident in the clothes he wore, the expensive things surrounding him, and the subtle blend of formality and casualness that informed his demeanor and speech.

Although scholars uniformly portray Goldfaden as a magnanimous generator of Yiddish culture for the poor and uneducated, Zilberbusch's record of his visit to Goldfaden calls attention to his preoccupation with social status and performance. Historians point to Goldfaden's devotion to cultivating Yiddish theater (as opposed to, say, Hebrew poetry) as proof enough of his populism. Indeed, aspects of his work and career seem to corroborate such a paradigm. Driven by song and, often, by comedy or melodrama, Goldfaden's theater struck historians as lowbrow, especially relative to the Yiddish prose generated during the same period. His contemporaries were the first to publicly dismiss the quality of his work. Goldfaden's friend, the writer Jacob Dineson, writes in his memoirs based on his first experience with Yiddish theater as he saw it in Warsaw: "With regards to the newborn Yiddish theater, the audience [alongside the theater itself] was practically childish and played with theater as one child plays with another."[4] Goldfaden's own complaints about the need to dilute his work to reach uneducated viewers and his reluctant dependence on folk singers to mediate his work seemed to confirm the theater's uncultivated "wide audience" (*braytern oylem*), as scholars would later call it. Goldfaden describes his early audiences as "cobblers and tailors and raw craftsmen" who would never have understood the sophisticated works he wished he could stage.[5] Theater critics and historians in the 1920s and 1930s turned Goldfaden's reliance on the uneducated into his theater's greatest virtue and referred to "a wide audience" as Goldfaden's creative source. Taking his cue from Goldfaden, the historian Jacob Shatzky insists that Goldfaden's audience was untutored and working class: "It is very important to understand Goldfaden's approach to theater. Goldfaden wanted to create a theater like other national theaters. But other nations had differentiated audiences (*diferentsirter oylem*) who satisfied their tastes each according to their own taste and education. At that time, however, the Yiddish theater had only one type of audience member—the common Jew (*dem folk mentsh*), the worker, the storekeeper, the petit-bourgeois element."[6]

In a number of works on this early period of the theater, Soviet critics Nusyinov and Y. Riminik argued that the contempt and anxiety expressed for Goldfaden's work by some was representative of the Jewish bourgeois "assimilated" class.[7] While "the bourgeoisie" voice controlled the press and they became the "enemy" of Goldfaden's theater, the folk organically participated in the theater as audience and actors. In fact, Goldfaden's continuous recruitment of new actors for his troupes "reinvigorated the folk element" of his theater.[8] Finally, the ubiquity of Goldfaden's work in shtetls throughout the Pale of Settlement by the turn of the century—the growth of his theatrical work into something of a mass commercial sensation—all but confirmed the theater's folkist orientation and popular reach.[9]

In this chapter, I take a markedly different perspective from that of my predecessors, both with regard to Goldfaden's intended audience and to the audience his troupe actually commanded during his first years (before the ban in October 1883). I push to the side the idea that with Yiddish theater Goldfaden sought to educate the benighted masses of shtetl-bound Jews. Although he was drawn to a form of folk culture, the idea of Goldfaden as a mediator of folk art has been overemphasized in the scholarship. I frame my discussion of Goldfaden with his strong identification with Russia's urban-based cultural intelligentsia, a social grouping distinguished by its education and affinity with Western culture and whose members were from the professional class, the enlightened gentry, and the bourgeoisie.[10] Though he never achieved its financial stability, Goldfaden came to identify with a Jewish middle class that grew up particularly in newer cities with merchant-heavy populations under the liberal rule of Alexander II (1855–1881): a Jewish middle class, it should be added, with attitude and behavior associated with the Russian aristocracy.[11] During the period under discussion, he played the part both of a member of the Russian Jewish elite, with an utter indifference to work, and a consumer and producer of art, who showed attentiveness to appearance and dress and who casually invoked the word "aristocratic" to describe himself. Goldfaden's attendance at the exclusive Russian Jewish teacher's seminary in Zhitomir was a vital ingredient of his manner of high self-regard: he emerged steeped in classic Russian literature as well as the social conventions of leisure activity with the self-presentation of the urban-dwelling merchant class. A self-fashioner of great resourcefulness, Goldfaden sought the attention and patronage of Russia's "middle classes" (Jew and Gentile, alike) even as he inflected his behavior with the more exaggerated habits of the nobility.

Thus, I marshal evidence from newspapers, memoirs, and biographical sources to assess the cultural project of the two (and at times as many as three) troupes under his stewardship from 1876 to 1883. I distinguish the first period of modern Yiddish theater ("Goldfaden elite") from the popular spread of Goldfaden's works that took place after 1883. While Odessa became the resident city of the modern Yiddish theater, the movement of Goldfaden's primary troupe from 1878 to 1883 reveals that Goldfaden favored theatrical venues in the cities with newer, more affluent, and more modern Jewish communities in which he sought an audience of his peers. I attempt to understand the genealogy of the playwright's refined demeanor and shift attention to how his preoccupation with self-presentation fueled a brand of urban and modern Yiddish performance imitated, most conspicuously, by his actors (explored in chap. 2). For many previous scholars, a writer's commitment to Yiddish letters is itself evidence of a populist commitment. By contrast, I believe that Goldfaden's aristocratic public persona begs articulation and analysis, as it is not simply ornamental or incidental to his theater but is rather the very substance of the life that he and many around him pursued.

Goldfaden's First Years (1840–1876)

Notwithstanding the variegated nature of Russia's bourgeoisie, Goldfaden barely qualified as a member, at least according to financial merit. Born July 12, 1840, in Old Constatine (Starokonstantinov, Volhynia province), Goldfaden grew up the son of Khane Rivke and Khayim Lipe Goldenfodem. His father was a clockmaker and, according to Avrom, the only craftsman in the shtetl of Old Constantine to organize a supplementary curriculum for his son.[12] Goldfaden writes, "When I arrived home from the *gemora* teacher, I would meet with a teacher who tutored me in German, Russian, and Tanakh [the Pentateuch] with German translation."[13] Among his tutors was Abraham Ber Gottlober, who by 1855 was already a prominent voice of the Russian Haskala and who composed poetry and song in Yiddish. Goldfaden's father considered his son to have extraordinary mental abilities, and he trained Goldfaden in Jewish and non-Jewish sources. Even as a boy, however, Goldfaden was also drawn to performance, something his father considered unserious, silly:

> It is hard for me to recall when I showed the penchant for rhyme-making. When I was about 6 or 7 already a student of *gemora* and knew by heart most of the two first books of the Torah, my mother took me along to a neighbor's wedding. There was a rotund man with a trimmed beard, with the visor of his hat askew who tucked his thumb in his belt and kicked his feet up like a scamp as he "sang to the bride" before the wedding canopy. . . . Everything he sang and said that night rhymed artfully. I observed his singing and his declamations with great attention. Later, when I went home with my mother, I pulled my cap askew, kicked my right foot before me and whatever I needed to tell my mother I did so in rhyme. My mother was in stitches. Overhearing, my father smiled beneath his moustache. He called me *Avremle* the Badkhn but soon his face grew serious and he said: It is not nice for a *gemora*-boy to be silly![14]

Finkel and Oyslender point out that the two volumes of poetry that Goldfaden would later publish exhibit the abiding respect and admiration he had for his traditional parents in the dedications he wrote to them. He did not wage rebellion against them, nor was he "banished from their table" as were some progressive intellectuals of his

Figure 1.1. Goldfaden in hat with tassel, c. 1882. Courtesy of the YIVO Institute for Jewish Research.

generation. By the time Goldfaden was eleven years old, he had written poetic verse in Hebrew that his father would prod him to recite before guests in their home.

Goldfaden remained close with his family throughout his career, though rifts occurred later between himself and his brothers, Naftoli and Wolf. Apparently, his younger brothers did not receive the extensive tutoring and schooling Avrom enjoyed, but they did achieve success in the theater alongside their brother.[15] Naftoli Goldfaden led a secondary troupe for Goldfaden, and Wolf Goldfaden (also known as Eugene Goldfaden) accrued fame as an actor in America. Goldfaden would parlay the intellectual achievements he cultivated early in his life at home into a higher social standing.

The cultivation of Goldfaden's talents at home earned him an unparalleled education in a special Russian-Jewish school and then a Russian-Jewish teachers' seminary. Set up by the Russian government to steer Jews away from traditional Jewish professions and to assimilate them more fully into Russian and Russian-language society, students were expected to graduate and then act as teachers and model good citizens (so to speak) in their communities. Students of the seminaries (there was a second one in Vilna) studied Hebrew as the refined Jewish language, and Goldfaden demonstrated particular mastery in memorizing and crafting Hebrew verse. His book of poetry, *Thorns and Flowers* (*Tsitsim u-ferakhim*), written while he was still a student, was reviewed enthusiastically by the Hebrew literary critic Avraham Kovner, who was known for his severe judgment.[16] But Goldfaden was also an exemplary student of Russian language and literature and, from the letters and documents of the school, as well as the memoirs penned by graduates later in their lives, Russian was the language most often spoken at the seminaries during Goldfaden's tenure. The faculty, comprised of Jews and non-Jews, was politically conservative and committed to the project of integrating Russia's Jews and to reforming their manners and appearance. It hoped to transmit to their students a mastery of secular knowledge that they the students would then teach to gymnasium students in cities throughout the empire. Underlying the concrete agenda of acculturation they shared with the government, Jewish reformers also looked forward to emancipation, to a future in which the rights and freedoms of Russian Jews would come to resemble those of their French brothers. Indeed, the gymnasiums seemed evidence enough of the good intentions on the part of the Russian government.

After graduating the crown school in 1857, Goldfaden attended a Russian-Jewish teachers' seminary in Zhitomir from the age of seventeen to twenty-six where he acquired the manners and tastes of the higher social classes. He studied and boarded in Zhitomir for a period of nine years. Though it did not possess the status of a university, the seminary offered a rarefied postsecondary education by any measure. In her book on the seminaries, *The Jewish Elite of the Russian Empire: Enlightenment and Integration in the Nineteenth Century*, historian Verena

Dohrn underscores the elite complexion of the lives of the schools' graduates and their shared outlook of privilege.[17] Goldfaden, the son of a clockmaker, was likely one of a small number of students (fewer than sixty-five) on scholarship while the others were from financially established families who paid their way. His fellow students exposed Goldfaden to the manners of the affluent, including their patterns of dress and grooming. Memoirs penned by former seminary students allude to the seminary's leisure time devoted to literature, poetry, theater, and music; Goldfaden learned how to play the piano in Zhitomir and participated in soirées of music and song. The songwriter Mark Warshavsky (1848–1907), composer of the celebrated Yiddish folk song "*Afn pripertshik*" ("On the Hearth"), recounts how his father's home in Zhitomir became a private venue of intimate performance to which local seminary students were regularly invited.[18] According to Shmuel Tsitron in his memoir *Three Literary Generations*, Gottlober, who knew "Avromele" first from when he was his tutor in Old Constantine, was a continuing musical and literary influence in Goldfaden's life when he assumed a position as a teacher in the seminary: "In Zhitomir, Gottlober would regularly host gatherings in his home to which the city's best musicians came. There were special musical evenings when music, general and Jewish, was discussed. These evenings had a big influence on the young Goldfaden who composed poetry and accompanying music to them during this time."[19]

Students and teachers integrated Hebrew and Yiddish culture into their diet of Russian-inflected leisure activity. The Hebrew critic and playwright Avraham Ya'akov Paperna (1840–1919), one of Goldfaden's fellow students, remembers that colleagues and teachers encouraged Goldfaden to write and perform Yiddish songs. Paperna also records Goldfaden's collaboration with Madame Slonimski (the wife of seminary director Hayim Zelig Slonimski, 1810–1904) to produce a private performance of the Yiddish play *Serkele* by Polish-Jewish Enlightenment figure Solomon Ettinger (1802–1856), which had circulated among seminary teachers and students in manuscript.[20] This was, apparently, not the first production of its kind at the seminary.[21] Goldfaden and his colleagues also studied how to recite poetry according to the prevailing declamatory practices of their day. The formal declamation of verse by seminary students reflects the close attention they paid to the conventions of the Russian intelligentsia and the empire's performance practices.[22]

Indeed, even as Jews, they sought to become men of culture equal to their non-Jewish counterparts. One of Goldfaden's fellow seminarians, for instance, Menashe Margolis (1837–1912) explains in his memoirs that he turned in a request to the director of the seminary about the significance of dance, especially to Jews for whom it is essential to learn grace and manners.[23] The request was acknowledged and triggered an epidemic of dance among students along with their attendance of masquerade balls. Even more so than balls was the importance of theater. As Goldfaden reports in his autobiography, he and his peers became avid consumers of theater by the time he arrived in Iași in 1876: "I had plenty of opportunity to see the best dramas and operas of that time, Polish, Russian, German, and all the smaller operettas from the most famous of Verdi and Meyerbeer and Halévy . . . and all of Wagner's works. I had the opportunity to see and hear the best actors of my day, not just Raissi, Salvini, etc., but also [Ira] Aldridge [1807–1867] an actual born Moor who played his role of Othello in English, while the rest of the cast spoke Polish."[24] Goldfaden began attending theater as a student. Along with his peers, Goldfaden was brought up to be a consumer of high culture and he was far more comfortable navigating the aisles of a city theater than he was a Jewish-owned tavern in the Romanian city of Iași.

While some students, like Goldfaden, considered themselves the intellectual heirs of their esteemed, autodidact teachers, the students were more intensely Russified than their teachers. Photographs from this period, for instance, reveal that teachers maintained more traditional appearances than their students, who decisively modeled their appearances after Russian urbanites. For instance, the seminary's director, the maskil Slonimski retained his traditional beard, while Goldfaden was clean-shaven or with just a well-groomed moustache and dressed in the fashion of the Russian intelligentsia.[25] Memoirs reflect that seminary students navigated Russian society with great facility, especially those who went on to attend university. Of course, there were still restrictions on their lives and the Jews of the empire, generally. The students of the seminaries, however, seemed to embody the promise of integration, if not integration itself; they were and behaved the part of the Chosen of the Chosen People. Not only did Goldfaden emerge with fluency in Russian literature and as a fluent speaker of the Russian language, but he also was permitted to travel freely beyond the Pale of Settlement.[26] And, like Russian teachers, many of the seminary graduates became published authors and teachers.[27] For Goldfaden, graduation from the seminary resulted in opportunity and a boost to his status that only army service or wealth were previously required by Jews to achieve. In its more intangible offerings, his nine years in Zhitomir afforded him the critical exposure to culture and language fluency that gave him a sense of Russian belonging.

The discrepancy between the more practical goals of the seminary to train teachers and its rarefied and elitist atmosphere became apparent in Goldfaden's life after graduation. As a stipendiary boarder at the rabbinical school, Goldfaden was obliged to serve as a teacher for a fixed number of years following his studies and, accordingly, was assigned to a post in the Crimean city of Simferopol.[28] Goldfaden's biographers Oyslender and Finkel speculate that Goldfaden could not tolerate life in the relative isolation of the small Crimean city. He abandoned his post a few months later for Odessa.[29] Historians depict Goldfaden as an intellectual who, at this point in his career, moved in a populist cultural direction, but

Figure 1.2. Hand-painted magic lantern slide of Avrom Goldfaden, c. 1910. Courtesy of the YIVO Institute for Jewish Research.

contemporary observers depict a man with an oversized sense of entitlement to an haute-bourgeois lifestyle devoted to cultural pursuits. He had spent nine of his formative years, ages seventeen to twenty-six, at the seminary, surrounded by members of an elite class of Russian Jews.[30] In Odessa, he avoided work and spent time attending theater and composing songs and theatrical materials with friends Sh. Trakhtman, Ulraykh Kalmus, and Sh. Bernshteyn, all of them published Yiddish writers.[31] Goldfaden would, according to Zilberbusch, point to his beginnings in Old Constantine as a sign of his modesty. But he did so only as part of a narrative about his innate nobility, and only after this nobility was allowed to flourish in him as an adult of impeccable manners and reputation. By the time he lived in Odessa, he behaved as though he were destined for Russian-Jewish greatness.

Goldfaden was hardly alone in enjoying a high self-regard. His biography illuminates a number of his fellow graduates of the Russian-Jewish seminaries who took pride in identifying with a privileged class. This departs from the impression of the seminary we might have from Jonathan Frankel's monumental study, *Prophecy and Politics*, which focuses on the trajectory of seminary student Aron Lieberman from Hebrew maskil to socialist revolutionary.[32] But Frankel himself reminds us that Lieberman was exceptional among maskilim in rejecting the moneyed Jewish establishment.[33] Even Goldfaden's fellow student and close colleague Yitskhak-Yoyel Linetski, for example—the son of a Hasidic rabbi of modest circumstances—quickly adopted a penchant for social formalities, which his protégé Reuven Granofsky remarks on in his memoirs.[34] Linetski enjoyed a brand of celebrity in Russian-Jewish Haskala circles for his anti-Hasidic novel, *The Polish Lad*. Even as Linetski relied on the money of patrons—mostly rich Odessa merchants—and complained bitterly about their lack of financial support. No matter his financial circumstances, he dressed daily in formal attire, including gloves, and groomed himself meticulously.

More important—and quite remarkably—Goldfaden was not alone in growing from Russian-Jewish seminary graduate to pioneer of modern Yiddish theater. Less known to scholars than Linetski are three seminary students who were all, apparently, born to wealthy, Russified Jewish families and who each came to play important roles in the nascent Yiddish theater alongside Goldfaden. One was the journalist and playwright Osip Lerner (discussed at greater length in chap. 4). A graduate of the seminary, Lerner was an important voice in Odessa's Russian-language press before he became a pioneer of a literary Yiddish theater in Odessa alongside Goldfaden. The writer N. B. Bazilinski (1836–1901) also graduated from the seminary, and his works were mounted by Lerner in Odessa, but there is almost no surviving information about him. Still, it is remarkable that the Russian Jewish teachers' seminary—with its more formal and public emphasis on Hebraism and Russian culture—was also the source of Yiddish-inflected literary, theatrical, and musical creativity. Put differently, Goldfaden and many of his fellow students point to the seminaries as instrumental in the rise of the modern Yiddish theater.

A final seminary student-cum-Yiddish theater pioneer is Yankev Spivakovski (1852–1919), whose role in the theater illuminates its special appeal among the Russian-speaking, acculturated Jewish bourgeoisie of Odessa. Spivakovski was born to a wealthy tea merchant in Moghilev-Podolski and, after graduating, became a journalist in Odessa.[35] Jacob Adler, who himself belonged to a wealthy and well-connected family (discussed in greater detail in chap. 2), describes Spivakovski's family as occupying a higher status than that of his own and as belonging to "Odessa's Jewish aristocracy."[36] As Adler notes, Spivakovski spoke French impeccably, and he was a darling of the "bourgeois-aristocratic" society for his Russian declamations and private theatrical performances.[37] Adler explains that Spivakovski had a reputation as an expert Russian declaimer "because of his authentic literary Russian expression and accent" and he would perform "with good taste" in Russian amateur theatrical performances.[38] It was no surprise that when Spivakovski would make an appearance in "bourgeois intelligentsia society" (*bal-habatish-intelligent gezelshaft*), he was met with happy ovations, Adler writes.[39] He explains that Spivakovski and his partner, Yisroel Rosenberg, are owed the true credit for bringing Yiddish theater to Russian soil and pulling it into the mainstream cultural purview of their fellow Russified Jews. While in Bucharest covering the Russo-Turkish War for a Russian newspaper, Spivakovski was struck by Goldfaden's theater, acted in it, and returned to Odessa to put on his own productions of Goldfaden's works. "Jewish children who had once idolized the Russian language and the Russian folk, now returned to their Jewish brothers and to Yiddish," Adler adds, contemplating Spivakovski's passion for Yiddish theater.[40] When Goldfaden returned to Odessa with the assumption that he would now take control of all matters pertaining to Yiddish theater, he sought out Spivakovski. But there was little love lost between the two, as they rivaled each other in attitudes of cultural superiority before becoming rivals in the theater. Always elegantly dressed with a top hat and silk gloves, Spivakovski shared Goldfaden's appreciation for the city's pleasures but saw Goldfaden as a competitor.[41] As Zylbercweig recounts, "Since [Spivakovski] was a member of the intelligentsia ("*intelligent*"), a good actor, and the first to have established Yiddish theater in Odessa, he expected Goldfaden to relate to him with great respect. Goldfaden, however, saw himself as the most important figure in the Yiddish theater and all others were merely window-dressing."[42] Spivakovski remained a Yiddish player all his life—and, apparently, reconciled with Goldfaden. Also, according to Adler, Spivakovski did not display the snobbery for which Goldfaden grew notorious. In any case, history has left the impression that Yiddish was the province of the charitable and selfless intelligentsia. Goldfaden's record of this period, which mentions none of these names, encourages such an understanding for reasons we will explore below. Yiddish culture however, here, among refined seminary graduates, is accompanied by a sense of cultural superiority, entrepreneurship, and competition.

While Spivakovski could afford to knock around Odessa as he did with Jacob Adler, a fellow flâneur, Goldfaden's ambition to do the same was harder to accomplish, given his family's modest financial circumstances. But there was no other city for Goldfaden. As much as the theater was an outgrowth of the seminary, it was also a product of Odessa and the complexion of this city's modern Jewish population, its entrepreneurialism, and the passion of its Jewish residents for the city's robust culture of theatrical performances and small-scale Yiddish musical evenings that were allowed to flourish in its taverns.[43] During the ten-year period between his graduation in 1866 and the first Yiddish-language performances he produced in Iaşi in the fall of 1876, Goldfaden sought, with growing unease, to reconcile the life of culture to which he felt entitled and the new and unwelcome challenge of supporting himself financially.[44]

After leaving Simferopol, he went to live in Odessa with a wealthy uncle, Nogid Yidl Keselman, about whom we know very little. For a time, Goldfaden enjoyed the enthusiastic hospitality of his extended family. Keselman's son Yoysef played piano and collaborated with Goldfaden to collect and compose melodies. According to the Russian biographer Riminik, Keselman prodded Goldfaden about what he planned to take up as a vocation, but Goldfaden was not preoccupied with the same question. He enjoyed days in the steppes beyond Odessa with intellectual confrères like Linetski as well as the Yiddish playwrights Ulrikh Kalmus and Sh. Trakhtman and the Yiddish poet Sh. Bernshteyn. Goldfaden also attended a good deal of German operetta and grew close to its troupe, among which were some Jewish actors. They composed songs together and published in the same newspapers.[45] At night he attended the theater and wouldn't return home until 2:00 or 3:00 a.m. by carriage.[46] Keselman asked Goldfaden to leave when he realized he did not plan on marrying his daughter.[47]

Goldfaden then began spending time with the family of the celebrated Hebraist and writer Eliahu Mordechai Verbel (1806–1880). He married Verbel's daughter Paulina, a woman brought up with a refined European education, who was fluent in English and French from a young age.[48] Verbel supported his son-in-law's theatrical endeavors financially and creatively. Verbel's epic poem *The Tomcat and the Well* (*Khulda ve-bor*), crafted in Hebrew, became the source text for Goldfaden's *Shulamis*. Verbel's son, Michel-Adolphe (Moyshe Avrom) Verbel, a graduate of L'École des Beaux-Arts in Paris, went on to serve as Goldfaden's set designer.[49] The elder Verbel supplied his daughter and new son-in-law with a monthly stipend. According to the memoirs of actors, Paulina would become notorious for the expensive clothing and jewelry she wore even as Goldfaden paid many of his actors very little. She also played a role in managing one of the Goldfaden troupes and, according to a review of a St. Petersburg performance, acted on the stage. They had a single son who died when he was an infant.[50]

Besides Goldfaden's circle of educated Russian Jewish colleagues and family—his own and Paulina's—the reputation Goldfaden had long garnered as a celebrated folk poet generated relationships with entertainers and other folk poets. His reputation as a folk poet was not what some historians of the theater took it to mean later; that is, Goldfaden was not an untutored generator of folk material. Though closely connected to Yiddish folk culture through his childhood and his native Yiddish tongue, Goldfaden ("father of the Yiddish theater") anticipates the work of Joel Engel (1868–1927, "father of Jewish music"), the Russian Jewish composer and pioneer of the Jewish art music movement.[51] Like Engel, Goldfaden turned to Yiddish song as a self-conscious gesture of making art songs from folk songs. He had written his books in the simple Yiddish language in the way the Russian intelligentsia had begun repackaging Russian folk culture. It is hardly irrelevant that Goldfaden was fluent in Russian, notwithstanding his commitment to Yiddish literature. In contrast, the Yiddish folk singers with whom he sometimes consorted had little formal education and did not necessarily speak a language other than their native Yiddish. Although some also composed poetry, folk singers were mostly associated with performing Yiddish songs and dramatic monologues. Many relied on the published works of Goldfaden and others for material to perform.

The relationship Goldfaden had with the folk singers reflected the subtleties of his social standing and the way the culture of Yiddish composition and performance bridged social worlds that were otherwise divided by class, education, and the measure of Jewish integration into Russian culture. During these pre-theater years, for instance, Goldfaden enjoyed a close friendship with folk poet and entertainer Velvl Zbarsher (born Benjamin Wolf Erenkrants, 1824–1884), who shared intellectual and social traits with both the Jewish intelligentsia and the primitive folk performers. On the one hand, Zbarsher was a virtuoso Hebrew and Yiddish wordsmith; on the other, he rejected bourgeois manner, was a known drunk, and performed in Galician taverns before large crowds. Goldfaden considered Zbarsher his intellectual equal, even his mentor: both men had much of the Tanach memorized as well as hundreds of poems—their own and those of other poets. After Zbarsher's death, Goldfaden wrote a poem that invoked the passage in Samuel I where King Saul consults a sorceress in order to commune with the dead: "Yes Sorceress, command the spirits/Let them do the hex dance/And bring up the master/Velvel Zbarsher Ehrenkrants."[52] In his memoirs, the maskil Zilberbusch reports that the two composers spent time with one another as equals, quoting long bits of poetry from the other. Folk singer and poet Avrom Fishzon, however, remembers his feeling of great awe and intimidation in Goldfaden's presence, even before Goldfaden became an impresario. Goldfaden was also acquainted with the rough-hewn folk singer-cum-actor Moyshe Finkel well enough to recruit him for his Iaşi productions; it's likely the educated folk poet took in one of his acts in an Odessa tavern. Unlike Finkel and Fishzon but like Engel, Goldfaden was a member of a formally educated crop of poets. He was more an insider of this culture than Engel and more an outsider than Finkel, Fishzon, and Zbarsher. His fluency in Yiddish and Russian as well his immersion in Russian middle-class life allowed Goldfaden to move comfortably between the worlds of the salon and the tavern. But in calling Goldfaden a folk poet, left-leaning historians of the 1920s and 1930s sought to identify him with the untutored masses more than he ever was. Goldfaden's embrace of Yiddish folk culture was good cover for those who would prefer to elide the bourgeois forces that gave rise to the modern Yiddish theater.

Proof of Goldfaden's modern sensibility at least as it applies to his Jewish roots can be found in his epic poem "Dos pintele yid" ("The Essence of a Jew"), which is folksy in tone but conflicted in its message. It appeared in one of the two volumes he published between 1869 and 1872 including *Dos yidele: yudishe lider af prost yudisher shprakh fun Avrom Goldenfodem*, a book of faux-naif nationalist Jewish poetry. It had been republished at least nine times by 1903.[53] Its overarching idea is that the irreducible essence of the Jew binds all Jews together, from the most modern Jew to the most devoted Hasid. It begins with a convention called the poet's affirmation of his commitment to his people. But if it is intended for a simple audience, Goldfaden wears his learning and sophistication on his shirtsleeve and he addresses his audience (traditional Jews) rather patronizingly as *yekele* (the Yiddish and diminutive name of Jacob, the typical stand-in for Israel). Goldfaden roams freely into areas of religious folk history and modern history and interpolates small pieces of dialogue. In its first section, for example, Goldfaden ventriloquizes a number of voices, including the voice of an anti-Semite: "Little Israel? . . . You are still alive? . . . We thought you already died!" and then reassures Yekele that "among noblemen you are just as noble." But the subsequent section repudiates this triumphal tone and proceeds with the narrative tone of a traditional jeremiad: "Only woe to the sheep that has strayed from his shepherd/ Not just one sacrifice has been brought to your altar."[54] Goldfaden's ruminations on "the essence of a Jew" turns on what he conceives of as the many paradoxes the Jew embodies: persecuted, but also self-persecuting; expelled from every place he goes, but finding his rest everywhere; always entreated, but asking nothing of anyone. However, the poem only grazes issues of a philosophical-historical kind, and there is no sense that Goldfaden has worked through the quandary the poem has marked out. We accompany Goldfaden in his efforts to recover his own connection to "his little Jews." As he states, his love for the Jewish people and their Torah feels visceral, so he must have imbibed it in his mother's milk. But Goldfaden does not conceive of a more conscious or principled embrace of Judaism. His words reflect dissatisfaction with the answers he musters to his own questions and of tensions unresolved and a work incomplete.

Notwithstanding his unstable income for his first married years in Odessa (1870–1875), Goldfaden did not let his lifestyle falter. To supplement his father-in-law's stipend, Goldfaden was forced to take a job as a clerk in a hat store. After opening his own hat store and then going bankrupt, he left his beloved Odessa for fear of debtors' prison. He lived in Munich briefly, where he considered studying medicine, and then repaired to the Black Eagle Hotel in Lemberg. He tried, once in collaboration with Linetski and another time on his own, to publish Yiddish-language newspapers. But without easy distribution in the Russian Empire, these efforts were not commercially sustainable.[55] In pursuit of patrons, Goldfaden made the trip to Iași on the invitation of Yitkhak Librescu, an admiring subscriber. Librescu was the leader of the local Lebanon Lodge, an organization funded by Alliance Israelite that promoted the modernization of Romania's Jewry in the face of worrying anti-Semitism.[56] The Librescus, who had "Romanianized" the family name Lieber, lived in an upper-class suburb of the city lined with asphalt streets and private gardens, far from the poverty of the cramped Jewish quarter.[57] Librescu offered Goldfaden a room in his home and an enthusiastic audience in the members of the Lebanon Lodge. The lodge subsidized Goldfaden's first productions in Iași and in Galați. The support and interest of the Lebanon Lodge members were crucial to the success of Goldfaden's productions.

In Iași, Goldfaden tested an audience that, besides his patrons, was composed of working-class and petty bourgeois consumers. As historians recount, Lebanon Lodge members had introduced Goldfaden to local tavern owner Shimon Mark, who invited him to declaim his poetry at the tavern. Goldfaden writes that the offer of money for a declamation was beneath a man of his social standing—he only declaimed before private audiences—but, given his dire financial circumstances, he had no choice but to accept it. Moreover, the offer revealed to him the commercial potential of Yiddish-language entertainment. Still, in his autobiography, Goldfaden is contemptuous of this first audience, which he believed lacked cultivation. In fact, while the educated Lebanon Lodge members admired his flawlessly executed declamation, Shimon Mark's customers preferred song, dance, and comedy. They drove Goldfaden from the stage. In Goldfaden's memoirs, his snobbery toward the less tutored masses is unmistakable:

> The night of the performance I was energized and dressed up in my formal evening wear: a black jacket, smooth white gloves; a white tie, I was accompanied by my good friend in a carriage to the garden.
>
> The garden was packed, overflowing, with . . . you know with what? I can't even tell you—whether they were people, or animals or beasts, because as soon as I got up on stage and began to declaim my well-known poem "*Dos pintele yid*," a dead silence reigned in the garden. And then I considered the situation: instead of a folksinger with shoes and socks they suddenly saw standing before them an elegant aristocrat in a frock jacket and my earnest demeanor commanded respect from them. . . . I declaimed with ecstasy. I concluded my poetry and the audience was silent. I left the stage and the audience was silent.[58]

Goldfaden's memory of the evening is informed not by embarrassment over his failure but by condescension toward an audience that could not appreciate his talent. He sees himself through the eyes of the audience as an "elegant aristocrat" to whom they cannot relate. Uneasy with Goldfaden's dismissive treatment of his lower-class audience, Soviet historians Oyslender and Finkel comment that Goldfaden is "too casual" with his language and imply that his snobbery was not representative of his general attitude toward the working class.[59] But it was. After Goldfaden exited the stage, celebrated Yiddish singer-entertainer Yisroel

Grodner performed a Goldfaden song that the audience loved. After this evening, Goldfaden and Grodner entered into collaboration and began pulling a troupe of actors together.[60]

Goldfaden's ever-growing nimbus of renown and activity was nourished by his expertise in self-promotion and not by his desire to enlighten the masses. When the theater began generating revenue, Goldfaden opened a headquarters for his theater company on Odessa's Richelevskaia Street. Mogulesco remembers that Goldfaden posted a valet outside his door to announce his guests before they entered the office.[61] Adler had already fashioned himself into a Yiddish actor under Spivakovski and Rosenberg's direction by the time of Goldfaden's arrival; he was nonetheless awed by the prospect of meeting the Yiddish impresario. According to his memoirs, only two episodes of his life—Adler's sighting of the tsar on a trip to Yalta and a pilgrimage to a Hasidic rebbe with his grandfather—compared to meeting Goldfaden:

> One trembled before [Goldfaden] . . . and just like a Tsar and a rebbe, he held court. He was always surrounded by people who looked up to him, who had a frightening respect for him. . . . To gain entry into the court of a rebbe you need a connection (*mekorev*). My connection was . . . Pukhhendler, a respected Odessa merchant and theater-lover. I knew him two ways, he was a close friend of my father's . . . and he had a restaurant . . . near the Mariinsky Theater and so he knew me as a theater-goer and he knew I had become a Yiddish actor.
>
> With the magic of Pukhhendler's words, the doors opened for me to an apartment on Preobrazhensky Street, onto a roomful of people. There were actors and actresses . . . the men smoking cigars or cigarettes and holding themselves comfortably. On the table were tea and cookies, and the clink of the spoons stirring the sugar created such a sweet and happy sound of the good life . . . loud conversations conducted in a casual and unrestrained tone animated the room. Falling into this "salon," I and Sonia (Adler's future first wife, the actress Sonia Oberlender) were confused. We sat down quietly off to the side and we cast searching glances around to figure out who among these people was Goldfaden. . . . Finally, ashamed, I quietly asked Pukhhendler: "Which one of these men is Goldfaden?"
>
> "Goldfaden here?" Pukhhendler looked at me with a mocking smile. "Goldfaden is not here. He is in his office. But he will make an appearance soon."
>
> A strange feeling came over me; a feeling of unrest and anticipation.[62]

As Pukhhendler makes clear to Adler, Goldfaden did not mingle freely with his actors; he generated a mystique about himself by making circumscribed and dramatic appearances even among his inner circle. The actor Dovid Kessler (discussed in chap. 2) recounts that only after he brought the house to its feet playing in Goldfaden's *Judah Maccabeus* (*Yehuda ha-makabi*) did the young actor even earn the opportunity to meet Goldfaden. He writes, "Then, Avrom Goldfaden appeared. It was the first time I met him. Goldfaden, with his aristocratic demeanor

Figure 1.3. Hand-painted magic lantern slide of David Kessler, c. 1910. Courtesy of the YIVO Institute for Jewish Research.

on his face at all times and with his intelligent eyes. He called me over, gave me a pat on my shoulder and said, 'I should burn the skin off your body! You should have told me earlier you could do such work!'"[63]

Just as in the exchange with Zilberbusch, Goldfaden's manner is that of a benign dictator. By cultivating an aura of intimate, unapproachable power, Goldfaden promoted both his name and image—not just in the cities he played but also in those beyond. Placards advertised his shows with his iconic trimmed moustache, goatee, and pince-nez.[64] So familiar was Goldfaden's mien that a Jewish immigrant to England who resembled the playwright managed to travel among far-flung communities of the country's Jewish immigrants impersonating Goldfaden and declaiming his words.[65] When troupes other than

Goldfaden's performed his works in shtetls, they announced them as works by Goldfaden because his name had cachet and commanded wide recognition. Goldfaden was arguably one of the first celebrities of nineteenth-century Jewish eastern Europe.

Goldfaden, the Father of the Yiddish Theater and the Problem of His Memoirs

For all the pomp and ceremony that Goldfaden was able to execute in person, his memoirs mirror the deflated person he became in his later years, vexed by crippling self-doubt. He could transmit neither his commanding presence nor his cultural and commercial triumphs. His paralysis was likely the result of the sudden downturn in his fortunes after the tsar banned Yiddish theater in late 1883. Adler writes in 1915 that "American Jews who had seen Avrom Goldfaden in his final years, an old, broken man, poor and abandoned, would have difficulty imagining the Avrom Goldfaden of 1878 following his success in Romania."[66] By the time he began reflecting on his accomplishments, Goldfaden had difficulty remembering the man he once was with stature undiminished and ego whole, untarnished by the blows of the Russian government and his fellow Jewish intellectuals. While on one level the memoirs transmit episodes of his life as readers might expect, between the lines—and in what they never transmit—his memoirs telegraph his depressed mental state.

Goldfaden's experience after the ban followed a downward slope until his death in 1908 and profoundly shaped—more accurately, profoundly diminished and distorted—the accounts of his life he managed to publish during his later years. In fact, he wrote no fewer than eight autobiographical works, some sketches, and one additional autobiography that, as he explained, doubled as a detailed history of the modern Yiddish theater.[67] At least that was his intention. So embittered was Goldfaden over what he considered the betrayal by his actors after all he had done for them, he barely mentions those actors who were still alive when he wrote his memoirs. As theater is collaborative, however, and as Goldfaden was unwilling to discuss the contribution of others to the enterprise of Yiddish theater, his accounts of the theater's beginnings are anemic, full of protestations about his hard work and the hurdles he had to overcome. The two actors to whom he gives the most credit are Max Karp and Yisroel Grodner, both long dead by the time he wrote. His memoirs are full of promises that he will return to a subject or person later on in his account. About the actor Karp, for instance, Goldfaden promises, "We will return to him later—the reader will meet him in Volume Two [of my memoirs entitled] 'Russia,' how his career was launched in St. Petersburg among the most talented of Jewish actors."[68] Goldfaden's story, however, does not advance beyond the year 1877. He never wrote Volume Two. He never returns to Karp and Grodner and mentions a paltry four or five names of the dozens of people who participated in pioneering Yiddish theater during its heyday. One version of his memoir edited by the scholar Moyshe Shtarkman is marked "*Der sof felt.*" ("The end is missing."). This could be said of each version he penned. And not just the end that is missing; most of the middle is missing as well. It occurs to no previous historian to wonder why Goldfaden never documented the heights of his cultural achievement and how to compensate for the lack of this record.

Omission marks, as well, the posthumously published memoir that was meant to be the most detailed version of his life, possibly the one he had gestured to in the earlier pieces he managed to publish during his lifetime. This, his lengthiest autobiographical work, although particularly absorbing in the details it furnishes, hews to the time-line of his previous memoirs; it, too, remarkably, does not extend past the year of 1877. Edited by the Yiddish theater impresario and historian Sholem Perlmutter and published in 1929, it does not address, to the great frustration of theater scholars, Goldfaden's most mature and successful works, which were first staged between 1879 and 1883 in Russia. It sheds some light on his days in Romania. But mostly, like the earlier published versions of his life, Goldfaden makes it to 1877, repeating the same set of anecdotes and laying claim to his legacy as the father of the Yiddish theater: "What am I to do in this work? The entire machinery of the 'Yiddish theater' turned on my 'self' (*mayn 'ikh'*)? What am I to do when my 'I' is the weight, the beginning point that allowed the wheels of the theater to begin turning? You cannot begin to fathom the machine without first understanding how the wheels and cogs began moving."

Goldfaden's assumption of the title "father of the Yiddish theater" is the most troubling aspect of his legacy as he shaped it. Throughout his autobiographical writings he continually talks about the theater as his child, haranguing his reader with a litany of abstract analogies that he uses to describe himself as the father and the theater as his child. The older he grew, the more he invoked these analogies of fatherhood and the less information he transmitted in his autobiographical narratives about his days as impresario; as he writes, he cannot free himself from the mental loop brought on by his fall from celebrity impresario. By 1906, Goldfaden's analogies grow nonsensical if not grotesque. "At that point, I had to take my newborn child and had to swaddle him. . . . He was not even able to wear a proper shirt." The level of emotion that accompanies these metaphors, metaphors to which he returns again and again, call to mind the only child Goldfaden had, who died young. It is revealing of his state of mind that he conflates the trauma of "losing his theater" with the trauma of losing his only child. While his fans and historians have embraced the title "Goldfaden, father of the Yiddish theater," and have thus—in these very words—made him into a cultural icon, the title was actually the product of his addled brain, his broken ego, and his utter desperation over feelings of detachment and abandonment.

At the same time, he uses the analogy of fatherhood to eschew responsibility for aspects of the theater that drew criticism. He quotes the Mishnah, "Against your will you were born," to explain that he did not opt to be an impresario of Yiddish theater, but rather destiny had chosen him to be its father. Like his fellow graduates at the seminary, he had planned to become a lawyer or doctor of medicine. He identified deeply with the class of Russian Jewish intellectual elite. So while he wants to take credit for the cultural achievement, he disavows the character of his work by blaming the audience, the actors, and even destiny for the choices he made as an impresario. "It meant nothing to me that I was forced into such debased situation," he explained regarding his first Yiddish theatrical productions, "but it pained me to see my people at such a low point . . . without a spark of its own nationalism, which it had already been seeking out in my national poetry."[69] Only some historical details turn up, wedged in between these grandiose claims. More of Goldfaden's memoirs followed. Again and again, Goldfaden raked over a brief period of his early theater activity in Romania but never produced an account of his far more impressive ascendancy as a celebrated impresario in Russia, most probably because doing so would mean conceding the cultural contribution of his colleagues toward whom he was too bitter to grant recognition. His memoirs illuminate little else besides his fragile state of mind during his two final decades.

The part of his life he never wrote about from 1878 to 1883—an era that is often dismissed as mere preparation for the theater's truer achievements of the twentieth century—was intensely creative and productive. Notwithstanding the criticism he attracted during this period, it was also an era that bore him the most positive recognition and celebrity. It was, in its own way, an unrivaled era of Yiddish theater and an unrivaled era of Jewish culture in imperial Russia. Without meaning to, Goldfaden deflates and diminishes his achievement in the few references to the Yiddish theater's first years that he manages to commit to paper. He writes nothing about his own accomplishments, the unprecedented appeal and renown he drew to modern Yiddish culture and its participants, first in Romania and then throughout the Russian Empire. With this small collection of references, historians have mischaracterized Goldfaden, his theatrical oeuvre, and the social and historical details that gave rise to the modern Yiddish theater.

Notes

1. In 1876 Eliezer-Isaac Shapiro, a Hebrew bookseller and publisher in Warsaw, wrote to a colleague about the arrival in Warsaw of "the important poet Mr. Goldfaden who is famous in our literature with his [Hebrew] book *Blossoms and Flowers*." The correspondence was published in 1876. Quoted in A. R. Malakhi, "Goldfaden-materialn," *Yivo-bleter* XV (1946): 330.

2. David Yeshayahu Zilberbush, *Mipinkas Zikhronotai* (Tel Aviv: va'ad yovel ha-shemonim, 1935). This part is excerpted in "Visiting Goldfaden, Father of the Yiddish Stage," in *The Golden Tradition: Jewish Life and Thought in Eastern Europe*, ed. Lucy Davidowicz (New York: Schocken Books, 1967), 322.

3. Ibid., 322.

4. Jacob Dineson, *Zikhroynes un bilder: shtetl, kinderyorn, shrayber* (Warsaw: Farlag Achiasaf, n.d.), 212.

5. Finkel, Uri, and Nokhem A. Oyslender. *Goldfadn: materyaln far a biografye* (Minsk: Institut far Vaysruslendisher Kultur, 1926).

6. Jacob Shatzky, "Goldfaden's Bibliografye," in *Goldfaden-bukh* (New York: Idisher Teater Muzey, 1926), 156.

7. See Y. Riminik, "Di ershte yorn funem yidishn teater (tsveyter teyl)," *Hamer* (April 1928): 59–64. Reprinted with both parts in Y. Riminik, "Di ershte yorn funem yidishn teater," *Di royte velt* Kharkov (12): 89–92.

8. Y. Riminik, "Di ershte yorn funem yidishn teater," 91.

9. On the widespread play of Goldfaden's works, see Jeffrey Veidlinger's "Jewish Public Culture in the Late Russian Empire" (Bloomington: Indiana University Press, 2009) and Nahma Sandrow, *Vagabond Stars: A World History of Yiddish Theater* (Syracuse: Syracuse University Press, 1996), 40–45.

10. See Richard Pipes, "The Historical View of the Russian Intelligentsia," *Daedulus*, 89 (Summer 1960), 488. Pipes defines two social groupings that came to be identified as the Russian intelligentsia. The one here invoked is a broader cultural group of like-minded, educated Russians that formed around the mid-nineteenth century and included part of the professional class, the enlightened gentry, the bourgeoisie, and provincial elite. A member was referred to as *intelligent*. The grouping of radical Russian intelligentsia that formed later was far narrower and accepted more extreme forms of contemporary French and German positivist thought and believed in socialism and revolution. Avraham Paperna makes a similar distinction when identifying himself as a member of the intelligentsia. See his *Zikhroynes* (Warsaw: Tsentral Farlag, 1923), 122.

11. As Clowes and Kassow point out, the term "bourgeoisie" lacks specificity in the complicated context of "loosening estates (*sosloviie*) of nineteenth-century Russia" but "bourgeois" (*meshchanin*) describes a number of "middle groupings" that emerged between the peasants and aristocracy during the age of Russian reform (1855–1881). See Steven J. Zipperstein, *The Jews of Odessa: A Cultural History, 1794–1881* (Stanford: Stanford University Press, 1985) and Natan Meir, *Kiev, Jewish Metropolis* (Bloomington: Indiana University Press, 2010) as a close study of the growth of a provincial city's Jewish community during this era, 36–51.

12. Reuven Goldberg supplies the most recent and authoritative account of the first period of his life. See Reuven Goldberg, ed., "Introduction" [Hebrew] in *Avraham Goldfadn: shirim ve-makhazot* (Jerusalem: Mosad Bialik, 1970), 9. The first study of Goldfaden was Wolf Heinreich Landau, *Abraham Goldfaden: Sein Leben und Wirken* (Vienna: Moriz Maizner, 1908). For a discussion of this sixteen-page work, see Mordekhe Kosover, "Di ershte goldfadn-biografye," *Yivo-bleter* XV (1946): 352–355.

13. Jacob Shatzky, "Goldfaden bibliografye," *Goldfaden-bukh*, 43.

14. Quoted based on an oral report in Nachman Maisel, *Noente un eygene: fun Yankev Dinezon biz Hersh Glik* (New York: IKUF, 1957), 7.

15. Wolf and Naftoli both lead Goldfaden troupes at some point during this era. Wolf had a long career as an actor in New York City. Binevich cites a reference to "Eugene Goldfaden" in the advertisement for a benefit performance of *Doctor Almosada.* See Binevich, "Obshie voprosi istorii. Personalii," *Istoriia evreiskogo teatra v rossii, 1876–1883. Annoturoviannaia bibliografia* (Moscow: Obshchestvo Nasledie, 1998). Both have entries in Zylbercweig's *Lekiskon.*

16. *Tsitsim u-ferakhim* (1865). Kovner's review appeared in *Ha-Melits*, no. 39–42 (1865). Goldfaden wrote Hebrew verse throughout his life. For a complete bibliography, see Shatzky, "Goldfaden shafn," *Goldfaden-bukh*, 80–96.

17. Verena Dohrn, *Jüdische Eliten im Russischen Reich: Aufklärung und Integration im 19. Jarhundert* (Cologne: Bohlau, 2008).

18. See Maisel, *Noente un eygene*, 35–53.

19. Tsitron, Sh. L. *Dray literarishe doyres: zikhroynes vegn yidishe shrifshteler* [Three Literary Generations] (Vilna: Sh. Shreberk, 1920), 14–15.

20. Avraham Paperna, "Di ershte yidishe drame" [The first Yiddish drama], *Pinkes: a fertlyoriker zhurnal far yidisher literaturgeshikhte, shprakhforshung, folklor un bibliografye* [*Pinkes*: a quarterly journal on Yiddish literary history, language research, folklore, and bibliography] 2 (1929): 187–188. For more on Ettinger and his literary work, see Shloyme Ettinger, *Ale ksovim*, ed. Max Weinreich (Vilna: B. Kletskin, 1925). On his most important work, *Serkele*, see my article, "The Currency of Yiddish: Ettinger's *Serkele* and the Reinvention of Shylock," *Prooftexts* 24 (2004): 99–115. For the staging of this work during this era, see chapter 4.

21. Menashe (Mikhail) Morgulis recalls two students at the seminary who put together a troupe in Berdichev one summer (1854–1855?) to perform songs in Yiddish and Ukrainian and a melodrama that some speculate was "The Kahal in Town" (*Kahal v mestechke*) for the benefit of the injured during the Crimean War. Margulis claims that there were objections to their cross-dressing in women's clothing. See his memoirs, M. Margulis, "Iz moikh vospomonanii," *Voskhod* (September 1895).

22. See, for instance, "Introduction of Declamation to the Russian Stage," document 218a in Laurence Senelick, ed., *National Theatre in Northern and Eastern Europe, 1746–1900* (Cambridge: Cambridge University Press, 1991), 328–332. The prominence of declamations of Yiddish literary works by "cultured Jews" in Odessa, Warsaw, Vilna, Berdichev, and Moghilev is mentioned by the maskil Joachim Tarnopol (1810–1900): "People pass the time in reading aloud, in the common Polish-Yiddish jargon, stories, dramatic scenes, whole pamphlets in verse or prose . . . which are declaimed before the entire assemblage." Osip Tarnopol, *Opyt sovremennoi I osmotritel'noireformy v oblasti iudaizma v Rossii: razmyshleniia o vnutrennem i vnieshnem bytiya russkikh evreev* (Odessa: 1868), 68. Zilberbush recounts his afternoon with Goldfaden and the poet Zbarsher Ehrenkrants, whose gift for memorizing and crafting spontaneous poetry was unsurpassed. See David Yeshayahu Zilberbush, *Mipinkas Zikhronotai* (Tel Aviv: va'ad yovel ha-shemonim, 1935), 81–90.

23. Quoted in Finkel and Oyslender, *A. Goldfaden*, 13.

24. A. Goldfaden, "Goldfadens groyse oytobiografye: fun yassi nokh bukarest ba'al kharkhekha ata molid," in *Goldfaden-bukh*, ed. Jacob Shatzky (New York: Idisher Teater Muzey, 1926), 46.

25. On Slonimski, see Ela Bauer, "In Warsaw and Beyond: The Contribution of Hayim Zelig Slonimski to Jewish Modernization," in *Warsaw, The Jewish Metropolis: Essays in Honor*

of the 75th Birthday of Professor Antony Polonsky, ed. Glenn Dynner and François Guesnet (Boston: Brill, 2015): 70–89.

26. For his familiarity with Russian literature, see Goldfaden's memoirs. The permission to travel is not recorded in any treatment of the schools that I know. In his memoirs, Isaac Librescu, the financial manager of Goldfaden's troupe, pointed out how much prestige and liberty his seminary medal afforded Goldfaden when he traveled.

27. As a group, the graduates of the Russian Jewish seminaries were sui generis in late imperial Russia, and as such joined the ranks of the *raznochintsy*, others likewise not easily categorized. Included here were, for instance, Russia's secondary teachers, men who were mostly married sons of the nobility, bureaucrats, and clergy and who entered the profession of teaching with privileges and ranks. Christiane Ruane and Ben Eklof, "The Teacher in Russian Society," in *Between Tsar and People*, ed. E. Clowes, S. Kassow, and J. West (Princeton, NJ: Princeton University Press, 1991), 200.

28. *Melits*, signed "Avraham ha-khut ha-zahav" (in Hebrew, "Abraham the Golden Thread"), advocated for the building of a school in Simferopol and for the entrance of a Simferopol resident to attend the seminary in Zhitomir. For bibliographical details, see J. Shatzky, "Goldfaden bibliografye," *Goldfaden Bukh*, 85.

29. See petitions sent to the government by seminary students asking to be released from their service in exchange for stipends: C. Freeze and J. Harris, eds., "Graduates of State Rabbinical Schools Who Had Received State Stipends," in *Everyday Jewish Life in Imperial Russia* (Waltham, MA: Brandeis University Press, 2013), 416.

30. A. Goldfaden, "Goldfadens groyse oytobiografye," *Goldfaden-bukh*, ed. Jacob Shatzky, 44. See Shatzky's discussion of Goldfaden's autobiographical works, "Goldfadens oytobiografishe material," *Goldfaden-bukh*, 40–42.

31. Nachmen Maisel, *Noente un eygnene*, 69.

32. Jonathan Frankel, *Prophecy and Politics: Socialism, Nationalism and the Russian Jews (1862–1917)* (Cambridge: Cambridge University Press, 1984), 29–31.

33. Ibid., 30. Finkel and Oyslender acknowledge what they deem the "reactionary" element in the seminary, which they claim was overwhelmed by the liberal and progressive ideas. See Finkel and Oyslender, *A. Goldfaden*, 12.

34. See the portrait of Linetski by Reuven Granofsky, "Yitskhok Yoyel Linetski: Zikhroynes," *Pinkes* I (1927–1928): 152.

35. Zalmen Zylbercweig, *Leksikon fun Yidishn teater*, vol. II (New York: Elisheva, 1931), 1528.

36. Yankev Adler, "40 yor af der bine: mayn lebn-geshikhte un di geshikhte fun yidishn teater," *Di varhayt*, August 30, 1916, 5. Adler's memoirs were serialized in *Di varhayt*. When possible, I will include a citation to the slightly abridged translation by Lulla Rosenfeld, *Bright Star of Exile: Jacob Adler and the Yiddish Theater* (New York: Thomas Y. Crowell Company), 1977.

37. Ibid., 5.

38. Ibid.

39. Ibid.

40. Ibid.

41. Riminik, "Di ershte yorn (tsveyte teyl)," 62.

42. Z. Zylbercweig, *Avrom Goldfaden un Zigmunt Mogulesko* (Buenos Aires: Elisheva, 1936), 159.

43. See Y. Riminik's "Ershte finf yor yidisher teater in odes (1879–1883)," *Di royte velt*, Kharkov (53): 89. Riminik writes that the city produced the cheap street singer and chanteurs. "Odessa was the crossroads and the theater market between Moscow and the smallest far-flung shtetl always traveled by the easy going actors from Mother Odessa" (90). In an effort to give their readers a sense of Odessa's theatrical offerings, Goldfaden and Adler both mention productions of works including Shakespeare, Schiller, Faust, Uriel Acosta, and Russian and Ukrainian fare. See Adler, "40 yor af der bine," *Di varhayt*, September 17, 1916, 5.

44. See Maisel, *Noente un eygene*, 15.

45. There are entries on all three figures in Zylbercweig's encyclopedia. Bernshteyn's lullabye, "Rozhinkes mit mandlen" ["Almonds and Raisins"], is the earliest published version of this song. Goldfaden wrote a version of it into *Shulamis*. See A. Quint and R. Robboy, eds., *Shulamis: A Critical Edition* (Dusseldorf: Dusseldorf University Press, forthcoming). Trakhtman was a pioneer of Jewish farming and colonization in Palestine and Argentina.

46. Zylbercweig, *Leksikon*, I: 278.

47. According to Riminik, Goldfaden's first drama that he finished around this time, *Aunt Sosya* (*Di mume sosya*), is an unflattering depiction of his Odessa-based extended family with whom he lodged for a period. In the play, the family tries unsuccessfully to court the interest of a visiting cousin, Zilberzayd—who himself is portrayed as sophisticated but also condescending and narcissistic. See Y. Riminik, "Tsu der geshikhte fun Goldfadens 'Mume sosya,'" *Shriftn*, Kiev (1928): 337–343.

48. Bertha Kalich [written with Tsvi-Hirsh Rubinshteyn], *Der Tog*, May 23, 1925, 5 (March 7–November 14, 1925). There are very few mentions of Paulina and the Verbel family generally.

49. See the brief entry on him in Zylbercweig, *Leksikon*, I: 731.

50. "Gol'dfadena v zale gostinitsy 'Demut,'" *Russkii Evrei*, no. 10 (1882): 387. According to the review, Paulina Goldfaden played the secondary female role of Avigail. There is a single reference to a son who apparently died at a young age in a brief memoir written by Isaac Perkoff, a British Jewish photographer who befriended the Goldfadens in their later years. See Perkoff's brief memoir of the Goldfadens that includes some of Goldfaden's letters to him. Isaac Perkoff, *Mayne memuaren un zayne briv* (London: Jouques Printing Works, 1908). Zylbercweig, *Leksikon*, I: 325.

51. On Engel, see James Loeffler, "Introduction," in *The Most Musical Nation: Jews and Culture in the Late Russian Empire* (New Haven, CT: Yale University Press, 2010).

52. Quoted in Finkel and Oyslender, *A. Goldfaden*, 32. For a discussion of folk poets and folk singers and the relationships among them, see my article "The Salon and the Tavern: Yiddish Folk Poetry of the Nineteenth Century," in *Inventing the Modern Yiddish Stage*, ed. J. Berkowitz and B. Henry (Detroit: Wayne State University Press, 2013), 40–63.

53. Shatzky, "Goldfaden bibliografye," *Goldfaden-bukh*, 85.

54. Avrom Goldfaden, *Dos yudele: yudishe lider oyf prost yudisher shprakh* (Warsaw: Y. Lidski, 1903), 8.

55. *Der alter yisrolik: tsaytungs-blat far kol yisroel* (July 1875–February 1876) lasted six months. Copies of *Bukowiner Israelitisches Volksblatt*, a newspaper he then founded in Czernowitz after *Yisrolik*, are no longer extant.

56. After a spate of anti-Semitic incidents, the United States Consul Benjamin Franklin Peixotto (1830–1890) believed that the only solution to the Romanian Jewish crisis was emigration, but until such a thing was possible, he helped put in place the Lebanon Lodge

network to keep acculturated Romanian Jews invested in the lives of the more traditional members of the community. The Lebanon Lodge would prove to be a good friend to Goldfaden and his troupe. Lloyd P. Gartner, "Documents on Romanian Jewry," *Salo Wittmayer Baron Jubilee Volume I* (Jerusalem: Columbia University Press, 1974), 483.

57. B. Lieber, "Zikhroynes vegn avrom goldfadn," *Yivo-bleter* XXXV (1951): 246.

58. A. Goldfaden, "Goldfadens groyse oytobiografye," *Goldfaden-bukh*, ed. Jacob Shatzky, 54–55. In his extended autobiography Goldfaden goes into greater detail about his "gala outfit": a black jacket, white gloves, and a white necktie and he was chauffeured into the garden in a horse-drawn carriage. With mock lament he writes "Oy, my jacket, oy, my white necktie!" *Der onfang fun yidishn teater Yidishe velt*, April 15, 1929, 11.

59. Finkel and Oyslender, *A. Goldfaden*, 41.

60. For a discussion of Goldfaden and Grodner's collaboration, see chapter 2.

61. Zylbercweig, *Leksikon*, I: 302. Adler has the same memory. In English, see Rosenfeld, 73.

62. Adler, "40 yor af der bine," *Di varhayt*, December 31, 1916, 6.

63. Dovid Kessler, "Goldfaden, Lerner, Shaykevitsh," *Der Tog*, January 21, 1917.

64. For a description of placards with Goldfaden's likeness, see B. Vaynshteyn's memoirs, "Di ershte yorn fun yidishn teater," in *Arkhiv far der geshikhte fun yidishn teater and drame* (Vilna and New York: YIVO, 1930), 245.

65. Zylbercweig, *Leksikon*, I: 318.

66. Adler, "40 yor af der bine," *Di varhayt*, December 27, 1916, 5.

67. He refers to this project in several places, including in an edition of *Shulamis*. Historian Yankev Shatzky contextualizes four of Goldfaden's autobiographical pieces in a short introductory essay in *Goldfaden-Bukh*. The first dates to 1887 and was published in Goldfaden's own short-lived periodical entitled *New-Yorker ilustrirter tsaytung*. The second was revised and published by Mordkhe Spektor as a third-person history of the Yiddish theater and published in *Hoyz-fraynd* in 1887. The third was published in *Varhayt* soon after his death in 1908, and the fourth he completed in 1901 in Paris and published in three segments in a quarterly called *Minikes bleter* that same year. These pieces are republished and edited by Shatzky in *Goldfaden-bukh* except for the missing second of three segments (Shatzky was unable to locate a surviving copy of the *peysakh* installment of *Minikes bleter*). Apparently, in 1926, Shatzky did not know about Goldfaden's longest autobiographical project that Perlmutter later discovered and published in serial form in 1929. See Sholem Perlmutter, "Der onfang funem idishn teater," *Yidishe velt*, Philadelphia (April 1930–June 1930). Moyshe Shtarkman edited and published one of his autobiographical pieces entitled "Fun Shmendrik biz Ben-Ami draysikyeriker epokhn-gang der antvikling fun mayn yidish teater-kind," in *Arkhiv far der geshikhte fun yidishn teater un drame* (New York and Vilna: YIVO, 1930), 265–272.

68. A. Goldfaden, "Goldfadens groyse oytobiografye," *Goldfaden-bukh*, ed. Jacob Shatzky, 62.

69. Ibid., 56.

2 The Rise of the Yiddish Actor

I was curious to meet a Yiddish actor. . . . I thought that as soon as I told him I wanted to write a play, he would start emoting; wipe his nose on his sleeve, jump on a chair, and recite one of his most popular tunes of the day. . . . Imagine to my surprise on meeting gentlemen with silk hats and handkerchiefs who talked intelligently.

Jacob Gordin

Goldfaden in Romania (1876–1878)

Beginning in the fall of 1876 in Romania, Goldfaden made two separate attempts at growing Yiddish-language vaudeville into full-blown operetta, failing first before he succeeded. After meeting a seasoned vaudeville entertainer named Yisroel Grodner in Iași, Goldfaden began composing content of one-act and two-act works that reflected the theater's vaudeville roots.[1] They played regularly at a modest café called for the proprietor Shimon Mark. They successfully recruited Sachar Goldshteyn, a pink-cheeked saddle-maker with a beautiful voice who could easily pass for a lady. Goldfaden also negotiated the entry of Sophie Karp (1859–1904, neé Sara Segal) into the troupe after arranging her marriage to Goldshteyn; he drew the character of a mute bride to acclimate her to the stage before she had to recite lines. Still, the troupe could not push the scale of its work beyond a vaudeville format with a small cast of actors, mostly because they could not raise ticket prices. Without more money, Goldfaden was stuck at Shimon Mark's café and could not attract more than a small and mostly working-class audience. About a year later, in the fall of 1877, history interrupted and Goldfaden and his troupe closed operations as the threat of war loomed on the horizon. The Romanian authorities began conducting a dragnet draft of all men of military age as they prepared for war against the Ottoman Empire. The three men went into hiding together in a cramped attic to wait out the recruitment.

Goldfaden emerged from hiding after the war began in the fall of 1877 when the Russian army had already begun moving down into Romania in anticipation of the Russo-Turkish War (1877–1878).[2] Russians fought alongside Romanians against the Ottomans for Romania's independence. The war was a difficult one for Russia's army, which sustained heavy losses.[3] But for many of the Russian merchants or "contractors" servicing the food and clothing needs of the Russian army, many of them Jews from the empire's southern provinces, the war was financially beneficial.[4] Strolling in Bucharest in the fall of 1877, after emerging from his hiding spot, Goldfaden bumped into an acquaintance from Odessa. "What are you doing here?" Goldfaden asked him. "Why are you so surprised?" his friend replied. "It is wartime; the whole world is about to descend on Bucharest to make money." By "the whole world," his acquaintance meant Russian Jewish merchants from Goldfaden's adopted city of Odessa, which was situated on the southern coast of the Black Sea in Crimea and was one of the empire's closest cities to Romania.

The war proved to be a boon as well to Goldfaden's second foray into the business of Yiddish theater for a moneyed audience. On hearing about his friends' lucrative prospects with the Russian army, Goldfaden's instinct was to abandon his theatrical efforts for business, but he reached the High Commission in Bucharest too late to secure a contract. Among the Russian contractors were Goldfaden's colleagues and fellow Odessans, but Goldfaden was sure to emphasize that they did not participate in his productions:

> As much as I tried to convince them to write a play for good money they weren't interested. [Avrom Ber] Gottlober was seeing good money from the contractors for his books, [Yitskhak Yoyel] Linetski had a contract to secure barrels to hold sauerkraut for the army, [Osip] Lerner was taking in a lot of bribe money in return for not denouncing the illegal contractors. [Nahum] Shaikevitsh, "the Jewish Eugene Sue" had not yet even dreamed of writing novels and adapting them for the stage, he was acquiring hay and oats for the army. The main point: all the work fell on my shoulders.[5]

Goldfaden's version of events contradicts the recollections of Jacob P. Adler, who explains that the Odessa bon vivant Yisroel Rosenberg and Goldfaden's seminary colleague, Yankev Spivakovski, enthusiastically participated in Goldfaden's productions. Adler's version is the likelier one: Goldfaden is careful not to give credit to fellow intellectuals—preferring to imagine himself as the theater's "father," the singular shaper of folk culture.[6]

Goldfaden does acknowledge the support his colleagues gave him in the form of an audience. When he mentioned his failed theatrical productions to them, as he recalls in his memoirs, his fellow Odessans urged him to try again and promised to bring thirty friends to attend the show. This time the whole world showed up. Goldfaden's productions became the regular entertainment of the Russian Jewish army contractors based in Romania. Until he was able to advertise with posters and newspaper advertisements, Goldfaden sent news about performances by word of mouth via a network of his friends and acquaintances.[7] Russian journalist N. D. Shigarin commissioned by the Society for the Promotion of Enlightenment (known as OPE, its Russian acronym) caught wind of one of Goldfaden's Bucharest productions and wrote about it in his book on Russian Jewish activity during the Russo-Turkish War. With a show of great elegance, Shigarin writes, Goldfaden and his wife led him to a reserved seat next to their own for one of the earliest Yiddish theatrical productions.[8] Fellow Russian Jewish businessmen, and not the Romanian Jewish working-class audience, lent Goldfaden's theater a crucial financial boast. With the proceeds from such an audience, Goldfaden assembled a theater troupe that rapidly grew to include a chorus and an orchestra, the first troupe of such scale to perform in Yiddish. Goldfaden's troupe was the first Jewish company to have female actors, as well as to use props and scenery, and the first also to have elaborate costumes and, eventually, sophisticated placards announcing shows.[9]

His troupes performed in the Romanian cities of Botaśani, Galați, and Bucharest in venues that included garden stages, halls, and theaters with loges.[10] Theater historian B. Gorin explains:

> The High Commission of the Russian Army established its headquarters in Bucharest and, with this, gold filled the pockets of anyone who wasn't too lazy to take it. There was nothing so cheap as money. Men who came to Bucharest poor became rich, and with the easily gotten money came the obligation of living for the moment, enjoying. The theater was created for them and the big, newly rich audience enjoyed this entertainment. Now, the theater houses were packed. There were no longer empty benches and the actors forgot about their hungry days. The audience also took on a different complexion. Instead of visitors from the very lowest level of society, one could now see householders, maskils, and the theater became a national institution of the people (*fun dem gantsn folk*). Also seen are Russian officers in the audience.[11]

By the first winter of his theatrical productions (1877), Goldfaden raised the price of a ticket from one franc to four to six and even as high as twenty francs. When he was once asked why a ticket was so expensive, he demanded of his interlocutor whether he himself had ever had as much money as he had now. "It is wartime, and I meant this in the best way possible," Goldfaden recalls saying.[12] Librescu estimates that Goldfaden had a yearlong track record of success. Theater tickets were so difficult to acquire that they were unavailable at the box office and could only be procured from agents. Goldfaden's acquaintances and colleagues—all of whom were making money from the war—created the inviting conditions for Goldfaden's theater: a sophisticated Russian Jewish audience beyond the legal reach of the Russian Empire where the law still prohibited Yiddish theater. Eventually, Goldfaden's theater productions attracted luminaries like the Romanian national poet Mikhail Eminescu (1850–1889), who reviewed his performances for Iași's local paper, and the esteemed Russian field marshal Count Iosif Vladimirovich Romeyko-Gurko, as well as members of the Romanian royal family. This second and successful attempt at theater by Goldfaden generated a community of

Yiddish actors that, in turn, allowed him to stage operettas on a greater scale. In 1877, less than two years into his experiment with Yiddish performance, Goldfaden wrote a five-act operetta called *The Sorceress.*

The Sorceress, a melodrama about the dangers of city life, opens onto the birthday celebration of Mirele at the home of her father Avromtshe (diminutive of Avrom, from the biblical name Abraham), a wealthy merchant and a member of the Galați bourgeoisie. Mirele is surrounded by friends, and Marcus, her fiancé, a young and educated Jew, is also by her side. Avromtshe has recently married a second wife, Basye, following the death of Mirele's beloved mother. Only interested in his money and in collusion with friends, Basye secretly frames Avromtshe, who is arrested by the end of the first act. As Avromtshe languishes in jail, Mirele is reduced to a servant in her stepmother's home. Impatient to get rid of Mirele for good, Basye enlists the help of the local sorceress, or fortune-teller, Bobe Yakhne, who kidnaps Mirele and sells her as an indentured servant to a Turkish merchant. A crook beneath her grandmotherly name and demeanor, Bobe Yakhne pretends to function as the spiritual leader of her community. A character named Hotsmakh, a folk singer and traveling haberdasher, is not crucial to the movement of the operetta's plot but has great thematic significance as an ally to the young Marcus. Marcus and Hotsmakh rescue Mirele and together they meet her father, recently released from his unjust imprisonment, and prevail over their common enemies.

In this chapter, I move between an analysis of Goldfaden's *The Sorceress* and the experience of his actors as recounted in memoirs and newspaper sources. Building on Goldfaden's own rise to elite status and celebrity recounted in chapter 1, I describe the social life of the Yiddish theater, first through Goldfaden's eyes, and then through his operetta and the memoirs of his actors. The characters of Hotsmakh and Marcus, each operating as the other's double, evoke the relationships that arose between the rough-hewn wedding jesters and the educated and multilingual Russian and Romanian Jews who joined the first Yiddish theater troupes after 1876. The double-protagonist structure in which a modern character works in tandem with a traditional and pious Jew recurs in a number of Goldfaden's comic operettas including *The Two Kuni-Lemls* (discussed in chap. 3) and his early comic farce *Shmendrik*. It also captures the ties that crystallized among the first actors of the modern Yiddish theater. Goldfaden's first troupe emerged from a diversity of social backgrounds to form a community of mutual cultural influence and creativity in which his performers remade themselves into *yidishe artistn* (Jewish artists or actors) in the images of one another and, of course, in the image of Goldfaden. The theater was fueled by the desire of the "folk" actors to be seen as modern actors, that is, to be like Marcus. With its references to premodern theater in Hotsmakh and the dangers of the city, *The Sorceress* advances the alliance of Hotsmakh and Marcus as the safeguard of modern Jewish life.

The Post-Sacred World of *The Sorceress*

Goldfaden's operetta *The Sorceress* is ample evidence of the richness of his theatrical imagination. Internalizing the criticism and sense of insult of his colleagues, Goldfaden dismissed his early operettas, including *The Sorceress*, as an instrument with which to acclimate untutored entertainers to his Westernized interpretation of the Yiddish stage. *The Sorceress* (called in Yiddish *Kaldunye*, *Di kishefmakherin*, or *Di bobe yakhne*—the latter translates as *Grandmother Yakhne*) was Goldfaden's most culturally relevant work by the time it was first staged in 1877 and it would go on to accrue a storied stage history.[13] The budding composer and impresario recognized its theatrical strength: the operetta marked Goldfaden's debut in Odessa when he transferred his troupe from Romania to the Russian Empire a year later. In August 1880, he staged *The Sorceress* fourteen times in Moscow, a city that was both beyond the Pale of Settlement and restricted to Jewish residents.[14] Contemporary press coverage suggests that it was one of the most popular Yiddish works of this period on a Russian stage and played by a number of the theater troupes active in the empire. It was one of the first Yiddish operettas to be performed in Polish translation (*Czarownica*) in Warsaw in 1888.[15] And it was the first full-scale Yiddish work on an American stage in July 1882, when Boris Thomashefsky (1868–1939) and Leon Golubok (1865–1918) organized a public performance of it in New York City's Turn Hall.[16]

In its very first performances, *The Sorceress* introduced a grand scale to the Yiddish stage. Goldfaden had gradually increased the number of actors on the stage by this point while adding costume, set design, and more dialogue to his works. Previously, plotlines were confined to intra-family conflicts that played out mostly against the backdrop of bourgeois living rooms. *The Sorceress* is lushly detailed with scenes that lift the action away from the domestic setting of his previous simple comedies to settings that include the bustling market in the Romanian city of Botoşani (in Yiddish, Botashan), the headquarters of a fortune-teller, a café in Constantinople, and a roadside tavern. Alongside *The Recruits* and his play *The Contractor*, *The Sorceress* is the most epic of his Romania-set works, apparently inspired by the work of the Romanian playwright Matei Millo, one of three founders of Romania's national theater, which dates to 1853. The copious notes that describe the costumes and backdrops detailed in the first published edition of the play reflect a sophisticated theatrical vision.[17]

The Sorceress plumbs the city's dangers and loneliness with the lens of melodrama and explores contradictory dimensions of *veltlekhkayt*, or worldliness. Instead of a domestic comedy driven by desire and romance, it presents an emerging urban merchant-class of Romanian Jews as the model of modernity denuded of their moral anchor in their Jewish heritage. As the evil sorceress says to her victim, the story's heroine Mirele, with feigned concern when she discovers her in rags at the marketplace, "Why, aren't you the daughter of Shifra Reb Yokhanan's daughter? Wasn't your grandfather the city rabbi?"[18] The fallen state of the granddaughter of the city's recent chief rabbi reveals the community's rapid secularization. Though Goldfaden was a creature of the city, *The Sorceress* reveals its urban backdrop, here the small city of Botoșani, to be a dangerous place, and where Jewish life is conspicuously absent, notwithstanding its sizable Jewish population.[19] The play's *yidishkayt*, or Jewishness, has a shrunken presence illuminated by the terms of what the literary theorist Peter Brooks calls the melodrama's "post-sacred world." Goldfaden deploys the melodramatic modality's basic principle "of uncovering, demonstrating, and making operative the essential moral universe in a post-sacred era." As Brooks goes on to explain in *The Melodramatic Imagination*,

> Melodrama starts from and expresses the anxiety brought by a frightening new world in which the traditional patterns of moral order no longer provide the necessary social glue. It plays out the force of that anxiety with the apparent triumph of villainy and it dissipates it with the eventual victory of virtue. It demonstrates over and over that ethical forces can be discovered and made legible. . . . Melodrama is indeed, typically, not only a moralistic drama but the drama of morality: it strives to find, to articulate, to demonstrate, to "prove" the existence of a moral universe which, though put into question, masked by villainy and perversions of judgment, does exist and can be made to assert its presence and its categorical force among men.[20]

The moral universe asserts its presence in the final scene of *The Sorceress* where it gathers the heroes in celebration at a tavern where Basye, Bobe Yakhne (the sorceress), and her assistant Elyokum set a fiery death trap for them. But the villains are foiled and burn to death themselves. A world mostly devoid of the sacred, as in *The Sorceress*, is only barely able to counter its inherent dangers. The libretto pits Bobe Yakhne and her entourage against the characters of Hotsmakh and Marcus, who move in tandem and in sympathy through the operetta.

Some of the most vocal first reviewers of the operetta overlooked the Hotsmakh-Marcus alliance and instead saw a close link between two traditional characters of Hotsmakh and the sorceress: both ugly Jewish caricatures and both invoking worldliness "*veltlekhkayt*" as their worldview. In 1880, for instance, a reader from Minsk wrote to the Russian-Jewish newspaper *The Russian Jew* (*Russki Evrei*) pointing to Hotsmakh as one of Goldfaden's most destructive characters: "In many Christian homes, the words 'Shmendrik,' 'Kuni-Leml,' 'Hotsmakh,' and others are becoming quite popular . . . go into a store and you will hear a nobleman-buyer turn to the Jewish shopkeeper and say: 'Are you measuring that according to the Hotsmakh theory in which four *arshin* becomes twelve *arshin*?'"[21] Accusing Goldfaden of anti-Semitism, one journalist wrote: "Hotsmakh depicts us [Jews] as swindlers and connivers. Even the most terrifying Judeo-phobe could not have amassed . . . [such] accusations of exploitation against the Jews."[22] Consciously or otherwise, actors also emphasized the link between the two characters in some renditions of the operetta with the same actor playing both old-world roles of Bobe Yakhne and Hotsmakh.[23]

Indeed, Hotsmakh and the evil Bobe Yakhne have analogously traditional bearing and both invoke the idea of worldliness as part of their outlook and way of life. In speech and action, their worldliness seems to characterize their lust for money, their cynicism, and their willingness to prey on the unsuspecting consumer. This is on display, for instance, when a young girl approaches Hotsmakh at the marketplace to buy sewing needles for her mother. Hotsmakh tricks the girl by deliberately miscounting the amount of needles she gives her. It is a hilarious scene that resembles a vaudeville sketch but it reveals Hotsmakh to be a common criminal:

> GIRL: Hotsmakh, English needles—do you have any?
>
> HOTSMAKH: So English they don't speak a word of French! How many do you need?
>
> GIRL: Twelve dozen needles.
>
> HOTSMAKH: Twelve dozen will cost you less. *(He puts his pack down and opens it.)*
>
> GIRL: How much do twelve dozen cost?
>
> HOTSMAKH: Not more than thirty kopeks.
>
> GIRL: Thirty kopeks, that much?
>
> HOTSMAKH: I need to survive going home to a wife and many children. They cost me more to buy, but it's Sabbath Eve and I'm prepared to give them away cheap.
>
> GIRL: It's too much. I'll give you only twenty kopeks.
>
> HOTSMAKH: Such a young girl and already smart enough to bargain. For that, I'll give it to you for twenty-five kopeks so hold out your little hand and let me count them. *(He takes his needles out and begins to count them)* One, two, three, four, five, six . . . How old are you that you can bargain so well?
>
> GIRL: I am thirteen.
>
> HOTSMAKH: Fourteen, fifteen, sixteen, seventeen, eighteen, nineteen, twenty. . . . And how old can that father of yours be, he should live a long life, you don't think I know him that red-haired bandit. How old is he now?
>
> GIRL: My father is thirty-five.
>
> HOTSMAKH: . . . I know your father to be at least forty, do you hear? Forty, forty-one, forty-two, forty-three, forty-four, forty-five, forty-six, forty-seven, forty-eight, forty-nine, fifty. Take a good look at me young lady and tell me how old you think I am with my little beard. (1.8)

And the dialogue continues. With each of his seemingly casual questions, Hotsmakh jumps numbers and finally gives the girl fewer needles for the same money. His deceitful mercantile practices, the play suggests, are routine: when the commissar first shows up at Avromtshe's house in act 1, Hotsmakh believes they are there to arrest him for dealing in false weights and fearfully offers an unsolicited confession to the bewildered officers. Hotsmakh attributes his savvy to his worldliness as he tells Marcus, "My merchandise takes me throughout the world" (4.5). Likewise, before Bobe Yakhne, the sorceress, agrees to help Basye, she sets her client straight on the nature of her magic powers and thus on the nature of the world:

> Still talking like a child? You are still convinced that I perform magic? You still believe that I stir cauldrons, . . . that I spin a wheel in an oven, that I stick a pair of scissors in the earth and cause something that way? Those tricks I do only to swindle money out of fools who are idiots enough to believe in such things. Really, those things have no worth—what constitutes my magic? *In the practical experience I gained in the world.* Life experience and wisdom. The expertise to swindle, that is the whole of my magic besides which there is nothing . . . Didn't the people themselves say that you placed Avromtshe under a spell when you got him to marry you? And you yourself know how it played out. *The whole thing was proof of my worldliness* (*genitshaft in der velt*), *and besides that nothing.* The only thing I "divined" was that Avromtshe is a rich widower and has but one child, and you were a poor and deprived widow so I ordered you to somehow become his neighbor and pretend to relate well to the child, smile, and smooth talk and serve her so she trusts you and Avromtshe would observe and take you as his wife. (2.4) (my italics)

Bobe Yakhne's extended monologue lays out what is akin to a religion of worldliness. Not only does she reject any otherworldly authority but also she arrogantly holds out the trappings of divine supremacy to manipulate those around her. Besides the worldliness of secular knowledge and Russian Jewish integration that Marcus embodies, with the introduction of the worldliness of Bobe Yakhne and of Hotsmakh, *The Sorceress* advances multiple and incongruous definitions of "worldliness."

As the operetta progresses, however, Bobe Yakhne's cynicism and boundless evil differentiate her from Hotsmakh who, albeit a thief, is self-effacing and steadfast in his commitment to Judaism and the Jewish People. Although the play suggests Bobe Yakhne is Jewish by default, any reference to a Jewish religious framework is astonishingly absent from her worldview. What remains is the power of deception and greed and the price tag that hangs not only from every false transaction she executes, but also from the weaker people whom she controls. As to how Basye may rid herself of Mirele, Bobe Yakhne proposes they take her hostage and sell her into servitude to a Turk. As Bobe Yakhne remarks with excitement, "And we can still make some money on her!" (1.4) Selling Mirele as if she were a piece of merchandise, so the play indicates, is true evidence of Bobe Yakhne's evil character on this otherwise slippery slope of worldly behavior.[24] Her actions set in motion Avromtshe's imprisonment and Mirele's indentured servitude in Constantinople.

Finally, Bobe Yakhne reveals the vulnerability of even the most sophisticated members of society in their attraction to her hollow magic. Marcus, for instance, is the paragon of a worldly Jew as signaled by his Western appearance and even his name. By the time Goldfaden wrote *The Sorceress* the name "Marcus" had become the name of the quintessential male hero in Yiddish-language Enlightenment plays. Marcus became the secular name for Mordechai, the uncle of Queen Esther in the Pentateuch's Scroll of Esther, read on the holiday of Purim.[25] His name, then, is associated with judiciousness and political intelligence as well as skill in navigating the non-Jewish world for the protection of the Jewish People—high expectations that Marcus barely fulfills. The operetta reveals that even Marcus follows the community—including his fiancée, Mirele—into spiritual dependence on the witch. In act 2, Mirele monologizes about her visit to the sorceress, "Why did you deal me such a bad hand, when you dealt others such good ones? . . . Oh, the good woman [the witch] tried to console me, but it was impossible, her words burrowed deeply into my heart and each morning when I awoke from my sleep my heart was heavy from the nightmares I suffered, they destroyed me" (2.1). Again, the possible inconsistencies of a belief system that accommodates Mirele's Jewish roots and her consultation with a fortune-telling witch are never at issue. And, except to Hotsmakh, her birthday party is similarly unexceptional. To the unsuspecting Mirele, her tragic circumstances are accounted for by the "bad deal" she was dealt. The audience learns that the witch's skill in "forecasting" Mirele's fate is due to the hand she has in orchestrating those events. Finally, the witch dupes the otherwise sharp-witted hero of the drama, Marcus, when he seeks out her expertise concerning Mirele's disappearance. She pretends to conjure an image of Mirele using magic when, in fact, Mirele herself, imprisoned for the time being in her lair, is what Marcus really sees. Who, good or evil, does not subscribe to the witch's counterfeit worldview?

Only Hotsmakh.

When we first meet him, Hotsmakh stumbles onto Mirele's birthday party and we relate to him initially as an object of entertainment. He comes uninvited and violates codes of dress and manner and yet the hosts of the party welcome him enthusiastically. He relieves a palpable emptiness felt as the partygoers try to shore up a distraction for themselves. "Oh, good, Hotsmakh is here, he will amuse us!" Marcus exclaims when he spies the peddler (1.2). Perplexed by the nature of the gathering—he knows it is not a Jewish holiday—Hotsmakh tries to peddle his tired wares to Avromtshe's refined guests. When Avromtshe and Mirele magnanimously urge him to set his wares aside and join the guests for a drink, Hotsmakh wonders aloud if there is any danger that the guests might steal his merchandise. This is meant to elicit laughter from the audience, for who among these refined representatives of Odessa's Jewish bourgeoisie would steal his wares? His host calls on him to sing a folk song, and Hotsmakh seems nothing more than an entertainer. But in his performance, his figure gathers significance. Hotsmakh takes the floor and sings a song about false behavior that proves to be the key to the partygoers.

> Today, people are false and affected,
> Everyone has his own opinion
> They are on top of the world when they speak aloud
> But in their hearts they are displeased
> Your friend might not be so rotten
> When he is visiting you at home
> He'll be friendly to your face
> But then he'll think to himself, "The hell with him." (1.3)

Each verse introduces another scenario in which the subject says one thing to his or her interlocutor but means something else: a lender is all smiles to his debtor but curses him in his heart just as a charlatan promises marriage to a young lady and thinks to himself, "to hell with her." Hotsmakh, a scam artist to be sure, is not referring to himself but rather to the people around him, for Hotsmakh is not just a peddler. He is a performer. And in castigating the audience, he channels the voice and message of the vaudeville players and wedding jesters who entertained Jewish crowds before the advent of the Yiddish theater. In this way, the character of Hotsmakh is wedded deeply to the rise of the modern Yiddish actor.

The Implacable Badkhn: Goldfaden's Account of the First Yiddish Actors

According to Goldfaden, he wrote the character of Hotsmakh to accommodate the limited talents of his first actors who only knew the stage as wedding jesters and folk singers. Although never referred to as such in the operetta's libretto, Hotsmakh is an example of the traditional Jewish entertainers called Brody singers (for the Galician city of Brody), *badkhonim* (wedding jesters), or folk singers (*folkzingers*), who became popular in some cities throughout Jewish eastern Europe by the 1850s and 1860s. As folk singers, they performed in the taverns that dotted merchant routes throughout the Pale of Settlement and stretched westward into cities like Lemberg (Lviv) and Vienna. The Russian government restricted public Yiddish-language performances but musical concerts of this smaller scale were allowed. Under this protection, entertainers did more than sing. Loosely defined as vaudeville, the shows included song, dance, costume, makeup, acting, and comedy routines always performed by men. The shows had an improvised feel and were sometimes accompanied by small three-piece ensembles.

While the Yiddish vaudeville shows were technically secular—they had no connection to the Jewish calendar, for instance—they worked off their connection to the Jewish sacred world. References to Jewish pious life infused the language of their shows. Moreover, Brody singers, many of whom had had vocal training with cantors, continued their work in synagogue choirs, which were quiet bastions of talent and creativity.[26] Although the appearance of the Brody singers varied, their dress often reflected a mixture of traditional and modern elements, and most folk singers maintained their beards as symbols of their continued piety and close identification with their audience. Folk singers also moralized to their audiences about maintaining their links to the Jewish community. By the time Hotsmakh enters the stage in act 1 of *The Sorceress*, Marcus and Avromtshe know he is an entertainer and have a familial relationship with him. They might even be relying on him as an anchor for their Jewishness. For a rising Jewish bourgeois audience, the songs of the Brody singers reconciled their modernizing lives with Jewish life and preached a brand of continued Jewish solidarity.

With Hotsmakh, Goldfaden embeds a piece of folk culture in an operetta, a genre that Goldfaden introduced to the Yiddish stage. It shared elements with vaudeville: it too combines song and spoken dialogue, has musical accompaniment, and also includes choreographed dance. At least as practiced on the Yiddish stage, both are conservative genres, socially and politically. An operetta, however, typically claims a larger orchestra, boasts a chorus, and is animated by plotlines that involve intrigue, villains, and, often, romantic love. Audiences are invited to lose themselves in a world and to suspend disbelief regarding the actors' identities. Hotsmakh singing his ditty before Avreml's gathered guests reminded viewers that Yiddish performance shifted away from a more intimate and vernacular experience.

Hotsmakh's song about men acting one way but thinking greedily or cynically is a signature genre of the folk singers.[27] Brody singers often castigated their audiences and warned against hypocrisy. Songs about social pretension and the superficialities of the modern world also urged listeners not to abandon Jewish law. Ironically, once Goldfaden began recruiting Brody singers to become actors, they themselves fell vulnerable to the same worldly allures their songs warned against. By the time Goldfaden wrote *The Sorceress*, a character like Hotsmakh was considered a throwback in the eyes of most city-dwelling theatergoers, a reference to an earlier cultural landscape. As one observer, Jacob Zizmor, wrote in 1888, "The people had become accustomed to operas, operettas, the ballet, and they were little interested in [the badkhn's] . . . songs and melodies."[28]

Looking back on the theater's first days in his memoirs, Goldfaden unintentionally feeds the narrative of the Yiddish theater as a product of the folk by denigrating his earliest productions. He complains bitterly that the "Hotsmakhs" are to blame for the purported inferiority of his theater: "You must understand, I had no actors. I took poor children who go around selling cigarettes on the street, and planted them on the stage. I had to write plays for them."[29] Responding to the charges by figures like Peretz and Sholom Aleichem who suggested his operettas lacked literary worth, Goldfaden blamed the plots he chose on the lack of acting talent. According to Goldfaden, the character of Hotsmakh was a product of the folk singers' implacability; their inability to be true actors forced him to create roles that allowed them to be versions of themselves. Consider his description of Mikhele Glikman. As Goldfaden tells it, he met Glikman as a brush seller and folk singer:

> He was a crude kid, he could not read or write, a bit of a clown who would play second fiddle to some local singers. . . . He placed his box of brushes down in front of me. . . . I asked him if he could get really angry . . . let's say he had a terrible mother-in-law whom he really needed to curse out. . . . Suddenly he let out a cry: "To hell with you and your father and your father's father! You think I'm scared of you? I'll hack you up like pieces of dumpling meat. You should contract cholera, and a growth should sprout from your nose." "Ok, Ok," I said to him. "Now you must shout the words that I tell you to shout." He memorized that piece, recited it very well, and from that moment the brush binder became a pretty good actor who went on to make quite a furor.[30]

According to Goldfaden, "actors" such as Glikman could do comic routines well but could not have handled a role that was any more sophisticated or demanding.

A similar tale is told regarding the beginnings of the Yiddish actor Moyshe Taykh who apparently came to meet the troupe when he sold the theater gas (before theaters went electric). A young man but half-deaf, colorful, and clownish, he had everyone in stitches each time he visited before he was recruited by Goldfaden to play Hotsmakh.[31] Goldfaden insists that the crude tastes of the folk singers hamstrung his high-minded vision of theater. "If bathhouse boys and street-girls were asked to recite the lines of de Silvio's philosophical monologues," Goldfaden writes elsewhere, "and the raw tailors and cobblers had to sit and listen to them, they would never have understood."[32] For Goldfaden, the Brody singers' inability to transform themselves on the stage mirrored an inability to alter their offstage conduct. In his autobiography, he claims his earliest actors were ragtag and mere "street urchins" that he dragged off the street. To the American Yiddish playwright Leon Kobrin (1873–1946), Goldfaden was particularly harsh, describing his actors as former prostitutes and johns.[33] At one point in his autobiography he describes an actor as "nameless," as if someone might have actually not had a name.

Goldfaden also diminishes the performance of comedy, the signature genre of the Brody singers. This seems inconsistent with his pleas to his reader to understand how great the challenge is to write comedy versus a realistic drama. Defensive of his early comic operettas like *Shmendrik*, Goldfaden argues that he found comedy a far greater challenge to write, saying, "To compose new witticisms and comedy is much more difficult than copying dramas [from other languages]. One need not even look for a realistic drama: every person you come across

Figure 2.1. *Schmendrik* souvenir portrait montage, 1885. Courtesy of the YIVO Institute for Jewish Research.

has his own interesting story ready to recount." When discussing the achievement of his first actors, however, he is unimpressed with the stage-work of the comedian: "The true test of an actor's talent is the dramatic role, and not the comic role which isn't so hard and for which no great effort must be exerted . . . a foolish turn of the head, a grimace with the mouth, a glance of the eye . . . is enough for anyone who wants to be a comic and to appeal to the sympathies of the crude public and earn thundering applause."[34] He claimed that former Brody singers-cum-actors were so limited in their acting range that, rather than prodding them to embody a character of his making on the stage, he drew characters that, to his mind, resembled the speech, appearance, and conduct of the *badkhns*.

Goldfaden portrays the cultivated and well-mannered actors who joined his troupe—those who did not cut the ragtag profile—as rare. He makes a fuss in his autobiography, for instance, about the modern Romanian Jewish lodge member Max Karp (1856–1898), who joined the troupe during its first days in Iași. The members of the lodge funded Goldfaden's first theatrical efforts and helped him arrange engagements throughout Romania, but they never participated in his shows until Karp expressed to Goldfaden his interest in acting on stage. As usual, Goldfaden portrays himself as the arbiter of the highest cultural standards—one of the few in his circle who had the capacity to appreciate Karp's classy demeanor and vocal splendor. So much the gentleman-actor was Karp in Goldfaden's eyes that he could not imagine Karp condescending to play on the Yiddish stage.

> That night among the invited guests was the young man Karp who I had met on an earlier occasion. He was a very elegant gentleman ("kavalier"), neatly costumed, educated, he spoke French, German and Romanian. He was a bookkeeper at a large Galați firm and was from a fine family. . . . Once, he paid me a visit and, on a lark, began to sing. I heard his remarkable native *basso profondo* and was stunned. I did not want to even mention the possibility of his joining the Yiddish stage which, as you know, was not even on the level to be called theater. It was easy for me to share with him, however, that he carried in his throat a God-given gift and if he would appear on a European stage he would do it justice for the sake of all Jewry.[35]

Karp was one of many men with middle-class backgrounds and good educations who joined the theater, only Goldfaden refuses to mention their names, let alone acknowledge their contribution.

Goldfaden's version of the theater's beginnings based on the implacable Hotsmakh-like actors shaped historians' conception of the rise of the Yiddish theater. Moyshe Zeifert (1851–1922) wrote for the Yiddish stage between 1890 and 1910 and also penned one of the first historical treatments of the Yiddish theater. Zeifert believed that folk singers were a boon to the theater for the Jewish types they provided Goldfaden for his operettas but that their acting techniques were in a poor state. He explains:

> Therefore, as we see, Goldfaden, from one side, did not have such big difficulties. The ground was already prepared and he himself was the man to establish the Yiddish theater. To that end he had a good literary breadth, good taste, and the main thing is, he had authentic Jewish types from which to create his characters. The *lider-zingers* would entertain the Jewish public for money with Jewish songs, and so it dawned on Goldfaden to establish a normal/normative (*normale*) Yiddish theater. This is proof that a Yiddish theater in miniature or in a sad state had already existed, and at the very least provided the ground to be adapted to become a normal Yiddish stage in the future. . . . On the other hand, there were no Yiddish actors.[36]

Zeifert suggests that the experience accrued by Brody singers was useful being "Jewish characters"—exaggerated depictions of traditional Jews with traditional roles like matchmakers, peddlers, and grandmothers—because the performers themselves were so closely related to the characters they played.

Biographer of the modern Yiddish theater, Zylbercweig opines similarly on the origins of the modern Yiddish actor in his extended entry on the actor Avrom Fishkind, one of Goldfaden's early recruits for the role of Hotsmakh. Fishkind was born in 1862 in Kherson, Ukraine, to a traditional *misnagdic* father who had served in the Russian military. According to Zylbercweig, Fishkind's theater career exemplifies Goldfaden's intervention in the lives of preexisting Yiddish performers. Based on an array of sources, including Goldfaden's autobiography, theater historian Zylbercweig writes:

> Goldfaden was especially good at "making" actors. . . . Goldfaden believed that anyone could be an actor if you find the appropriate role for him and this is what he did. He would consider a candidate, evaluate his "mimic," his gait, the way he holds himself, the way he speaks, and for each man he met he wrote a role that fit him so well, that he had not needed to become someone else, rather the role would be like him. In English theater today this is called "casting." One doesn't recruit a man to transform into a type that is required by the theater, one looks first for a person who resembles this type.

The concept of typecasting that Zylbercweig invokes is not precise. An actor who is typecast is one who is habitually cast in very similar roles; however, the type of role may require the actor to display personality traits that are different from his true personality. Fishkind was, at the time, a peddler with a hoarse voice who would travel to homes with a box of merchandise. According to Zylbercweig, when Goldfaden saw him and heard his scratchy voice and saw his eyes, he decided to write the famous role of the raspy-voiced Hotsmakh.[37] Like Zeifert, he suggests that Goldfaden's invention of actors had to do with creating a character for an actor to play on stage that echoed his personality, appearance, and sensibility. Hotsmakh and other Jewish caricatures grew out of the implacable characteristics of the so-called actors that Goldfaden was forced to draw upon.

For Goldfaden, Yisroel Grodner epitomized the *badhkn*'s implacability. The men's meeting in Iași is a piece of often repeated theater lore. After observing Goldfaden's failed attempt at performing a formal declamation of his poetry to a crowd at Shimon Mark's café (chap. 1), Grodner replaced him on the stage and the audience went wild for him. Goldfaden recounts, "As quick as lightning Grodner threw himself into socks and shoes and a long caftan with a *shtrayml* and *payes* . . . and announced: 'I will now sing for you the song "The Happy Hasid" written by the famous author Avrom Goldfaden' and began to sing and make crazy hand gestures and dance a Russian folk dance. God knows why they could not appreciate the same author for whose work they would constantly clamor."[38] Goldfaden's discovery of Grodner's onstage talent and its commercial value motivated him to explore a partnership with Grodner and other entertainers like him. In his version of events, Goldfaden downplays Grodner's intelligence and talent. He refers to him as an illiterate *papirosn yingl*, a cigarette-maker, and describes him along the lines of other artless folk singers for whom he made compromises on the stage: "Grodner had many talents. He was in possession of good looks, a rather uncultivated baritone voice. He was naturally talented. His movement and 'mimic' were still exaggerated, but satisfying; he was in need of regimented training."[39]

Besides the rawness of his vocals, according to Goldfaden, he felt that Grodner could not take on dramatic roles. Grodner asked Goldfaden to create a dramatic role for him, telling him, "I do not want to be a clown." But Goldfaden writes that Grodner's onstage skill was too limited to execute a dramatic role: "In this respect he fooled himself. A congenital flaw of the actor: he educates himself more than his capability allows."[40] And elsewhere Goldfaden recounts: "I tried to teach him the art of . . . assuming a natural manner . . . but he had no interest." According to Goldfaden, Grodner was so limited that he could not play the role of a leading man or affect a natural demeanor on the stage. Goldfaden awarded the more distinguished parts to the more educated and cultured actors like Karp. In a state of frustration, Grodner left the troupe. Goldfaden emphasizes anecdotes about Grodner that portray him as primitive and in need of guidance, which he alone provided, magnifying his own hand in cultivating the theater. Beyond the limits of Goldfaden's misshapen memory and record, the first community of actors was far more capable of transformation. Moreover, *The Sorceress* reveals Goldfaden's earlier view of his folk singer–actors was not as implacable but as moral anchor.

The Sorceress's Hotsmakh and the *Badkhn* as Hermeneutic

While some early reviewers of the operetta dismissed him as an anti-Jewish caricature, Hotsmakh, as Goldfaden constructed him, is in fact the hermeneutic of his world. Goldfaden hints at this in his name. Peculiar and without precedent, the name Hotsmakh sounds funny to the Yiddish ear but, on further consideration, might suggest *er "hot smakh"* (he "has authority") from the word *smikha*, rabbinic authority. Mirele's friends, gathered in Avromtshe's illuminated garden with its flowers and—worse—its marble statuary, have not heeded the warnings of the *badkhn* and have allowed the trappings of money and urban life to erode Jewish cohesion. Consider, again, the grand birthday celebration at Avromtshe's house that constitutes the "destroyed feast" that typically initiates the melodrama's conflict. Such a point of departure is naturally suited to a Jewish ritual occasion establishing the cohesion of the community in its state of stability. In fact, that it is anything other than a Jewish festive occasion feels affected and conspicuous. Avromtshe even likens it to a religious occasion: "Seventeen years earlier than today my Mirele was born and therefore today is a festival," he explains to his single less worldly guest (1.3). Goldfaden suggests that the birthday celebration is a symptom of a kind of narcissism that characterizes the play's community. Hotsmakh deflates the importance of it with a joke of self-deprecation. "I don't know about you but I curse the day I was born!" (1.3) he answers and jokingly asks about the proper prayers he must say on the "festival" day. Against the figure of Hotsmakh, the audience is implicitly invited to assess how much Avromtshe, named for one of the three biblical patriarchs (as well as the name of the playwright), has displaced the celebration of a collective Jewish festival (*yontef*) with a nonsacred celebration.

Although the audience observes Hotsmakh cheat his customer, his speech in act 1 points out the darker villainy of Avromtshe's new wife Basye that is still imperceptible to everyone else. Only two scenes earlier she is consoling Mirele, who is still suffering from the recent death of her mother. Avromtshe does not know what more he could do to placate his daughter, for whose sake he married their doting neighbor Basye. Basye, he explains, will provide Mirele the maternal love that she has been without since her mother's death. In a scene that seems meant to provide just another laugh, Hotsmakh reproaches Basye for the money she owes him for a shawl she bought from him. His mention of her debt undermines the propriety that Avromtshe and his guests try to uphold. Moreover, Hotsmakh remains intransigent in his religious worldview, speaking of time according to the Jewish calendar: she owes him since before the holiday of Shavuot (1.3). Something is amiss when someone's accounts are not balanced. The next act reveals Basye's true colors, as she reduces Mirele to a slave in her own home and strategizes with Bobe Yakhne, the sorceress, on how to get rid of her for good. And by the end of the drama, Hotsmakh's innocent if curious hawker's pitch that he repeats in the first act and throughout the play, "Whosoever cheats a buyer, he will burn in fire," takes on prophetic resonance during the last scene of the drama when the witch and her cronies burn to death in the tavern.

Finally, when the police suddenly appear to see Avromtshe during the festivities, Hotsmakh's nervousness also turns out to be on the mark. At first, he thinks they are out to get him. "I have proper weights," he protests, revealing to everyone how he cheats his customers (1.4). When they demand to see the head of the household, Hotsmakh remains frightened, now on Avromtshe's part, and employs what was the coded distress signal among eastern European Jews. The biblical term "And he fled" or "*va-yivrakh*"—said in Hebrew, even less familiar to the Russian ear than Yiddish—conveys to Avromtshe that he is being pursued by enemies and must try to escape.[41] Avromtshe, who finds Hotsmakh's attitude laughably archaic, acts on the enlightened notion that an innocent man need not fear the Russian authorities and graciously welcomes the policeman into his home. While acting according to the worldly code of conduct, Avromtshe is nonetheless arrested before the eyes of his aggrieved and shocked guests. While Avromtshe's arrest turns out to be a mistake that is corrected by the play's end, it costs him many months in jail as well as the abduction of his daughter in his absence. By the end of the series of scenes comprising act 1, the character of Hotsmakh has effectively dismantled the picture of stability and harmony that Avromtshe, Basye, and the others present at the beginning of the operetta. He works his own brand of white magic on the play's society, showing the good to be evil in the case of Basye and that the Russian police are not the protectors of order and welfare, as believed, but the source of rash judgment and danger.

Acts 2 and 3 demonstrate Hotsmakh to be spiritually invulnerable to the evil worldliness of the sorceress. For the most part, Hotsmakh's character follows the same path as Marcus: they both visit the witch and they both end up in a café in Constantinople in act 4. Marcus seeks the advice and magic of the sorceress in finding Mirele after her mysterious disappearance. The sorceress dupes him into believing that she has conjured her image. Hotsmakh instead knows to approach the witch with suspicion. When Hotsmakh approaches the witch's lair, her demimondaine entourage of young girls informs him through the closed door that the witch is not in and they cannot allow him inside. Remarkably, the scene vaguely recalls elements of the biblical Sodomites who trap Lot and demand he surrender his daughters for use in their sexual pleasure. Both narrative episodes involve the motifs of sexual violence and blindness. Goldfaden describes the witch's "girls" as a band of sexualized handmaidens "dressed in red décolleté dresses with loose and straggly hair." Anxious to have their fun at Hotsmakh's expense, they blindfold him and lead him into the lair. When the blindfold comes off, Hotsmakh grows increasingly upset by the lair's pagan décor—particularly of a picture of a snake that he describes suggestively as one that "can swallow me whole with my box of goods." Hotsmakh begs to be released. But the girls insist on "completing their brew" and demand of Hotsmakh some hair from his head—an analogy to the guests that Lot is pressed to surrender. Already very agitated, Hotsmakh weakly negotiates: "But no more than three [hairs]" (3.5). The girls ignore him and wantonly cut off his entire side-lock. When he realizes what they have done, Hotsmakh is aggrieved and finally manages to escape.

> HOTSMAKH: Let me feel how much you took. *(He takes his hand to his left side-lock and jumps back with a mournful cry)* Woe is me! Woe is me! What have you done . . . *(He stamps his feet on the ground)* My side-lock. Take a look at me, do I have a Jewish face any longer? (3.5)

Unlike the hollow grandmotherly appearance of the witch, Hotsmakh's appearance is invested with the vitality and strength of his religion. Nonetheless, his lost side-lock makes him no more spiritually vulnerable to the witch's charms or machinations. Confirmation of Hotsmakh's relative purity of heart in contrast to the witch, despite his moral lapses, does not lie in his victimization but in the final words he utters before escaping the lair: "My heart told me not to come in here, but a spirit delivered me to see if Mirele might be here" (3.5). Hotsmakh risks danger to rescue the daughter of a friend, a daughter of Israel. He is not duped by the sorceress, rather he suspects that she is behind Mirele's disappearance.

In the scene in Constantinople when Hotsmakh and Marcus discover Mirele, the distinction between the witch and Hotsmakh sharpens further. When the organ-grinder demands to be compensated for relinquishing Mirele, Hotsmakh spontaneously offers to contribute to her release. While negotiating her release, the organ-grinder makes it a point to demand "ten more" than what he paid for Mirele; why should he lose out on the profit he would otherwise make because they are personally acquainted with her? His suggestion is enough to enrage Hotsmakh. The schlemiel-like character gets physically violent and tries to grab the organ-grinder by the beard: "Were you to have a beard, I would rip it out," he yells (4.6). Implied in this comic line are the narrow limits of Hotsmakh's physical and intellectual prowess. But Hotsmakh also suggests that the organ-grinder is so far from the terms of his world that it is impossible for him even to engage him. Seemingly trivial religious rituals of hair—of side-locks and beard—tether him to Judaism and a code of modesty. The exchange between Hotsmakh and the organ-grinder comments similarly on what sets Hotsmakh apart from Bobe Yakhne: for all his reverence for money, Hotsmakh cannot conceive of assigning a price to a human being, and the thought of Mirele having been bought and sold like cattle offends his sense of morality.

The historical subtext of these scenes of the witch's lair and Mirele scantily dressed in a café visited only by male customers is the white slavery industry that posed a grave danger to Jewish women of this time period. Reviewers complained that there is nothing culturally authentic or true to Jewish life in Goldfaden's play, for who ever heard of a Jewish witch? But the play provides hints that Bobe Yakhne is a madam, the young ladies in her lair are prostitutes, and

Mirele's kidnapping is part of a prostitution ring. As Edward Bristow shows in *Prostitution and Prejudice*, by 1889 an official census of prostitution recorded that Jewesses ran 203 of the 289 licensed houses, or 70 percent of the total number of brothels throughout the Pale of Settlement. Bristow argues that we can assume the brothels in Odessa (along with those in Warsaw accounting for thirty-eight of fifty-seven brothels in 1889) to have been open for at least ten years.[42] This brings us back to 1879, a year after Goldfaden composed *The Sorceress*. Prostitution and brothel life among Jews would become an important theme on the Yiddish stage, due in no small measure to the number of Jewish victims it claimed and Jewish men and women who participated in their operation.[43] But in *The Sorceress*, Goldfaden was the first to explore it as a subject of literature.

By the end of the play, Marcus and Hotsmakh remain standing as the villains fall. In act 5, Bobe Yakhne, Elyokum, and Basye burn in a purifying pyre from which the heroes desist rescuing them. Hotsmakh celebrates their demise with a reinstatement of God's name: "God has punished them very well/And has protected us from their iniquity" (5.6). But Goldfaden stays true to the melodramatic mode and accordingly never goes so far as to imply that God is the author of the retributive act. The world remains desacralized; through Hotsmakh, it rests on the ethics deriving from a godly universe but does not constitute a godly universe itself. The operetta thus suggests that it is dangerous to equate a birthday and a Jewish festival (act I) as Avromtshe does unwittingly in act I when he compares Mirele's birthday to a holiday. The introduction of new codes of ethics into society leaves it more vulnerable to the corrupting forces of someone like Bobe Yakhne. In fact, there is no full restoration of an ideal society in a melodrama, just the promise that the moral fiber of society is strong enough to resist and survive the corrupting forces that are bound to resurface.

The Rise of the Yiddish Actor: Between Marcus and Hotsmakh

In contrast to Goldfaden's self-serving narrative about Grodner and the others of his "unreformable" first actors, the rise of the Yiddish actor was rapid and noticeably so to those around them. This first generation of actors "caught up" rapidly with their worldlier counterparts on other modern stages throughout Europe. The experience of Yiddish actors came to resemble the life and experiences of actors in other European societies.[44] Almost immediately, for instance, the Yiddish theater generated troupes that enjoyed longevity due to a number of stabilizing effects, including the evolution of acting-family dynasties (e.g., the Kaminskas, the Thomashefskys, the Turkows, the Fishzons, and the Adlers, to name the most celebrated).[45] Family troupes kept the excesses of theater life at bay and fed the stage with a continuous, well-trained stream of fresh talent. Performers who juggled various ways of earning a living and lived marginal lives throughout most of the nineteenth century evolved into members of a kind of middle class and, depending on the country in which they lived, became established members of their communities. The culture of theater life took on patterns of other modern theaters. Quick to materialize, for instance, were claques (in Yiddish, *patriotn*) and amateur theater groups (*libhobers*), which date to the theater's earliest days in Odessa.[46] To those who knew the first actors in the earlier chapters of their lives—many of them bearded and in traditional clothing—the thumbnail pictures of clean-shaven men in suits and ties that accompany each of Zylbercweig's lexicon entries confirm the transformation of the Yiddish actors. As a group, their strict observance of Jewish law fell away and they had more disposable income, but more importantly they presented themselves to the public as more modern with more money and prestige than in the past. Their acculturation played out in the city, not through the exposure to new ideas per se but to new forms of Jewish social behavior, through imitation and performance.

The Yiddish language reflects the theaters' accelerated growth and institutionalization.[47] Choristers in synagogue choirs referred to by the culturally parochial Hebrew loanword *meshoyrerim* became, on the Yiddish stage, *khoristn* (a female chorister was referred to as a *khoristike*). The first chorus leaders, often former cantors (*khazonim*) or synagogue choir leaders, became *dirigantn* (or *dirizhors*). The most prestigious roles were the male leads or *libhobers* for the men and the *primadonas* for the women. If one did not start out in the choir, one might have begun theater work as a prompter (*supler*) or undertaken minor roles (*episodn roln* or *nebn-roln*) as a *statist* that provided for brief appearances on stage and then graduated to *kharaktur roln* character roles such as *foter roln* or *bobe roln*, both played regularly by men. An actor with the specialized skill of *kupletist* performed entr'acte much as he did he before the advent of Goldfaden's theater. Most importantly, Yiddish performers who were also known as Brody singers, *badkhns* (wedding jesters), or *lider-zingers* became "actors," according to the Russian word *aktyor(n)* or the German term *shoyshpilers/shoyshpilerins*. Borrowed from the Russian language, backstage is referred to as *hinter di kulisn* and, finally, the Yiddish word for stage fright (*lompn-fiber*) likely dates to this period as well.

The self-consciousness that accompanied the new vocabulary of Yiddish performance is an indication of how rapidly the late nineteenth-century Yiddish theater grew out of older forms of Yiddish-language performance. According to actor Hersh Amasya, for example, whose short memoir was found after his death in 1927 and posthumously published, he, along with nine other children from his music school in Odessa, were invited to be choristers in Goldfaden's production of *The Recruits* (*Di rekrutn*) in 1878. He recounts the day that Dunayevski, the school's musical director, chose ten members of his class and taught them a batch of Yiddish songs over a two-week period after which he announced that they will perform in the theater: "We looked at each other with a sense of thrill

Figure 2.2. A portrait of the actors, *left to right*: Jacob P. Adler, David Kessler, Krastochinsky, Sigmund Mogulesco, Sigmund Feinman, Rudolf Marks, and Max Abramovitsh, 1888. Courtesy of the YIVO Institute for Jewish Research.

that we would be singing in the theater. One of us asked, 'What type of theater?' Dunayevski then explained to us that there is now Yiddish theater whose director is a man named Goldfaden who made a play about the war contractors that called for ten children. How foreign it seemed to us then: Theater! What do you eat with such a thing?"[48] Similarly, the actor Leon Blank also recalls: "I still remember how my parents, who never in their lives stepped foot in a theater, recounted news about the 'aptyor' [*sic*] Mogulesco even though they had never seen him perform" in person.[49] According to many memoirs, the rise of the Yiddish theater was unexpected and thrilling and offered a cultural product with which Russian Jews felt an instant intimacy, an irresistible familiarity.

Notwithstanding the novelty the theater represented to some—and notwithstanding Goldfaden's complaints about the lack of talent with which he was forced to contend—Goldfaden's troupes (and those troupes that competed with them) included many actors besides rough-hewn wedding jesters. Giving the early troupes instant heft were crops of former choristers. And not just any choristers: The Yiddish theater drew on the most talented synagogue choristers who had acquired such an advanced level of training under the direction of cantors and choirmasters that local non-Jewish operetta companies had already been actively recruiting from their ranks before Goldfaden's arrival.[50] Among such recruits was the Yiddish theater celebrity Mogulesco, born in Zlatopolye, Bessarabia, who apprenticed with his local cantor at the age of nine and advanced through a regimented system in which he learned musical notation by the age of ten. Soon after, he was recruited by a more prestigious cantor, according to Mark Slobin:

> Mogulesco had not yet reached the bar mitzvah age of thirteen before he was poached from his first master by a rival *khazn*. The competitor was none other than the celebrated Nisn Belzer, one of the best known cantors of the late nineteenth-century. Nisn was famous . . . for his innate musicality and his ability to put together exceptional choirs. No wonder then, that he got his *meshoyrers* by hook or by crook. But Nisi's activities were not without redeeming features: he raised Zeligl's salary to sixty rubles a year plus 12 percent of whatever the choir earned on the side, a generous offer by any standards. Mogulesco now found himself in Kishinev.[51]

Once in Kishinev, Mogulesco was again poached by Cantor Israel Kupfer, who worked out of a synagogue in Bucharest. There he sang alongside Leyzer Zuckerman (1850–1922), a native of Korets, Ukraine, who had a similar experience to that of Mogulesco, including being "kidnapped" by some young toughs (*shtarke yungn*) on behalf of Cantor Hershele in Berdichev after word had gotten around about his remarkable singing talent. Cantor Nisi himself plucked Zuckerman from the choir in Berdichev for his own in Bucharest where the boy sang until the age of eighteen. According to a fellow actor named Kornblit, Mogulesco and Zuckerman were multitalented: "Both knew how to dance, act, sing, and enliven an audience. There was not one wedding or circumcision, not one celebration in the city in which Mogulesco and Zuckerman did not appear. They were both talented comedians before they knew the word 'comedian' existed."[52]

With other choristers, including the future actor Simkhe Dinman, Zuckerman and Mogulesco had already tried to make a living performing in a quartet but could not juggle the demands of finding venues with the cultivation of their show.[53] All four members of the quartet were "discovered" and recruited by Goldfaden, but only after they accrued significant performance experience as choristers, including experience in the choir of a French operetta company usually nourished by graduates of the Romanian Conservatory. Another of Goldfaden's first actors, Shmuel Tabatshnikov (1861–1930), was also a former chorister from Kamenets-Podolsk (Ukraine) who grew up with voice training and traditional Jewish learning.[54] Tabatshnikov, who would eventually immigrate to the United States and cofound the Hebrew Actors' Union (1899), also began his career in a synagogue choir and small roles in an Italian opera company. He joined Goldfaden's troupe in Kharkov and was immediately embraced as a leading man. While they were not graduates of the conservatory, the crop of choristers was a

Figure 2.3. Hand-painted magic lantern slide of Sigmund Mogulesco, c. 1910. Courtesy of the YIVO Institute for Jewish Research.

boon to the burgeoning Yiddish theater as products of a rarefied vocal training informed by the high standards of city life; they were hardly examples of "primitive folk culture."

In contrast to what Goldfaden writes emphatically in his memoirs, there is no other evidence that educated men of good social standing felt any shame in participating in Yiddish theater. On the contrary, in the brief years that constitute the first era of the modern Yiddish theater, at least ten of the fifteen of its most important impresario entrepreneurs went to great lengths to promote Yiddish theater in association with their good names among like-minded peers.[55] They published advertisements of their Yiddish shows in the pages of the local Russian press. Alongside ten other producers, playwrights, and actors, including Hebrew writer Moses Lilienblum (1843–1910) and Hebrew and Yiddish novelist S. Y. Abramovitsh (1835–1917), the Yiddish theater community boasted a remarkable number of Russian Jewish intellectuals. Among the Yiddish theater impresarios—or "entrepreneurs" as the Russian press referred to them—many came from families with wealth and were fluent speakers of Russian or Romanian and typically other languages besides. While the Soviet literary critic Riminik describes the maskilim and Russified Jews as the enemy of the Yiddish theater, he also acknowledges "the best of the *maskilim* became a lively force that brought them into close contact with the folk through language. A few of these '*folkishe maskilim*' even felt the pull to work in this field."[56]

In fact their numbers were substantial. After graduating the teachers' seminary in Zhitomir, Russian Jewish journalist Yaakov Spivakovski, already a passionate consumer of Russian theater, acted under Goldfaden and then became a producer of Yiddish theater alongside Yisroel Rosenberg and Jacob Adler. Another early joiner was Goldfaden's future competitor, Joseph Lateiner. Like Goldfaden, his intellectual trajectory transcended his origins of a relatively modest household, but he was hardly a rough-hewn folk singer. He spent some years studying in yeshiva before joining the Iaşi branch of the Lebanon Lodge where, because of his language proficiency, he read German works aloud to entertain his peers.[57] Actor and playwright Sigmund Faynman (born Asher Zelig, 1862–1909), the son of a manufacturing merchant in Kishinev, joined a Goldfaden troupe at the age of seventeen after attending gymnasium.[58] These well-spoken, well-dressed, and well-mannered men set the tone and modeled behavior for those who did not have backgrounds of privilege and education.

Yisroel Grodner, Jacob P. Adler, and Yiddish Theater as Self-Realization

In contrast to Goldfaden's demeaning report of the Yiddish theater, Adler (1855–1926), the Yiddish theater's first dramatic actor, presents the theater as having great social cachet, even in the eyes of Jews belonging to Odessa's higher social classes.[59] In his memoirs, he portrays himself as obsessed with status and preoccupied with details of dress and manner well before Yiddish theater emerged on the cultural landscape. He did not embrace the theater from a position of natural talent (for singing, composition, or performance) as did Goldfaden, Grodner, Fishzon, Spivakovski, and others. Instead, Adler's embrace of the theater flowed naturally from his love of the stage and as a devoted social performer of the good life. As he recounts: "I was a dandy, my cape, my top hat, my gloves, attractive neckties and patent shoes, even my walking stick that I bandied about when I walked down the street, sung in my hands."[60] Born to an established merchant family in Odessa that expected him to become a doctor, Adler explains in his memoirs, he lived the life of an Odessan boulevardier. Before coming into contact with Yiddish theater, he had already achieved great social status. With the help of Avraham Brodskii (1816–1884) of the famous Brodskii sugar empire, who was also a member of Odessa's city council, Adler had secured a government job as an agent of the Weights and Measures Department: "[In this position], I lived what one calls the good life." With the ample free time that the position afforded him, Adler explains, he became intensely interested, along with a group of other privileged gymnasium graduates, in theater. "I loved the works of realism," he writes.[61] Together, Adler and his colleagues decided which works were worthy of applause or whistles.

Adler was hardly the only Russified Jew drawn to Yiddish theater. He notes, for instance, that even Spivakovski, a virtual aristocrat in Adler's eyes, also had friendships with traditional folk singers before he considered getting involved in Yiddish theater. He had regularly enjoyed attending their shows in Odessa's taverns. When Spivakovski and Rosenberg returned from Romania to Odessa with the opportunity to mount Goldfaden's productions on his behalf, they had already been in contact with Adler and other entertainers by mail to tell them about their plans. As a result, a gaggle of folk singers turned up on the train station platform to greet them on their arrival. Adler describes the different crowds that showed up at the train station to wait for Spivakovski in a way that makes clear that Jews of different classes didn't mingle as freely as they themselves (i.e., Adler, Rosenberg, and Spivakovski) did:

> Such a meeting was once in a million. There were Rosenberg's parents, an old patriarchal Jewish couple, and his brothers and sister, respectable people. There were Spivakovski's brothers, pure gentlemen . . . who belonged to the Odessa Jewish aristocracy, and there was me with my gang who lurk around at night attracted to female company and not averse to scandal, and there were also a couple of singers, poor people, with rumpled clothing, white shirts and stovepipe hats, a motley crew: a piece of klezmer, a little small-shtetl-teacher, a kind of big-city jack-of-all-trades, and at the other end, the refined women of Spivakovski's family.[62]

Adler here presents the social and class diversity that would come to characterize many Yiddish theater companies of this era. Notwithstanding Rosenberg's respectable parents, Rosenberg himself had the reputation of a jobless ne'er-do-well with no family of his own, who dressed impeccably (with the help of a valet) and dined "always in restaurants, but never alone."[63] Neither education, nor ideology, nor social class determined entry to the theater. For these were trumped by talent and passion. The Yiddish theater pushed its participants beyond the barriers of social class and estate and, like Marcus and Hotsmakh, they collaborated.

Actors who emerged from the higher social echelons of Russian Jewish society report a change of outlook on discovering Yiddish theater. Hardly desperate to reinvent himself given his good breeding and good position, Adler's encounter with Yiddish theater nonetheless moved him profoundly. Adler explains that he might as well have been born in the wheat store in the Russian city of Kherson where he performed Yiddish theater for the first time under Spivakovski and Rosenberg.

He was born anew, he explains, while participating in their modest production of Goldfaden's *The Sorceress*. Adler continues: "I jumped into the role of Marcus, my face new, my appearance, my height, my gaze, my manner, all new."[64] The theater was a perfect outlet for his aspirations to social status and celebrity. As Irving Howe observes of him, "The growth of [Adler's] powers as an actor depended, first, on his ability to create for himself that public personality which soon took over the whole of his being."[65] Adler recalls with great clarity one of his first appearances on a stage in Kherson in Goldfaden's *Bluebeard* spoof called *Brayndele the Cossack*: "Stage fright got to me [that evening] and I delivered my lines so mechanically . . . and I felt as if I had failed. But I was surprised when, at the end of the act, they shouted, 'Adler' along with the names of the other artists. At the end of the performance Rosenberg shook my hand and remarked, 'Adler, brother, you have become an overnight star (*krasavets*). The girls and women are crazy about you. Have you ever heard such bravos?'"[66] As Howe observes, audience attention gave Adler confidence on the boards. After another successful night in Kishinev, Adler remembers waking up earlier than usual in his hotel to see it besieged with "Jews, women, and children who awaited the cashier [of the troupe] with money for tickets. The police were forced to intervene to prevent scandal."[67]

The American Yiddish theater actor Dovid Kessler had also found himself bewitched as a young boy in Kishinev by the sudden access to celebrity that the Yiddish theater afforded fellow Jews. From a pious family, Kessler was drawn like a magnet to the Yiddish theater troupe and to the hope of achieving the actors' social status.[68] "Everyone was jealous of the Jewish actor," wrote American Yiddish journalist Bernard Vaynshteyn (1866–1946), who had observed the first performances of Yiddish theater in Odessa as a teenager before moving to America: "All the young people, men and women, dreamed of becoming Jewish actors."[69]

Goldfaden portrays Grodner as a rough-hewn performer, but by all other accounts, Grodner was already an evolved gentleman actor by the time the two men met. The memoirs of Fishzon and Adler describe Grodner as a man who briskly transcended his humble beginnings with savvy and talent. Among his Yiddish acting peers, Grodner was legendary even before he met Goldfaden: an actor of great range and intelligence and the most innovative and celebrated impresario of Yiddish performance before 1876. It was, therefore, no accident that Goldfaden proposed they collaborate (even though Goldfaden portrays their meeting as an utter accident). He was not a composer of music or libretti, but Grodner was a pioneer of theatrical production and was well acquainted with the landscape of existing Yiddish-language talent. According to witnesses, Grodner sought to apply the same production standards to his café and tavern shows as seen in those he had attended in theaters before he had even met Goldfaden. He had amplified the dramatic element of his stage shows by shifting them away from straightforward concerts (while still framing them as concerts to placate Russian authorities). According to Adler, Grodner, even as a tavern performer, was a celebrity before Goldfaden discovered him: "[Grodner] was the first I saw as a Brody singer in big local venues [in Odessa] who put together scenes and acts of Jewish life."[70] Fishzon explains that Grodner doggedly tried to pull together troupes of performers to put on theater and that he rallied his fellow cigarette-rollers to attend shows. They followed him as claques eventually tracked their favorite actors. In 1867, a young Moyshe Heine-Haimovitsh—eventually a star of the American Yiddish stage—reports that he left his hometown of Vasilkov (Kiev Province) for Odessa at the age of fourteen, to take in Grodner's show at the legendary Meir Yentshe's tavern. Based on his performance, he pulled together a similar show that he put on in another tavern. To Heine-Haimovitsh's great satisfaction, Grodner came to see him perform and eventually hired him.[71] Grodner was the most celebrated Yiddish performer to see and to imitate, known for his modern theatrical style. When interviewed by Zylbercweig, the great comic actor and composer Mogulesco spoke about Grodner's sophistication as an actor, telling him, "If [Grodner] had made it to America he would be a dramatist on the level of Adler."[72]

Fishzon's memoir, probably the richest document of this transitional time from pre-theater entertainment to modern Yiddish theater, corroborates this portrait of Grodner as a man of great sophistication well before he met Goldfaden; he was modern and entrepreneurial even as he continued to rely on his cigarette-rolling job to earn a living. When Grodner began managing Fishzon's career as a performer for private Jewish gatherings in the early 1870s, the two men began to make money. Demonstrating savvy in fashion and style, Grodner bought Fishzon two bespoke suits, "aristocratic costume . . . with a short jacket,"[73] which gave him a much more modern appearance. Grodner, a man of far less formal education than well-bred, middle-class Fishzon, taught Fishzon how to refine his bearings and his conduct. Once, when Fishzon accumulated some money from some shows, he bought himself a wallet, a penknife, and handkerchief "*take vi a laytisher mentsh*" ("like a man of means"). Fishzon remembers how Grodner surveyed his new accouterments with disapproval because they were so flimsy. Fishzon explains the blades of the penknife were of tin, the wallet felt like paper, and the handkerchief was not soft. "Next time, he said to me, please consult me first," Grodner advised him.[74] Grodner encouraged Fishzon to assume not just the appearance of class but its substance as well.

While many of the first folk singers modeled themselves on the persona of Goldfaden, Grodner had embraced the art of social performance long before his encounter with the impresario. And he believed that everyone had the potential to behave as if they belonged to polite society and would thereby belong to polite society. In 1875, when Fishzon and Grodner tried to assemble a small theater troupe to put on a three-act play, they came upon a beggar named Dovid in the courtyard of the Berdichev Inn with a singing voice that astonished them. Grodner approached him, invited him for a drink in their room, and offered him a job. Soon after, Grodner left the hotel room with Dovid promising Fishzon to return by evening. Fishzon recounts: "[When they returned], *Reb Dovidn* was unrecognizable. He was dressed in clean clothing, with a white collared shirt and new hat—a completely different person. Yisroel looked at him with eyes full of happiness, as one might say, '*me-ashpos yarim evyon*' ['He raises the needy from the dust']."[75] To Grodner, the act of being a gentleman offstage functioned similarly to what one did onstage. The difference between a beggar and an actor was the suit and the offstage demeanor of a gentleman. Grodner was able to play Hotsmakh, but he could just as easily play Marcus.

Rather than two groups of "Hotsmakhs" and "Marcuses," actors began their trajectories from a diversity of intellectual and social origins, and many underwent moments of transformation and self-realization in the theater. There were the *intelligenty* like Lateiner and Goldfaden, the educated and wealthy like Spivakovski, the well-educated bon vivants like Adler, and then there were choristers. The choristers, who generally shared working-class backgrounds and some Jewish learning, nonetheless accrued diverse levels of worldliness or sophistication. Their experience training in city synagogue choruses exposed some of them to cosmopolitan Jewish audiences who hired them for private functions in their homes while others like Mogulesco acted on the stage of French, German, Romanian, and Italian operetta companies. The relationships among these were far more nuanced than what is implied in the narrative of Goldfaden's despised folk singers.

According to Adler, the American Yiddish actor Maurice Finkel (1852–1904) was a blabbering tavern beggar before going to Romania.[76] Even so, he had a sufficient reputation as a talented performer that Goldfaden sent him a formal letter of invitation to travel to Romania to join his troupe. Goldfaden reached out to Finkel with a very civilized note that expresses not even a hint of the condescension found in his later memoirs.

> My friend Moyshe Finkel!
>
> I am now in Iași and have heard about your performances, I decided to invite you to gather a troupe of the best artists and to arrange them in a European manner. . . . In Iași, we will be building a permanent Yiddish theater . . . besides which I have a batch of fresh songs that I have written only recently as well as plays and I will surely write new material for this theater, and it will be the only one of its kind in the entire world, with women taking part . . . when you receive this letter you should not think too long about this [proposition] and come to me immediately. . . . I would have sent you a bill [of the performance] but I want no one in Odessa to know about my readings in Iași . . .
>
> Your friend, A. Goldfaden[77]

Figure 2.4. Hand-painted magic lantern slide of Maurice Finkel, c. 1910. Courtesy of the YIVO Institute for Jewish Research.

Whatever his starting point in terms of social class and education, Finkel's career bloomed after meeting Goldfaden: he not only became an actor but is also named as an entrepreneur with his own company in some of the press coverage of the Yiddish theater during this era. "You should see what the theater made of him in Romania," Rosenberg apparently said to a group of folk singers he and Adler had assembled in Odessa in as early as 1878 in an effort to recruit them for a Yiddish theater troupe of their own. "How stately he appears, without facial hair and wearing a top hat. No more Moyshele who disgraces himself playing women's parts."[78] The theater had changed him. Moyshe became Maurice, manager of New York City's Grand Theater, Yiddish theater's first permanent residence in New York City. Married first to Annette Schwartz and then to Emma

Thomashefsky, Finkel emerged a member of American Yiddish theater royalty by the turn of the century.[79]

Likewise, when Adler saw Spivakovski and Rosenberg step off the train after the year they spent in Romania with Goldfaden, Adler remembers feeling alienated from them who defied social class, and feeling, also, a sense of "wonder" (*farvunderung*): "I shrugged to myself. They were the same men, I guess, but they were also different. Rosenberg, who used to wear a full beard with a moustache, as was the style of an Odessa lawyer, was completely clean-shaven, without any sign of a beard or moustache, without a hair on his face, a real priest. So, too, Spivakovski who would groom and cultivate his facial hair with great care and pride; he was also completely shaved. And both of them wore high top hats, lacquered spats and gloves—in one word, two barons. Two vagabonds."[80]

In Adler's eyes, they returned from Romania at once "barons" and "vagabonds." Rosenberg insisted that he was a "new man" to Adler after discovering Goldfaden's theater: "The old Rosenberg no longer stands before you, the charlatan, the good-for-nothing. . . . Yiddish theater is not small-time business with thievish practices . . . it is a gentle calling."[81] When Adler, Rosenberg, and Spivakovski decided to work together in Odessa, Rosenberg turned to Adler, saying, "Yankele, since I have known you have always been with a walking stick. That will not do. That is not the way it's done by an actor (*Dos is nit mayse artist*). We Jewish [Yiddish] actors must be like the Romanian Christian actors."[82] Even the dandies recrafted their appearance with care and strategy.

The Post-Sacred World of *The Sorceress*, Part II

In contrast to the tweaks made by Rosenberg and Adler to their appearances, the former folk singers underwent more abrupt changes Goldfaden might have had in mind when he refers to Hotsmakh's facial hair in *The Sorceress*. Recall when Hotsmakh and Marcus try to rescue Mirele in Constantinople, Mirele's owner in the café demands money in exchange for her freedom. Hotsmakh threatens him, "If only you had a beard, I would take you by it" (4.6). And earlier, the sorceress's minions cut one of Hotsmakh's side-locks off, causing him much distress. Hotsmakh's awareness of his hair, his side-locks and beard, is akin to his awareness of his role as a Jew in the world, and in Constantinople he goes so far as to equate his beard with a code of conduct. Mirele's owner is ethically so far gone there is no beard for Hotsmakh to pull on in order to set him straight. Similarly, the folk singer's beard was the final frontier in a shift to the modern Yiddish stage. In addition to the social significance their facial hair had on the street, for Jewish performers, their beards signaled a shared code of piety with their audiences. No matter what they satirized on the stage, their beard signified that their ultimate loyalty was to the Jewish People.

Grodner is a case in point. Notwithstanding the sophistication he accrued before meeting Goldfaden, for instance, Grodner did not shave his beard until he was firmly planted in Goldfaden's troupe—until he could allow himself to covet male lead roles. Even as a folk singer in taverns, when he performed female roles on the stage, an observer explains, Grodner gingerly glued his beard beneath his chin in order to de-empashize its presence without having to shave it. Goldfaden's financial manager Librescu remembers that only for Goldfaden's theater did Grodner finally shave: "We sent for Grodner and recounted our idea to him to put on theater. Grodner was in agreement and told us that Romanian actors who would hear him perform with his sidekick Sakhar Goldshteyn often kissed him and begged him to put on real theatrical productions '*vi bay laytn*' ('like those of other people') but he had never done so because he never had what to put on. *Grodner himself shaved his beard*" (my emphasis).[83] This last sentence might seem not to follow from what comes before but, in fact, it makes sense to readers initiated in the conventions of Jewish performance: *badkhns* and folk singers maintained their beards but actors shaved them. "It's no problem," Adler remembers Rosenberg saying to him when they shared their ideas on how best to pull together a troupe from so many disparate traditional performers, including folk singers. "We'll shave their beards, shave their moustaches, crop their wild heads of hair, put glasses on them, top hats and nice clothes, you won't recognize them."[84] In a section of his memoirs entitled "The folk singers part with their beards," Adler recalls that before they put on their comic performance in the restaurant in which they planned to appear, "a terrifying burlesque" played out offstage when the newly shaven folk singers arrived:

> All the faces of the ones we knew so well, old friends, faces that were so *heymish*, had become utterly strange, unfamiliar, so strange, so weird, so forced, such grimaces, where once there was a moustache, there was just lips, where once there was a beard, there was now a sickly or ruddy, wrinkled, shameful cheek. We could not recognize them and we were frightened and only with time could we figure out who was who and then we laughed, but a laughter . . . as if from a hen about to be slaughtered, a kind of hysterical grating sound, and at that point someone with bitterness and derision said to someone else what he looked like, and discontented and shame-faced grabbed a look at themselves in the mirrors of the restaurant and touched their cheeks searching for the disappeared hair. [85]

This scene of the folk singers contemplating the disappearance of their ritual hair with sadness and shame is reminiscent of Hotsmakh's reaction to the sorceress's prostitutes when they brazenly cut off his side-lock. "Woe is me, where is my side-lock?" he cries out mournfully. And it connects, further, to a section of Goldfaden's autobiography that he called "Why I never became an actor." In it, Goldfaden claims emphatically that acting was, in his eyes, a corrupt act, that is, "*fardorben*," which is a startling statement coming from a man so devoted to the cultivation of the Yiddish stage in the name of the enlightenment of the masses.

Figure 2.5. Studio portrait of three unknown actors and Yisroel Grodner (*far right*), c. 1886. Courtesy of the YIVO Institute for Jewish Research.

It is a baldly stated admission of Goldfaden's ambivalence about his cultural project, and he contradicts it many times over when he touts his theater as a force of moral education. Still, it is there. He attributes this sentiment to Grodner, his first collaborator whom he portrays in his memoirs as a lowly folk singer: so, while Goldfaden gives little credit to Grodner as one of Yiddish theater's pioneers, he understands Grodner as a moral anchor of a kind. The corrupt girls in

Bobe Yakhne's headquarters who cut Hotsmakh's side-lock and the clean-shaven organ-grinder connect a version of worldliness with corruption. The shearing of facial hair is a palpable indication of the secularization of Yiddish performance that played out in more subtle gestures of manner, speech, and mentality. These symbols express Goldfaden's guilty conscience about introducing theater and performance to the folk singers.

Conclusion

While most intensely felt by its actors, the impact of Goldfaden's theater radiated outward from its tight communities of acting troupes. Besides providing entertainment, its actors provided models of self-transformation to a broad audience in imitation of Goldfaden. The journalist N. D. Shigarin who visited one of Goldfaden's early productions suggests that some actors did not differentiate completely their onstage lives from their lives offstage. While Shigarin was generally impressed with how much Goldfaden's troupe reproduced the elements of seasoned theater, he shared the following doubts about the professionalism of this newly formed troupe of performers: "Only one thing struck me as strange. During intermissions, the actors and actresses emerge from backstage and appear publicly, mingling with the audience; they talk, drink and smoke and then return to the stage to appear in the next scene. Such behavior weakens the impression of their performance, at least in so far as it struck me."[86]

The social performance that Yiddish actors modeled legitimized self-fashioning among swaths of devoted fans, some of whom became part of a troupe's entourage. Adler wrote that fans would call actors on the street by the roles they had played the night before. Yiddish theater historian Mendl Osherovitsh explains that the first theater troupes attracted entourages of social performers: "The easy-going 'nouveau riche' who enjoy sitting around with friends in a tavern and calling out 'it's on me tonight' . . . such people, who were by nature inclined toward play and performance in life, had in those first years fastened themselves to the Yiddish theater and the backstage as bees to honey; they felt a particular fondness for those who perform and their greatest pleasure was, after the performance, going out to a restaurant with the actors, living it up with them."[87]

It is a paradox of the modern Yiddish theater that with the rise of the modern Jewish actor came the rising demand for authentic Jewish types on the stage: for caftans and *payes*, not Jews with trimmed moustaches and short jackets, or not just modernized Jews. It was this demand that created Hotsmakh. Goldfaden drew on the appearance and the acts of some of his first wedding jester actors, but not because they did not hunger to appear more refined, and not because they were so stunted in their range and talent as he portrays, but because they enriched the ethnic authenticity and appeal of Goldfaden's shows. As Goldfaden realized, these types that had animated intimate vaudeville routines and private performances would now appeal to new audiences on public urban stages.

Chapters 3 and 4 are twin chapters that shift our attention from the actors to the audience and playwrights of the Yiddish stage. In them, we discuss episodes of social performance native to eastern European Jewish society that emerged from the encounter between personal initiative and ingenuity—Hotsmakh might call it worldliness—and boundaries of religion and ideology that were policed by appearance, manner, and even one's name. As Goldfaden's critics suggested, his operettas are translations of popular European novels and operettas, but in their Yiddish iterations they are nonetheless alive to the particulars of Jewish life in late imperial Russia. In chapter 3, we explore an operetta in which a modern Jew dresses up as a pious Hasid, and in chapter 4 we look at another Goldfaden operetta that features a Jew pretending to be a gentile. The latter is explored against the backdrop of the community of Yiddish playwrights that quickly arose in the wake of Goldfaden's first productions. The former, the modern-as-Hasid, is discussed in relation to the audience that determines his meaning on the stage.

Notes

1. For a list of these vaudeville works, see Jacob Shatzky's annotated bibliography "Goldfadens shafn," in *Goldfaden-bukh* (New York: Idisher Teater Muzey, 1926), 80–81.
2. For primary documents on Jewish activity during the Russo-Turkish War, see A. E. Kaufman, "Evrei v russko-turkoi voine 1877 g.: po sovremennym istochnikam i lichnim vospominaniiam," *Evreiskaia Starina* VIII (1915): 176–182.
3. The Treaty of Paris of 1856, which ended the Crimean War between the Ottoman Empire and Russia, established Moldavia and Walachia as principalities that would continue to pay tribute to the Ottoman Empire and Russia was obliged to return southern Bessarabia to Moldavia. In 1857 the councils of Moldavia and Walachia voted for union under the name Romania. The last traces of Ottoman rule, which had lasted for nearly five hundred years, finally disappeared as a result of a Russian-Romanian victory over the Ottomans in the Russo-Turkish War of 1877 and 1878.
4. A sketch called "Plevne" calls attention to the discrepancy between the war's impact on Russia and how it was felt by southern Russia's merchant Jews. See a description of this play in "Vnutrenee obozrenie" [Domestic review], *Russkii Evrei*, no. 7 (1880): 247–249.
5. Avrom Goldfaden, "Der onfang fun yidishn teater," ed. Sholem Perlmutter, *Yidishe velt* (January 26, 1929): 6 (serialized publication from April 5, 1929–July 6, 1929). According to Reisen's Lexicon, Lerner worked as a journalist during the war and wrote a pamphlet on the Jewish contribution to the Russian war effort.

6. Adler himself was not in Romania but, after a brief period, Rosenberg and Spivakovski returned to Odessa to direct their own production of Goldfaden's works, which they invited Adler to join.

7. For the most accurate description of Goldfaden's early repertory and a glimpse at the first Yiddish theater posters, see an article by Bucharest-based historian Shas Roman, "Der repertuar fun yidishn teater in bukaresht in 1877," in *Arkhiv far der geshikhte fun yidishn teater un drame*, ed. Jacob Shatzky (Vilna: Vilner Farlag B. Kletskin, 1930), 280–285.

8. N. D. Shigarin, *Russkie evrei za granitsei* [Russian Jews Abroad] (Kiev: n.p., 1878).

9. For more detail on these months, see Zalmen Zylbercweig, ed., *Avrom Goldfaden un Zigmunt Mogulesko* (Buenos Aires: Elisheva, 1936), 45.

10. In Bucharest Goldfaden's troupe played at the salon Lazăr Cafegion, in the Jewish neighborhood of Văcăreşti, and then at the Jigniţa beer garden on Negru Vodă Street. For the best treatment of Goldfaden's Romanian period, see Romanian actor and writer Israil Bercovici's (1921–1988) *Hundert yor yidishe teater in Romania 1876–1976* (Bucharest: Editura Kriterion, 1976). The first theoretical and critical work about the fledgling Yiddish theater was in Hebrew, by a Romanian Maskil Abramsky (Avraham Hagershoni Abramsky), *Bamat yitskhak o gey chizayon* (Bucharest 1877).

11. B. Gorin, *Di geshikhte fun yidishn teater: tsvey toyznt yor yidish teater* [The History of the Yiddish Theater], 2 vols. (New York: Max N. Mayzel), 1923.

12. Avrom Goldfaden,"Der onheyb funem yidishn teater," ed. Sholem Perlmutter, *Yidishe velt* (January 26, 1929): 3.

13. Shatzky bases this date on Goldfaden's *kurtse oytobiografye*. See "Goldfadens kurtse oytobiografye," *Goldfaden-bukh*.

14. It ran between August 3 and September 16, 1880, as part of a longer stint during which he showcased a number of his works. Binevich finds advertisements for productions of the operetta by Rosenberg and Spivakovski in Rostov-on-Don in 1881 and by Goldfaden in St. Petersburg in August 1881; J. Shatzky, "Klenere arbetn tsu der geshikhte fun yidishn teater," *Arkhiv fun yidishn teater*, 499. The Central Police Bureau kept records of the placards Goldfaden posted.

15. See a positive review of the performance in A. R. Malachi, "Goldfadn-materialn," *A Centenary of Abraham Goldfaden*, ed. Jacob Shatzky (New York: YIVO, 1940), 4–75.

16. See Aaron Seidman, "The First Performance of Yiddish Theatre in America," *Jewish Social Studies* 10 (1948): 67–70. Zalmen Zylbercweig, "Golobuk," *Leksikon fun Yidishn teater*, vol. I (New York: Elisheva, 1931), 386–387.

17. For a fascinating description of the lighting effect on Goldfaden's stage, author interviewed stagehands. See L. Dushman, "A. Goldfaden in Minsk," *Literarishe Bleter* 95 (1926): 141.

18. All references to *The Sorceress* are from my translation that appears in Appendix II of this volume. See Appendix II for complete bibliographic information. This quotation is from act 1, scene 10. The translation is based on Avrom Goldfaden, *Di kishefmakherin (tsoyberin)*: operete in 5 akten un in 8 bilder. Warsaw: 1887.

19. There is only one reference in the entire operetta to its setting as Botoşani in act 1, scene 3, where Goldfaden refers to the animated market scene of the operetta (scene 3): "The market in Botoşani" ("Der mark in Botashan"). Goldfaden staged Yiddish theater in Botoşani successfully, and the small city (that for some resembled a large town at this time with under 25,000 residents) was one of the largest Jewish-proportioned settlements in late nineteenth-century eastern Europe and home to many wealthy Jewish merchants. At moments, however,

it feels more like Odessa with Russian references (police are called *komisar* and Basye tells Marcus that Mirele has run off with a member of the *Duma*). It's possible that these references suggest the presence of Russian officials in Botoşani as was the case during the war.

20. Peter Brooks, *The Melodramatic Imagination: Balzac, Henry James, Melodrama, and the Mode of Excess* (New Haven, CT: Yale University Press, 1976), 20.

21. N. I-s., "Vnutrennii obosprenie," *Russki Evrei*, no. 44 (1880): 1739. Quoted in A. Gurshteyn, "Toward the History of *The Sorceress*" [Yiddish], *Literarishe bleter* 95 (1926): 159.

22. In B. Brand, "Motif of Jewish Drama," [Russian] in *Russki Evrei* 33 (1880): 1308. The original is in Russian but I quote from Gurshteyn's article, "Towards the History of '*The Sorceress*.'"

23. See the biography of Leo Golubok (1865–1918) in Zylbercweig's *Leksikon*, I: 386–387. Other well-known actors who played Hotsmakh include Yisroel Vaynblat Tsukerman (1853–1918) (Zylbercweig, *Leksikon*, I: 679), Avrom Lipovetski, and Moyshe Taykh (Zylbercweig, *Leksikon*, II: 879).

24. The characters also plot the death of all the heroes in one of the drama's last scenes, which is arguably a worse crime. But the crime of selling Mirele is placed at the center of the action and is explored thematically in the drama's constant discussion of buying and selling. The last scene feels more like a *deus ex machina* or an episode that does not flow organically from the rest of the drama.

25. Chone Shmeruk, "Ha-shem ha-mashma'uti Mordekhai-Markus: gilgulo ha-sifruti shel ide'al khevrati" [The significant name Mordekhai-Markus: The literary transformation of a societal ideal], *Tarbiz* 1 (1959).

26. Mark Slobin, *Tenement Songs: The Popular Music of the Jewish Immigrants* (Urbana: University of Illinois Press, 1982).

27. See the composition, for instance, by Shmuel Khayim Levin quoted in Ariela Krasney, *Habadkhan* [The Wedding Jester] (Ramat Gan: Bar Ilan University Press, 1998), 158: "Ver es vil zikh tsayt farginen/Tsu batrakhtn ayer velt/Vet ir in yeder zakh gefinen/Di ales iz mit a maske farshtelt." Also quoted in Krasney is Elyokum Zunser's song about bourgeois Jewish life as masquerade, p. 159. Moyshe Danzig, in his book of songs he published sometime in the mid-1860s entitled *Di litvitshke*: farshaydene yudishe lider datsu eyn lid 'Di litvitshke,' is even bleaker in depicting the habits of those around him with biting sarcasm: "A sheyne velt iz haynt gevorn/Sheyne tsaytn mit sheyne yorn/Mentshn mit sheyne penimer oysgetshtelt/Sheyne—mit a sheyne velt/Nishto keyn foter, nishto keyn muter/Nishto keyn shvester, oder a bruder a guter/Yeder lebt far zikh vi der ber in der nare/A sheyn shtikl velt on a hora." The definition of what a *badkhn* was in late nineteenth-century eastern Europe is debatable to an extent. Krasney's book extends the definition to include songwriters who performed in public secular venues. She even refers to Goldfaden as a *badkhn* based on the folksy attributes that earlier scholars falsely attributed to him. For a list of those she considers *badkhns*, see Krasney, "Shemot badkhanim," 242–243.

28. Quoted in E. Lifschutz, "Merrymakers and Jesters Among Jews (Materials for a Lexicon)," in *YIVO Annual of Jewish Social Sciences*: 7 (New York: YIVO, 1952), 64–65.

29. Quoted in Sholem Perlmutter. *Yidishe dramaturgn un teater-kompozitors* [Yiddish Playwrights and Theater Composers] (New York: YKUF, 1952), 54.

30. Goldfaden, "Der onfang fun yidishn teater," *Yidishe velt* (June 7, 1929), 7.

31. The story is told in Y. Riminik, "Di ershte yorn funem yidishn teater (tsveyter teyl)," *Hamer* (April 1928): 63.

32. "Avrom Goldfadn un zayn teater: tsum yuvilium," *A Centenary of Abraham Goldfaden*, ed. Jacob Shatzky (New York: YIVO, 1940), 155–157.

33. Leon Kobrin, *Erinerungen fun a yidishn dramaturg*, vol. 1 (New York: National Yiddish Book Center, 1925), 92.

34. Goldfaden, "Der onfang fun yidishn teater," *Yidishe velt*, July 6, 1929, 6.

35. Quoted in Zylbercweig, *Leksikon*, IV: 2586.

36. Moshe Zeifert, "Di geshikhte fun yidishn teater," *Di yidishe bine* (New York, 1897), 27.

37. Zylbercweig, *Leksikon*, VI: 5307–5308.

38. Goldfaden, "Der onfang fun yidishn teater," *Yidishe velt* (June 7, 1929): 7.

39. Sholem Permlutter, ed., "Der onfang fun yidishn teater," *Yidishe velt* (April 16, 1905): 6.

40. Ibid., 5.

41. This translates as "And he fled" and is part of a passage that refers to Jacob fleeing his brother Esau. Eastern European Jews switched to Hebrew when trying to communicate an urgent message that they did not want to be understood by non-Jewish observers who might have been acquainted with some Yiddish or enough German to understand the Yiddish.

42. See Edward Bristow, *Prostitution and Prejudice: The Jewish Fight against White Slavery 1870–1939* (New York: Schocken Books, 1983), 55.

43. See Joel Berkowitz's essay "The Brothel as Symbolic Space in Yiddish Drama," in *Sholem Asch Reconsidered* (New Haven, CT: Yale University Press, 2004), 35–50.

44. See *The Rise of the Victorian Actor*, a sociological study of actors' growing respectability and status over time until they come to enjoy middle-class mainstream lives. For a treatment of the professionalization of the actor in imperial Russia, see Murray Frame, "Commercial Theatre and Professionalization in Late Imperial Russia," *The Historical Journal* 48, no. 4 (2005): 1025–1053. Other indicators of the theater's institutional heft in North America is evident in Zylbercweig's references to the myriad theaters across the Northeast and theater people who participated in gathering funds or information for *The Encyclopedia of Modern Yiddish Theater* during the 1920s.

45. On acting families, see Nahma Sandrow, *Vagabond Stars: A World History of Yiddish Theater* (Syracuse: Syracuse University Press, 1996), 55.

46. Nina Warnke, "*Patriotn* and Their Stars: Male Youth Culture on the Galleries of the New York Yiddish Theatre," in *Inventing the Modern Yiddish Stage: Essays on Drama, Theatre, and Performance*, ed. Joel Berkowitz and Barbara Henry (Detroit: Wayne State University Press, 2012), 161–183.

47. See Mark Shveyd, "Aktyorn-shprakh," *Pinkes 1927–1928*, ed. Jacob Shatzky (New York: YIVO, 1928), 257–259. See also Noakh Prilutski, "Di yidish bine-shprakh," *Yidish teater: kvartar-bukh*, II (1927): 1–9.

48. Hersh Amasya, "Zikhroynes," *Yidish teater* (1927): 200–213. For a review of the premiere of "The Contractors or the Russo-Turkish War" in the Marinski Theater, see "Zametka o prem'era 'Podriachika' A. Gol'dfadena. Mariinski Teatr," *Odesskii Vestnik*, January 15, 1881, 2.

49. Quoted in Zylbercweig, *Goldfaden un Mogulesko*, 155.

50. On the modernizing of cantorial practices during the late nineteenth century, see ChaeRan Freeze and Jay Harris, *Everyday Jewish Life in Imperial Russia* (Waltham, MA: Brandeis University Press, 2013), documents 1 (61–71) and document 7 (131) and 8 (132–134).

51. Mark Slobin, *Tenement Songs: The Popular Music of Jewish Immigrants* (Urbana: University of Illinois Press, 1982), 34. For more on Nisn Belzer's celebrity, see ChaeRan Y. Freeze

and Jay M. Harris, eds., *Everyday Jewish Life in Imperial Russia* (Waltham, MA: Brandeis University Press, 2013), 62.

52. Quoted in Zylbercweig, *Leksikon*, II: 2513.

53. Zylbercweig, *Leksikon*, I: 562.

54. M. Osherowitz, "Geshtorben samuel tobias, eyner fun di gor ershte idishe aktyoren," *Forverts*, July 1, 1930.

55. See Binevich's extensive and annotated bibliography of the Yiddish theater that includes the multitude of advertisements impresarios placed in Russian-language, mostly non-Jewish newspapers.

56. Y. Riminik, "Di ershte tri funem yidishn teater (tsveyter teyl)," *Hamer* (April 1928).

57. This is according to Zylbercweig, *Leksikon*, II: 964.

58. Ibid., IV: 2544. Riminik also mentions Yakov-Moyshe Trachtenberg.

59. Adler wrote reams of autobiographical material. Only some of it was translated and abridged for a volume of memoirs by Lulla Adler Rosenfeld, *Bright Star of Exile: Jacob Adler and the Yiddish Theatre* (New York: Thomas Y. Crowell, 1977). He wrote at least three memoirs including one serialized in *Teater Zhurnal* (1901); "Mayn Leben," *Di naye varhayt*, March 14–July 18, 1925; also serialized is "40 yor af der bine: mayn lebens-geshikhte un di geshikhte fun yidishn teater," *Di varhayt*, April 30, 1916–February 22, 1919.

60. Adler, "40 yor af der bine," 5.

61. Ibid.

62. Ibid.

63. Zylbercweig, *Leksikon*, II: 456.

64. Adler, "40 yor af der bine," *Di varhayt*, December, 10, 1916, 6.

65. Irving Howe, *World of Our Fathers* (New York: Harcourt Brace Jovanovich, 1976), 474.

66. Adler, "Mayn lebensbashraybung," *Der teater zhurnal*, October 1, 1901, 11–12.

67. Ibid., 12.

68. Mendl Osherovitsh, "Dovid Kessler," *Arkhiv* (1928): 302–340.

69. B. Vaynshteyn, "Di ershte yorn fun yidishn teater in odes un in New York," *Arkhiv far der geshikhte fun yidishn teater un drame*, ed. Jacob Shatsky (Vilna, YIVO1930), 245.

70. Quoted in Zylbercweig, *Leksikon*, I: 514. Grodner died young and never wrote a memoir.

71. Ibid, 608.

72. Ibid.

73. Avrom Fishzon. "Fuftsik yor yidish teater," *Morgn zhurnal* (November 21, 1925): 5.

74. Zylbercweig, *Leksikon*, I: 4.

75. The reference is to Psalms 113. Avrom Fishzon, "Fuftsik yor yidish teater," *Morgn zhurnal* (January 9, 1925): 4.

76. Adler recounts in his memoirs that he explained to folk singers in Odessa how much Finkel rose socially when he went from being a folk singer to an actor. See Adler, "40 yor af der bine," *Di varhayt* 11, September 13, 1916, 4.

77. Quoted in Moyshe Shtarkman, "Materialn far Avrom Goldfadens biografye," *Arkhiv far der geshikhte funem yidishn teater un drame*, ed. Jacob Shatzky (Vilna: YIVO, 1930), 255–256.

78. Adler, "40 yor af der yiddisher bine," *Di varhayt* 11, September 13, 1916, 5.

79. For more on Moyshe Finkel, see Zylbercweig, *Leksikon*, III: 2668. Also see Faith Jones, "Stage Killing: An Attempted Murder-Suicide," *The Forward*, October 13, 2006.

80. Adler, "40 yor af der yidisher bine," *Di varhayt*, October 4, 1916, 5.
81. Ibid.
82. Adler, "40 yor af der yidisher bine," *Di varhayt* 11, September 20, 1916, 5.
83. Librescu quoted in Zylbercweig, *Leksikon*, I: 512.
84. Adler, "40 yor af der bine," *Di varhayt* 11, September 17, 1916, 5.
85. Ibid.
86. Quoted in Nahum Oyslender, *A. Goldfadn* (Minsk: Institute of White Russian Culture, 1926), 96.
87. Osherovitsh, "Dovid Kessler," *Arkhiv far der geshikhte funem yidishn teater un drame* (Vilna: YIVO, 1930), 320.

3 The Rise of the Yiddish Theater Audience

There are also some gentiles who insist on attending almost every single performance.

A. Zamkovoi

Goldfaden in Odessa

Although the birthplace of the modern Yiddish theater is most closely associated with Romania, it enjoyed a symbiotic relationship with Russian audiences. In fact, Goldfaden's core audience was the Jews of Odessa: modern and Russified Jews, many of them members of the bourgeoisie. This relationship was already in evidence in Romania, as explored in chapter 2. Goldfaden relied on the financial support of a network of modern Romanian Jewish lodges. He had drawn on choristers who were trained by Bucharest's preeminent Cantor Israel Kupfer, and he had even sought models for his first farces in Romania's fledgling national theater. Although his sojourn to Iaşi began as a visit to an admirer of his poetry, Goldfaden discovered that Romania offered freedom from the stifling laws imposed on entrepreneurial theater in Russia, all of which had made Romania far more hospitable to Goldfaden's first experiments in Yiddish theater. Romanian hospitality alone, however, was not enough to launch the Yiddish theater. Only with Russia's participation in the Russo-Turkish War, which drew Russian Jewish cultural consumers onto Romanian soil, was the commercial and cultural potential of the modern Yiddish theater revealed to Goldfaden. Therein lies the significance of the historical accident of the war as it intersected chronologically with Goldfaden's theatrical experiments: had the war not taken place, it is likely Goldfaden would have abandoned Yiddish performance. Romanian consumers alone did not bring in enough money for him to recruit more talent or grow his productions to his artistic satisfaction. The war made obvious that Russian Jewish merchants could afford to buy enough tickets at the right prices to finance the growth of the theater. When the Russian Jewish contractors returned home after the end of the Russo-Turkish War in 1878, Goldfaden made arrangements to follow his core audience to Odessa.

By this time, Goldfaden, based in Bucharest, had received a number of letters from his father-in-law, Mordechai Verbel, in Odessa describing the success of Spivakovski and Rosenberg in producing Goldfaden's work in one of the city's prestigious theater venues. Both Odessa natives were friends of Goldfaden and had enthusiastically participated in his productions in Bucharest at the beginning of the Russo-Turkish War. Only a few months later, they decided to return to Odessa where they would try to duplicate Goldfaden's success. Rosenberg struck a deal with the manager of a seven-hundred-seat performance hall called the Craftsmen's Club, a theatrical venue commonly used for German-language theater located on Evreiskaia Street. Here, Yiddish-language shows could be produced under the legal loophole "Evenings of Literary Entertainment."[1] Public Yiddish-language performance was otherwise banned. From the first shaky show they put on the boards, the productions were well attended. The eminent Hebraist Verbel might have been there only to represent the interests of the operetta's composer, to be the eyes of Goldfaden, his son-in-law, on the production of his works. But, according to Adler's memoirs, others of the Odessa Jewish intelligentsia were also in regular attendance, including the celebrated Odessa cantor, Nisn Blumenthal (1805–1903). With these first productions, modern Yiddish theater took root in Odessa as early as 1877 at one of the city's prominent theatrical venues.

No matter the success of Rosenberg and Spivakovski, curious Jewish Odessa residents who avidly read the press coverage of the war knew Goldfaden's troupe to be the genuine article. He and his troupe pulled into Odessa's train station to great fanfare in April 1878 and, soon after, Goldfaden launched his first theatrical production. Displacing Rosenberg and Spivakovski at the Craftsmen's Club, Goldfaden launched his troupe with a performance of *The Sorceress*. It played five times a week.[2] Initially, the government shut Goldfaden down for failure to vet his work, either with the local censor or the Bureau of Censorship in St. Petersburg. Goldfaden, however, was undeterred. With the freedom to travel beyond the Pale of Settlement he had earned from graduating the seminary, he immediately traveled to St. Petersburg to negotiate in person with the censor's office. Meanwhile, in order to ensure steady income, he sent Librescu, now acting as the company's manager, with the troupe back to Bucharest to put on shows on familiar territory. A few months later, Librescu received a telegram from Goldfaden announcing that he had secured permission to stage Yiddish theater, not just in Odessa but throughout the empire.[3] There are no surviving details about this extraordinary coup that Goldfaden accomplished for the Yiddish theater. Adler and Librescu confirm that Goldfaden did this on his own. He secured legal rights that in 1879 far exceeded even the rights of Russian-language entrepreneurial theaters of his day—to say nothing of more comparable minority-language theaters, like the Ukrainian theater, which was also in its infancy.[4] By the last months of

1879, Goldfaden and his troupe were back in Odessa and, soon after, competing Yiddish theater troupes surfaced in the city.[5] In January 1880, Goldfaden brought two of his most popular operettas, *The Sorceress* and *The Two Kuni-Lemls*, to Odessa's majestic Mariinsky Theater.

In little time, Odessa became the seat of the Yiddish theater, and its large Jewish population, with its modern sensibility, became its ideal audience. And this was no accident. Odessa's residents and particularly its Jewish residents had long been active participants in the city's cultural life. As early as 1839, one visitor to the city called Odessa Jews music "fanatics." As Steven Zipperstein reports: "The opera, in particular, was the rave of Odessa society. . . . Local Jews, even those who had no knowledge of foreign languages, found the opera enjoyable and for the mere price of a ticket (tickets were priced quite low) they could appreciate a sense of belonging to, and participating in, the larger cultural milieu."[6] Shaikevitsh, a playwright and producer of Yiddish theater during this era, explains in his memoir that the enthusiasm Odessa Jews already felt for the theater was magnified and channeled toward the Yiddish theater. One who has never seen the passion in play has no conception what "visiting the theater" meant. He recalled, "All the seats were sold out three nights before every show. And even though the shows were populated by dilettantes and other actors who had no experience on a stage, the applause and bravos were deafening."[7] "Odessa was the center of the theater's market," Avrom Fishzon explains about this period. "Whoever needed an actor or actress came to Odessa. And an actor or actress looking for work came to Odessa. Even agents sprang up."[8] Betty Vinovits, the daughter of Goldfaden's conductor, recalls the popularity of his shows: "People would rise at night to secure a ticket. Tickets would sometimes transfer three or four hands. The best business was made by the agents. None of the Russian-language theaters with the best actors did such business."[9] Odessa embraced theater and particularly Yiddish theater. Even without imperial subsidies and with no protection from the caprices of local government and government censors, Goldfaden—and soon competing Yiddish theater impresarios—found success.

Although the majority of Goldfaden's audience was presumably Jewish, his move to Odessa's 1,500-seat Mariinsky Theater signaled that his Yiddish-language operettas were on exhibit for an audience that was not only Jewish. The Mariinsky was the regular venue of the city's government-sponsored Italian and French operetta companies, and it was the city's largest theatrical venue during the period that Goldfaden's theater was allowed to operate in the Russian Empire (1879–1883).[10] We cannot determine how many Jews versus non-Jews attended the Yiddish theater during this period. But although historical sources like newspapers and memoirs are not forthcoming with numbers, they do offer impressions. Advertisements and reviews, for instance, appear in the non-Jewish press alongside reviews and ads for non-Jewish theater. More explicit references are made by reporters and theater critics who were intrigued by the question of who attended Yiddish-language productions. "[*The Two Kuni-Lemls*] drew a big audience among whom the residents of Zaryadye and their families were represented in great number,"[11] one non-Jewish reporter observed wryly referring to a neighborhood of Moscow known for its Jewish residents. In Odessa, Goldfaden's core audience—the audience that sustained Yiddish theater financially during these first years—was a version of the preexisting (non-Jewish) theater audience that included a disproportionately large number of Russified Jews and at least some gentiles.[12] In this chapter, we explore the rise of the Yiddish theater audience, mostly urban and Jewish, to be sure, but unmistakably conditioned by the non-Jewish gaze. How did its Jewish audience members understand the meaning of Goldfaden's operettas assuming gentiles were taking it in alongside them?

Goldfaden's *The Fanatic* or *The Two Kuni-Lemls*

Perhaps a better question to consider initially is the following: If Goldfaden sought and succeeded in attracting the interest of sophisticated and secular theatergoing urbanites to his theater—and not the untutored masses—why was he writing what many contemporaries and scholars of Goldfaden's work describe as anti-Hasidic propaganda? His comic operetta *The Two Kuni-Lemls* (*Di tsvey Kuni-lemlekh*, also called *Der Fanatik* or *Di beyde Kuni-lemlekh*) is a fitting starting point in exploring this question.

The operetta's action begins in the well-appointed home of an Odessa merchant named Pinkhes, "a refined Jew . . . dressed in Hasidic garb" who presides over a Saturday night celebratory meal with his Hasidic guests. His wife Rivke is dismissive of his newfound passion for Hasidism, while Pinkhes believes that his wife's modern ways have ruined their only daughter, Carolina. Rivke allowed Carolina to study literature with a tutor, a university student named Max, but Pinkhes has recently put an end to their lessons. He rightly suspects that they are falling in love. Before Carolina is lost to worldly ways, Pinkhes reports to his wife in act 1, he has begun negotiations with Kalmen, a traditional Jewish matchmaker, who promises him a groom of fine Hasidic lineage for Carolina. The groom's name is—quite preposterously—Kuni-Leml, two words that have no record as Jewish names and little meaning except that *leml* means "lemon." "Kuni-Leml" sounds as silly in Yiddish as it does in English. Kuni-Leml is the stepson of Shloyme, the respected Galician sexton and alderman and as such gives Pinkhes access to prestige. Kalmen arranges for Kuni-Leml to arrive in Odessa from Cracow at which time he will present himself to Pinkhes in his home to finalize the match and pick up his dowry. After hearing about her arranged match, Carolina goes out to meet Max in the park and complains to Max about her betrothal to Kuni-Leml. As luck has it, Max knows Kuni-Leml and explains to Carolina that not only is her future bridegroom's name silly, but he also limps, has a stutter, and lacks intelligence. Max then devises a plan to dress up as Kuni-Leml in order to replace him in Pinkhes's home and win over Pinkhes. Once he has Pinkhes's allegiance as Kuni-Leml, according to Max, he will reveal himself and claim his bride.

While earlier scholars applauded *The Two Kuni-Lemls* as the composer's finest anti-Hasidic work, there is no historical evidence from this period to indicate that Goldfaden's intention with the operetta was to stage anti-Hasidic propaganda. The proof of audience's reactions that does survive demonstrates that Goldfaden's depiction of Hasids entertained theatergoers who enjoyed the staging of Jewish ethnicity, the deployment of Hasidic tunes, and effective comedy.[13] About a production of *The Two Kuni-Lemls*, for example, a non-Jewish reporter wrote the following review:

> You are probably thinking that this is an operetta of Jewish life and not more? It is *à la lettre* a Jewish work, written in the same language that sounds loudest than the others in places like Shklov, Zhitomir, Berdichev, etc. and played by pure-blooded Jewish royalty. . . . The play began with a fiery table song, presented not at all badly and might even be an original. After this, we suddenly found ourselves navigating a variety of "*oy veys*" and "*gevalds*" that we heard but could not understand for our lives. We turned to our neighbors, and from every direction, one interrupting the other, they made everything clear to us.[14]

Albeit with a hint of condescension, the reporter celebrates the ethnic otherness he enjoys in attending Jewish theater notwithstanding the Yiddish-language barrier. Other reactions were lukewarm, especially among critics who initially assumed Goldfaden sought to create anti-Hasidic propaganda. Writing in *The Russian Jew*, a critic that signed his work B. Brand is scornful of Goldfaden because he does not play Berdichev, a city with a dense Jewish population susceptible to Hasidism and a place where his anti-Hasidic message would have propaganda value. Brand guesses that Goldfaden does not bother with Berdichev because its Jews do not have a lot of money.[15] Remarkably, another review in the *Odessa Herald* takes issue with the operetta's ideological ambiguity:

> On Wednesday the twenty-second and Saturday the twentieth-sixth of January, two of A. Goldfaden's best plays, "The Sorceress" and "The Fanatic" [*The Two Kuni-Lemls*] whose subjects are drawn from the lives of the most conservative traditional Jews, were presented on the stage of the Mariinsky Theatre. Apparently, Mr. Goldfaden wrote these plays with some particular goal, but the problem is that the audience . . . does not consider the plays' heroes to be zealots. . . . This is one of the deficiencies of all of A. Goldfaden's plays. These plays would produce a different impression and influence, and have a different conclusion to their plots, if Goldfaden introduced serious heroes into his plays, and not the motley assortment of personalities that appear on the stage to amuse the audience.[16]

The reviewer suggests that the young heroes of these two plays, Marcus in *The Sorceress* and Max in *The Two Kuni-Lemls*, do not differentiate themselves enough from the other characters on the stage and that the operettas adds up ideologically to nothing more than toothless satire. One might recall how Hotsmakh shadows Marcus and collaborates with him to find Mirele (as discussed in chap. 1). In *The Two Kuni-Lemls*, Uncle Sholem, a prominent Hasidic sexton, likewise champions his modern nephew's desire for Carolina's hand in marriage. In both cases, the traditional characters—Hotsmakh, the wedding jester, in *The Sorceress* and Sholem, the Hasid, in *The Two Kuni-Lemls*—are effective in achieving their desire and do so in collaboration with the modern and conventional heroes. The reviewer explains to his readers that Goldfaden's work does not contain enough ideological definition for it to be an effective anti-Hasidic tool.

Building on this striking reaction to *The Two Kuni-Lemls*, I explore Goldfaden's libretto as a meditation on Jewish visibility in late nineteenth-century Russia from the perspective of a modern Jew. Beneath the comedy and hijinks, the operetta depicts its two most important male protagonists as both maskilic *and* Hasidic. With this thesis, we shift the focus of this legendary comedy away from the first Kuni-Leml and onto Max, the disguised or second Kuni-Leml. Max, the young hero, and his Uncle Sholem are at the heart of this reading as each, in his own way, embodies the modern maskil as harboring inextricable ties with his inner (or outer), tradition-bound Hasid. Max's decision to masquerade as Carolina's Hasidic groom seems incidental to his identity, but it is really a key to his character. Max, costumed as a Hasid, indicates his reluctant identification with the Hasid and his vociferous opposition to the Hasid. Max-as-Kuni-Leml represents the new, urban-based Jewish audience to which the Yiddish theater gave rise: it identified itself as the object of Goldfaden's anti-Hasidic caricatures and vociferously attacked his work as a result.

Alongside Max's embodiment of Haskala and Hasidism that is fraught with aggression, Uncle Sholem also identifies with both the Hasidic and progressive Jewish communities in a way that, according to Max, involves a kind of benign trickery or social performance. For, as Max put it, his Uncle Sholem, a high-profile Hasidic sexton, is secretly sympathic to Haskala. Caught in the strident discourse of the reformers, Max's Hasidic and modern sides clash inside of him while Sholem's two sides are reconciled by his deft social chameleonism that the operetta ultimately sponsors; Sholem, who makes "sholem" or peace at the end of the play, emerges as the authority of the operetta. *The Two Kuni-Lemls* is Goldfaden's deployment of Jewish visibility on the modern, postideological Jewish stage. Whether applied to the public theatrical stage or to the city streets beyond, Goldfaden wrote about how the portrayal of Jews by fellow Jews on the public stage matters deeply to how others see them and how they see themselves.

Not Kuni-Leml, Max as Kuni-Leml

The operetta's opening scene anticipates Goldfaden's softer ideological stance vis a vis Hasidism and also offers a depiction of a milieu that is evocative of his own personal experience with friends and colleagues in Odessa. The first act of *The Two Kuni-Lemls* shifts between two celebrations that lay out two Jewish cultures of the libretto's Odessa in a split stage: from a scene in the home of Pinkhes, celebrating with his Hasidic guests, to his daughter's modern tutor Max, celebrating together with friends in the city's municipal garden. At twenty-one years old, Max is the privileged son of a wealthy Jewish merchant and attends university; he and his peers have just completed their final exams and they sing about the hard work they have accomplished and the rest with which they will reward themselves.

> Now let's relax
> We're done with our tasks,
> Now we start everything over again,
> Together we crammed,
> For all our exams—
> We've been most successful and feel like new men.
> Remember: our professors deserve thanks,
> They're the ones who showed us the light.
> They've filled our heads, which used to be blanks,
> And now we are erudite. (1.5)[17]

Lounging and singing in the park together, his colleagues ask about his romantic pursuit of his beloved Carolina, the student to whom he has been giving private lessons in literature. "So, Max, still head over heels in love?" a student asks him. They are worldly young men, students in Odessa's Russian university and not self-conscious with discussions of romantic love.

The plot is set in motion not only by Max's love for Carolina but also by his resentment of Pinkhes, Carolina's father, who is the obstacle to the young couple's mutual love. Max explains with brazenness that Carolina's mother is not a "fool" like her father who "runs in the other direction" when he sees a modern Jew. Max is angry with Pinkhes for putting a stop to the lessons he was giving Carolina. When Carolina arrives in the park, she describes her father's plans to betroth her to the offspring of the illustrious Hasid Reb Shloymenyu—the final and irreversible step in depriving Max of the object of his desire. Max realizes that Carolina is talking about his own father's brother and his stepson Kuni-Leml. Max explains his plan to undermine the wedding: "I'll get dressed up as this Kuni-Leml, I'll limp like him and speak like him, and make myself blind like him . . . and then you'll see me at your house, dressed as the real Kuni-Leml, and the rest you'll see for yourself" (1.6). Carolina agrees to the plan.

Max's plan takes an unexpected turn as early as act 3, scene 6, when, masquerading as Kuni-Leml in Pinkhes's home, he encounters the real Kuni-Leml. Max was supposed to arrive at Pinkhes's home well before the real Kuni-Leml so as to usurp his place, but Kuni-Leml has arrived earlier than usual. The presence of two Kuni-Lemls in Pinkhes's home causes comic confusion: at one point, for instance, Carolina mistakes the real Kuni-Leml for a disguised version of Max and tries to kiss him. With time, Carolina and Max run into each other and this time she is convinced that she is looking at Kuni-Leml. The two men have, indeed, become indistinguishable, just as Max promised in act 1! When the young couple figures out Carolina's error and they are able to successfully identify each other, they steal a romantic moment together only to be interrupted when the real Kuni-Leml stumbles upon them. Carolina frets that Kuni-Leml will bring their caper to her father's attention and this will surely undermine their plan. But Max reassures her and asks Carolina to leave him alone with the hapless Hasid. The mirror-like encounter of Kuni-Leml and Max-as-Kuni-Leml is thus initiated. Hence, "the two Kuni-Lemls" of the title: the one real, the other an imposter. Both dressed in full Hasidic regalia, they size each other up; each gazes at the other, the mirror image of himself.

While Max's mirror experience is given equal weight in the play, it is ignored by critics. Berkowitz and Dauber's recent analysis of the libretto provides the normative anti-Hasidic reading of the operetta that focuses on Kuni-Leml's crisis of identity: "If I wasn't sure I am me, I would think he is me" (3.6). Berkowitz and Dauber write, "One can argue that Goldfaden had brought the satirization of Hasidism to its logical conclusion; in his hands, Hasidism had seen itself in the mirror, and was left with no identity of its own."[18] So befuddled is he by seeing a mirror image of himself, Kuni-Leml decides to return to the matchmaker for confirmation of his own identity—written proof that he is who he thinks and says he is.

Meanwhile, Max's successful colonization of Kuni-Leml leaves him with two versions of himself. The real Kuni-Leml has surrendered his identity; "both" Kuni-Lemls thus "belong" to Max—an episode of reproduction that, according to the comedy's conventions, is expected to happen at the end of the comedy and between the bride and groom. In the comedy, the hero's desire is what drives the plot that, according to Northrop Frye, concludes in the hero "getting his will" and wedding his betrothed in the final scene.[19] Accordingly, in act 1, scene 2, Max says to Carolina: "When you can't succeed either by being nice or getting rough you have to rely on desire." Desire pushes past the comedy's obstacles so that the hero has his bride. Thus the hero claims the operetta's future society by way of marriage and reproduction. In the mirror scene, however, Max's desire drives him to reproduce himself just as Carolina absents herself from the stage. His reproduction of himself—albeit symbolic—cuts Carolina out of the process. "How will you disguise yourself so well as to approximate the appearance of Kuni-Leml?" Carolina asks Max in act 1. "Even you will not recognize me," Max replies (1.2).

Max's mirror experience exaggerates an identity crisis or ambivalence that is arguably already at play in his dressing up as Kuni-Leml: he identifies himself all the more vehemently with Kuni-Leml while he wants to be rid of or destroy (the other) Kuni-Leml. Both of these instincts play out simultaneously. The two men, clad in Hasidic garb, survey one another as if they are surveying themselves in a mirror; face-to-face, Max copies Kuni-Leml's gestures. Max begins.

> MAX: You can walk and see and speak like everyone else, you're just in disguise.
>
> KUNI-LEML: I can swear on my f-father and m-mother that I was born b-blind and l-lame and with a s-stutter.
>
> MAX: Q-quiet you liar. You better tell me right now why you d-disguised yourself. (3.6)

The logic and language of Max's argument against Kuni-Leml are very specific. Not only does Max accuse his weak and befuddled rival of impersonating him, but also he accuses Kuni-Leml of being physically whole or normal and only pretending to be crippled and stuttering. Kuni-Leml is befuddled by such an attack. So eager is he to calm Max down that he submissively calls Max by his own name, "Kuni-Leml." Max, however, continues his aggressive stance and insists on written proof of Kuni-Leml's identity.

> MAX: Q-quiet you liar. You better tell me right now why you d-disguised yourself as me. What are you doing here?
>
> KUNI-LEML: What am I doing here? Reb P-pinkhes wrote me a l-letter that I should c-come and take the one thousand rubles' dowry and take his girl for my w—oh here's the letter (*Takes a letter out of the breast pocket of his coat and shows Max.*)
>
> MAX: (*Skims through the letter.*) Now I see what a s-schemer you are. This letter is c-counterfeit. . . . I'm taking this letter to the p-police, and I'm g-going to show them what a s-swindler you are unless you bring a s-signature from home that this is you.
>
> KUNI-LEML: (*Runs after him and stops him.*) Reb K-kuni Leml, come here. (*Pleading.*) What do you need the p-police for? I'll run home right n-now to get the proof in b-black and white. But is it f-fair for me to leave here without a name?
>
> MAX: (*Grabs him by the lapels and speaks to him as if angry.*) No, no, you're a swindler. C-come with me to the police. (3.6)

The scene is played for laughs. However, Max's hostility and threats betray anxiety born of clashing impulses: for Max's defensiveness further entrenches himself in his identity as Kuni-Leml, while his desire to destroy Kuni-Leml grows ever stronger.

Anti-Hasidic or Anti-Jewish?

A vocal minority of Goldfaden's core Jewish audience was critical of Goldfaden's work and condemned many of his comic operettas for their anti-Jewish caricatures. In a city theater with an audience of Jewish and non-Jewish viewers, Goldfaden's caricatures of mostly Hasidic Jews struck members of the Jewish intelligentsia as satirizing not just Hasids—but all Jewish people. In fact, rather remarkably, Hasidic Jews were not among those who condemned Goldfaden's works during the first years of their production in the empire. Goldfaden's portrayals of Hasids triggered the anxieties of acculturated Jews because they were the ones attending his shows and they were the ones concerned about Jewish visibility.

To be sure, Goldfaden's Hasidic works are of a piece with a body of anti-Hasidic works published throughout the nineteenth century with the intention of curbing the spread of Hasidism. Many reformers believed Hasidism to be a corruption of Judaism and sought to quell its spread with literature and anti-Hasidic propaganda throughout much of the nineteenth century.[20] Both traditionalist non-Hasids (or, as they would come to be known, *misnagdim*, literally "opponents") and maskils generated satirical literature that depicted Hasidim as retrograde or laughable.[21] As Jeremy Dauber and Joel Berkowitz have demonstrated, *The Two Kuni-Lemls* is derivative of a number of these works, most prominently A. B. Gottlober's *The Two Wedding Canopies*, a work that expressed the playwright's outspoken vitriol for his Hasidic subject matter. For the most part, before Goldfaden began mounting his plays on public stages, anti-Hasidic literary tropes had remained a phenomenon of "*nor tsvishn-undz*" or "only among us": an intramural conflict that had played out internally, in Yiddish and Hebrew-language books accessible to Jewish people for private consumption.

By the time Goldfaden had begun writing in the 1860s, however, these sectarian conflicts had mellowed considerably. In a discussion of his poetry, the literary critic Shmuel Niger remarked that his poetry is unfettered by sectarian gripes: "The superstition, the orthodoxy, the silly traditions, the fanaticism, and all the other religious issues that claimed such an important place in the Hebrew Haskala literature—Goldfaden has little interest in."[22] Goldfaden had no personal or ideological issue with Hasidism as did Gottlober. And in contrast to Gottlober's all-Jewish readership, Goldfaden sought to appeal to non-Jews.[23] For his part, Goldfaden could hope that *The Two Kuni-Lemls* would attract the sophisticated theater-goers he needed to survive commercially. He drew on his anti-Hasidic sources for familiar ethnic material, for ready-made narratives, and for jokes and tunes native to his coreligionists. Soldout shows testified to his operettas' broad appeal.

Goldfaden himself generated the idea that he sought to combat Hasidism with his plays and this idea found currency with willing colleagues and later scholars of the theater. Embarrassed by the notoriety he had earned with his Jewish caricatures, and on the defensive while writing his memoirs, Goldfaden framed his operettas as anti-Hasidic propaganda. He excuses his Hasidic caricatures by explaining that he sought to warn his audience against the perils of religious "fanaticism."[24] The aging impresario argued that his anti-Hasidic works were part of a larger effort to enlighten the masses of Russian Jews. Historians like Dobrushin, Oyslender and Finkel, among others, accepted this as a key component of Goldfaden's works.[25] "With his caricatures Shmendrik and Kuni-Leml, he did more to extract fanatics from their mud of fanaticism than a thousand teachers of his era," Perlmutter gushed approvingly in a tribute to Goldfaden as if the fact that his work functioned as anti-Hasidic propaganda was incontrovertible.[26] There is no evidence, however, that *The Two Kuni-Lemls* ever caused viewers to revise their opinion of Hasidism during this first period.

In the eyes of his audience, however, the Hasidic characters shifted from representing Hasidic Jews to representing all Jews. It did not matter whether the actors played the Hasidic characters with ideological intensity or with a sense of benign ribbing; acculturated Jews seeing the performances "through the eyes of gentiles" became convinced that the Hasid represented an ugly caricature—not just of retrograde traditionalists or devotees of Hasidism—but of all Russian Jews no matter how enlightened or integrated. The Russian press already referred to Yiddish theater troupes as "Jewish Troupes" (*Evreiskie truppiy*), calling attention to the Jewish character of the troupes' players and the ethnic content of the operettas they performed. Indeed, the interchangeability of Hasid with Jew is evident in reviews and dovetails with the anxieties voiced by Russian Jewish critics. None other than Romanian national poet Mikhail Eminescu (1850–1889) covered Goldfaden's theater in the (non-Jewish) Romanian *Iaşi Courier* (*Curierul de Jassy*) as a young journalist in 1876. In his review of one of the very first shows Goldfaden produced, Eminescu praises the acting but, in doing so, blurs the distinction between the Hasid and the Jew: "In the second play, the actor played a *Hasid* with such fidelity that he seemed a Jew that we are used to seeing every day: hotheaded, with hurried and drooling speech, superstitious, tittering, and beady eyed—and he deserves his due as the great talent that he is. Another, the best of the troupe, played a stupefied Jew."[27] Eminescu seems familiar with two differentiated terms ("Hasid" and "Jew") but proceeds to use them interchangeably. Understandable elisions of this kind suggested to modern viewers that the Yiddish theater was, indeed, slandering "Jews," which made them react with shame and hostility to Goldfaden's Hasidic portraits.

As a play about the identity crisis of Max (not Kuni-Leml) and intended for an acculturated audience (rather than "benighted" Jews susceptible to Hasidism),

The Two Kuni-Lemls intersects with Goldfaden's personal crisis as a generator of scandalous public Jewish caricature. Although Goldfaden had steadfastly identified as a reformer of Russian Jewry throughout his life, the angry reaction to his theater by fellow reformers put him on the other side of the battle line over Jewish visibility. He was now Hasid-like: inspiring self-consciousness on the part of socially integrated Jews. They, more importantly, were Max-like: reluctantly identifying with the Kuni-Lemls on the boards, and lashing out at Goldfaden, both in person and in the form of negative reviews in the Russian press.

The Russian press coverage of Goldfaden's shows testify to the broad interest they sparked. The Soviet scholars of the Yiddish theater have framed the negative press coverage of Goldfaden's theater as the vitriolic voice of the Jewish bourgeoisie trying to suppress the voice of the working class. They are correct in identifying the source of these negative reviews but refuse to acknowledge that Goldfaden was reviewed so often by the liberal press because its bourgeois readers mostly embraced Yiddish theater alongside their diet of non-Jewish theater (meaning, theater in the Russian, French, or Italian language).[28] A critic in Odessa made this disparaging observation about the reception of Goldfaden's productions—one that is not so much expressive of the social anxieties under discussion here but, rather, revealing of the profile of Goldfaden's audience: "It is strange to see how the public that yesterday applauded Salvini (*Othello* or *Hamlet*) is thrilled today by *The Sorceress* performed by local celebrities. Frankly speaking, this parallel seems a bit offensive and we wonder what [Salvini] the great artist thought of this."[29] Even as he puts down Goldfaden's productions, the critic registers his popularity. (And he is right to wonder what the great actor Salvini thought of the Yiddish theater as the celebrated actor attended the Yiddish theater while in Odessa). The Soviet scholars rightly differentiate intra-Jewish criticism from anti-Semitism: a letter in Odessa's Judeophobic newspaper, the *New Russian Telegraph* (*Novorossiyski Telegraf*), lamented the "Jewish takeover" of one of the city's most important cultural institutions to which the editor added that no one would be willing to suffer the "Jewish atmosphere" required to attend the performances.[30] Most negative press, however, flowed from Jewish journalists (in Jewish and non-Jewish newspapers) protective of the Jewish community in general and the relatively high social standing they had attained. In fact, by the time *The Two Kuni-Lemls* was on the boards in January 1880, Goldfaden had become the most publicly censured Russian Jewish artist in the empire.

Goldfaden might have predicted this reaction based on even his earliest tavern-based theater experiments. Indeed, the negative reaction by first audiences to the characters in his earlier shows had become a regular part of his life as an impresario and a blemish on what was otherwise a colossal cultural achievement. In his memoirs, Goldfaden recalls a similar episode surrounding his operetta called *The Recruits*—a play he staged in Romania during the Russo-Turkish War (1877). It features a hapless Hasid who is wrenched from his yeshiva for military service and later rejected by the army for his utter incompetence. In bidding farewell to his *shtender*, the pew that holds the sacred text of study, the schlemiel Zadok breaks into a song to the tune of Joan's farewell in Schiller's *The Young Maid of Orleans*.[31] Here, Goldfaden mischievously deployed Schiller's music to contrast the bravery of Joan of Arc with Zadok's cowardice. As Goldfaden recounts, however, Russian Jewish soldiers seated in the audience one evening—not Hasids—became incensed at what they understood to be a depiction of them on the stage and, with threats of violence, forced the show to close.[32]

Before *The Two Kuni-Lemls* was on the boards, particularly striking were the reactions to Goldfaden's notorious caricature Shmendrik, the title character of one of his earliest operettas whose pathetic and intellectually stunted behavior is overtly associated with his superstitious Judaism in a way that anticipates Kuni-Leml. While its popularity was without precedent on the Yiddish stage, *Shmendrik* enraged some members of the Jewish intelligentsia. *The Russian Jew* published a particularly derisive review about a production of *Shmendrik* that was staged in an outdoor venue in St. Petersburg's Krestovsky Park. The critic warned that instead of the Jewish audience Goldfaden sought to attract, members of the Russian petite bourgeoisie were attending his shows: "Bored dacha inhabitants of Krestovsky Island . . . wandered out . . . to watch the Jews romp about."[33] The reviewer grudgingly recognized the talent of the actors but continued, "We can find no good reason for the appearance of Goldfaden's play [*Shmendrik*] on the boards of a capital-city theater."[34] A Jewish journalist complained that non-Jewish attendees of the Yiddish theater had begun calling the acculturated Jewish residents of Moscow "Shmendrik."[35] A banker and an influential member of Minsk's plutocracy, Khonen Wengeroff (husband of the memoirist Paulina Wengeroff) tried to shut down a performance of *Shmendrik* that played in Minsk's municipal theater. During intermission, Wengeroff made his way backstage demanding, "Do you know that the Chief of Police is in a loge taking all this in?"[36] Apparently writing in defense of Goldfaden's work many years after the night in question, the memoirist Shmuel Tsitron writes, "Wengeroff belonged to a class of half-assimilated maskilim who aspired to one thing only: to find grace and acceptance in the eyes of the non-Jews and for that reason would erase anything that would emphasize its Jewishness."[37]

The Soft Ideological Center of *The Two Kuni-Lemls*

Following the mirror scene, Max ingratiates himself in Pinkhes's eyes by making of himself an idealized pious Hasid, a son-in-law that men like Pinkhes dream of. Max has averted disaster by intimidating Kuni-Leml and convincing the hapless Hasid that he is not himself and sends Kuni-Leml back to the home of the matchmaker in search of his identity. As if Carolina has not been made sufficiently peripheral to Max's desire, she also leaves the scene at this time. In pursuit of Carolina's hand in marriage, Max-as-Kuni-Leml pursues a kind of courtship, albeit laced with trickery, of Pinkhes. For Max to "get his will," he has impersonated the daft, stuttering, and limping Kuni-Leml to gain entry into Pinkhes's home. But here, to further impress Pinkhes and to mock him simultaneously for his belief in what non-Hasids believed was superstitious, he pretends to be a *lamed-vavnik* (literally a "thirty-sixer"), one of the thirty-six righteous Jews with magical powers who wander the earth disguised as the poor or otherwise wretched. Ironically, the Hasidic folk idea of the shape-shifting *lamed-vavnik* lends itself well to the protean Max who so deftly manipulates his appearance. With such supernatural powers at his disposal, Max sheds all of Kuni-Leml's most distinctive features like his stutter, his limp, and his shortsightedness. He becomes the ideal groom: a man of great lineage and piety, a man who reads Talmud and who is physically whole.

Like all traditional Jewish betrothals typically negotiated between the fathers of the bride and groom (or his family), the relationship of Max-as-Kuni-Leml and Pinkhes may be plotted on Eve Sedgwick's concept of male-male love that "is set firmly within a structure of institutionalized social relations that are carried out via women: marriage, name, family." Such homosocial relationships make use of women in a way that enables the bonds between men.[38] Here, however—again, notwithstanding the trickery—there are distinctly erotic overtones. "If you don't want me, you may say so," Max knowingly teases Pinkhes when the latter notices how physically appealing "Kuni-Leml" has become. Pinkhes responds with an explicit expression of desire: "God forbid! Who wouldn't want you? All I want is you" (3.7). As a refashioned Kuni-Leml, Max easily convinces Pinkhes that he is a worthy son-in-law. Pinkhes hurries to sign the conditions for marriage and he hands the dowry over to Max. Max is no longer a duplicate of Kuni-Leml; he becomes distinct from Kuni-Leml and even closer to his true self.

As the operetta proceeds, its ideological edge is softened, as the characters' language draws the audience's attention away from ideological divisions and toward the bifurcated selves of its characters. Act 3, scene 3, in which Carolina's arranged groom, Kuni-Leml, arrives at the house to claim his dowry and meet his bride is a case in point. Before this scene, we have come to know Carolina for her love of Max and his modern ideas and for her resentment of her father Pinkhes, who has reluctantly allowed her a modern tutor, according to the custom of his class, but forbids their marriage when he discovers that they have fallen in love. She sings her first aria in the solitude of her bedroom where she complains that her father imprisons her in the shadows of his Hasidic superstitions. Her parents are justly surprised, then, when Carolina consents to meeting Kuni-Leml. She does so expecting he will be Max disguised as Kuni-Leml. When he arrives, Carolina plays the provocateur, scandalizing her father and—as the audience quickly deduces—the real Kuni-Leml who arrived at the house before Max. She insists on introducing herself by her non-Jewish name, Carolina, and not by her Jewish name, Khayele:

> CAROLINA: Allow me the honor of presenting myself to you—your bride Carolina!
>
> KUNI-LEML: Why is she using such funny language?
>
> CAROLINA: (*With a smile.*) I am your bride.
>
> KUNI-LEML: My b-bride? . . . What's this C-crinolina? (*To Pinkhes who has been gesturing to Rivke this entire time as if they are arguing.*) Reb P-pinkhes, oy, she is a he-r-etic! Can a Jewish girl have such an aristocratic name?
>
> PINKHES: (*Goes to Carolina and whispers in her ear.*) You should have said "Khayele" to him. (3.3)

In the case of Carolina/Khayele, who is being introduced to her pious groom by her Hasidic father in the precincts of the home, the expectation is that she calls herself by her Jewish name, for the sake of her father.

Kuni-Leml's speech also picks up on Carolina's evolved sexuality when he confuses her name with "crinoline," the hooplike petticoat that women wore beneath their dresses, a word that became a shibboleth of Jewish eastern European sartorial tensions. Kuni-Leml's slip of the tongue was surely meant to elicit laughter as it references the Jewish battle with the crinoline, dated by Ginzburg to be almost a century old by the time Goldfaden wrote his operetta. Still, it continued to raise the ire of the rabbinic establishment. The memoirist Paulina Wengeroff (1833–1916) records her parents' rage against the makeshift crinoline that her sister crafted on her own and innocently modeled for her parents. Furious, Wengeroff's parents quickly made firewood of it. Her last words on the subject hint at the item's sexual connotations: "the flames grabbed eagerly at the new fashion."[39] A Hasidic community leader claimed the wearing of crinolines to be responsible for the spread of cholera while another rabbi put the garment in *herem*. Multiple articles in the conservative maskilic organ *The Preacher* (*Ha-magid*) evidence the suspicion assigned to this piece of clothing even by more moderate voices in the community. A brief article reminded readers that "a judicious rabbi" had outlawed crinolines. It concluded: "These days, even girls of Israel, in order to appear plump and healthy of flesh wear crinolines. This is a wild custom that is unprecedented among Jews."[40] Goldfaden refers to the discourse on the crinoline among eastern European Jews only obliquely in the operetta; we do not even know if Carolina's character wears a crinoline since Goldfaden does not indicate as much in his costume notes (although others of his young lady characters do). And yet, in one word, Goldfaden references modern fashion and the contentiousness it spawned among Russian Jews. Invariably, the crinoline among Jewish women of this time had much in common with its initial resistance by, say, the English and its role in women asserting their control over their appearance.[41] Kuni-Leml's stuttered slippage from "Carolina" to "crinoline" signifies his attentiveness to his betrothed's sexual awakening as it comically expresses his fear of and instinctive outrage for it.

In contrast to Carolina, whose appearance announces her new sensibility, the character of Sholem practices a self-conscious social chameleonism. Sholem, who takes on special prominence by the end of the operetta, is unique in Yiddish literature. In literature—as opposed to public theater—maskilic writers were particularly contemptuous of Hasidic leaders, rebbes, and sextons.[42] Here, instead, Sholem the sexton is judicious and is woven tightly into the play's community of characters. Related to "both Kuni-Lemls," who vie to inherit the comedy's future—he is the stepfather to Kuni-Leml and the uncle of Max—Sholem identifies with everyone without regard to their ideological orientation. Sholem is also the Hasidic sect's member of the *kahal*, the executive board democratically elected by the Jewish community's householders. We see his supporters cheering him on in act 1, scene 3. Thus his authority stems from the people and from his close-knit relations to the operetta's main characters and, presumably, from the trust he has earned in the rebbe's eyes. While Max presides over the first three acts of the play, Sholem asserts his authority in the final fourth act to bring (as his name suggests) peace and compromise to the explosive situation that Max has choreographed.

Sholem's importance compensates for the absence of an organic denouement of the operetta, which is at once a flaw and a curiosity of the operetta. For the most part, Goldfaden hewed closely to his literary models for this work: Gottlober's *Bridal Veil*, which also features an antagonist named Leml who is entangled in a plot of mistaken identities, depicts a maskilic hero who marries his beloved before his ruse can be unmasked. While everyone assumes one bride is beneath the veil, it is another. This occurs, too, in *Shmendrik*. In both cases, the protagonist's goal in tricking the beloved's father is to force upon him a marriage that, in his narrow-mindedness, he had initially rejected. In the case of *The Two Kuni-Lemls*, just as the prenuptial contract is settled in Max's favor, the real Kuni-Leml reappears on the scene and this time with Liba, the matchmaker's daughter, to reveal to all those gathered in Pinkhes's home that Max is an imposter. Max's ruse is over before there is a wedding canopy; the modern couple now hangs by the thread of a handshake and dowry between Pinkhes and a disguised Max—hardly legitimate and irreversible if Pinkhes believed he was shaking the hand of the real Kuni-Leml. Why didn't Goldfaden opt for a bridal canopy so as to cut Pinkhes out of the equation as he did in *Shmendrik*? In any case, while Pinkhes processes the trick played on him, Max exits the stage. At this point,

Sholem enters and convinces Pinkhes that Max and Carolina should marry. Pinkhes eventually agrees.

After seeing the evidence of Pinkhes's religious devotion to his Hasidic belief over three acts, how are we to believe that Sholem can convince him that Max—as he truly is, a modern, secular student—is the better match for Carolina? Moreover, why would Sholem, a Hasid, hope to see the daughter of a Hasid marry a progressive non-Hasid? These questions are never answered with great satisfaction. The operetta's convoluted plot ties together in the character of Sholem whose identity lies in the eyes of the beholders, those beholders within the frame of the operetta and those beyond. Max, for instance, is convinced from act 1 that his uncle is sympathetic to his ideological cause. He says to Carolina about Sholem: "Don't think my uncle is a Hasid like your father assumes him to be. He is a free thinker like my father. But, because he was the eldest brother, he never had the opportunity to study and was left to play the pious role (*er iz geblibn shpiln di frume role*) and leads the rebbe and his followers by the nose."[43] The most important man in the Hasidic community, but for the rebbe, is not a Hasid at all, according to Max, but a freethinker. While Max frames his uncle's identity as a committed reformer who pretends to be a Hasid to mock his rebbe, none of Sholem's actions support this claim. In fact, Sholem expresses attachment to both communities and navigates his conflicting loyalties by practicing a form of benign social chameleonism that allows him to "make peace" (*sholem*) with whichever social context he is in at the moment. [44] Goldfaden does not suggest that Sholem is corrupt as an apparent Hasid or as a supposed maskil. In fact, his moral uprightness and accrual of authority depend on his modulation of behavior according to the perception and expectations of the community that he moves within at the moment.

Forced to differentiate between the two Kuni-Lemls in the final act of the operetta, Sholem takes control of the situation and becomes the final arbiter of fairness. The language Goldfaden deploys in the scene is fascinating for how the character hedges with regard to his loyalties and identity. Sholem confirms Max's general take on him but suggests that his nephew was slightly more wishful about his uncle's progressive ways than is the case. Before an audience that combines Hasids and progressive Jews, Sholem begins with the following tautology: "Don't think I am a Hasid of the kind you think I am." And he continues, "More than once I have envied my brother who attained such a high level, and made of his children civilized people (*layt*). We must play old roles since we are of the old world, but in our heads, we need not be deceived." Such a statement would suggest that Sholem practices Hasidic piety in his (outward) behavior only.

But Sholem complicates this scenario. In an attempt to convince Pinkhes of Max's quality as a groom, Sholem does what Max did earlier in the play; that is, Sholem likens him (Max) to himself (Sholem). When Max and Carolina first conceived of their machinations, Max likens his uncle to himself and calls him a closeted "free-thinker." Now, Sholem depicts Max as the same as himself: "He is pious, possibly as much as I am, besides which he is also educated. That is, to God and to People." Here, Max is "as pious" as Sholem, a Hasidic sexton—albeit one who also confesses his modern/wayward thinking. Who Max and Sholem are is expressed in a series of vague and relative likenesses. Just as in life, their performances encourage their interlocutors to relate to them as like-minded.

The operetta's finale is one of optimism and intramural peaceful coexistence that hinges on identities being left as ambiguous as reason permits. Max's persuasive performance as Kuni-Leml with his knowledge of Hasidic practice in the previous act confirms what Sholem says: Max could be more observant and knowledgeable and even more emotionally wedded to Jewish piety than he represents. Perhaps in a conciliatory gesture, Max offers half his dowry to fund the match between Kuni-Leml and Liba, the matchmaker's daughter. Similarly, Max's mockery of certain Hasidic practices in act 3 is mitigated by the fact that Pinkhes adopted his Hasidic practice later in life, which the operetta seems to suggest is a rather exaggerated gesture especially as Pinkhes forces it on the rest of the family that finds it unnatural.

Hasidism, it suggests, might be deserving of a greater show of tolerance by Max if only Pinkhes was born Hasidic and if Kuni-Leml weren't so unappealing. Might. The marriages of the two young couples, each matched ideologically, are accepted equally by the operetta's society to claim its future. In the last moments of *The Two Kuni-Lemls*, it is not known with great specificity where everyone lands since it is a scenario orchestrated by Sholem who prioritizes social harmony over ideological purity.

Mapped on the ideological divisions of the characters are familial relationships that function to soften the ideological edge even more. Even in such scenarios of rivalry, so Goldfaden might be reminding his audience, Jews are all related, are all family. Sholem may be expected to favor his blood relative, Max, a valence that mitigates his harsher treatment of Kuni-Leml who is only his stepson. Perhaps, so this familial structure suggests, Sholem would favor the Hasid if he were the blood relative. Family and blood trump ideology in Goldfaden's world. His desire to be at once Max and Max-as-Kuni-Leml reinforces his kinship with his Uncle Sholem. It is no wonder the critic of the *Odessa Herald* felt the operetta's characters were not sufficiently differentiated. The identities of Max and Sholem are blurred by the adjustments, visual and verbal, that they make to their identities throughout the operetta. Finally, we can never know their identities with precision; who they are depends on where they are and their ever-changing social circumstances. While Max might not have accepted this about himself, his uncle has. He is at peace with being his multiple selves. The character of Sholem anticipates the character of Alonso in Goldfaden's *Doctor Almasada*, another important social chameleon of Goldfaden's oeuvre examined in chapter 4.

Conclusion

A famous scene in Woody Allen's *Annie Hall* succinctly echoes the experience of the modern Russian Jews who recoiled at Goldfaden's theater. In it, the male Jewish protagonist Alvy Singer visits Annie's grandmother, Grammy Hall, for Easter. While sitting at the family's Easter dinner, pushing through an awkward conversation with her, Alvy has a vision of himself as a Hasid with sidelocks and *shtrayml*, the round, fur-lined hat donned by some Hasidic sects. His feelings of cultural alienation triggered an involuntary vision of himself as he imagined how he looks in the eyes of Grammy Hall. It is not the way he would ever elect to see himself. It is not even the image Granny Hall conjures of him—for she has no access to these associations. Alvy cannot help but see himself "through her eyes" in a sense but constructed according to his own visual vocabulary that is intimately aware of the appearance with which he wants least to associate. Similarly, when modern Russian Jews visited the theater, the theater did for them what Alvy's imagination does in *Annie Hall*: it identified them most closely with those ethnic features of their lives that they had worked so hard to slough off. They left the theater believing that gentiles in the audience would identify the exaggerated traditional types on Goldfaden's stage with the refined and acculturated Jews among them. If *The Two Kuni-Lemls* is Goldfaden's reflection on his peers' anxiety, it suggests that their embarrassment is their only hurdle to overcome and the way to happiness is Sholem-like acceptance. A paradox, perhaps, but the ideal audience of the modern Yiddish theater was one that included those for whom the most familiar images were the most unsettling.

Notes

1. Jacob P. Adler, "Mayn lebensbashraybung," *Di naye varhayt* 15, 18, and 21 (March 1925). Funding came from a financier by the name of Kheykl Bern. Adler provides ample description of the success of these first productions in his memoirs.

2. A number of brief articles mention Goldfaden's activity in Odessa. See "Evreiskie spektakli," *Pravda*, no. 176 (August 11, 1879): 2. For a comprehensive bibliography of references to Goldfaden and Yiddish theater, see Evgeni Binevich, *Istoriia evreiskogo teatra v rossii, 1876–1883. Annotirovannaia bibliografiia* (Moscow: Obshchestvo Naslednie, 1998). Also see Zylbercweig work that collates a number of earlier Yiddish sources, Zalmen Zylbercweig, ed., [o]*Avrom Goldfaden un Zigmunt Mogulesko* (Buenos Aires: Elisheva, 1936), 66.

3. Zalmen Zylbercweig, ed., "Di zikhroynes fun yitskhak libresku der initsyator fun Goldfadns teater," in *Hintern forhang* (Vilna: Vilner farlag fun B. Kletskin, 1928), 54–58.

4. Ibid. Librescu provides the most detail on this period. During the 1870s, the Russian Empire saw the rise of entrepreneurial theaters funded by private money. Officially, the government banned the theaters but nonetheless, during this era, came to tolerate such private initiatives. Ironically, in 1883, when Yiddish theater was banned, private theaters were officially given full rights. See Paul du Quenoy, *Stage Fright: Politics and the Performing Arts in Late Imperial Russia* (University Park, PA: The Pennsylvania State University Press, 2009), 24–25.

5. For a discussion of Goldfaden's troupe in Odessa, see Y. Riminik, "Ershte finf yor yidisher teater in odes (1879–1883)," *Di royte velt* 12 (1926): 89–107.

6. Steven Zipperstein, *The Jews of Odessa: A Cultural History, 1794–1881* (Stanford, CA: Stanford University Press, 1986), 65.

7. Nahum Shaikevitsh, "Dos yidishe teater," *Der menshenfraynd: beletristishe vokhnshrift (farlag N/M/ shaykevitsh)*, no. 10 (1891).

8. Avom Fishzon, "Fuftsik yor yidish teater," *Morgn zhurnal*, November 21, 1925.

9. Quoted in Y. Riminik, "Di ershte yorn fun yidishn teater (tsveyter teyl)," *Hamer* (April 1928): 62. Here Vinovits might have only been referring to shows in Odessa. She does not specify time or place. A similar report about Goldfaden's shows in Minsk by a stagehand name Samsonov includes an anecdote that agents would line up and cluster around the box office and guards were hired to keep order. In L. Dushman, "A. Goldfaden in Minsk," *Literarishe Bleter* 95 (1926): 141.

10. The Opera and Ballet Theater, historically Odessa's grandest theater, was destroyed by fire in 1873 and only rebuilt in 1887.

11. Quoted in Y. Riminik, "Di ershte yorn fun yidishn teater (tsveyter teyl)," *Hamer* (April 1928): 62.

12. See Adler's remark on how Jews in Odessa attended theater in disproportionate numbers: Jacob Adler, "40 yor af der bine," *Varhayt*, September 17, 1916, 5.

13. Initially, the Jewish press welcomed news of Goldfaden's theater for what it assumed to be its educational goals: "Thank God that we live in such fortunate times, that we Jews have lived long enough to see our very own theatre," Abramsky wrote. See Avraham Hagershoni Abramsky, *Bamat yitskhak o gey chizayon* (Bucharest, 1877). The maskil Bernard Nathanson trumpeted, "Great benefits can flow from a mass theatre towards the enlightenment of the Jews wherever they may live," in an untitled article in *Hamelits* 15 (1878): 290–291. For another adulatory treatment of Goldfaden and the "educational" nature of his theater, see a letter to the Hebrew newspaper *Ha-magid* 15 (1883), A. R. Malachi, trans., "Materialn," *A Centenary of Abraham Goldfaden*, ed. Jacob Shatzky (New York: YIVO, 1940), 77.

14. "Evreiskaia operetka 'Fanatik,'" *Russkie Vedomosti* (August 10, 1880): 1. Signed "X." Quoted in A. Gurshteyn, "Tsu A. Goldfaden-forshung," *Literarishe bleter*, 109 (1926).

15. B. Brand, "Ucheno-literaturnyi otdel: Motivy evreiskoi dramy," *Russkii Evrei* [The Russian Jew], no. 33 (1880): 1307–1310. This is the second of a multipart essay on Goldfaden. The other parts appear in no. 32 (1880): 1265–1269; no. 35 (1880): 1382–1384; no. 36 (1880): 1424–1426. Oyslender and Finkel also acknowledge that Goldfaden never sought out theatrical audiences in Hasidic population centers or where Jewish communities were vulnerable to Hasidism's attraction. At one point they wonder why Goldfaden's troupe never reached the dense Jewish population centers of Warsaw, Vilna, and Cracow if he sought out uneducated masses of Jews.

16. This review is quoted in *Russkii Evrei* in a broader review of Goldfaden's works. See "Vnutrenee obozrenie [Domestic review[o]]," *Russkii Evrei*, no. 7 (1880): 247–249.

17. I rely on Berkowitz and Dauber's translation of *The Two Kuni-Lemls* in *Landmark Yiddish Plays: A Critical Anthology*, trans. and eds. Joel Berkowitz and Jeremy Dauber (Albany: State University of New York, 2006), 13. The translation strongly resembles a manuscript of the play that has a censorship date of April 1882. "Fanatik" ms. 1882. St. Petersburg. Abraham Goldfaden Collection RG219; folder 20.

18. Berkowitz and Dauber, "Introduction," 44.

19. Northrop Frye, *Anatomy of Criticism* (Princeton, NJ: Princeton University Press, 1957), 43.

20. As his competitor Joseph Lateiner had complained, Goldfaden probably drew unfairly on his operetta, *Di tsvey Shmuel Shmuelkes*. It is clear that he borrowed from Gottlober's (1801–1899) anti-Hasidic play, *Dos dektukh: tsvey khasenes in eyn nakht* [The Bridal Veil: Two Weddings in One Night] (Warsaw: Yozef Verbeynski, 1876). On Gottlober as an influence, see Berkowitz and Dauber, "Introduction." Lateiner's *Di tsvey Shmuel Shmuelkes* was mounted briefly in February 1879 by Rosenberg and Spivakovski in Odessa before it was shut down by the Russian authorities. It is possible that this work was among those Lateiner handed over to Goldfaden when he worked for him as a prompter. There is no extant copy of Lateiner's operetta.

21. So significantly did the battle with Hasidism figure in the maskilic creative imagination that scholars like Raphael Mahler attribute the early growth of Yiddish literature to reformers' ideological zeal to counter the spread of Hasidic propaganda. See R. Mahler, *Hasidism and the Jewish Enlightenment: Their Confrontation in Galicia and Poland in the First Half of the Nineteenth Century*, trans. from the Yiddish by Eugene Orenstein and from the Hebrew by Aaron Klein and Jenny Machlowitz Klein (Philadelphia: Jewish Publication Society of America, 1985), chap. 2. See also Chone Shmeruk, *Sifrut yidish be-Polin* (Jerusalem: Hotsa'at sefarim 'a. sh. Y.L. Magnes, ha-Universiṭah ha-'Ivrit, 1981), 119–184.

22. Shmuel Niger, "Di lider fun avrom goldfadn," *Tsukunft* 3 (1926): 150–154.

23. The interest by assimilated Jews of Goldfaden's harshest portrayal of Hasids might be indicated by the Russian translation of his Hasidic play *Neither Beh, Nor Moo, Nor Cock-a-doodle-Doo* (*Ni be, ni me, ni kukuriku*). It is the only one of Goldfaden's works translated into Russian. On its popularity in Odessa, see Y. Riminik, "Di ershte finf yor yidishn teater in odes," *Di royte velt* 12, Kharkov, vol. 12 (1926): 100.

24. Avrom Goldfaden, "Fun Shmendrik biz Ben-Ami (Autobiography)," in *Avrom Goldfadn: Oysgeklibene Shriftn*, ed. Shmuel Rozhinski (Buenos Aires: Literatur gezelshaft baym YIVO, 1907).

25. See Chone Shmeruk and Chava Turniansky, eds., *Di yidishe literatur in nayntsenten yorhundert: zamlung fun yidisher literatur-forshung un kritik* (Jerusalem: Y. L. Magnes, 1993); Uri Finkel, "Sotsiale figurn in A. Goldfaden's ershte verk (materialn tsu der karateristik fun A. Goldfaden's shafn" and Yekhezkel Dobrushin, "Goldfaden's dramaturgye," in *Di yidishe literatur in naytstn yorhundert*.

26. Sholem Perlmutter, "Avrom Goldfaden, der grinder fun yidishn teater." A newspaper clipping dated to 1926, YIVO Archives RG 298, file folder titled "Avrom Goldfaden tsaytung oysshnitn."

27. Quoted in Shas Roman, "The Earliest Critical Reviews of the Jewish Theater," in *A Centenary of Abraham Goldfaden*, ed. Jacob Shatzky (New York: Yiddish Scientific Institute, 1940), 43–45.

28. See a two-part article on Goldfaden's theater by B. Brand who wonders why Odessa's Jews needed Yiddish-language theater to enlighten them when most of its potential Jewish

visitors were already regulars of non-Jewish theater. B. Brand, "Motivy evreiskoi dramy," *Russki Evrei*, no. 32 (1880): 1265; and B. Brand, "Motivy evreiskoi dramy," *Russki Evrei*, no. 33 (1880): 1307.

29. *Vedomosti Odesskogo Gradonachal'stva*, January 18, 1880. Salvini himself would visit the Yiddish theater and effuse about it publicly.

30. Quoted in Y. Riminik, "Redifes kegn yidishn teater in rusland in di 80-er un 90-er yorn," *Teater-bukh*, Kiev (1927): 87.

31. For a synopsis and excerpt of the song, see Gorin, B. *Di geshikhte fun yidishn teater: tsvey toyznt yor yidish teater* [The History of the Yiddish Theater], 2 vols. New York: Max N. Mayzel, 1923, 174–178.

The play was never published. Incomplete ms. at YIVO. *Di rekrutn*, 1877; Abraham Goldfaden Collection; RG 219; folder 1; YIVO Institute for Jewish Research. See more bibliographical information as well as a translated excerpt from one of the show's songs entitled "Dos Hsidishe militer" [The Hasidic Soldier] in Donny Inbar, "A Closeted Jester: Abraham Goldfaden between Haskalah Ideology and Jewish Show Business" (doctoral dissertation, Graduate Theological Union, Ann Arbor, MI: ProQuest, UMI, June 2007, 3289818), 115.

32. See Zalmen Zylbercweig, *Leksikon fun Yidishn teater*, vol. I (New York: Elisheva, 1931), 287–288.

33. "Trupa G. Shmuel, Gold'fadena v. Peterburge," *Russkii Evrei*, no. 32 (1881): 1229–1230.

34. Ibid., 1230.

35. Article is quoted in A. Gurshteyn, "A. Goldfadn in moskve," *Literarishe bleter* 95 (1926), 138–139.

36. Tsitron, Sh. L. *Dray literarishe doyres: zikhroynes vegn yidishe shrifshteler* [Three Literary Generations]. Vilna: Sh. Shreberk, 1920, 97.

37. Ibid., 98.

38. Eve Kosofsky Sedgwick, *Between Men: English Literature and Male Homosocial Desire* (New York: Columbia University Press, 1985), 35. See Naomi Seidman, *The Marriage Plot* (Stanford, CA: Stanford University Press, 2013).

39. Pauline Wengeroff, *Rememberings: The World of a Russian-Jewish Woman in the Nineteenth Century*, trans. Henny Wenkart and ed. Bernard D. Cooperman (Potomac: University Press of Maryland, 2000), 110.

40. Ginzburg, "Redifes af yidishe begodim," 281.

41. Kimberly Chrisman, "Unhoop the Fair Sex: The Campaign against the Hoop Petticoat in Eighteenth-Century England," *Eighteenth-Century Studies* 30, no. 1 (1996): 7,

42. See, for instance, Aksenfeld's *Kabtsn-oysher shpil* [Pauper–Rich Man Play]. For a far more conventional depiction by Goldfaden of a Hasidic sexton who controls the rebbe's court life, see A. Goldfadn, *Ni Me, Ni Be, Ni Kukuriku* (Odessa, St. Petersburg: 1880, 1881). Published only in Russian translation, a Yiddish version of this play did not survive. For a historical treatment of the Hasidic court, see David Assaf, "Money for Household Expenses," *Scripta Hierosolymitana* 38 (1998): 14–50.

43. Berkowitz and Dauber, *The Two Kuni-Lemls*, 212.

44. However remarkable he is as a theatrical character, Sholem was not anomalous in the social life of eastern European Jews. Memoirs evidence a trend of social chameleonism, specifically of Jewish men manipulating their clothing throughout the nineteenth century so they could be perceived to be more pious in some circles and less so in others. The maskil Mordechai Ginzburg[o] (1795–1846) provides an early example. See Joseph Klausner,

Historiah Shel Ha-Sifrut Ha-Ivrit Ha-Khadasha, vol. 3 (Jerusalem, 1954), 125. Jacob Shatzky, *Geshikhte Fun Yidn in Varshe*. vol. 2 (New York: YIVO, 1948), 82. See also the memoirs of Yehezkel Kotik and Alexander Zederbaum, Yekhezkel Kotik, *Mah She-Ra'iti: Zikhronotav Shel Yehezkel Kotik. Meturgemet U-Mevo'eret Bi-Yede David Asaf, Sefer* 132 (Tel-Aviv: Universtat Tel-Aviv, 1998), 120. Originally published in Yiddish in 1922.

4 The Rise of the Yiddish Playwright

The Yiddish Theater Beyond Odessa

While Goldfaden's memoirs supply little information about his experience producing Yiddish performance in its resident city of Odessa, the memoirs of his colleague and sometimes competitor Nahum Shaikevitsh (1849–1905) do. Shaikevitsh serialized "The Yiddish Theater," in 1891 in a weekly periodical he published in New York City called *The Philanthropist* (*Dos Menshenfraynd*).[1] By this time, Shaikevitsh was already best known as a Yiddish pulp-fiction novelist (known by the name of Shomer to his readers), a career to which he turned only after his involvement in the Yiddish theater. "The Yiddish Theater" is half history and half personal recollection of a period that still lived clearly in Shaikevitsh's memory by the time he committed it to paper.

Born to a wealthy family in Nesvizh, Lithuania, Shaikevitsh began his career writing for the Hebrew journal *Ha-Melits* and then turned to publishing stories in Yiddish in the early 1870s. He interrupted his creative work in order to service a lucrative contract with the Russian military in Romania during the Russo-Turkish War (1877–78). Following the war, he spent time in Odessa, where one evening in 1880 he attended the Yiddish theater with his colleague Avrom Gottlober, who at the time was visiting the city from Zhitomir. Together, they took in a production of Joseph Lateiner's *The Dybbuk* (*Der dibek*, not to be confused with S. Y. Ansky's *The Dybbuk*) at the elegant Mariinsky Theater. After seeing the performance, the two gentlemen decided that *The Dybbuk* was mediocre at best. While they conceded that it showcased the talent of the lead comic, Mogulesco, they recognized that it was only a hodgepodge of Goldfaden scenes and strategies. By the time of Shaikevitsh and Gottlober's visit to the theater, no composer or playwright had yet approached Goldfaden's success in crafting a winning Yiddish operetta, although a number had tried to plagiarize his work.

Goldfaden himself was in charge of the Yiddish-language repertoire at the Mariinsky Theater under its manager, a man referred to as Homer in historical sources. But Homer removed Goldfaden from his lease after the men had a falling out and turned, with the lucrative lease for the theater's Yiddish slot, to the Russian Jewish writer and journalist Osip (Yoysef Yehuda) Lerner (about him we will say more later in this chapter). By this point, Lerner's reputation preceded him as an accomplished journalist and, in Yiddish literary circles, for his defense of Yiddish in a (Russian-language) booklet (1868), among other polemical writings. Lerner translated works for the stage and also sought out content from playwrights other than Goldfaden under his production. Goldfaden, it seems, refused to permit the production of his works without producing and directing the shows himself.

At Gottlober's suggestion, Shaikevitsh approached Lerner with his first play, a comic tragedy called *The Jewish Nobleman* (*Der yidisher porets*). Lerner paid him a hundred rubles for its first performance and fifteen rubles for every subsequent night that it remained on the boards. *The Jewish Nobleman* played to packed houses. With this happy experience, Shaikevitsh awoke to the commercial potential of Yiddish theatrical culture. By 1881, Shaikevitsh was holding tryouts in the living room of his Odessa apartment for a troupe of his own that he planned to take on the road to cities in close proximity to Odessa. He managed to set himself up in Nikolaev only to be disrupted by the assassination of Alexander II on March 13, 1881. The assassination led to a temporary closure of most newspapers and theaters throughout the empire as well as the threat of pogroms. Shaikevitsh returned to Odessa to wait out the crisis. When the political climate cooled and theaters and newspapers began to reopen, Shaikevitsh's troupe was one of a number of Yiddish theater companies that had discovered hospitable venues for Yiddish theater in Russia's borderland cities.

The theater's growing pool of playwrights, along with positive reviews signaled an unprecedented level of acceptance of the Yiddish theater in the Russian Empire as well as an unprecedented acceptance of European material on the Yiddish stage.[2] The introduction of historical operettas to the Yiddish stage was an important milestone in this regard. Defined until this point mostly by Goldfaden's farces and comic operettas, the Yiddish theater boasted a broad array of historical operettas that brought it into line with popular European operetta. A combination of song, dialogue, and dance, often with a conservative bent, operettas of many languages dominated the larger opera houses in Odessa, not to mention those in Moscow and St. Petersburg. But while Goldfaden generated original Jewish content, competing impresarios relied on translations and adaptations of European works, especially those that featured Jewish characters. The translations raised the literary level of the Yiddish stage. More important in the following pages, these translations expanded the idea of what stories and ideas might be transmitted on a Jewish stage and who may author such stories—that is, who might write a play or operetta that commands the attention of a mostly Jewish public in its mostly vernacular language of Yiddish.

Indeed, Goldfaden inspired fruitful and fierce competition during this era that has been half forgotten beneath the myth of his fatherhood but is indisputably in evidence in the contemporary Russian press. Historian Evgenii

Binevich reports that between 1878 and 1883 at least ten discrete Yiddish theater troupes formed and mounted at least fifty-three separate works. While most were original Yiddish-language libretti, others were translations and adaptations. All would require approval by the Bureau of Censorship in St. Petersburg. Goldfaden's operettas account for only twenty of these titles. Who wrote and submitted these other Yiddish-language theatrical works to the Bureau of Censorship? Beside three troupes under Goldfaden's control (two of which were run by the actors Tsukerman and Kessler or Kessler's brothers) and the troupe organized by Spivakovski and Rosenberg based in Rostov-On-Don, the press named the following as "entrepreneurs," leaders of commercial Yiddish theater companies: the former Goldfaden actors Finkel, Mogulesco, and Adler who sought success in Kishinev; the playwright Shaikevitsh;[3] an impresario named Yakov Hartenshteyn; and the journalist, Yiddish literary critic turned impresario Osip Lerner.[4] A flurry of announcements in *The Prompter* (*Sufler*) from March to May 1883 located Hartenshteyn and his theater company in Moscow putting on works by Goldfaden, among others.[5] Russian sources do not supply an abundance of details about of the experiences of impresarios staging Yiddish theater in the Russian Empire during this period and many of the actual censored materials have not survived.[6] Still, the Yiddish theater generated Yiddish playwrights beyond just Goldfaden in cities beyond just Odessa and, finally, with ideas that lay beyond what many would consider Jewish. To the extent we can reconstruct the biographies and activities of the gallery of playwrights at work during this era, they animate a far richer cultural story of the rise of the modern Yiddish theater that has been, until now, eclipsed by the dominance of the Goldfaden legend.

In his memoirs, to the extent Goldfaden reckons with the record of his competitors' achievement, he spitefully questions their Jewish credentials: he insists that his "fatherhood" of the Yiddish theater is legitimate while his competitors were illegitimate polluters of the theater. Writing in the 1890s, Goldfaden could not bring himself to share the credit for creating the Yiddish theater with his pioneering colleagues. He levels such arguments at his contemporaries in Russia as well as those who wrote in the 1890s against whom Goldfaden struggled a great deal for attention. Indulging in colorful name-calling, Goldfaden wrote to his friend Adolf Lichtenshtein, a French Jewish writer in 1904, complaining about the plethora of foreign adaptations performed on the Yiddish stage: "Guilty for this are our Jewish-authors-anti-Semitic apostates who have sought to make the stage gentile."[7] Here and elsewhere, Goldfaden associates the post-Goldfaden Yiddish theater of the 1890s and 1900s with apostasy and invokes the presence of the non-Jew as a dangerous specter haunting the Yiddish culture of performance. Among his first victims of such attacks were playwrights who began their careers in Russia and some of whom converted to Christianity.[8] Against the background

Figure 4.1. Hand-painted magic lantern slide of Yakov Hartenshteyn, c. 1910. Courtesy of the YIVO Institute for Jewish Research.

of American fears about assimilation, Goldfaden portrays himself as the defender of the theater's Jewish honor.

Goldfaden's historical operetta *Doctor Almasada or the Jews of Palermo* (*Doktor Almasada oder di yidn fun Palermo*, from now on *Doctor Almasada*) is an important resource in exploring his later comments regarding the growing gentile complexion of the Yiddish theater. Newspaper announcements indicate that he mounted the operetta for the first time in 1882, at the height of his success in Russia.[9] *Doctor Almasada*'s ostensible subject is Jewish-Christian relations under the Crown of Aragon in the fourteenth-century Sicilian city of Palermo.[10] The story moves between two main camps of characters. The first camp includes the governor of Palermo, Don Pedro, and his wife, Isabella, whose daughter Elvira is dying of a mysterious illness. The second group is the elderly Jewish Dr. Almasada and his daughter. At the start of the play, Palermo's Jews have been driven out of the city by royal decree. Alonso, Dr. Almasada's Christian apprentice, recognizes that only Dr. Almasada can heal Elvira, but Jews are forbidden from treating Christian patients. Dr. Almasada and Alonso collaborate to convince the governor that he should be allowed to bring Almasada's Jewish medical genius to bear on Elvira's grave situation. Thus, Dr. Almasada saves Elvira, and her restoration convinces the governor to influence the ruling tsar to repeal the anti-Jewish laws. Among the other plotlines of the play are a false accusation of murder followed by a stint in jail for Dr. Almasada, the exploits of a band of Christian robbers, and what appears to be a forbidden romance between Alonso and the doctor's Jewish daughter Miriam.

Alonso is particularly revealing of Goldfaden's thinking about Jewish-Christian relations. He is the doctor to the royal family and loyal to his teacher, Dr. Almasada. And toward the end of the operetta, Alonso reveals himself to be Jewish. Alonso, in my coinage, is a gentile Jew: a Jew who behaves like a gentile in order to advance the cause of humanity in general and that of the Jewish People in particular. Out of line with Goldfaden's later accusations of apostasy against his competitors, the character of Alonso reveals his thinking on the question of Jewish and gentile identity to be subtle and complicated. Although projected onto historical Palermo, Alonso calls to mind the historical realities of baptized Jews in Russia, as well as those Jews who pretended to be Christian to improve their personal situation in Russia.

In what follows, I investigate Goldfaden's claims about the lives of the Yiddish theater's first playwrights including the plays they generated for the stage and their relationships with Christianity. I also offer a reading of *Doctor Almasada* that, I suggest, is Goldfaden's conservative rejoinder to his fellow Yiddish playwrights who embraced the liberal narratives—many of them direct translations of Western plays, operas, and operettas—that depicted Judaism as inferior or religions as ideologies of intolerance. Alonso's comfort with social performance is balanced by his protective posture toward his Jewish identity. That is, the gentile Jew is palatable to Goldfaden—as long as a man's blood and his primary loyalties remain Jewish. This reading of *Doctor Almasada* is particularly clear alongside the French opera *La juive* (*The Jewess*, originally performed in 1835) by Fromenthal Halévy and Eugene Scribe that became a favorite on European and Russian stages well into Goldfaden's day and enjoyed resurgence in Yiddish during this early era of the modern theater's development. Goldfaden was eager to see the integration of Russian Jewry, but not at the cost of compromising the physical integrity of the Jewish People. As with the questions of social performance, Goldfaden had a double-edged approach regarding Jewish politics. He did not have a quarrel with gentile Jews per se; in fact, *Dr. Almasada* endorses the gentile Jew. But Goldfaden could not abide Scribe's depiction of interreligious romance and friendship as transcending Jewish solidarity.

Unintentionally, so he claims, Goldfaden's enterprise unleashed the rise of Yiddish playwrights who generated works that were hardly attentive to any kind of "Jewish principles." Goldfaden's comedies articulated Jewish solidarity across ideological divides while his histories promoted obedience toward host governments alongside Jewish fealty and paternalism. The staged works of his fellow pioneers, however, reflected liberal universalist ideas, and sometimes even the desire to propagate Christianity. A number of playwrights did not abide what Goldfaden insisted were the strict ideological boundaries of his world. With little precedent in the arena of Yiddish performance, the Yiddish language more than Jewish ideology defined a work of the Yiddish stage. Such plays, much to Goldfaden's chagrin, signaled the rise of the Yiddish playwright. Goldfaden remained, in his own eyes, a Jewish playwright. Or so it seems. Goldfaden's allegiances were ever-shifting and colored by his native opportunism. The gentile Jew afforded him a reassuring measure of ambiguity and latitude to navigate a world still divided by religious and geographic borders.

Jewish History on the Expanding Yiddish Stage

Following in the wake of a number of his comic operettas that some audience members found offensive, *Doctor Almasada* along with *Shulamis*, *Bar Kochba* (*Bar Kokhve*, 1881), and *Judah the Maccabean (Yehuda ha-Makabi*, 1882) constitute four operettas that redeemed Goldfaden in the eyes of his contemporaries.[11] Notwithstanding the relative infancy of the Yiddish theater and its scant financial resources compared to the generous subsidies received by authorized state theater troupes that competed for venues, Russian theatergoers continued to track Goldfaden's troupe with curiosity. Still, not least because of the lack of substantive commentary on this period of his career by Goldfaden himself, we cannot confirm conclusions drawn by a number of observers about his artistic decisions. Building on the comic/history divide in Goldfaden's career, the Yiddish ethnographer and playwright S. Y. Ansky suggested that Goldfaden pivoted toward historical content in order to assuage his critics.[12] Finkel and Oyslender suggest that the histories are evidence of Goldfaden's sense of Jewish nationalism that he felt after the wave of pogroms that occurred in the southern provinces in 1881 and1882. "In general terms, the historical plays animated Goldfaden's new voice that he formulated after the pogroms; a voice of a man that wants to repent, and wants to reverse the effects of his earlier biting satires [and replace the satirical characters] with traditional Jewish figures."[13]

Goldfaden seems to contradict the idea that his histories were a response to the pogroms. His only reference to the 1881–1882 pogroms is the inconvenience they caused when the government temporarily shuttered the Yiddish theater after the assassination of Alexander II. Instead, he singles out the Kishinev pogroms of 1903 as having an impact on his Jewish politics and his attitude toward Russia. Indeed, his last operetta, *Ben-Ami* (1908), which he writes when he is in America, addresses anti-Semitic persecution on the part of the Russian government. This was over twenty years later. While the pogroms of 1881 and 1882 have become an important milestone in nineteenth-century Russian Jewish intellectual history, there is no evidence that they had an effect on Goldfaden's ideological orientation. The histories in general and *Doctor Almasada* in particular reflect Goldfaden's enduring optimism about the future of Russian Jewry: *Bar Kokhve* cautions against the post-Temple period leader who led rebellions against the Romans while *Doctor Almasada* demonstrates how Jews are better deployed by their host countries for their unique ingenuity rather than persecuted for their otherness.

It is likely that Yiddish-language historical opera was Goldfaden's aspiration from the beginning. Historical opera had an important presence in Russian theaters and Goldfaden attended a great deal of opera, historical and otherwise. As early as 1877, Goldfaden began incorporating quotations from Western opera into his stage works. A smaller work of his called by the nonsensical title *Iks Miks Driks*, for example, quotes Richard Wagner's *Flying Dutchman*, and Goldfaden's very popular *Brayndele Cossack* was a parody of Jacques Offenbach's *Bluebeard*. From the beginning, Goldfaden claims in his memoirs, he had looked forward to growing his troupe to a size large enough to put on full-scale historical operas, and he was not the only Yiddish playwright who wanted to do so: competition among the growing clutch of Yiddish impresarios fueled the rapid growth of troupes and prestige of the stage. By 1881, histories—adapted and original compositions—represented at least half of the Yiddish theater's offerings.[14]

Western and Russian historical operas that favored Jewish themes and characters had already set the stage for the appearance of Yiddish-language histories. The historical opera *Judith*, a Russian adaptation of *Yudith* based on the Italian opera *Giuditta* by Paolo Giacometti, made Alexander Serov (1820–1861) imperial Russia's most important composer of the 1860s.[15] The opera, which recounts the story of Judith's slaying of the Assyrian King Holofernes (from the Apocrypha), was later adapted for the Yiddish stage in 1880 by the Yiddish playwright Osip Lerner.[16] Goldfaden also adapted the story for the stage as a satire or ironic version.[17] Although not performed widely, the Russian composer Anton Rubinstein's *The Maccabees* (*Die Maccabaer*) premiered in 1875.[18] Duplicating the popularity it enjoyed on the Russian stage, Karl Gutzkow's (1811–1878) *Uriel Acosta* was the most popular translated historical work of the Yiddish stage. Lerner's adaptation of this work about the Jewish philosopher excommunicated by his community's rabbis was the most celebrated.[19] While it was originally "performed in many European languages and countries," *Uriel Acosta* came to be associated most with the Yiddish theater after its 1881 premiere in Odessa.[20] But in Goldfaden's day, of all the theatrical works that featured Jewish characters, unsurpassed in popularity was Fromenthal Halévy's *La juive* (1835). *Zhidovka* (its Russian translation) was first absorbed into the empire's Russian-language repertoire and, under its Russian name, a Yiddish adaptation enjoyed a considerable run on the Yiddish stage in Odessa during this period as its popularity continued across Europe and in America.[21] *La juive* and what I suggest was Goldfaden's disapproval of its plot and characters had an indelible effect on *Doctor Almasada*.

Christianity and Goldfaden's Playwright Contemporaries[22]

Goldfaden's operettas were the most performed works on the Russian Yiddish stage from 1878 to 1883; their performance in the empire's big cities and the subsequent popularization of his work obscured the presence of his competitors. Presumably, Goldfaden, whose agenda was to claim sole proprietorship of the Yiddish theater's cultural legacy, was not broken up about this: he had personal relationships with most every playwright in the business of Yiddish theater of the time, and each relationship ended in feuding and acrimony. Moreover, when the Yiddish theater shifted westward, to London and New York, as a consequence of the ban, his competitors benefitted from the new opportunities they found to continue producing Yiddish theater, while Goldfaden had nothing to focus on but his legacy. His claim of fatherhood was intended to leave in the shadows the memory of other Yiddish playwrights of this early era. And for those who could not be ignored, Goldfaden reserved a special brand of self-righteous derision aimed at their loyalty to the Jewish People.

Of course, not all of the theater's half-forgotten Yiddish playwrights flirted with Christianity. According to scholar Leo Wiener, a playwright named Isaac Katznellenbogen was "the most original and most literary" of the assembly of Yiddish playwrights who conveniently go unmentioned by Goldfaden. As none of his dramas have survived and there is no memoir by Katznellenbogen, we cannot test the accuracy of this statement. The press was especially enthusiastic about his work *Rashi*, presumably about the French-Jewish Torah commentator, Shlomo Yitzchaki (1040–1105).[23] Likewise, the playwright Jacob Ter is associated with New York's thriving commercial Yiddish theater of the 1890s and later. (The New York Public Library has a large collection of his plays and operettas, both published and in manuscript form.) But Ter's career as a Yiddish playwright began in Russia before the ban. The son of a merchant from Neustadt, near the Prussian-Polish border and a former student of Slonim's prestigious misnagdic yeshiva, Ter found himself in Rostov-on-Don in 1883 on business where he fell in with Finkel's Yiddish theater troupe. Impressed with what he saw, he began to write. At the age of twenty-two, he saw his first works of drama mounted on the Russian stage in that city.[24]

In addition, neither Shaikevitsh nor Lateiner, the most prolific writers of original works for the Yiddish stage during this period after Goldfaden, earns mention in the memoiristic writings of the father of the Yiddish theater. His colleague and sometime collaborator Shaikevitsh was referred to routinely as both playwright and "entrepreneur" in the Russian press. It may be surprising to scholars familiar with Shaikevitsh's reputation as a peddler of Yiddish potboilers (a reputation generated almost single-handedly by Sholem Aleichem five years later) that he participated in efforts to elevate the Yiddish stage. Shaikevitsh, for instance, translated Nikolai Gogol's (1809–1852) satirical comedy *The Government Inspector*, which was mounted by Lerner in 1883.[25] Lateiner lost his association with the first era of Yiddish theater in Russia even though his experience writing for the Russian stage was extensive.[26] Likely his Romanian background forced him to rely on Russian-born impresarios to mount his works, and so we see them produced on the stage under Lerner and Adler. In his failure to mention these men as the pioneers they were, Goldfaden's memoirs are hardly the complete record of the early Yiddish theater that he claims it to be.

On the other hand, Benedict Ben Tsiyon is an example of a Yiddish playwright of this era who was an unapologetic propagator of Christian propaganda on the Yiddish stage and yet did not become a target of Goldfaden's vitriol. Ben-Tsiyon was born in 1839 in Kiev and spent time in Romania and Berlin, where he converted in 1863.[27] As a Christian, he was allowed to enroll as a student at the University of Würzburg, where he earned his medical degree in 1867. In England, he was in contact with a missionary group and returned to Romania and then to Odessa as one of its emissaries to spread Christianity among Jews. In Odessa, Ben-Tsiyon began writing for the Yiddish theater.

Ben-Tsiyon penned a Yiddish translation of the Italian librettist Silvio Pellico's *Esther in Ein Gedi*.[28] A single ad for a production of this operetta under Adler's direction ran in a local circular in Rostov-on-Don in 1882.[29] The libretto features the Christian martyr Eliezer, who has been sentenced to death by her daughter's husband, the Jewish High Priest Azaria. Before his execution, he has sought out a final and secret meeting with his daughter Esther. Esther, who dies in the opera's final scene, is torn between the two men throughout the drama and a conversation she has with her father touches on the theme of social performance. As the drama takes place in the second century of the Common Era, Esther is referring, not to Jews posing as Christians, but to a persecuted Christian posing as a Jew:

> ELIEZER: Can we never look forward to a time when we can be together freely?
>
> ESTHER: I hope. When you are prepared to pretend a bit.
>
> ELIEZER: What do you mean, pretend?
>
> ESTHER: Just understand: I have respect for your religion since it is yours. Please, do not take this the wrong way. You just need to hide it . . . in your heart.
>
> ELIEZER: Should I be ashamed of the truth?[30]

For Eliezer, pretending to be something he is not is hypocrisy even if it invites the threat of death. Here, Eliezer has opted to be Christian, and insists on being openly Christian, even at the threat of his life.

There is no evidence that Goldfaden had Ben-Tsiyon's overt Christian-themed plays in mind when he ranted against the Christianizing of the Yiddish stage. He never mentions Ben-Tsiyon and Ben-Tsiyon's play were seldom performed, according to Zylbercweig. But also absent is any indication that his themes caused any discomfort among Yiddish impresarios. *Esther in Ein Gedi* played in 1881 and another play with a provocative title, *The Baptized Daughter* (*Der getoyfter tokhter*), was sold to Thomashefsky in New York City—surprising given Thomashefsky's conservative portrayal of Jewishness generally.[31] Russian newspapers do not register more than that one performance, but there are manuscripts censored by the Bureau of Censorship in St. Petersburg that are now in the Thomashefsky Collection at the New York Public Library that suggest his plays were mounted regularly.

After pursuing missionary work for England's Presbyterian Church in Odessa, Ben-Tsiyon moved to New York City. According to Gorin's index of Yiddish productions, eight of his works were produced between 1881 and 1888.[32] These productions do not include his version of *La juive*, staged by the celebrated Yiddish actor Dovid Kessler as early as 1881, and another two plays sold to Boris Thomashefsky in 1884 in New York City, one of them called *The Baptized Daughter*. The Russian Jewish writer Reuven Waisman, who remained Ben-Tsiyon's friend in New York, recounts that Ben-Tsiyon autographed a book of his with the following words, "The former Hornostopolye sexton's son, now in the topsy-turvy world of New York City. Doctor Benedict (Barukh) Ben-Tsiyon."[33] From all accounts, Ben-Tsiyon pursued a career as a playwright in the world of Yiddish theater. It is unlikely he enjoyed a high profile but it seems he was tolerated as an apostate.[34] In his memoirs, Goldfaden never bothers with Ben-Tsiyon.

In contrast, Goldfaden is hostile toward Hurvits, a commercially successful playwright of the American Yiddish stage from around 1890 to 1910—a time when Goldfaden tried and failed to break into Yiddish theater in New York City—and, thus, an ongoing threat to Goldfaden's ego and career. His biography is vague. "Professor" Moyshe Hurvits (1844–1910), as he announced on theater placards, was born in Galicia in 1844 into a Hasidic family but moved to Romania when he was eighteen and eventually became the director of a modern Jewish school in Bucharest.[35] According to Zylbercweig, when he was kicked out, he promptly converted to Christianity and became a missionary. Goldfaden contends that he met Hurvits in Bucharest in 1877 when Hurvits asked him to look at some dramas he had written for the stage. In his rendering of their encounter, Goldfaden refers to Hurvits as the "missionary-writer": "The author of the play was a missionary, was known as such in Bucharest. When I asked him why he converted, the missionary-writer told me that he was very desperate for work and that his family was subsisting on potato peels, things were so bad. . . . And as the new God bought him over for 90 francs a month, he had no choice but to take the position. As he himself was able to appreciate, I could not take his plays to mount on the new fresh Yiddish stage. The audience would think that my theater had converted!"[36] For a "missionary writer," it should be noted, none of Hurvits's works transmit a Christian or Universalist message.

Still, Goldfaden spares no sensational detail regarding his meeting with Hurvits. He explains that as a result of their meeting, "the missionary" (Hurvits) headed to the local tavern, where he staged his conversion back to Judaism over a lot of schnapps before a quorum of wagon drivers who happened to be hanging around. This show earned Hurvits no points; Goldfaden claims that he outright refused the young Hurvits a job in his theater. The high profile he achieved in New York notwithstanding, we know surprisingly little about Hurvits, and there is no competing narrative or biography of his meeting with Goldfaden or his path to producing Yiddish theater. This story has been repeated multiple times in Yiddish theater literature, but each rendition quotes Goldfaden's autobiography as its only source. Hurvits's experience of being baptized and his return to Judaism has never been corroborated. More relevant: his operettas, while accused of lacking taste and quality, were never guilty of undermining Jewish values. Goldfaden had plenty of motivation to have imagined retrospectively his indignation at what he presents as Hurvits's cynical performance at the tavern. Notwithstanding Goldfaden's dismissal of him, Hurvits pulled a troupe together. In the earliest surviving newspaper advertisements for Yiddish theater, dating to 1877, Hurvits's shows are the only shows represented other than those produced by Goldfaden.[37] He wrote and directed some theater in Romania but, according to the early theater historian B. Gorin, Goldfaden undercut him and, as result, Hurvits eventually left for America.[38] Hurvits's colossal success in New York City was Goldfaden's comeuppance.

Goldfaden also attacks the Jewish credentials of Jacob Gordin, recognized during his lifetime and by critics ever since as one of the greatest Yiddish playwrights.[39] In doing so, Goldfaden reveals himself to be just as parochial as the Yiddish gatekeepers who sought to keep him and his work outside the Yiddish literary canon. Before arriving in America, Gordin had served as a cofounder of the Spiritual-Biblical Brotherhood, which devoted itself to Jewish renewal and communal and agrarian life. While the group wasn't conventionally Christian, it made no claim of continuity with Judaism and was attacked by Jewish enlighteners as a "profoundly misguided evangelical effort."[40] Some Jews found it so hostile to Judaism that they besieged the Brotherhood's headquarters in Elizavetgrad. In her book on Gordin, *Rewriting Russia: Jacob Gordin's Yiddish Drama*, historian Barbara Henry shows that Gordin himself sought to cover up

Figure 4.2. Hand-painted magic lantern slide of "Professor" Moyshe Hurvits, c. 1910. Courtesy of the YIVO Institute for Jewish Research.

or dismiss his Brotherhood activities but that his involvement had, in fact, been extensive. Goldfaden was not alone in gesturing toward the compromised past that Gordin preferred to keep buried. As Henry recounts, "Gordin's perpetual antagonist, Lilienblum, denounced him as a hypocrite: 'To the authorities and the Russian press he presented himself as a reformer, and to the Jews he presented himself as a socialist, or a Tolstoyan.'"[41] Raising the specter of the "*sheygets*" or bastard theater, Goldfaden complained about Gordin to American Yiddish actor and playwright Leon Kobrin soon after he arrived in New York in 1905: "What did he do with my child! He took my beloved child, my Jewish child, my Benjamin and converted him! My holy of holies he made impure. He is a missionary; how did he get involved in the Yiddish theater?"[42] Goldfaden's critique of Gordin included an attack on the substance of his theatrical works that offered its audiences moments of dramatic realism (leavened, albeit, with melodrama) that was new to the Yiddish stage. Plays like *The Jewish Queen Lear or Mirele Efros* (*Di yidishe kenigin lir oder Mirele Efros*, 1898) that offered a dissection of a dysfunctional family under the sway of a powerful matriarch or *The Kreutzer Sonata* (*Di kreytser sonata*, 1902) that told the story of an illegitimate pregnancy amounted to airing dirty Jewish laundry more than using the stage for Christian propaganda.[43]

Goldfaden's insinuations about Osip Lerner, arguably the greatest "gentile threat" to the integrity of the Jewish stage, is the most fascinating of the half-known pioneers. Despite playing a central role in the world of Jewish Odessa, and the Yiddish theater in particular, we know little about the life of Osip (Yoysef Yehudah) Lerner (1849–1909).[44] This might be due to his decision to be baptized, a fact that might have informed the way his Jewish biographers told his life story. He was born in Berdichev in 1847 to traditional parents who sent him to *kheyder* and then to a secular Russian high school. As a young man he studied law, but after receiving his degree he settled in Odessa, where he devoted himself to literary and journalistic work in Russian, Hebrew, and Yiddish. Among his early writings is an 1868 Russian-language pamphlet that champions the Yiddish language for its literary potential and includes an appreciation of one of modern Yiddish literature's first serious writers, Israel Aksenfeld (1787–1866).[45] Lerner's efforts on behalf of Yiddish predate Sholem Aleichem's *Folksbibliotek* by twenty years.[46] In 1877 and 1878, Lerner was in Romania reporting on the Russo-Turkish War for the Russian newspaper *The Odessa Herald* (*Odesskii Vestnik*); there and after it moved its residence to Odessa, he observed Goldfaden's theatrical troupe firsthand.[47]

When Lerner became the manager of the Mariinsky Theater in 1880, he tried for success with highbrow literary material. Since Goldfaden had secured permission to produce Yiddish theater in the empire a year earlier, the theater had featured his operettas on a regular basis. But after a falling out with the manager, Goldfaden was banished from the opera house and left Odessa with his troupe for nearby Nikolaev. When Lerner assumed management of the opera house, he sought to put on Yiddish theater of higher artistic aspiration than the shows produced by Goldfaden. He staged over a dozen Yiddish works, including *The Bigamist* by the Hebrew writer and nationalist Moses Leyb Lilienblum (1843–1910) and *Rashi* by Katznellenbogen.[48] He also adapted the classic Yiddish drama *Serkele*, which the reformer and medical doctor Shlomo Ettinger penned in 1830 for consumption in private Russian Jewish salons, as public Yiddish theater was prohibited.[49] In his memoirs mentioned earlier, Shaikevitsh claims that although Goldfaden was the first to stage Yiddish theater in Romania, the theater blossomed into its true artistic form only under the hand of Lerner in Odessa, particularly in the Mariinsky Theater. Shaikevitsh writes in 1891, "From then on [1880], the Yiddish theater began to bloom. Mr. Lerner translated the renowned plays *La juive*, *Uriel Acosta*, and *Deborah* [by the German Jewish librettist, Salomon Hermann Mosenthal, 1821–1877] into Yiddish and staged them in their full splendor.[50] He spared no cost on the costumes, and the sets, and hired Mr. Grodsky, who studied theater in Vienna, to teach the actors how to deliver their lines and how to act."[51]Lerner represented the highest form of Yiddish theater in his day and, according to the Yiddish playwright Zishe Kornblit (1872–1929), Lerner put to use his many connections in the literary and government world to advance Yiddish theater.[52]

Lerner was baptized sometime in the 1890s (no source provides a definite date), but according to the bibliographer Zalmen Reyzen, who offers a sensitive first glance at this figure, his religious ambivalence predated his apostasy by decades. Reyzen describes Lerner's apostasy as shocking in light of his intense commitment to Yiddish literature and language, but yet of a piece with a second literary life Lerner apparently pursued, alongside his career in Yiddish and Hebrew, in (non-Jewish) Russian newspapers and books. A former student from Lerner's days as a teacher in Odessa claims that Lerner wrote anti-Semitic articles published in *The New Telegraph* (*Novyi Telegraf*) and other journals and newspapers from the 1870s into the 1890s. Although his entry on this intriguing figure is probing, Reyzen suggests that Lerner's extensive trilingual literary career demands more attention and analysis. By the turn of the century, Lerner was participating in a collaborative revision of the Yiddish translation of the New Testament.[53] Until recently, Yiddish scholars, perhaps embarrassed by his apostasy, had largely excised Lerner from the literary record, with the exception of Reyzen, Gorin, and Nachum Minkov (who occupies himself only with Lerner's Yiddish literary criticism, not his life or his Hebrew and Russian-language writings).[54] For similar reasons, the unprecedented writing career of Lerner's wife Maria (née Miriam, 1860–1927) still awaits scholarly attention.[55] She was the first modern female Yiddish playwright and one of the first published Yiddish short-story writers in a literature that has few female voices. Her drama, *The Chained Widow* (*Di agunah*), was staged in October 1881 and January 1883.[56]

While Goldfaden was guilty of trying to tar his competitors, there was, in fact, a basis for the fear of what Goldfaden referred to as "*sheygets theater*." The umbrage Goldfaden takes is with his most prominent competitors, not necessarily the most committed Christians or most vociferous Christian proselytizers. There is no evidence that he avoided recruiting actors who flirted with Christianity or that he avoided collaborating with Lerner. He did not work with Hurvits in Romania or Russia but—from what we know from Lateiner—he might have worried that collaborating with him would make of him a fierce competitor. He likely targeted Gordin, who only began writing for the theater in the United

States and in the 1890s, for instance, because he was operating successfully in New York, while Goldfaden was sidelined and writing his memoirs. His anxieties regarding the Christian character of some Yiddish theatrical works did not align with the competitors he tried to vilify.

Still, in contrast to Hurvits and Gordin, Yiddish playwrights Lerner and Ben-Tsiyon saw the Yiddish stage as a legitimate forum for a Christian or universalist message, one in which they both strongly believed.[57] In Lerner's case, this is not necessarily apparent in his translation of *La Juive,* that might have been driven more by the popularity of the opera in other languages than Lerner's embrace of its ideological slant. His original play *Uncle Moses Mendelssohn* (*Der feter Moyshe Mendelson*), however, apparently staged during the Yiddish theater's first period (1876–1883), reflects his strong dual interest in both Yiddish culture and radical assimilation. In it, the German Jewish philosopher Moses Mendelssohn is portrayed as a wise and doting uncle to Esther, who converts to Christianity in order to marry Heinrich, with whom she has fallen in love. Mendelssohn does not admonish her because her apostasy is morally wrong, as he explains to her, since "in the world of ideas there are no differences between religious beliefs," but because her baptism is too hard emotionally for her traditional father to bear. And Mendelssohn continues:

> And are you a believing Christian? Obviously not. You changed your religion only to make your love lawful with marriage and in this you are guilty, since you have given up on improving the lives of all. Religion is a necessity placed on every moral person. It is a garment of many colors that each nation holds tight to its nakedness. With time, this coat will grow purer and with time all the colors will disappear and it will become a mantle of Truth and Understanding and cover all of mankind. . . . How can you take part in this work if you have thrown your coat off? [58]

Uncle Mendelssohn's assumption that Esther's conversion is not genuine evokes the instrumental gentile Jew. But his abstract ideas about religious devotion and the interchangeable nature of Judaism and Christianity represented a radical religious alternative for the Jewish audience of the Yiddish theater in the 1880s. As Goldfaden's provocative words suggest, the positive Jewish characters who animate the works of Ben-Tsiyon and Lerner are those who are willing to recognize the goodness of Christianity. Both adapted *La juive,* which prioritizes interfaith humanism over the maintenance of Judaism and the Jewish People.[59]

Notwithstanding the explicit commitment to Christian ideas of these playwrights, there is no evidence that Goldfaden distanced himself from Lerner. They collaborated in Odessa for as long as they were on good business terms, according to Shaikevitsh, as late as 1882 when Goldfaden returned from his tour.[60] Lerner possessed the lease and Goldfaden possessed the hits and censored manuscript copies of them, which were required by the government. Their partnership crumbled over business affairs. Questions of ideology and religion do not surface in any account of their relationship. Still, Goldfaden's disapproval of the ideological tenor of his plays registers in his historical operetta *Doctor Almasada*.

The Gentile Jew in St. Petersburg

Though we know little about the exact circumstances under which Goldfaden wrote *Doctor Almasada*, moments of it feel particularly apropos of Jewish life in St. Petersburg, where he first put the play on the boards. Only twenty years earlier, Jews were prohibited from residing in the empire's capital, but by the 1860s and 1870s, Jews began to migrate to the city by the thousands. The historian Benjamin Nathans explains that during this time, "Petersburg Jewry gave rise in Russia to a new image of the Jew as modern, cosmopolitan, and strikingly successful in urban professions (such as law, banking, and journalism) that were emerging in the wake of the Great Reforms."[61] According to the historian Eugene Avrutin, considerably more Jews lived in St. Petersburg "than were documented by either city or police census[es]." By the time Goldfaden and his troupe arrived in St. Petersburg, soon before they staged the play in January 1881, the capital city had "a sizable Jewish migrant population," a good number of whom resided in the city illegally, according to Eugene Avrutin.[62] Palermo, the setting of *Doctor Almasada* on whose streets the intolerant thug Don Diego would prefer Jewish feet did not tread, doubles well as the city of St. Petersburg, which traditionally boasted a reputation in the Russian imagination as a city free of Jews.[63] "Why do they ramble around our land? Why do they still tread Palermo's beautiful streets?"[64] The ruler of Palermo is not referred to as "King" but as "Tsar," and Dr. Almasada's cry in prison invokes the random passport checks conducted by Russian gendarmes in cities like St. Petersburg: "I am not a foreigner/You know me well/I have my documents."[65]

The relationships between the doctor and his student, and the student and his gentile mask might have resonated considerably with a Russian Jewish audience. In general, Jews of late imperial Russia constituted a population that was shifting uneasily between increasingly fungible estate and confessional categories and, in particular, baptism was a viable choice. According to Avrutin in his recent study *Jews and the Imperial State*, "Most Jews [who] chose to convert [did so] for strategic reasons—to alleviate the existential burdens of Jewishness, marry a Christian spouse, work in the profession of their choice, attend institutions of higher education, or receive residential privileges in the interior provinces." He continues, "Conversion entitled Jews to the legal rights to leave the Pale of Settlement and work in the profession of their choice. . . . By law, conversion erased much of the discrimination Jews faced in their daily lives—in the process improving their civil and material plight by allowing them to escape from the professional, geographic, and social stigmas attached to Judaism."[66]More recently, Ellie Schainker has argued that Jewish nationalists "went to great lengths to emphasize the instrumental nature of conversions and the ongoing Jewish commitments—emotional, social, and religious—of many apostates"; patterns of conversion were complex, especially beyond city limits.[67] Even among the playwrights, motivations to convert varied. Instead, Alonso's character represents converts as loyal and pure Jews.

By the time *Doctor Almasada* was on the boards, the gentile Jew had assumed considerable cultural currency among Jewish reformers in eastern Europe. Jacob Shatzky reports that as early as 1840 a group of baptized Jews in Warsaw contributed money to a Jewish orphanage in order to prevent Jewish orphans from falling prey to missionaries. "This institution was the first demonstration of Jewish unity in Warsaw. It united all sides."[68] Here, ironically, the apostates used their elevated status as non-Jews to protect Judaism from more apostates. The Yiddish newspaper *A Heralding Voice* (*Kol mevaser*), with which Goldfaden was closely associated, makes peace with the Jewish apostate in an unsigned editorial, probably penned by the newspaper's editor Zederbaum, by legitimizing the contribution of baptized Jews to Russian Jewish society: "It is a well-considered question that those Jews who adopt a new religion—and it appears on the exterior as if they have utterly renounced their old religion—remain, for the most part, true to Judaism in their hearts and seek out ways to express this at every turn. Among such people, we come across the most loyal representatives of the Jewish nation, who do us more favors than even many of our Jewish youth who, as soon as they begin studying, think they must sever all ties with their Jewish brothers."[69]

The writer speaks of the "exterior" of such converts versus whatever feelings or convictions that reside in their "hearts" and goes so far as to compare apostates favorably to Jews who seek personal acceptance in non-Jewish Russian institutions at the expense of their connection to the Jewish People. Presumably the latter feel the pressure to prove their Russian loyalty, whereas converts are unburdened by this obligation. As to why he pretended to be a Christian, Alonso explains in the fifth and final act of the play:

> Since I began practicing in Palermo
> And Jews have been forbidden to treat Christians
> I have impersonated a Christian and assumed the name of Alonso.
> My plan was to achieve an important position, and, like an agent,
> I could be of use in a time of need for the Whole of Israel (*Klal Yisroel*). (57)

Like the markers of Christianity assumed by the subjects of Zederbaum's editorial, Alonso's Christian mask is justifiable and even laudable, since he puts it to the service of his people—Jewish and otherwise.

To a mostly Jewish audience in St. Petersburg, Alonso might have particularly resonated as a Jew who did not convert but exercised a more temporary brand of social opportunism by assuming a Christian name. Nowhere in his explanation does he mention that he was actually baptized—only that he "impersonated" a Christian by adopting the name Alonso in place of his Jewish name Menashe. Goldfaden may have been intentionally vague on that point. In the 1860s and 1870s, administrators in the provinces and in St. Petersburg reviewed "countless requests from Jews wishing to change their nicknames to their Russian equivalent."[70] Although such requests were arguably a welcome sign of the Jews' acculturation to Russian society, they were denied. As Avrutin explains, "Like so many members of the Ministry of the Interior, [one official] reasoned that Jews could easily invent fictitious identities and avoid recognition by changing their names."[71] Official anxiety over distinguishing Jews from Christians ran deep, and it reflects the widespread social chameleonism that was practiced by Russian Jews. Although officials stated that their worries stemmed from the commission of possible crimes, Jews just as often deployed a Christian name to further business and professional interests as well as to reside in a restricted city. Goldfaden's Alonso/Menashe addresses himself to Russian Jews of all backgrounds: he invites the former to maintain their sense of allegiance to their people and the latter to consider their baptized brothers as sympathetic crypto-Jews.

The Jewess and the Gentile Jew on the Yiddish Stage

While the character of Alonso/Menashe resonates with the particularities of a certain class of late imperial Russian Jews, it is also Goldfaden's response to Scribe's libretto to the opera *La juive*, which enjoyed substantial popularity in Russia since it premiered in Paris in 1835. Historian Richard Stites explains that the Russian Empire's policy that "prohibited the representation of the Russian empire's Jews as people with decent moral principles was balanced occasionally by the staging of sympathetic or at least complex figures in *Merchant of Venice*, Lessing's *Nathan the Wise*, Scott's *Ivanhoe*, Richard Cumberland's *The Jew*, *La juive* and a dramatic version of Scribe's libretto for that opera."[72] In January 1881, *The Odessa Herald* ran an announcement of a Yiddish translation of *La juive* mounted by Lerner at the Mariinsky Theater.[73]

Scribe wrote the libretto in the wake of legislation that granted French Jews full civic rights. Notwithstanding the nuances of its politics that a more recent scholar has suggested were anti-Semitic, *La juive* was at the time considered a coup for the cultural and political profile of Jews throughout Europe and Russia.[74] Indeed, its musical composer was the French Jew, Halévy. *La juive*'s decidedly liberal anticlerical bent treated Jews and Christians as equally susceptible to religious fanaticism. The operetta takes place in the city of Constance in the year 1414 soon after the reconquest of the town by the Catholic Church. Christians and

Jews are forbidden to marry. Prince Léopold, the emperor's son, is married but enthralled by a Jewess named Rachel, the daughter of the pious Eleazar, and Léopold pretends to be a poor craftsman named Samuel in order to court her. When Cardinal Brogni discovers the romance and Léopold's identity, he pronounces an anathema on the father and daughter. The only way Eleazar and Rachel can save themselves from a death sentence is for them to proclaim themselves Christian, but they stubbornly refuse. After Rachel is cast into a seething cauldron of water, Eleazar reveals to Brogni that Rachel was, in fact, not his own child but the daughter of Brogni whom he believed had died in a fire many years earlier. The play depicts religious fealty to be divisive, antihumanistic, and a weapon of the most spiteful and stubborn characters, Brogni and Eleazar.

If a comparison of the two operettas does not confirm the sincerity of Goldfaden's anxieties about the Christianizing of the Yiddish stage, it at least suggests that his Jewish politics were quite conservative even as he considered himself a loyal Russian subject. In *Doctor Almasada*, Goldfaden borrows some of Scribe's plot strategies but rejects the French librettist's universalism and responds with his own nationalist gentile Jew. Whereas Alonso is a Jew disguised as a gentile, *La juive* features a Christian who masquerades as a Jew in order to court the Jewess Rachel. Whatever plot point it shares with *La juive* in its masquerading male protagonist, however, *Doctor Almasada* does not preach the destructive divisiveness of religion. The relationship between Alonso and the Jewish doctor's family would only be an inspiring example of Christian-Jewish relations if Alonso were really Christian. But it is a setup. The danger and forbidden thrill of a Jewish-Christian love affair that climbs with each scene dissolve in act 5 when Miriam learns Alonso's true Jewish identity. In the final act, Goldfaden reunites the titular hero with his daughter Miriam after her mysterious disappearance. Then, to her utter disbelief, the aging doctor proceeds to marry Miriam off to his Christian apprentice.

> Miriam is stunned: Alonso?
> Doctor Almasada: No, not Alonso, but really Menashe
> He has been your groom for ages
> His father Yoysef of Toledo was my dearest friend in our youth
> And we swore to each other that we would be in-laws one day.[75]

As Alonso explains in the operetta's final act, he is actually a Jew, not a Christian. The romance brewing between Alonso and Miriam, then, was always legitimate. Although Miriam secretly pursued Alonso, her father presumably encouraged the development of their romance. Alonso and Miriam's mutual love and Alonso's disguise are a rebuke to *La juive*. In contrast to Prince Léopold, who disguises himself as a Jew to pursue an adulterous affair with Rachel, Alonso's purer motives for disguise are to learn and practice medicine. Most important is that

Miriam loves Alonso precisely because he is unlike Christian men (i.e., Léopold) lusting after Jewish women. The audience looks on as they trade confessions of love in act 1, while Dr. Almasada is away from home:

> Miriam: I thank you, Alonso, you gentle Christian
> You are our only consolation
> . . .
> My love of my religion could not rob me
> Of my love for you of another belief
> No one could compromise my love of my religion
> **But I see how different you are than other Christians**
> . . .
> Alonso! You have won my love for yourself.[76]

In *La juive*, religious loyalties corrode interpersonal love; in *Doctor Almasada* religious loyalties are aligned with Miriam's intuition about Alonso. Miriam could not possibly love a Christian man, since Christian men do not have the same sexual restraint as Jewish men. As Miriam explains, before Alonso arrived she walked outside her home looking for her father, who had intended to return from a patient at around that time. Two (Christian) bandits seized her arms and would have had their way with her had Alonso not been approaching. This is typical Christian behavior. The "difference" that Miriam recognizes in Alonso on a subconscious level is later confirmed by her father's announcement. Jewish men do not lust over Jewish women; they do not see them as objects of sexual desire and do not pursue them the way Prince Léopold pursues Rachel. Christian men do.

Compared to Jewish historical fiction generated at the same time in western Europe, *Doctor Almasada* is both politically conservative and nationalistic; it expresses Jewish solidarity that is untroubled by loyal service to one's country. Historical fiction by French Jewish authors like David Schornstein promoted history in lieu of religion and promoted positive relations between Jews and gentiles. As the scholar Maurice Samuels observes, "The general devaluation of Jewish religious observance in Schornstein's historical fiction also serves to promote other aspects of the ideological program of emancipation which continued to influence Jewish thinking in post-emancipation-France . . . [like] the importance of forming bonds with Christians, with breaking down the literal and symbolic walls of the Jewish ghetto."[77]

This is consistent with the liberal philosophy in Scribe's *La juive* that disapproves, ultimately, of all forms of religious devotion. Instead, in Doctor *Almasada*, Jewish onlookers are victims of an ignorant government and the non-Jewish population—its leaders most of all—must slough off its superstitious ideas about the Jews and change its restrictive policies. Alonso can reveal his true identity to Miriam only when Palermo's Jews have been invited to return to live within the city walls. His need to disguise himself is a consequence of the ignorance of Christian Palermo. According to the enlightened Dr. Almasada, with time the people of Palermo as well as their leaders will learn and embrace their Jews.

> Yes, this is our lot and the lot of our brothers
> They drive us out, then stop, then drive us further
> But we shall not complain about our country
> God will strengthen the Tsar's heart for the good
> He will return to us our grace and our rights
> So we shall always pray for his life.[78]

God is responsible for hardening the tsar's heart just as he was responsible for hardening Pharoah's heart against the Israelites. The fate of the Jews is ultimately in God's hands. Goldfaden's utopian vision does not involve dissolving differences between people or religion. It involves those who persecute Jews to stop doing so and to begin appreciating their unique contributions. Dr. Almasada, in jail for a crime he did not commit, pleads for his life and is released. The government of Palermo speaks openly and apologetically about its earlier mistreatment of its Jewish population and reverses anti-Jewish legislation. In the context of Russian Jewish life, such a picture would undoubtedly be resonant, if aspirational. Goldfaden does not advance a progressive idea of Jewish-gentile friendship or love. He champions the idea of Jewish stewardship and cohesion. The operetta's grand moments turn on Jewish nationalist and religious sentiment and celebrate God and Torah. When the Jews are forced to leave their homes in the city, they maintain their dignity and sing:

> Holy Torah, accompany us
> Wherever we go, we cannot be without you
> You are our rapier.
> God is there
> Everywhere
> Where one calls for him.[79]

The religious practice of the Jews of Palermo does not stand between them and their ability to be peaceful citizens of the city. While it doesn't say so in so many words, the best gentiles, according to *Doctor Almasada*, are Jewish gentiles.

Conclusion

An ingredient that distinguishes the modern Yiddish theater from the Yiddish performance that preceded it is the broad ideological spectrum of its material. Moreover, those who generated its content were, themselves, not necessarily Jewish.

Next to Lerner or Ben-Tsiyon (both Christian), who used the platform of the Yiddish stage to advance an openness to Christianity and religious universalism in the vein of Scribe's *La juive*, Goldfaden is decidedly conservative. But his conservative stance is only relative. It is hardly conservative, for instance, compared to the popular traditional Yiddish translations of the Spanish Expulsion, Solomon Ibn Verga's *Shevet Yehudah*, whose original theme of Jewish banishment mirrors the theme of *Doctor Almasada* that was so popular among traditional eastern European Jews.[80] The bowdlerized translations of *Shevet Yehudah* do not even acknowledge the existence of conversos, since its author could not imagine a Jew whose identity is complicated by a false mask. An operetta called *Exile from Russia* or *The Apostate (Der meshumed)* by Lateiner that was written and staged in New York in 1891—about a decade later than Goldfaden's *Doctor Almasada*—is also more conservative regarding Jewish gentiles. In it, the Jewish protagonist Osip converts to Christianity in order to become a university student. Notwithstanding the mere instrumental nature of his decision—like Alonso's—his father Mikhele rejects him.[81] Protesting his father's fears, Osip insists that he remains a Jew even as a gentile: "The [baptism] ceremony will not transform (*ibermakhn*) me." Mikhele responds, "Who needs such Jews! (*Azoyne yidn af kapores*)."[82] He thanks God that he now lives in America "and need not be ashamed." America's freedoms dispose of any need to pretend to be Christian.

Alonso's true Jewish identity lends stability and resolution to the romantic narrative between him and Miriam: now her love for Alonso makes sense on some physical or primal level, where Jews must remain differentiated from gentiles. The stability that is achieved in this deep realm of love and flesh, however, results in a destabilizing of Alonso's social identity. His adoption of a Christian persona extends license to Russian Jews to exercise significant latitude including baptism, the adoption of a Christian name, and the adoption of Christian behavior in overcoming social and professional barriers or in residing in a restricted city. Especially for a people who underscore observance and the act (performance?) in their religious practice, one would think that behaving like a Christian poses great risk to Jewish cohesiveness. Perhaps that is the greatest gentile threat of all that goes unacknowledged by Goldfaden and his like-minded colleagues. *Doctor Almasada* endorses the gentile Jew for his service to the Jewish People and, at the same time, endorses his gentile manners and his ability to move among gentiles undetected. The character of Alonso calls into question the integrity of Goldfaden's later self-righteous indignation regarding the apostates who sought to contribute to the Yiddish theater. It suggests that, at least during those formative years of the theater, Goldfaden sympathized with the complexities of identity upon which baptized Jews acted and felt comfortable justifying their apostasy to his audience by explaining their enduring commitment to the needs of the Jewish People. The purity of the Jewess is paramount. And her purity, which characterizes the introduction of female actors to the Jewish stage, is discussed in the following chapter.

Notes

1. Nahum Shaikevitsh, "Dos yidishe teater," *Der menshenfraynd: beletristishe vokhnshrift (farlag N/M/ shaykevitsh*, nos. 5–32 (1891).

2. Gorin's discussion of Goldfaden's theater shifts to its historical circumstances. See his *Geshikhte*: chapter 10. S. Y. Ansky, *Narod i kniga: opyt kharakteristiki narodnogo chitatelia* [*The People and the Book*] (Moscow: L. A. Stoliar, 1914).

3. Binevich includes a number of reviews of Shaikevitsh's productions in his bibliography. See Evgenii Mikhailovich Binevich, *Istoriia evreiskogo teatra v rossii, 1876–1883. Annoturoviannaia bibliografia* (Moscow: Obshchestvo evreiskoe nasledie, 1997), 48 and 51.

4. According to a brief entry by Zylbercweig, Hartenshteyn worked with Naftoli Goldfaden, and then with Thomashefsky after emigrating to the United States (*Leksikon*, I: 462). But Binevich's bibliography demonstrates that Hartenshteyn's activities in Russia, before emigrating, were far more extensive than Zylbercweig captured in his biography. See Binevich for bibliographies of announcements associating Hartenshteyn with his own theatrical troupe in Odessa throughout 1882 and Moscow in 1883. Binevich, *Istoriia evreiskogo teatra v rossii, 1876–1883*, 36 and 42.

5. These names are among the fifty mentioned by the press in association with Yiddish theater. The rest are those of actors singled out in reviews or for whom benefit performances were arranged. See the section entitled "Ukazatel' imën," in Binevich, *Istoriia evreiskogo teatra v rossii, 1876–1883*, 50–51.Two other names of impresarios that appeared in the press, Kriko (who worked briefly in Simferopol) and a man named Katsanov, do not have biographies in Zylbercweig's *Encyclopedia*.

6. Nikolaev (10,000 Jews in 1880), Rostov-on-Don (5,000 Jews), Minsk (present-day Belarus, 30,000 Jews at the time), Berdichev, and Poltava and Kremenchug in Poltava province and Moscow all figure as hospitable destinations for Yiddish theater. Later, two of Goldfaden's competitors, Spivakovski and Rosenberg, and also Adler found success in Rostov-on-Don, mounting a number of modest productions there, including many of Goldfaden's operettas, from October 1881 to January 1882. See "Evreiskaia truppa Spivakovski i regisserstvom Rosenberga. Rostov-na-Donu. 1881/1882" in E. Binevich, *Istoria evreiskogo teatra v rossii. 1876–1883*, n.p. Newspapers refer to their troupe as "itinerant," in brief announcements in local newspapers including *Listok Obiavlenii* and *Donskaia Pchenia*. Rostov-on-Don had about 5,000 Jewish residents in 1880 and was located beyond the Pale of Settlement. For Kishinev, where Shaikevitsh tried to dominate, see B. Dvinets, "Laughter and Grief: Feuilleton on Traveling Troupe" ("Smekh i gore: feleton o gastroliakh truppi"), *Rassvet*, no. 51 (1880): 2003. Also "Vnutrennie obozrenie," *Russki evrei*, no. 44 (1880): 1739.

7. Y. Sh., "Goldfadens a briv fun yor 1904," *Goldfaden bukh*, ed. Jacob Shatzky (New York: Idisher Teater Muzey, 1926), 74.

8. It is worth noting that converting to Christianity represented an appealing alternative to some working-class performers had Goldfaden not absorbed them into his troupes. On the

temptation of the actors Mogulesco, Dinman, and Zilberman to convert, see Mark Slobin's *Tenement Songs: The Popular Music of the Jewish Immigrants* (Urbana: University of Illinois Press, 1982), 35. For brief biographies of Dinman and Zilberman, see Zybercweig, *Leksikon*, I: 562–563, 782–783. On Kessler's interest in missionaries, see Dovid Kessler, "Erinerungen fun dem idishn teater," *Der Tog* (January 1917): (14). Also M. Osherovits, "Dovid Kessler," *Arkhiv far der geshikhte fun yidishn teater un drame* (Vilna: YIVO, 1930), 302.

9. The operetta was first produced in St. Petersburg, January 10, 1882. The play was first published in 1887. A copy of this edition is found in Princeton University's Rare Books and Special Collections. See *Doktor Almasada: oder di yuden in Palermo: historishe opereta bearbayt nokh eynem Daytshn roman* (Varsha: Baumritter and Gonsior, 1887). I am working from a duplicate published by the Hebrew Publishing Co. See *Doktor Almasada oder di yidn in palermo: historishe opereta in 5 akten un in 11 bilder* (New York: Hebrew Publishing Co., n.d.).

10. The title cover of the printed edition states that Goldfaden wrote it based on a German novel but does not supply the title of the novel. I have not found a source text. Zylbercweig recounts the theory that Goldfaden created his operetta from a play written by a colleague of his from the Zhitomir seminary named N. B. Bazilinski, who published a number of plays during the theater's heyday in Russia (before 1883) including a play entitled *The Libel* (*Der bilbl*). See his book of theater anecdotes, *Teater-mozaik* (New York: 1941), 144–145. Goldfaden was an avid reader of Jewish history and mentions the work of Jewish historians Isaac Marcus Jost (1793–1860) and Heinrich Graetz (1817–1891) in his autobiography. For a recent treatment of Palermo's Jewish life, see Eliyahu Ashtor, "Palermitan Jewry in the Fifteenth Century," in *Hebrew Union College Annual* 50 (1979): 219–241.

11. See my article, "Ha-makhaze *Bar Kochba* shel Avraham Goldfaden," *Khulyot* 6 (Fall 2003): 79–90. For a negative review of *Judah the Maccabean*, see *Odesskii Vestnik* 11 (January 15, 1883): 2.

12. See his *Geshikhte*: chapter 10. S. Y. Ansky, *Narod i kniga: opyt kharakteristiki narodnogo chitatelia* [*The People and the Book*] (Moscow: L. A. Stoliar, 1914).

13. Uri Finkel and Nokhem A. Oyslender. *Goldfadn: materyaln far a biografye* (Minsk: Institut far Vaysruslendisher Kultur, 1926), 70.

14. Based on my own count of the Yiddish theater advertisements collected in Binevich's annotated bibliography. See Binevich, *Istoriia evreiskogo teatra v rossii, 1876–1883*.

15. Taruskin, Richard. *Defining Russia Musically*. Princeton, NJ: Princeton University Press, 1997, 229.

16. See the published libretto, *Yehudis: a historishe drama in fir aktn un finf bilder* (Warsaw: Y. Alapin, 1888). For a review of Lerner's adaptation, see K. "Zhidovkana evreiskom zhargon," *Odesskii Vestnik* (February 1, 1881): 2. Announcements of the performance appeared in *Russkii Evrei*, no. 4 (1881). Serov's maternal grandfather was Jewish. According to Shatzky's bibliography of Goldfaden's work, Goldfaden also composed a version of this opera. See *Goldfaden-bukh*, 84.

17. "Uriel Akosta," ms. n.d., Abraham Goldfaden Collection; RG 219; folder 46 and 47; YIVO Institute for Jewish Research.

18. According to Shatzky, it was penned in 1890 and was not published but an advertisement of it appeared in 1883. Zylbercweig also reports that it was staged in Odessa's Mariinsky Theater in February 1883 (I: 310). On Rubinstein, see James Loeffler, *The Most Musical Nation: Jews and Culture in the Late Russian* (New Haven, CT: Yale University Press, 2010).

19. For *Uriel Acosta* on the Russian stage, see "Russian Theater," in *The YIVO Encyclopedia of Jews in Eastern Europe* (New Haven, CT: Yale University Press, 2008).

20. See Seth Wolitz's detailed article, "Translations of Karl Gutzkow's *Uriel Acosta* as Iconic Moments in Yiddish Theatre," in *Inventing the Modern Yiddish Stage*, ed. J. Berkowitz and B. Henry (Detroit: Wayne State University Press, 2012), 87–115.

21. Joseph Judah Lerner, *Zhidovka: di yudin: a tragedye in finf akten* (Varsha: Y. Lidski, 1903).

22. For a discussion of Christians (from birth) who performed on the Yiddish stage, see Zylbercweig, Zalmen, N. B. *Teater-mozaik* (New York: Itshe Biderman, 1941), 187–193.

23. It is unclear if Wiener bases this opinion on Katznellenbogen's songs (apparently taken from his dramas) that he printed in songbooks, if he came to know the dramas himself, or if he is accepting the opinion of others. Wiener mentions that none of his dramas were printed. *Leksikon fun der nayer yidisher literatur* lists eight dramas. There was no love lost for Goldfaden on the part of Katznellenbogen. See his "Satirical Eulogy for the Yiddish Theater" [Yiddish] printed by Shatzky in *Arkhiv: far der geshikhte fun yidishn teater un drame*, ed. Jacob Shatzky (Vilna: Vilner Farlag B. Kletskin, 1930), 445. French cultural critic Leroux urged his readers to see a performance of Katznellenbogen's drama in Paris in 1889. For mention of this review, see Zylbercweig, *Leksikon*, VI:5342. Announcements of the production of his plays appeared in "Chast' neofitsional'na," *Vedomosti Odesskogo Gradonachal'stva*, January 20 and January 28, 1882, 2.

24. A number of the manuscripts in the collection in the New York Public Library bear the Russian censor's mark from 1883. Ter's works were advertised in the local press in Rostov-on-Don where its Jewish population of about five thousand comprised 5 percent of the city's population in 1880. See E. Binevich, "Obshchestvo evreiskikh operetochnikh i dramaticheskikh artistov pod rezh. M. Finkelia, Rostov-na-Donu, 1883," in Binevich, *Istoriia evreiskogo teatra v rossii, 1876–1883.*; Zylbercweig, *Leksikon*, II: 889. For the Jewish community of Rostov-on-Don, see "Rostov-on-Don," in *YIVO Encyclopedia*, vol. 2 (New Haven, CT: Yale University Press, 2008), 1595–1596.

25. "'Revizor' na evreiskoi stsene," *Odesskii Vestnik*, March 18, 1883, 2. For a short period, the local authorities were provoked to close down the theater by a Yiddish production of Gogol's *The Government Inspector* in Kiev that Shaikevitsh staged. Russian-speaking audience members who attended the first performances were angered by the changes he made to it and possibly were bewildered as to why it was staged in Yiddish and not in Russian. Posters advertising performances were ordinarily in Russian and, taking the same name as the original, the audience may not have identified that his was an adaptation and translation of the original. It caused an uproar, and the local government shut him down for a period. "Tsulib gogols 'revizor' hot men aroys gegebn dem ershtn farbot tsu shpiln yidish teater in rusland," *Teater tsaytshrift* (1928): 4. Shaikevitsh published his translation. See N. Shaikevitsh, *Der revizor* (Odessa: 1883).

26. Zylbercweig depicts Lateiner as marginalized by Goldfaden, and Lateiner never published the operettas he staged during this period. It is more accurate to suggest that Lateiner's American career upstaged these four years in Russia. But Lateiner's operettas were produced repeatedly from 1880 to 1883. His works "Libe fun Yerushalayim" and "Der Dibek" survive in manuscript. See YIVO RG8. For mention of Lateiner's works in the press, see Binevich, "Truppe O. Lernera Odessa. 1880/1," *Istoriia evreiskogo teatra v rossii, 1876–1883*, 23-24.

27. Some of Ben-Tsiyon's plays are part of the collection of manuscript plays housed in the Jewish Division of the New York Public Library. He is also mentioned by the online edition of

the 1906 *Jewish Encyclopedia* under the name "Benzion, Benedix" and mentioned in passing in a newspaper published by the Presbyterian Church in an article entitled "Presbyterian Church in Odessa, Russia," *The Westminister* (1905): 17.

28. For an insightful treatment of Pellico, see Jesse Rosenberg, "Notes on Philo-Judaism and Its Limits in Nineteenth-Century Italian Opera," *Ad Parnassum Studies* (forthcoming).

29. "Anons segodniashnei premiery tragedii Y. Adlera 'Ester-en-gedi,'" *Listok ob"iavlenii*, Rostov-on-Don (March 13, 1882): 1. Mention of a performance of *Esther in Ein Gedi* under Adler's direction appeared in "Chronika," *Charkovskie gubernskie Vedomosti*, January 8, 1883, 2.

30. Benedikt Ben-Tsiyon, *Ester in ein-gedi*, m.s. New York Public Library, n.p.

31. See Joel Berkowitz, "This Is Not Europe, You Know: The Counter-Maskilic Impulse of American Yiddish Drama," in *Yiddish in America: Essays on Yiddish Culture in the Golden Land*, ed. Edward S. Shapiro (Scranton: University of Scranton Press, 2008), 135–167.

32. B. Gorin, *Di geshikhte fun idishn teater*, vol. 2 (New York: Literarisher Farlag, 1918), 233.

33. Quoted in Zylbercweig, *Leksikon*, I: 187.

34. Ibid.

35. Ibid., 591.

36. A. Goldfaden, "Di onfang fun idishn teater," *Yidish velt* (1929): 7–8.

37. See Shas-Roman, "Der repetuar fun yidishn teater in bukaresht in 1877," *Arkhiv far der geshikhte* (1930).

38. Gorin, *Geshikhte farn idishn teater*, 198. Hurvits's biography is curiously incomplete given his prominent and extended presence on the American Yiddish theater scene. His activities require more investigation and analysis. Lateiner's unpublished memoirs and the memoiristic work of Cesar Grinberg, both quoted by Zylbercweig in his *Encyclopedia*, would go far in providing such details, but both apparently were lost and I have had no success in finding them in the original.

39. Barbara Henry, *Re-Writing Russia: Jacob Gordin's Yiddish Drama* (Seattle: Washington University Press, 2011).

40. Ibid., 52.

41. Ibid., 53.

42. Leon Kobrin, *Erinerungen fun a yidishn dramaturg*, vol. 2 (New York: Komitet far Kobrins shriftn, 1925), 158.

43. See Henry on these and the discussion of realism prompted by Gordin's work, *Rewriting Russia*.

44. Zylbercweig, *Goldfaden un Mogulesco*, 85.

45. This analysis of Aksenfeld's work in Russian, *Kriticheskii razbor: na evreisko-nemetskom zhargone* (Odessa, 1868) is likely the first piece of literary criticism on a work of Yiddish literature.

46. For the most comprehensive biography of Lerner, see Reyzen, Zalmen. *Leksikon fun der yidisher literatur, prese, un filologye*. 5 vols. (Vilna: B. Kletskin, 1926–1929), 269–278 and B. Gorin, *Di geshikhte fun yidishn teater*, vol. 1 (New York: Literarishe Farlag, 1918).

47. According to Reyzen, Lerner worked as a journalist during the war and wrote a pamphlet on the Jewish contribution to the Russian war effort.

48. Zylbercweig's entry on Lilienblum claims an Odessa performance and Binevich's bibliography includes an ad in a Rostov-on-Don local paper. "Anons segodniashnego spektaklia

'Dvoeschenets' D. Lilienbluma." *Listok Ob"iavlenii* (June 5 1882): 1. Zylbercweig, *Leksikon*, III: 1084–1086. See Binevich for a list of about twenty announcements, reviews, and news items on the Yiddish theater under Lerner's stewardship in Odessa newspapers.

49. An ad for Lerner's production of *Serkele* that indicates it was a benefit performance ran in *Odesski Listok*, December 2, 1880, 2. For a positive review, see "Zametka o spektakle 'Serkele' Dr. Ettingera v peredelke O. Lernera," *Odesskii Vestnik*, August 13, 1880, 2.

50. For more on *Deborah* see Jonathan M. Hess, *Deborah and Her Sisters*: How One Nineteenth-Century Melodrama and a Host of Celebrated Actresses Put Judaism on the World Stage (Philadelphia: University of Pennsylvania Press, 2018).

51. Nahum Shaikevitsh, "Dos yidishe teater," *Menshenfraynd* 14 (1901): 3–28.

52. See his oral report to Zylbercweig in the latter's entry on the actor/impresario Spivakovski. Zylbercweig, *Leksikon*, II: 1532.

53. In 1901, J. Rabinowitz, W. I. Nelom, and Joseph Lerner, native speakers, respectively, of Bessarabian, Lithuanian, and Galician Yiddish, were invited to revise Hershon's New Testament translation. The Mildmay Mission to the Jews (whose main center was in Whitechapel, London) distributed one hundred thousand copies of this edition. See Leonard Prager, *Yiddish Culture in Britain: A Guide* (Frankfurt: Peter Lang, 1990), 558.

54. Compare, remarkably, the entry on Lerner in Zalmen Reyzen's *Leksikon* (New York: Alṿelṭlekhn Yidishn ḳulṭur-ḳongres, 1956–1981) with the one in the *Leksikon fun der nayer yiddisher literatur* (New York, Congress for Jewish Culture: 1965).

55. See an informative entry on Maria Lerner by Zylbercweig, *Leksikon*, III: 1169–1170. Among her works are plays that were censored in St. Petersburg for public performance and contributions to the prominent journal edited by Mordkhe Spektor, *Hoyz-fraynd* and the *Chovevei-Tsiyon* periodical *Der veker.*

56. Maria Lerner, *Di agune: A drame in 4 aktn un 6 bilder* (Warsaw, Farlag yudishe bine, 1908).

57. Later in his career, Lerner contributed to the Yiddish translation of the B.F.B.S. New Testament Bible (published in Berlin in 1901), which was distributed by the Mildmay Mission to the Jews. See Prager, *Yiddish Culture in Britain*, 558.

58. Osip Lerner, *Der feter Moyshe Mendelsohn: A dramatishes bild in eyn akt* (Warsaw: Boymritter ve-khatano Gonshor, 1889).

59. Lerner published his adaptation and Ben-Tsiyon's survives only in manuscript.

60. This is also reported in Zylbercweig, *Goldfaden un Mogulesko*, 90.

61. Benjamin Nathans, *Beyond the Pale: The Jewish Encounter with Late Imperial Russia* (Berkeley: University of California Press, 2002).

62. Eugene Avrutin, *Jews and the Imperial State: Identification Politics in Tsarist Russia* (Ithaca, NY: Cornell University Press, 2010), 7. See also page 98.

63. Nathans, *Beyond the Pale*, 123–126.

64. *Doktor Almasada*, 9.

65. Ibid., 35.

66. Avrutin, *Jews and the Imperial State*, 119. According to Avrutin, toward the end of the century, the Russian government questioned the sincerity of Jewish baptisms and began introducing laws to help divide converts "from the core of the Christian population by making their integration into Russian society increasingly difficult." See page 120.

67. Ellie Schainker, "When Life Imitates Art: Shtetl Sociability and Conversion in Imperial Russia," unpublished, with permission of the author.

68. Jacob Shatzky, *Geshikhte fun yidn in varshe* (New York: Biblyotek fun YIVO, 1948), 152.

69. Alexander Zederbaum, "Algemeyne bagebnhaytn," *Kol mevaser* 2 (1870): 14–15.

70. Avrutin, *Jews and the Imperial State*, 153.

71. Ibid., 152.

72. Richard Stites, *Serfdom, Society and the Arts in Imperial Russia* (New Haven, CT: Yale University Press, 2005), 198–199. He adds that in 1860 "the censors about-faced and began prohibiting Judeophobic works on stage." On its success in Russia, see Michael Weiskopf, *The Veil of Moses: Jewish Themes in Russian Literature of the Romantic Era*, trans. Lydia Wechsler (London: Brill, 2012), 63.

73. For the full citation see Binevich, *Istoriia evreiskogo teatra v rossii, 1876–1883*, 24.

74. See the article by Olivier Bara, "*La juive* de Scribe et Halévy (1835). Un opéra juif?" *Romantisme* 34, no. 125 (2004): 75–89.

75. *Doktor Almasada*, 59.

76. Ibid., 15.

77. Maurice Samuels, "David Schornstein and the Rise of Jewish Historical Fiction in Nineteenth-Century France," *Jewish Social Studies* 14, no. 3 (2008): 48.

78. *Doktor Almasada*, 17.

79. Ibid., 21.

80. The work was originally published in Adrianople in 1553 and published in Yiddish as early as 1591 in Cracow with more editions to follow, one as late as 1810. See Michael Stanislawski, "The Yiddish *Shevet Yehudah*: A Study in 'Ashkenization' of a Spanish-Jewish Classic," in *Jewish History and Jewish Memory: Essays in Honor of Yosef Hayim Yerushalmi*, ed. Elisheva Carlebach, John M. Efron, and David N. Myers (Hanover, NH: Brandeis University Press, 1998), chap. 8.

81. As recounted in Irving Howe, *World of Our Fathers* (New York: Harcourt, Brace, Jovanovich, 1976), 465–466.

82. Manuscript in Esther-Rachel Kaminska Collection RG 8; folder 170514, YIVO Institute for Jewish Research.

5 The Rise of the Female Yiddish Actor

Goldfaden in Moscow and St. Petersburg

A measure of the Yiddish theater's success during its first era under Goldfaden is its presence in Moscow and St. Petersburg, the twin capitals of imperial Russia, and the twin capitals of Russia's theatrical life. Unfortunately, the record of these episodes is paltry. In one of his memoirs about his Yiddish theater troupe, Goldfaden provides a single reference to a period of time he spent in St. Petersburg on tour with his theater company. With cloying flourishes typical of Goldfaden's style, he implores his reader: "You must commit to following me from the dirtiest of taverns, to the [performance space at the] most splendid Demuth Hotel in St. Petersburg, which is located not far from the Tsar's Winter Palace; you cannot feel ashamed to speak to a simple poor girl because soon, with my help, she will become a princess with a golden crown and will amaze you with her acting and singing! . . . All will be described in a chronological order as every event came to pass."[1] Overcome by a kind of paralysis when writing about his most productive years, Goldfaden never provides us with further details about this moment of acclaim or any others he and his troupe experienced in Russia's interior during these years.

The press, however, is more revealing. Although hardly complimentary, the St. Petersburg-based *Svetoch* reports Goldfaden's progress from outdoor stages in St. Petersburg to the city's prestigious small theatrical venues including the Demuth Hotel.[2] In January 1881 the popular daily *Peterburgskaya gazeta* reported Goldfaden's arrival to the capital city in 1880 in a way that it might have announced any of the other theatrical troupes authorized by the tsar: "a big troupe of actors and actresses" of "the well-known Goldfaden" will present "historical plays" written in "*zhargon*" (Yiddish). It goes on to report: "the troupe owns a large number of costumes that are exceptional in their historical authenticity."[3] Announcements of his shows indicate that one of Goldfaden's troupes did at least two tours in Moscow and St. Petersburg, and Goldfaden's contemporary Shmuel Tsitron reports that Moscow was particularly hospitable to Yiddish theater.[4] Both cities, the capitals of Russia's theatrical life, lay beyond the Pale of Settlement and were highly restricted to Jewish residents: it is estimated that each of the Jewish populations of Moscow and St. Petersburg at the time numbered only thirty-two thousand (of whom only half were officially registered as legal residents).[5] Such tours are additional evidence that Goldfaden did not seek the benighted Yiddish-speaking masses but instead sought out Russia's big-city seasoned theatergoers.[6] Announcements of Goldfaden's shows also appeared in St. Petersburg's *Alarm Clock* (*Poriadok*), the theater journal, *The Prompter* (*Suflior*), and *St. Petersburg Record* (*Sankt-Petersburgkie Vedomosti*). Goldfaden, as well as his competitors, were well reviewed by a number of Moscow newspapers, including *The Russian Courier* (*Russkii Kur'er*) and the most influential newspaper in the empire at the time, *The Russian Record* (*Russkie Vedomosti*), the organ of liberal landowners and bourgeoisie. With the exception of the period following the assassination of Alexander II, which temporarily halted the theater, the press coverage of the Yiddish theater grew more robust with time and included a growing number of advertisements, more mentions of the movement and activities of Yiddish impresarios, and more reviews of their shows.[7] Its presence even in Moscow and St. Petersburg suggests that the Yiddish theater was at its peak in 1883 when the government shuttered Yiddish theaters across the empire. It is an irony that Goldfaden, who so anxiously sought to claim his title as the father of modern Yiddish theater, never recorded his most triumphant years. Unconcerned with Goldfaden's success with middle-class audiences, historians of the Yiddish theater allowed this remarkable milestone of his cultural project to fall away.[8]

Among the productions that attracted Russian theatergoers in St. Petersburg was the operetta *Shulamis: Or, the Daughter of Jerusalem*, Goldfaden's most important work of this period and one of the most storied works of modern Jewish culture. Its early stage history during these years is difficult to pin down with certainty, but according to a news item in *The Odessa Report* (*Odesskii listok ob"iavlenii*), Goldfaden secured permission from the dramatic censor in St. Petersburg to stage *Shulamis* as early as February 1880.[9] While Zylbercweig speculates that Goldfaden first mounted it in Nikolaev later that year, the earliest known review of *Shulamis* appears in *Kharkov Provincial News* (*Khar'kovskie gubernskie vedomosti*) in July 1880.[10] Following the production of Goldfaden comedies and Jewish caricatures that so many fellow Jews found offensive, Jewish critics welcomed it with cautious optimism. *The Russian Jew*, based in St. Petersburg, wrote as follows:

> In terms of the decorations, the play was presented relatively well. Relative to the means available to a Jewish troupe, the scenery depicting the luxury and sumptuous nature of the East was completed artfully and richly. The decoration of the temple was quite solemn. In the appearance of a bobcat with live, wild eyes and shadowy figure, the staging was carried off well. The use of electric light gave certain scenes a picturesque quality. . . . The ensemble gave a fair performance. The performances of Miss Schwartz and Mister Schrago (as always) were especially noteworthy. Mister Tabachnakov's appearance was heart-felt. In short, all the artists carried out their parts quite well.[11]

The reviewer emphasizes to his readers that the content of the play will not embarrass them with satirical portraits of Jews and that, with *Shulamis*, Goldfaden has made Yiddish theater deserving of his readers' attention.[12]

Goldfaden's persistent recruitment and integration of women into his theater troupe were essential to the seriousness with which so many theatergoers and critics received Yiddish theater.[13] Indeed, the participation of female actors on the stage was the most revolutionary dimension of the rise of the modern Yiddish theater. The tone of triumph struck by early historians with regard to the theater's first women is therefore legitimate, though it has been supported by more tokenism than profound historical inquiry. Before 1876, the year Goldfaden gathered the first professional theatrical troupe to put on Yiddish-language theater, there is no evidence that a woman played a role on a private or public "Jewish" stage. As discussed in chapter 2, a great deal of seasoned Yiddish-speaking male talent preexisted theater. Women, however, had had no experience participating in public Jewish performance. The religious prohibition of women singing in public, "The Voice of a Woman is lewd" ("*Kol isha*"), not only suppressed female performance in Jewish public and sacred spaces, but also informed a larger cultural practice that went unchallenged for centuries. Groups of Yiddish-language vaudeville entertainers that performed in taverns and were theoretically independent of Jewish ritual maintained continuity with the religious world. They cultivated good relations with local synagogues where they also continued to perform, circumstances that would be undermined with the appearance of female performers. The tavern itself posed its own social stigma for women. Once Goldfaden and his troupe made the participation of female actors a priority, the cultural momentum was immediately apparent. With time, almost every professional Yiddish theater company mentioned in the Russian press of this period was in the position to stage serious national dramas or historical operettas with strong female leads.

Shulamis: Or, the Daughter of Jerusalem (*Shulamis: der bas yerushalayim*) is Goldfaden's most significant operetta precisely because it is so attuned to the rise of the female Yiddish actor.[14] Based on a legend that appears in the Talmud, the story of Shulamis is set in the Second Temple period during the Hasmonean reign (c. 140–116 BCE) and begins with Shulamis, a shepherdess who tends her father's flock while he makes his obligatory pilgrimage to the Temple in Jerusalem. Accompanying her father, Manoakh, for the first steps of his journey, Shulamis turns to go home but instead gets lost in the desert, where a prince of Jerusalem named Avsholem rescues her from an abandoned well. They make an oath to marry as soon as they can be reunited with only a well and a bobcat as their witnesses. Act 2 demonstrates to the audience that Avsholem forgets his oath after returning to Jerusalem. He marries the beautiful Avigail and they have two children together. Meanwhile, Shulamis is steadfast in her loyalty to Avsholem. She feigns madness in order to discourage suitors. Avsholem's memory of his oath

Figure 5.1. Goldfaden (*center*) posing with a group of actors including Bina Abromovitch (*to his right*), c. 1880. Courtesy of the YIVO Institute for Jewish Research.

to Shulamis returns when his children die in terrible accidents: one drowns in a well and the other is attacked by a bobcat. Avsholem seeks out Shulamis in the operetta's final scenes and they marry.

Strong-willed and a devoted daughter to her father, the character of Shulamis breaks from the mostly passive young ladies who populated Goldfaden's other operettas alongside his gallery of spiteful old Jewish women. Shulamis is still a product of convention: she embodies sexual purity in contrast to temptresses in the operetta (Avigail and the ladies-in-waiting in Avsholem's court), but she is distinct from Goldfaden's previous female heroines like Miriam (*Doctor Almasada*) and Dina (*Bar Kokhve*), who are classic virtuous Jewesses but are also depicted as objects of male lust and desire. For Shulamis is, quite emphatically, not an object of desire. She is, thus, a key to Goldfaden's abiding ambivalence about women; for Goldfaden subscribed to a bourgeois model of Jewish women where, under ideal circumstances, they pursued lives of refined domesticity. Shulamis reveals, however, that Goldfaden understood the need for the Jewish actress to take possession of her role as a Jewish performer—and to carve out her place in what was considered a Jewish male cultural space.

This chapter describes the integration of women into public Jewish performance alongside a reading of *Shulamis*. While there is a rich abundance of memoiristic literature by and about the men in these first theater troupes, almost nothing was penned by the troupes' first women. I draw on men's narratives that include valuable details about their female counterparts even as I come to terms with the limitations of documenting women's history with few women-authored sources. The men's memoirs also illuminate the significant role they played in introducing femininity to the Yiddish stage. I hope to map this phenomenon alongside a discussion of one of Goldfaden's earliest operettas, *Bontsye the Wick-Layer or the Grandmother and the Granddaughter* (*Bontsye di kneytlekhlegerin oder di bobe mitn eynikl*, from now on referred to as *Bontsye*).[15] This operetta's libretto, itself a fascinating work of Yiddish literature that has garnered little previous scholarly attention, is all the more significant for the social life it accumulated among those first male actors who established their acting careers by playing female roles. Ironically, the experiences of male actors—here playing the roles of the grandmother and the granddaughter or damsel in distress—provide Goldfaden's creative pathway to his construction of *Shulamis*.

There are few surprises when it comes to Goldfaden's female characters: they hew to bourgeois convention and reflect Goldfaden's discomfort with feminine desire and sexuality. Even Shulamis does not deviate profoundly from this mind-set. So spiritual a character is Shulamis she is hardly of the body. Avsholem discovers her as a disembodied voice that comes to him from an underground cistern into which she fell. She enters an oath of marriage with the young warrior Avsholem but insists that she cannot compete with the erotic appeal of the women he meets in the city. She is a figure of spirit and piety, practically androgynous, and engages Jewish text with the devotion of a devout Jewish male. In this respect, she owes much to the character of Bontsye of Goldfaden's earlier comic operetta. Aged but also devout, Bontsye is a master of her piety; in Shulamis, this trait becomes the legitimizing female claim to the Jewish stage.

The Female of Goldfaden's Imagination

Goldfaden's cultivation of women actors created a paradoxical situation in which he empowered women but also created female characters that reveal the special contempt he had for a number of his actresses and a hostility he harbored for women generally.[16] The latter is reflected even in the schematic damsels in distress like Mirele of *The Sorceress*. Modeled after Western female protagonists and inspired by bourgeois values, the young heroines are well mannered but reliant on men to rescue them from the dangers of the world. Moving toward the other end of the spectrum, Goldfaden's powerful women are antagonistic. Goldfaden is less preoccupied with Haskala values like the education of Jewish girls and the liberation of young men and women from the structures of traditional marriage, like matchmaking and dowries. He was invested in "restricting women to hearth and home." David Biale puts it succinctly in *Eros and the Jews*:

> While [the *maskilim*] experienced their mothers-in-law and, to a lesser extent, their wives as powerful and domineering, they imagined an ideal family in which power implicitly lay in the hands of the husband. Their revolt against the traditional family was a revolt against a perceived matriarchal family. . . . While the *maskilim* directed their polemics against a specifically Jewish system of marriage and family, their goal was the same as that of other nineteenth-century advocates of domesticity—upholding such values as privacy and chastity. Their solution to what they saw as the promiscuity and sexual dysfunction of traditional Jewish society was the imposition of bourgeois constraints upon desire.[17]

Goldfaden never suffered the emotional hardship of an imposed match and apparently had a loving relationship with his mother; his view of women coalesced along the lines that Biale delineates here. Caricatures of overbearing mothers (as in Goldfaden's classic operetta *Shmendrik*) as mercenary businesspeople (*Shmendrik*, *The Sorceress*) or as domineering, shrewish, or even murderous (*Aunt Sosya* and *Sambatyon, The Sorceress, Brayndele the Cossack*) have become icons of the Yiddish theater and of Yiddish culture generally. They are inherited models that also reflect the impresario's disdain for strong women. Goldfaden's theatrical vision endorsed a view of women that promised cultural authenticity that was mostly out of step with the unconventional lives of actresses.

Goldfaden was hailed legitimately as the first impresario to introduce females to the Yiddish stage, but he was not one to hide his contempt for the very actresses who helped him realize his theatrical vision. In his autobiography, he writes about a woman named Golditse, whose precocity for onstage acting he could only think to equate with a corrupt nature: "The new little actress (*aktrisele*) quickly progressed on the stage because she was a wild one (*hefkerkind*) even before the stage, and was used to not being scared by people; she had strength and brazenness."[18] Zylbercweig offers nothing more about Golditse. We learn slightly more about an actress named Rosa Fridman and the lascivious "man-eating" female character Goldfaden called *Brayndele the Cossack*, which he based, in part, on her.[19] The operetta, which featured song and dance and comedy, was inspired by Offenbach's operetta *Bluebeard* in which a man marries women only to murder them. Goldfaden reversed the gender of the victim and victimizer; the serial murderer is a woman who seduces and kills her husbands. In his autobiography, Goldfaden claims that the role was inspired by Fridman who, he suggests, was sexually experienced, besides having accrued experience as an entertainer and singer in Constantinople. The role of the eponymous villain, *Brayndele the Cossack*, turned Fridman into a celebrity the likes of which was, until then, unknown to eastern European Jewish culture. "They pointed at her in the streets and said, 'Hey, there is Brayndele,'" Librescu claims. According to Librescu, Goldfaden tried replacing Fridman with another actress when she became demanding and "unruly." The threat of banishment was the primary way Goldfaden kept his actors in check.[20] But when he tried staging *Brayndele the Cossack* without Fridman in Odessa, members of the audience who had seen the show in Romania felt short-changed and demanded Fridman, the "real" Brayndele.[21] Goldfaden tracked her down in Romania, they struck a deal, and she took a train to Odessa.[22] Eventually, Fridman broke from Goldfaden and returned to Bucharest and played her best-known roles either as part of a troupe or in cabaret format. Notwithstanding her popularity and longevity on the stage, especially in Romania, many actors were disapproving and disdainful of her. All Lateiner could muster when Zylbercweig asked about her was the following anecdote: "At first, Fridman played the role of the young granddaughter but she was neither young nor beautiful and had a raspy voice."[23] Fridman and Golditse are acknowledged as two of the first women on the stage, but they are spoken about in ugly innuendo.

Goldfaden's portraits of women are also illuminating, particularly when they do not hew to convention. Carolina (of *The Two Kuni-Lemls* discussed in chap. 3) does: she is educated and uppity, but her only aspiration is to marry Max and to move from one male-dominated home to another. The same is true of Mirele in *The Sorceress*. An operetta Goldfaden composed during this period named *The Picky Bride or Kabtsenson et Hungerman* (*Di kaprizne kale-moyd oder Kabtsenson et Hungerman*), however, is remarkable for how it begins as a comedy and then turns tragic.[24] In it, twenty-eight-year-old Hannah is a kind of unmarried Madame Bovary. The daughter of a doting and progressive father, a medical doctor, Hannah is an avid reader and she becomes infatuated with a literary figure named Franz, the male protagonist of her favorite romance novels. An otherwise eligible match, beautiful and educated, Hannah insists to her father that she marry a dashing man with a moustache who must go by the name Franz, just like the hero in her book. We process this demand through the eyes of her father who thinks his daughter's demand is absurd. But she does not let it go. After a male childhood friend returns to town, now also a doctor, Hannah's father convinces him to call himself Franz and court her in the style she expects. At first, the young man complies. As it unfolds, however, the operetta, which begins with a comic brand of absurdity, grows increasingly tragic until both father and daughter are dead. Hannah is a nightmarish version of a bourgeois lady: feminine but made mad by the bourgeois pursuit of novel reading. Except his earliest vaudeville routines, Goldfaden never discusses his works and so it remains unclear how he was comfortable staging such a morose portrait of Enlightenment.

Goldfaden's Operetta, *Bontsye the Wick-Layer*

The trajectory of the young and educated Adele in *Bontsye the Wick-Layer or the Grandmother and the Granddaughter* also strays from the course of a typical comedy in a way that is germane to the character of Shulamis. Adele is swayed by the books of German Romantic poetry that she studies with her German tutor Ignats, and she deploys her poetry in resisting the traditionalism of her grandmother, Bontsye, a wick-layer who is also a devout Hasid of the Saruga rebbe.[25] Bontsye's daughter (Adele's mother) has died, and in act 1, we see Bontsye finalize the arrangement of a match for Adele, the granddaughter entrusted to her care. When Adele finds out she is to be married to a relative of the rebbe whom she does not know, she and Ignats plot to run away together and marry. In the last act, Bontsye lies dying, abandoned by her granddaughter and foiled in her dream to see the Land of Israel. But as the titles implies, the figure of Bontsye dominates the play. However unimpeachable her case against her traditional family—however much moral weight she has—Adele cannot compete with the centrality of her grandmother. Bontsye is old and lends herself easily to satire, especially early in the libretto. In the end, however, Bontsye is a spiritual leader more than anything else, and her devotion to Jewish text, to the Jewish people, and to the Yiddish language—and even her discomfort with sexuality make of her a kind of prototype for Shulamis.

Bontsye's occupation as a wick-layer is a central motif of the play: it lends a gothic atmosphere to the play and also highlights Bontsye's spirituality and commitment to the People of Israel. Laying wicks was a practice associated with Jewish women who followed the ritual of "*keyver-mestn*" (measuring the circumference of a loved one's grave with candlewick while reciting *tkhines*, women's prayers). Families would then make candles with the wicks and burn them on Yom Kippur. Making candles in memory of dead relatives, called "laying wicks," was a specialized task performed by an older woman known for her piety. With the dead "beholden" to the living on receiving their prayers, they must reciprocate the favor by interceding on behalf of their living relatives while God judges them during the "Days of Awe" before Yom Kippur. The wick-layer also boasted a special connection with the Land of Israel. As the scholar Chava Weissler notes, by measuring graves, "the wick-layer hoped to rouse the souls of those in that cemetery to communicate with other souls through space, and so on and so forth, all the way back to the patriarchs and matriarchs buried in the Land of Israel to pray for the living."[26] We meet Bontsye at the conclusion of the Sabbath as she and Tuvye Shemaya, the matchmaker, are saying the *havdole* blessing, the blessing that separates the Jewish Sabbath from the rest of the week. When they conclude, her language teems with allusions to the divine. "Journey with good health and the right foot, the Supreme One should endow your trip with luck and success," she says to Tuvye. While Goldfaden's belligerent matriarchs are known to curse those around them, Bontsye introduces us to her world with a surfeit of blessings.[27]

Act 1 reveals an emotional and ideological gulf between the eighteen-year-old Adele, an enthusiastic student of Enlightenment, and her seventy-year-old grandmother steeped in arcane Jewish ritual and eschatological folklore. It starts down a plot familiar to the reader of the Haskala drama in its satirical treatment of the Hasidic grandmother opposite the wit and rationalism of Adele. Bontsye tells Adele the grisly details of a dream in which an angel took her on a tour of hell where she witnessed "*daytshn*" (modern Jews) being skinned alive and dismembered because they allowed their Jewish observance to lapse. Intelligent and dignified or, as her name Adele indicates, literally noble and gentle, the granddaughter deciphers the wick-layer's dream matter-of-factly: the angel is Bontsye and the "*daytshn*" are the chickens that she skinned, dismembered, and tossed into a seething pot to make her blood-red Passover borsht. As the refined young lady points out in familiar Enlightenment rhetoric: if only her grandmother would open her eyes to the world around her, she would see how wondrous reality is compared to her contrived dreams. When Bontsye hires Reb Tuvye to find her granddaughter a pious Hasidic groom, she enrages Adele, who accuses her grandmother of wanting this match so "you can have it good in the world-to-come, a *likhtikn gan eden*, while, in this world, I must suffer a hell." She adds, "You are pulled toward the graves"—a reference to her practice as a wick-layer—"and I am pulled toward the living" (act 1).[28] Adele bemoans her personal suffering and launches what seems a well-deserved assault on her grandmother's manipulations and religious fanaticism.

But even as Adele's romance with Ignats develops according to convention, her heroic stature diminishes. Adele sits down with her German books and Ignats as an uncomprehending Bontsye looks on; the only language she knows is Yiddish. In a previous scene, German was established as the language of education, love, and purity—linguistic purity and purity of character. But the young heroes' subsequent actions compromise this maskilic tableau. When Bontsye is curious about her granddaughter's modern book, Adele and Ignats deliberately mistranslate it. Ignats pretends to read the book but instead he romances Adele; Adele then fabricates a Yiddish "translation" that earns her grandmother's favor:

> THE TUTOR: [in German] Show me no doubt and endow me with your trust and I will make everything right.
>
> BONTSYE: What does that mean in Yiddish?

Adele: It means that there is no other way to be an honest Jew unless one follows the entirety of the 613 laws.

Bontsye: Is that what it says? May you be blessed with a long life. Continue. (act 1)

Adele's trickery is in the eye of the beholder. Although Bontsye is a tyrant, she hired Ignats as a concession to the modern world; though old and old-fashioned, she accepted the need for her granddaughter to know other languages than Yiddish. "If only one didn't need such languages, but in today's world one must," she mutters to herself. The danger of Adele's mediating role between German-speaking Ignats and Yiddish-speaking Bontsye comes to a head in an unexpected botched kiss, an idiosyncratic element in Goldfaden's oeuvre that shapes the poetics of his literary world.[29] Relieved to hear of the pious content of her granddaughter's books, Bontsye moves to give her a kiss of approval but fumbles and accidentally kisses Ignats:

Bontsye: Adele, let me give you a kiss. Now, you are worthy.

(*In the same moment, the tutor runs between them and bends to say goodnight to Bontsye. Meaning to embrace Adele, Bontsye embraces the tutor and kisses him.*)

Bontsye: (*Shocked.*) *Tfu! Tfu!* Woe is me, what have I done? *Tfu, tfu!* (*Bontsye wipes her mouth.*) Woe is me, Adele, run and get me a glass of water. (act 1)

The deceit that lay cruelly beyond Bontsye's understanding seemingly rises to the surface here in a wordless gesture carrying a different charge than the pious "translations" that had flowed from her granddaughter's mouth.

From this point, as a comedy, the play moves off course or charts two courses: one in which Goldfaden retains a maskilic attitude with Adele as the heroine of the play, and another in which he becomes increasingly invested in Bontsye. Competing to be the central voice of the play, the two women describe parallel emotional trajectories and have parallel reflective experiences. Each laments her plight in similar language. Adele bemoans her arranged betrothal as the result of Tuvye's entrance into her grandmother's home: "Since my Grandma let her beloved Tuvye into our home (*arayn genumen in shtub arayn*) things have gotten worse for me." Steeped in shame over the botched kiss, Bontsye similarly describes the botched kiss episode to Tuvye so he may ask the rebbe on her behalf how she may repent: "And when I opened my mouth the entire tutor came into my mouth, *tfu, tfu* (*un vi ikh hob geefnt dos moyl iz mir der gantser lerer arayn in moyl arayn*)." Unlike the unreformed "phallic monsters" that are Goldfaden's signature, characters like the Sorceress or Aunt Sosya, Bontsye grows more vulnerable and sympathetic in her shame, defeat, and sense of remorse. References to heaven and hell recur, as do allusions to a lost paradise: "*Vos felt dir?*" "What are you missing?" (act 2) Bontsye asks her granddaughter before Adele abandons her. Bontsye's sacred worldview never admitted of any lack; it is only with the introduction of Ignats's German books that Adele notices an absence in her life.

These parallel story lines—one maskilic, one traditional—merge into a layered narrative of admonition and guilt. The women appear on opposite sides of a split stage, each suggestively in her bedroom. Our attention shifts between Adele, who recites Ignats's love letters to herself, and Bontsye, who reads her *tsena-urena*, a Yiddish translation of Bible stories that engages the letters' erotic content:

> ADELE: [reading Ignats's letter aloud] You are mine, my dear Adele! (*to herself*) Yes, I am yours, my dear!
>
> BONTSYE: And she understood that she was naked and she sewed fig leaves and she gave her husband [the fruit] so he may also eat from the Tree of Knowledge.
>
> ADELE: (*Reading the letter.*) Oh my dear Adele! Your heavenly look, your tragic life follows me in sleep and wakefulness. I see your divine image in my dreams. Yes, my dear!
>
> BONTSYE: (*Continues to read.*) And Joseph had a dream. My brothers and I were sheaths in the field and yours bowed down to me as mine remained standing. . . . And he left a piece of his clothing with Potiphar's [wife] because there was a great hunger. (act 2)[30]

Adele swoons over Ignats's histrionic poetry as Bontsye piously studies the Torah. But the dialogue between the letters and the *tsena-urena* expresses guilt and condemnation. Ignats's letters express a love inflamed by desire as Bontsye's selections from the *tsena-urena* warn against this same physical desire. The biblical stories condemn Adele who has turned away from biblical notions of good and evil. The *tsena-urena* offers the only categories Bontsye knows and she uses them to make sense of her world. In the end, the meaning of this evocative scene is ambiguous: is the *tsena-urena* a running commentary on Ignats's letters, or is the romantic love of the young couple intended to contrast with what Goldfaden advances as Jewish tradition's modesty toward romance and sexuality? By the act's end, Bontsye discovers the romance blooming between Ignats and Adele and the young couple flees.

In the third and final act, the drama shifts from comedy to tragedy as it revises its earlier attitude of Yiddish as inferior to German. In act 2, when Goldfaden demonstrates Adele's and Bontsye's reliance on discrete languages with their own cultural codes (for Bontsye, the Yiddish *tsena-urena*; for Adele, German romantic love), he points out that language dominates and organizes human thought and behavior. The communication gap that characterizes the "translation" scene and the "bedroom" scene blames neither German nor Yiddish for the strife between the women. In the final moments of the play, however, Goldfaden treats Yiddish in *Bontsye* with a mounting tenderness. In the final scene, Bontsye lies solitary, on her deathbed, a volume of Yiddish stories her only company; her setting and her subsequent death mark the play's radical shift from comic to tragic mode. Throughout much of the drama, Adele has been the play's heroine, its moral center. In the end, however, the playwright adopts the tragic perspective of Bontsye instead of the predictably happy ending of the Europeanized Adele and Ignats. Bontsye's loss of her insular, Yiddish-glossed world follows the progress of Adam and Eve's fall from the Garden of Eden. The German books—their Germanness just as much as their modern content—represent the intrusion of experience on innocence. And although Goldfaden integrates German speech into his text, Yiddish recuperates its dominance by act 3 and remains the language of the drama's universe. In *Serkele*, a modern Yiddish play that Goldfaden knew well and admired, German dominates the last scene of the play as the language spoken by the young Jewish heroes.[31] Here however, by preferring German to Yiddish, the young couple in effect writes itself out of Goldfaden's text. We catch a glimpse of the young couple but only as mediated through Bontsye's failing consciousness. The final scene delivers tragedy's autumnal mood. As Frye defines tragedy, "The hero's death or isolation thus has the effect of a spirit passing out of nature, and evokes a mood best described as elegiac . . . [that is] often accompanied by a diffused, resigned, melancholy sense of passing of time."[32] Instead of the comedy's attention to the noble young heroes, the scene focuses on the death of Bontsye. Goldfaden's preoccupation with the character of Bontsye effectively derails the comedy. The drama seems to think twice about her: first as the obstacle to young love, a Hasidic target for ridicule, and second as having so much love in her that, in the final reckoning, she set aside her religious notions for the sake of her granddaughter. Bontsye, as distrustful of romance, as a male-like practitioner of Jewish spirituality, and as a protector of Yiddish as sacred language, leads Goldfaden to the character of Shulamis.

Men as Women on the Yiddish Stage

The deep connection between the aged character of Bontsye and the youthful Shulamis begins in the play's break from the tavern theater. *Bontsye* dominated the repertoire of the theater's first days; references to this operetta recur more than any other in the early experiences of male actors. Its small cast made it a good fit for burgeoning troupes just starting to perform together. For some actors, playing in *Bontsye* was their first experience on the stage and, in particular, it made a deep impression on those men who played female parts. Traditional folk singers had already been bringing great ingenuity to the performance of female parts to the tavern stage.[33] Realism was not the concern in these early sketches; vaudeville highlighted an actor's ability to shift among a variety of characters (male and female) with the audience's complicity. In contrast, *Bontsye* is closely associated with an intermediate stage that transitions from all-male tavern vaudeville to the integrated modern Yiddish stage where females are beginning to be introduced to the theater. At this point, men began playing female roles with a far greater measure of realism than in the tavern shows; in a sense, they competed with the first female actors in elegance and femininity. The distinctive social experience of this operetta reflects a form of self-realization that the Yiddish theater offered its male players in its formative years. The elision of gender in their experiences with this play anticipates the elision of gender that occurs with the role of Shulamis.

During this early period of Yiddish theater, cross-dressing on the Yiddish stage mostly invokes men playing Jewish grandmothers. Alongside Hotsmakh, the wedding jester, male-performed Jewish grandmothers in Goldfaden's shows like *The Sorceress*, *Aunt Sosya*, *Sambatyon*, and *Bontsye* are redolent of the theater's vaudeville roots. Grandmother roles were the calling card of many of the first actors, emblems of their talent and especially their comic prowess. In the very act of cross-dressing, the actors parodied the grandmothers' aged and sexless bodies and the idea of the "masculine" economic power they wielded over their families. Both male and female were drawn to what they recognized as the ethnic inflected elements of the pious Jewish grandmother. It was an intuitive introduction to performance for the Yiddish actor Dina Feinman (1870–1946). According to her daughter, Tsili Adler, who relays her mother's memory in her mother's voice:

> What constituted my crazy sketches and wild and crazy episodes? They were theater. I would wear a long skirt, would wrap my head with a kerchief, and stand before a mirror in our dining room and make all kinds of faces and movements of an old lady. I would scrunch up my face so it would appear like the wrinkled face of an old lady, squinted and would start talking and complaining with a raspy voice. The words would come out as if I had no teeth in my mouth. I would also imitate the professional mourning women (*klogvayber*) that I would hear at funerals in our shtetl. And I attracted an audience. When our elders napped after the Sabbath *cholent*, my friends would gather at our place and I would begin my ritual of performance (*praven mayn shtik*). . . . I would devote quite a bit of time to these sketches during the week. Hours long I would stand in front of the mirror and prepare a new sketch.[34]

Male or female, the actor as the grandmother temporarily gained possession of the grandmother's earnest commitment to Jewish law and parodied it before a knowing audience.

Historical sources reveal, however, that under Goldfaden cross-dressing was far more varied than men playing the hoary Jewish grandmother and more elaborately executed due to the dearth of women during the theater's first days.

The Yiddish playwright and theater historian Zeifert describes, for instance, how Goldfaden prepared male actors for their female roles. While Goldfaden draws attention to his search for female actors in his memoirs, Zeifert mentions the impresario's investment in costuming and training men in "female" manner and behavior:

> The first Yiddish performances were staged without women. In his entire troupe of actors, Goldfaden had not one woman, that is, not one actress (*shoyshpilerin*) who could go out onto the stage in one of Goldfaden's romantic roles (*roman-roln*). This absence naturally slowed the progress of the Yiddish theater, but even in this respect Goldfaden knew what to do. He taught a good many of his actors how to play female roles; he put their make-up on just like women, and showed them how to play their roles like women with more or less success. Some of them developed so well as actors in their female roles that the audience would prefer to see them in female roles rather than in male roles. For a considerable amount of time, men played female roles.[35]

This, the earliest history of the modern Yiddish stage, is one of the only records of its kind to furnish information about male-played femininity that was mostly eclipsed by the more momentous advent of actual women on the Jewish stage. Among memoirists, however, such episodes figure prominently, reflecting the formative influence they had on the lives and careers of the theater's Jewish men.

The achievement of authentic femininity represented an introduction to the rigors of performance for the so-called *aktyorn vayber* ("male ladies") who were held to high standards in their attention to speech and gesture. The editor Sh. Tsitron relays one such anecdote in his literary memoir, *Three Literary Generations* (*Dray literarishe doyres*), about the experience of a legendary *aktyor-vayb* Shaul Vaynshteyn who played opposite a (biological) woman in a play Goldfaden wrote called *The Mute Bride* (*Di shtume kale*) to accommodate an uninitiated female actor.[36] Little is known about Vaynshteyn's (d. 1896) life before he arrived in Odessa with a "yellow beard" and began performing in Rosenberg and Spivakovski's troupe.[37] Goldfaden had come upon a woman who had agreed to perform and appear on stage as long as she didn't have to say any lines. The other female characters were played by men and one of them, Tsitron recalls Goldfaden explaining to him one evening in Warsaw, was particularly demanding. Tsitron summarizes his discussion with the impresario: The actor is required to correctly imitate, with all the details, not just the general posture of a woman in the various moments, but also her voice in all its possible variations. This art was known best to one of Goldfaden's actors, Shaul Vaynshteyn (d. 1896), who had previously served as a bass to the Minsk Synagogue Cantor Yisroelke Shavlson. Vaynshteyn had always played the most difficult female roles masterfully, the different poses, from a young lady to an old lady of eighty years."[38] In his memoirs, Adler shifts from telling his reader about seeing the first female actor on a Jewish stage through the eyes of his uninitiated audiences to remarking on Vaynshteyn's expertise who appeared as the grandmother in a rendition of *Bontsye the Wick-Layer*: "His gestures and make-up were so good that it was impossible to recognize that it was a man and not a woman. He held himself so well, he gesticulated so expertly, and was such the old woman, the Jewish grandmother with all the nuances. Even more, it was as if the grandmother was never young and that she was an old woman straight from her mother's belly."[39] It is hard to deduce who attracted more attention, one of the first females to perform on a public Jewish stage or Vaynshteyn, the skilled cross-dresser. Elsewhere, Adler recalls that Vaynshteyn began in the theater with a yellow beard that he later shaved in order to play his role.[40]

Whether their own or those of others, documentarians of these experiences of men playing women craft them as competitive with (biological) women. While their cross-dressing act might have stemmed from the tavern stage, the presence of a biological woman on the stage challenged *aktyorn-vayber* to play their roles as realistically as possible. The reaction of onlookers suggests that this was done with great success. Consider the following anecdote about the rare appearance of Goldfaden on the stage, which also suggests that Goldfaden went to great lengths to achieve verisimilitude: "In Goldfaden's comedy 'Dvosye the Gossip,' Mogulesco played two roles, one of them a female role. As there was a scarcity of actors at the time, Avraham Goldfaden played a part himself. In the beginning of the theater, Mrs. Goldfaden would sit and watch the shows, especially the premiers. When she saw her husband, playing his role, kissing another woman she became very jealous. The beautiful woman was, in the end, Mogulesco, but he had played his role as a woman so well, he was able to arouse jealousy in Mrs. Goldfaden."[41]

Moments like these make the reader wonder about the inner lives of some of these cross-dressing actors. As was the case about the first women players who never wrote memoirs, their inner lives did not yet have a language or cultural framework. But Goldfaden's female roles were a more evolved version of what took place on the tavern stage. Even those women roles that Goldfaden knew he would cast with men (at least at first) required a greater degree of verisimilitude because they anticipated the introduction of women actors. It was a heightened form of cross-dressing that became a discrete step in the transformation of Yiddish-language performance in foreclosing the social play of vaudeville.

The centrality cross-dressing claims in the actors' personal narratives reflects how much the Jewish stage invited its men to reinvent themselves in a way that is not necessarily reflected in the libretti of the operettas. While Goldfaden complains about the dearth of talented women in his autobiography, one senses from the sources that he and his male colleagues enjoyed performing as women. Goldfaden participated in an amateur production of the Yiddish play *Serkele* as a seminary student and played the title role. Expecting us to believe that female actors could never achieve what their male counterparts did, Zylbercweig writes, "The audience was so used to seeing Grodner's interpretation of the role of the grandmother, a woman could not possibly play the female roles."[42] In recalling his meeting with Jacob Katsman, Adler writes, "At the time, Katsman was so young, still utterly childlike, a beautiful boy from a respectable family with an authentically boyish love for dressing up as a girl, a wife."[43] The American Yiddish actor and memoirist Mendel Teplitski is frank about the pleasure he derived, not just from acting, but also from playing the role of a woman. He was born in 1866 to an Odessa grain merchant. At the age of ten, his family moved to Nikolaev, and Mendel worked in a tavern there that showcased Yiddish-language vaudeville. He would act on the stage in secondary roles. Notwithstanding the rabbinic prohibition against dressing as a female or any possible social stigma, Teplitski was more than comfortable substituting in vaudeville shows in female roles. In a brief memoir about the advent of the Yiddish theater, he recalled first hearing about the appearance of Goldfaden's troupe in Odessa:

> All the folksingers became actors. My boss, Yekhiel Vayner, tried traveling to Odessa to recruit one of the older entertainers for his establishment. But it was as if they disappeared. I asked him, "Where did they all go?" He replied that there came along a fellow named Goldfaden and made a Yiddish theater. "Oy Mendele," he said, "I am afraid that it is the end to your dream to live long enough to once again play the role of a woman. I took in some theater in Odessa; the roles of women are being played by real girls and real women (*emese meydlekh un emese vayblekh*)."[44]

Teplitski was right; eventually women would come to claim the female roles, but it was a process that took about a decade. In fact, it's possible that some of the actors that his boss Vayner thought he saw on the Odessa stage were men in drag.

The richly detailed memoirs of the Yiddish actor and impresario Alter Fishzon describes the pleasure he experienced in cross-dressing. As a chorister and the son of a pious and bourgeois family, Fishzon was inspired by a concert organized by the city's Jewish community in the Polish theater that stood opposite his home on Makhnovker Street in Berdichev.[45] The first modern concert of its kind in the Berdichev Jewish community, it featured Chief Cantor Herr Shpitsberg singing—not Hebrew liturgy—but songs in Yiddish. "The words and melodies robbed me of any sleep . . . [and] the entire night I lay still and repeated the songs from memory."[46] Soon Fishzon was trotted out before his parents' guests to regale them with the songs of Shpitsberg's concert. In need of fresh material, he began to compose his own songs, which earned him a reputation as a songwriter that reached the future actor Yisroel Grodner, at that time a Berdichev street urchin who worked at the local Titan Cigarette factory. Grodner knocked at the door of the Fishzon family's middle-class home offering him tobacco in exchange for his songs: "We began [matching my poetry] with the melodies sung on the Sabbath, then those of the holidays . . . we pasted everything together, composed refrains, and it began to work like a song."[47] With little exposure to non-Jewish forms of entertainment, Fishzon and Grodner performed the songs in private homes of Berdichev in appearances that Grodner arranged. "But when the first day of [the Hebrew calendar month] of Elul arrived, I could only moonlight because during the Days of Penitence I continued to sing for Cantor Yerukham . . . and at that time I distanced myself somewhat from Yisroel [Grodner] although he would often appear at our rehearsals in the little synagogue. . . . And this is how the days of Elul passed slowly with sweet tea and bagels [at the homes of the wealthy Jews where they performed] and I considered myself a very happy man."[48]

Fishzon's career as a Broder singer was launched. After the holidays, Grodner and Fishzon took their act on the road after buying as many books of Yiddish poetry as they could afford from a traveling book peddler. "One night we sat with our pals and Yisrolik asked me to read the part of the granddaughter. . . . When it came time in the book for the granddaughter to sing I brought my voice up to the highest tenor I could manage and it was an outstanding performance. Yisrolik was bewitched by the combination of my voice with that song and said to me: 'You know what, Alter-Avrom son of Fishl Fishzon? You will play the role of the granddaughter.' I surged with happiness and my feet began to dance."[49]

Fishzon describes the details of his physical and material preparation for the role of Adele. Yisroel hired a local tailor and had Fishzon fitted for three costly dresses, one for each of the drama's acts. He writes: "For the first act, a Hasidic Sabbath dress of real silk; for the second act, an aristocratic dress in keeping with the day's fashion, with a wide hoop and crinoline . . . and the third, a white wedding dress of the most expensive satin." Fishzon was also fitted with an authentic-looking wig and three pairs of women's shoes (each pair bought to match a particular dress). When he wrote his memoirs years later, Fishzon effectively transmitted the excitement he felt at being outfitted for a costume that was new, expensive, and feminine. Once he was fully attired in wig, makeup, dress, and shoes, Fishzon remembers glancing at his reflection in the mirror. "I studied myself in the mirror, my face, and what had become of me—of me, the little boy in the enclosed little world of the schoolhouse . . . a reader of Torah. . . . But what's the use? What is it my grandfather used to say? There is no going back. (lit. Returning [*tsurik*] is not sellable goods)."[50]

His cross-dressing experience transports Fishzon to memories of his childhood and a sense of cultural wholeness that is evoked in the all-male performance space from which the Yiddish theater shifted away.[51] Hence, the unmistakably elegiac tone. An all-male stage nourished a sense of cultural wholeness among its actors; it released the actors from contact with male-female eroticism, scripted or otherwise. At least in some moments, presumably, homoeroticism was on full display. The theater's first days provided men with a prepubescent world free of cultural norms and expectations that is the liberating essence of acting itself.

The Rise of the Yiddish Actress, Its History, and Documentation

The ambivalence on the part of Jewish men regarding the integration of women into the Yiddish theater had to do not just with the men's love of playing women but also the prevailing bourgeois Jewish ideas regarding women's roles in society. Theater, generally, is associated with female immodesty, and though the beginning of modern, integrated theater plays out belatedly in the Jewish milieu, women are still subject to these ideas. Goldfaden never overcame his fetish for Jewish feminine sexual virtue and the theater's first historians shared his views. Consider B. Gorin on the introduction of women to the Yiddish stage:

> With time, Goldfaden knew he had to get (*krign*) a woman for the stage in Bucharest. As was already mentioned, males played the female roles at the beginning, since Jewish girls were afraid to compromise their reputations. The theater did not have a good name, and visitors to the theater were of the lowest/dirtiest element. Most of the actors conducted themselves without control (*vi hefker yungn*) and for a girl or a woman (*vaybl*) to get on stage was as if she was entering a bar with bad company. But the pull [of the stage] was so great that it bypassed the Jewish woman's native modesty.[52]

Gorin's account is based to some extent on Goldfaden's report of his first days, including his suggestions that his first actors would have remained the pimps and prostitutes they were before he found them if not for his intervention.[53] Of course, for some actors, the theater was their first taste of a life unregimented by strict codes of behavior. A number of the first female Yiddish actors emerged from such dire economic backgrounds—far worse, on the whole, than their male counterparts—that they might have considered prostitution to support themselves. We know of at least one actress who was a prostitute for a time before joining the theater. Moreover, the white slave trade posed an enduring threat to Russian Jewish women traveling beyond the borders of their communities (see chap. 2). As the Yiddish theater scholar Joel Berkowitz has demonstrated, Yiddish operettas and dramas register the presence of prostitution in the lives of Jewish women from the theater's earliest days.[54] Indeed, the story of the rise of the female Yiddish actress poses a dilemma well known to historians of women's history: the only surviving sources are shaped by rigid, biased ideas about women. Here, more than the overt threat of the white slave trade, subtler prejudices regarding the purity of the Jewish woman shaped the rise of the female Yiddish actress, as well as our account of the rise of the female Yiddish actor. Few memoirs penned by the first Yiddish actresses exist. They include Bina Abramovich, Khine Braginska, Ester-Rokhl Kaminska, and Bertha Kalich (1875–1939), all of whom published their memoirs in 1925 or later—late relative to the publication of the memoirs of the Yiddish theater's men, which proliferated between 1900 and 1920.[55] A strong preoccupation with "the Jewish woman's native modesty," as Gorin explains it—more than the actual menace of prostitution—accounts for prostitution as theatrical subject matter. A concern for female propriety weighed heavily on (male) historians and checked everything they wrote. As a result, only paltry and vague details about these exceptional historical figures survive and even less inform our historical narratives of the theater. While some Jewish women were held back from the theater (mostly by their families) for fear of sullying their reputations, it was the idea of Jewish female modesty in the mind of the theater's male participants that profoundly shaped the theater's first years as well as its historical record.[56]

At the same time, the rise of the modern Yiddish actress seemed to take place overnight. At least three female actors earned the moniker of the first female of the Yiddish theater, suggesting that the supply of actresses more than met the sudden demand. The casts of Goldfaden's operettas as outlined in the published libretti seem to confirm the overnight rise of a robust stock of female actors, as most of the fourteen operettas he wrote from 1876 to 1883 have almost as many female as male roles. When London and New York City became the centers of Yiddish theater by the late 1880s, a substantial number of female Yiddish actors enjoyed celebrity equal with their male counterparts.

As with the rise of the actor in other European cultures, the social status of the Yiddish female actor rose, and acting on the Yiddish stage became a viable and respectable profession. As wives and mothers to child actors, female actors had a stabilizing effect on theater troupes. Yiddish theater dynasties were born: the Adlers and Thomashefskys, most famously, but just about every troupe was organized around a husband and wife team, including the Vaysmans, Shors, Treittlers, Kompanyetzes, Glickmans, and Fishzons.[57] A substantial number of twentieth-century Yiddish theater troupes had female leaders, most famously, Esther-Rokhl Kaminska (née Halpern, 1870–1925); her daughter, the director and founder of the legendary Warsaw Yiddish Art Theater (*Varshever Yidisher Kunst Teater*), Ida Kaminska (1899–1980); and Molly Picon (1898–1992) as well as lesser-known actresses like Clara Desser (b. 1892), Rukhl Akselrad, and Penny Schwarz.[58] The Yiddish actress became the subject matter of plays written for the American Yiddish stage.[59]

As cultural producers, women accumulated more stature in the Yiddish theater than in any other Yiddish-language cultural realm—especially compared to literature—by a remarkable margin.[60] The domesticating forces of embourgeoisement likely worked against potential female writers of Yiddish literature.[61] Women with enough education or enough money to write without compensation (before being established) were those who succumbed to the expectations of middle-class life, like bearing and raising children and tending to the home. The theater was more available to women of lower-income backgrounds. To become an actress, natural vocal talent was crucial while formal education was virtually unnecessary. The Yiddish theater absorbed many women of working-class backgrounds, some of whom experienced a kind of embourgeoisement—an embrace of marriage, family, and middle-class accouterments—but one that they shaped to the peculiarities of theater life. Generally, actors were compensated, or their basic needs met, as soon as they were hired. Notwithstanding the demands of evening performances and travel, the Yiddish theater retained a good number of families consisting of husband, wife, and children. Some pursued their careers into middle age, as the culture of the Yiddish theater evolved to accommodate Jewish family structures that are not necessarily typical to theater life.

Still, an analysis of the first community of Yiddish actors reveals that only a small number of women participated in theater during the first era of modern Yiddish theater (1876–1883). The dearth of female actors did not go unnoticed by audience members. When Goldfaden played a venue in St. Petersburg in 1882—six years into his run as theater impresario—a reviewer criticized the insufficient number of actresses.[62] Zylbercweig's *Encyclopedia* includes no more than twenty biographies of women whose biographies place them on the Yiddish stage during this first period before the ban of 1883.[63] To put that figure in perspective, Goldfaden's financial manager in 1878, Isaac Librescu (discussed in chap. 3), reports that one troupe and its entourage numbered forty when it arrived in Odessa from Romania. Based on the women named in various sources about the period before Goldfaden shifted his headquarters to Odessa, I would estimate that of these forty, only two were women. The size of the most important city troupes was, on average, about thirty including a choir and the number of female actors remained at about three to five. To extrapolate further from the biographical entries in Zylbercweig's *Encyclopedia*, of a population of over a hundred actors, only about thirty were women during the entire period under discussion. Even after the troupe had actresses as members, Goldfaden continued deploying male actors to play female roles.

Goldfaden recruited his first actresses one by one and most were from working-class backgrounds. When Grodner and Goldfaden decided to collaborate in Iași in 1876, they agreed that the Yiddish stage's most conspicuous deficiency was its lack of females. The presence of women in their productions, they knew, would quite starkly and immediately differentiate them from the vaudeville shows put on by Yiddish folk singers, wedding jesters, and choristers. Shimon Mark, the tavern owner who first hired Goldfaden to sing, for instance, overheard the daughter of another tavern owner down the road singing as she did her laundry and put her in touch with Goldfaden and Grodner. This young woman became the American Yiddish prima donna Sophie Karp (discussed in greater detail below). Bertha Tantsman (née Berlin, 1856–1926) was born to a tailor in Riga where

Spivakovski and Rosenberg discovered her. According to her biography, she was taken secretly from her home, presumably because her parents did not approve. The narrative of a future Yiddish actress being secreted away from her pious family was made iconic in Sholem Aleichem's novel about traveling Yiddish theater troupes, *Wandering Stars.* Indeed, some actors were forced to contend with parental disapproval and there were others who were orphaned. Unlike in the novel, feelings of disapproval did not necessarily stem from strict religious observance but from a sense of propriety. If only sources were more forthcoming with biographical details of these women. After some training, Tantsman began playing prima donna roles in Goldfaden's repertoire including the role of Shulamis. The American Yiddish stage actress Bina Abramovich (née Fuks, b. 1865) was born in Saratov to a former Cantonist soldier who died while she was still young. Her grandparents raised her for a time in a small village outside Odessa. She had seen the Broder singer acts when she accompanied her grandfather to a local tavern, according to Zylbercweig, and was entranced with theater at a young age. She moved to Odessa to live with two older sisters who supported her while she tried to find work. During this time, she was able to see the theater and, according to Zylbercweig, thoughts of the theater kept her up at night. With the help of her sister, she approached a doorman at the theater for an introduction to the troupe manager. He introduced her to Mogulesco, who hired her to be in the choir if she sang for free for the first months. She eventually graduated to playing mother roles and stabilized her status in the theater by marrying the actor Max Abromovitch.

We know the most about Khine Braginskaia-Fishzon (b. 1872, for now on Braginskaia). In her memoirs Braginskaia describes her childhood as the daughter of a wealthy Russian-Jewish merchant, Leyb Braginskaia, and a mother who died when she was an infant. She attended a Russian gymnasium in Kiev before her father and older brother were killed in a pogrom. Yiddish-speaking and more observant of Jewish law, the extended family found her and her sister apprenticeships in the lace shop of the Luria family. The Lurias were a prominent Jewish family in Kiev and had access to government authorities, and residents often approached them to intercede on their behalf. It is likely that such a request brought Goldfaden, in Kiev with his troupe, to the Luria's store one day when he overheard Braginskaia singing from the workshop behind the store. With the Lurias' permission, Goldfaden recruited her immediately even though she did not speak or understand Yiddish, and theater barely figured in her life or imagination:

> After greeting me and paying me a compliment on my lovely singing, our guest asked me if I wanted to appear on the Yiddish stage as an actress.
>
> To me, his question seemed wild. I had never even dreamed of acting in a theater. The expression that he had used, "a career in the theater," was

> completely new and incomprehensible to me. Our conversation took place in Russian, because I did not yet speak Yiddish. Confused, I responded with a question:
>
> "How can I act in your Yiddish theater, if I don't speak any Yiddish?"
>
> "Don't worry about that, child," he replied. "After all, Yiddish is the language of your people. You'll learn it quickly."
>
> Then he asked Mrs. Luria to bring me to the hotel where he was staying with his wife that evening at 7 o' clock.
>
> At seven o'clock sharp, we—my sister, Madame Luria, and myself—arrived at the hotel. We came done up in our very best garments. We found him in his room with his wife and another man—a pianist.
>
> Goldfaden presented me to his wife and their friend. He told them that I was the girl whom he had mentioned. They soon asked me to sing the aria from *The Queen of Spades* that I had sung in the morning at the workstation.
>
> I obeyed, although at that moment it was very difficult for me to sing. It was the first time in my life that I had sung for elegant strangers, let alone with piano accompaniment! I felt disoriented, but I did sing, and as soon as I finished, Madame Goldfaden was the first to react:
>
> "Child, you have a wonderful career ahead of you!"
>
> I stood intoxicated before my unfamiliar audience, and everything seemed strange. A career—what was that? How could I have one of those? After all, I knew nothing! Not to mention Yiddish—I didn't know the language, and I wasn't used to studying![64]

Goldfaden sent her to his parents in Old Constantine for eight months to learn enough Yiddish to sing and perform. After that, she started in his smallest troupe under the direction of Goldfaden's brother in which she made her way from the choir, then to small roles, and finally, to her debut in the town of Priluki in Poltava province (now in Ukraine) as the lead female in his oddly named opera *Neither Moo, nor Beh, nor Cock-a-Doodle-Do* at the age of fifteen. On that occasion, as Braginskaia recalls, Goldfaden sent Braginskaia lorgnettes or opera glasses engraved with her name, a symbol of theater as it was lived in urban centers by its cosmopolitan residents. Soon after her debut, Braginskaia migrated to Lerner's troupe and played the role of Rachel in his Yiddish adaptation of *La juive.* She performed in Odessa and toured shtetls with one of his troupes. She met her husband, Avrom Fishzon, who was, at the time, acting in a competing troupe. Braginskaia performed for about a year before the Russian government banned Yiddish theater.

Gymnasium-educated girls were also among the theater's first actresses. The press mentions "Miss Moshkovits" or Masha Moshkovits, who Adler remembered seeing for the first time when Rosenberg produced a photograph of her from his breast pocket in 1878.[65] He was convinced that she would be a perfect candidate for Yiddish theater for her talent and beauty. She played opposite Spivakovski in the first production of *Bontsye* in Odessa's prestigious German theater.

We cannot know with certainty, but Liza Einhorn (b. 1865) was likely the first to play the role of Shulamis. While other female actors before her had no formal training, Einhorn had studied in conservatory and would later sing prima donna roles in the Royal National Theater of Romania under the direction of Niko Poyanaru. She went by the stage name of Elisa Odesana.[66] Although she was so important to the first chapter of the modern theater and eventually immigrated to America, there is little information on Einhorn beyond the few paragraphs Zylbercweig provides. She was born in Iași to owners of a restaurant that was located not far from the Pomul Verde, the site of Goldfaden's first small productions. She was only fifteen years old when she played the role of Shulamis in one of Goldfaden's troupes in Kishinev. During this period she met her husband, Goldfaden's first choir leader, Hershl Goldenberg (d. 1927). Goldenberg left the theater to devote himself full-time to his career as a cantor, but Einhorn continued to act. Margaretta and Annetta Schwartz, sisters who grew up in Romania and were trained in classical music, also joined the Yiddish stage early in 1877. Annetta would eventually marry Moyshe Finkel. Sofia Oberlender (1862–1884), a graduate of gymnasium in Odessa, began acting at the age of eighteen under a pseudonym (Fraulein Mikhelson) to protect her reputation.[67] Her brother, Alexander Oberlander (1854–1913), accompanied her for at least a time, to protect her reputation from being sullied. Eventually, she would become Jacob Adler's first wife. Goldfaden found it difficult to find and recruit females for the Yiddish stage, but it had less to do with its lack of respectability and far more to do with the need to cultivate talent. Most remarkable—due in part to the fact that Goldfaden failed to even mention it—is that his wife Paulina had a theater career, evidenced by multiple mentions in the press of her appearance on the stage in Odessa and St. Petersburg.

The history of female actors on the stage during the first years of the theater is paltry and, among its many deficiencies, fails to register even one female voice before the publication of Bertha Kalich's memoirs in 1925 (Braginskaia, who began acting earlier than Kalich, only published her memoirs in 1934).[68] Compared to those of their male counterparts, the biographies of female actors in Zylbercweig's encyclopedia too often lack even basic information. Sarah Berkovitsh (n.d.) played prima donna roles, including Shulamis, and played opposite Adler. But all we learn about her from Zylbercweig is that she had a beautiful voice.[69] Remarkably, this is also the case regarding Clara Sheyngold (d. 1902), the wife of the Yiddish stage celebrity Abba (Albert) Sheyngold. The Sheyngolds consistently played leading roles on Goldfaden's stage and then played secondary stages after immigrating to the United States. Nonetheless, Clara's biography by Zylbercweig begins thus: "It is not known where she was born, what her name was at home, and how she came to act in the Yiddish theater."[70] The theater's historical consciousness was forming by the first decade of the twentieth century and a number of the first females on the Yiddish stage had emigrated to its new nerve center in New York City, and even lived close to some of the theater's first historians. Still, their biographies in Zylbercweig's encyclopedia are marked by brevity and scant source materials.

The lack of first-person reports from this era sometimes reflects the relatively shorter careers of Yiddish female actors and, perhaps, their discomfort with writing. But it also reflects the more socially precarious status of Yiddish stage actresses. Yiddish actresses were not encouraged to have public personas and were not venerated with the same enthusiasm as were their male counterparts. While actresses are mentioned by name in reviews and were often praised for their talent, reviewers never provided information about the lives of the actors. Benefit performances, which were dedicated to raising money for particular actors—and which were preceded by newspaper ads—included the names of the actor. A number were dedicated to actresses including Margaretta Schwartz and a woman the newspaper announcement refers to as "S. Natanson," who debuted in a performance led by the former Goldfaden actor Moyshe Finkel, who produced his own performances for a time in Rostov-on-Don.[71] Claques revolved almost exclusively around male actors. Alongside the less educated of Goldfaden's male actors, female actors were the most exploited. Marriage to a fellow actor was the most reliable way to boost and secure one's status.

The curiously thin biographical material on Sophia Karp (1859–1904, née Sara Segal, also known as Sara Goldshteyn), despite her accomplished trajectory and her stardom in New York City, makes this case. Sophia was only in her teens when she debuted in 1877 in her native Romanian city of Galați. After her mother objected to her appearance on the public stage, Sara married the actor Sachar Goldshteyn so she could remain with the troupe. She eventually became known as Sophia Karp after her immigration to New York in 1882 and her second marriage to the Yiddish actor Max Karp after Goldshteyn's death. In New York, Sophia continued her acting career and was one of the original comanagers of the Grand Theater. By this time, her second husband Max Karp had died (in 1898). As her daughter Rosa Karp explained, "She wanted to have her own home and so she put down a lot of money and invested a lot of her energy into having her own theater. [When she worked with] other theaters, she was exploited so she decided she needed her own home." [72] A lengthy article in *The New York Times* commented that the Grand Theater represented the first of the foreign-language immigrant populations to succeed in building its own theater and the first attempt in the United States to put into practice the actor-manager system that was already in place in England. Sophia acted as the vice

Figure 5.2. Hand-painted magic lantern slide of Sophia Karp, c. 1910. Courtesy of the YIVO Institute for Jewish Research.

president of the theater's board as well as its prima donna until her untimely death a year later. There is no evidence that she ever penned a memoir. It's possible that she (like other actresses) did not have enough formal education to write her story on her own, but this reason alone does not explain why none of her female contemporaries wrote memoirs. The absence of any thorough account of Karp's life reveals how much historians of the theater sidelined its female participants.

The preoccupation with female modesty explains the pinched accounts of Yiddish actresses' lives by the exclusively male biographers of their day. In his memoirs, Adler is careful to mention that Annetta Schwartz was "respectable." Likewise, about the Romanian-born American Yiddish actress Sabina Lasker (1871–1927), a fellow actor named Botwinik is quoted as saying that she was beautiful and as noble as a princess on stage as well as in "her private life" and that "she was opposed to vulgarities" indulged in by many other actresses "on the stage and in their private lives."[73] Female modesty played an oversized role in the narrative of the celebrated actress Keni Liptzin (1856–1918). She began her career in one of Goldfaden's secondary troupes on the stage in 1882, in the city of Rostov-on-Don, as Carolina in *The Two Kuni-Lemls*. She played opposite Jacob Adler who praised Liptzin but did not furnish any details of her life.[74] She was a star on the American Yiddish stage. In "Sex and Scandal in the *Encyclopedia of the Yiddish Theatre*," Faith Jones brings to light a controversy between the *Encyclopedia*'s editor, Zylbercweig, and the theater historian, Jacob Shatzky, over Liptzin's past that played out publicly in 1928 in the pages of *Literarishe Bleter*.[75] The exchange touched on a number of aspects of a prospectus Zylbercweig drew up to solicit funds for his encyclopedia including some of its sample biographies. Shatzky was most irate about a biography of Liptzin that he dismissed as "vileness" because it suggested that she may have been a prostitute. As Jones explains, "Zylbercweig defends his facts, stating baldly that Liptzin almost certainly supported herself through prostitution as a young woman, and since she had left no children or close relatives to be hurt by a public discourse, it was important to tell the truth. He even claims it shed light on her abilities as an artist to rise above her tainted past, particularly in her portrayal of genteel characters such as Mirele Efros."[76]

Notwithstanding Zylbercweig's principled defense of the inclusion of unbecoming details in the biographies of his actors, in his response to Shatzky (quoted above) and in another article ("Is Not Speaking Ill of the Dead a Custom or a Law?"), Jones believes that Zylbercweig ceded to the pressure to "moderate socially-charged information such as that pertaining to sexual matters."[77] The evidence of this lies in the revised biography of Liptzin published in the second volume of the encyclopedia (1934), which makes mention of her early failed marriage but not of her prostitution. Such a report would dovetail with L. Elbe's sugarcoated biography published while Liptzin was still alive, which claimed that Liptzin ran away from her middle-class home to join the theater. "*A balebatish kind zol vern an aktrise*?" her parents apparently countered, when she told them of her aspirations, "A child of a good family should become an actress?" [78] Liptzin herself never told her story. In the history of women in the modern Yiddish theater, such anecdotes qualify as biographical information. But they paper over relevant facts to which we have no access. The public shaming of Zylbercweig made it clear to him and others in the Yiddish theater community that the fewer details divulged about actresses, the better.[79] And so it was the case.

Shulamis Androgynous

The role of Shulamis offered Yiddish actresses a bona fide prima donna role in an operetta, *Shulamis; Or, the Daughter of Jerusalem*, that became the most iconic and monumental of Yiddish operettas.[80] More than any other moment on the Yiddish stage, this aria expressed, in unprecedented terms, the claim of women to the Yiddish stage. In *Shulamis*, Goldfaden explores female piety and performance in a Jewish pastoral informed by the diasporic Palestinophilism, a genre already well developed in Hebrew in his intellectual milieu. Against this setting, the youthful Shulamis re-embodies the elderly Bontsye's spirituality and devotion to the sacred world. Seth Wolitz correctly observed that "[with *Shulamis*], Yiddish theater re-sacralized Jewish history, its traditions, and its people: the Jewish stage dared to become the lost sovereign land of Israel."[81] The source text for *Shulamis* is a classic piece of Hebrew maskilic literature, *Trusted Witness or a Story of the Weasel and a Well* (1852). Penned by his father-in-law, the maskil and Hebrew teacher Mordechai Verbel, *Trusted Witness* was itself based on rabbinic sources that Verbel claimed to faithfully convey in his rendition of carefully crafted metered poetry.[82] Indeed, *Shulamis* is only the best known of the estimated fifteen maskilic adaptations of this tale.[83] Just like its Hebraist counterparts and source text, *Shulamis* is neither Zionist nor a traditional religious yearning for Zion. In it Goldfaden deploys the ancient pastoral setting to wrestle with the dilemma of romantic desire while he expresses the Haskala's Romantic yearning for messianic wholeness, a Jewish Paradise of cyclical time.[84] *Shulamis* is emphatically not a mere Yiddish translation of a Hebraist work as is the Yiddish translation of, say, the Hebraist pastoral Avraham Mapu's *Love of Zion* (*Ahavat Tsiyon*).[85] It reflects the moralism and Romantic nationalism that many Jewish (non-Yiddish) writers of his age associated with "continued viability of the Jewish collective," and the unique "character of Jewish erotic ideals and experience."[86] Goldfaden transposes the Haskala's reverence for Hebrew on to the Yiddish language; in doing so, *Shulamis* became a manifesto for the voice and presence of the Jewish actress.

Even as a female character, however, Shulamis transcends gender because she is so spiritual and identifies most with the beauty of language and words. Like her namesake from *Song of Songs* she is the object of allegory: she is both shepherdess to her father's flock and a spiritual shepherdess, a divine presence who cares for the Jewish People. She also is the shaper of sacred language like a rabbinic poet. When Avsholem rescues Shulamis, for instance, she offers a prayer of gratitude to God:

> I thank you God, unreservedly,
> for showing me two miracles.
> First, I almost choked with thirst.
> You sent me the spring of water.
> Then it wanted to swallow me like a lion
> One glance from you—I live. (1.5)[87]

For Shulamis, words are nothing less than divine, or in the service of the divine. Her speech amazes Avsholem: "From your mouth come not mere words, but pearls. From your eyes shines wisdom" (1.5). Shulamis is a walking inscription, a living articulation of divine purity:

> And on your golden forehead is engraved
> Your purest innocence and virtuous ways. (1.5)

Shulamis behaves with a deep sense of the divine, with a strong belief in God's engagement in the earthly world that is not simply rhetorical or metaphorical. She interprets her rescue from thirst as God's doing and wonders aloud if Avsholem might be an angel: "God's messenger? God bless you" (1.5). Shulamis's ethereality is summarized in her description of the pilgrimage to Jerusalem that results in her entrapment in the well:

> My father left Bethlehem for Zion for the holiday.
> I came to see him off. And oh! The way
> The pilgrims marched, inspired - turned glad faces
> Toward God's holy land, toward Zion's holy places!
> For soon the Temple's towers, its golden spires that touch the skies
> Would flash like lightning in their eyes.
> Soon they would kneel in the Temple's high halls,
> Its marble hallways, gold-encrusted walls.
> Soon they'd see the priests before the altar,
> Soon smell the fresh fragrance of incense smoke rising,
> Soon hear the Levites' lovely voices singing:
> Sweet sounds of rams' horns, drums, and harp strings ringing.
> "How lovely are thy tents, O Jacob, thy dwelling place, O Israel!"
> If only I might someday live to see it all, as well. (1.5)

Transfixed by the pilgrims' progress toward Jerusalem, Shulamis plays the opposite of Lot's wife, who turns to see God's destruction of Sodom and Gomorrah and is herself destroyed. In this rendition, God's splendor that beams radiantly from Jerusalem is reflected in the faces of the pilgrims who, in turn, allow Shulamis to absorb the divine brilliance from afar. Like Lot's wife, she is frozen by a vision of a place to which she feels intimately connected. Overcome by her "holy passions," Shulamis forgets her way home and is lost in the desolate landscape of the desert. Avsholem recognizes her holiness and cannot but fall in love with her and propose marriage.

In contrast to Shulamis and her spirituality, are the maidens who Avsholem encounters on his return to Jerusalem. In particular, he is smitten with a woman named Avigail. Recall, Avsholem and Shulamis only pledge they will marry in the future; they are not yet married when they part in the desert. Shulamis

Figure 5.3. Aba Kompanyets as Bobe Yakhne in *The Sorceress*. Courtesy of the YIVO Institute for Jewish Research.

must defer her visit to Jerusalem in order to care for her flock, and she worries to Avsholem that while they are apart the worldly women of Jerusalem will distract him. She, in turn, draws out of him his sense of historical mission that, he claims, will trump his desire for worldly women:

> I know those worldly women all too well.
> So when I found you, I could tell
> You're what I've dreamed of for so long:
> Shulamis, like your namesake in the Song of Songs. (1.5)

Act 2 in Jerusalem demonstrates that Avsholem is more conflicted on the topic than he admits. At a celebration in the royal gardens, Avsholem and his friends are invited to participate in a mating game where he catches Avigail and they marry immediately. How can Avsholem forget or disregard the oath of love and commitment that he swore to Shulamis only two months earlier? According to Seidman, the story highlights "the fickleness of male youth" or, perhaps, to Avsholem, Shulamis represents a maternal presence that is so otherworldly that there is no cognitive dissonance when he pursues Avigail in Jerusalem and proposes marriage to her. Goldfaden couples the transgression of Avsholem's oath to Shulamis with wrongdoing against his close friend Khananye, whom he presses to reveal which woman he would pursue in the mating game only to pursue her himself. His servant, Tsingitang, whom Avsholem constantly tries to tame without success, functions as a personification of his undisciplined id. When tragedy has struck the couple, Avsholem in weak defense says to the beautiful Avigail: "I saw a goddess. Your beauty enchanted me./And I forgot my vow entirely" (3.10).

In act 3, two years into Avsholem's forgetfulness, Shulamis's character assumes a weightier and a more traditionally masculine role in her claim to Jewish spirituality. She has retreated into a feigned madness, the strategy she has found to avoid the suitors who continually approach her father for her hand in marriage. In her most enduring solo aria, "Sabbath, Holiday, and the New Month" ("*Shabes, yontef un rosh-khoydesh*"), Shulamis sings of her deep connection to her house of prayer where she spends her time in solitude. Remarkably, her aria departs from the Second Temple Era in which the operetta is set, studded as it is with language of the nineteenth-century eastern European synagogue and religious practice. Shulamis herself takes the form of the structure: "She has her own ark that allows only her to enter, her 'heavy heart' is her pew (*amud*) that holds the prayer book, and her love the synagogue's eternal light." It is one of several moments in the operetta that overtly invokes Ashkenazi culture—here, the elements of the eastern European *shul*—instead of abiding by the logic of its Second Temple setting. Shulamis also claims male religious space and duties without

Figure 5.4. Frontispiece for *Shulamis*, 1887. Courtesy of the YIVO Institute for Jewish Research.

explanation. She assumes the role of prayer leader and cantor (*khazn*), religious positions that were strictly reserved for men.

> I am the Cantor, and I sing alone.
> My griefs my only choir make.
> We sing sad melodies in perfect tone;
> At joyful tunes, our voices break. (3.1)

She moves from being the *khazn*, a role that could only have been fulfilled by a man in eastern Europe, to reminding the audience of the specialized prayers Jewish women said, called *tkhines*, prayers in the Yiddish vernacular for women who could not read the Hebrew-language liturgy of the prayer book, or *sidur*.[88] For the character Bontsye (analyzed earlier), the Yiddish *tsena-urena* was the vehicle of a female connection to God, an expression of her particular pains and grief and one that exhibits her piety and learnedness. Goldfaden includes this as well as the male forms of piety and the vocabulary of the male-dominated synagogue—the cantor, the *ner tomid* (eternal light), the *aron koydesh* (the ark)—that transform her expression of loneliness into one of strength and independence. She neither dismisses nor surrenders the feminine pathway to the divine.

While Avsholem fails to honor his "word"—fails to appreciate the divine weight of words—Shulamis feigns madness, and emits cryptic riddles when eligible bachelors approach. Her words remain perfectly expressive and meaningful to the audience, but to her father and suitors, who are oblivious to the oath the lovers made, her speech becomes frighteningly opaque. In a mad rage, Shulamis screams:

> I am holy, do not come near.
> I will kill anybody, my dear.
> Go away, away, away from me.
> Witness. Heaven. Well. Cat. Wild beast.! (*faster*)
> Witness. Cat. Well. Heaven.
> All turn in a circle! (3.6)

Shulamis plays the role of the mad prophet, imprisoned by her own words.[89] When Tsingitang appears at Shulamis's home without his master, she thinks Avsholem is dead and loses her power of speech: "His servant! Oh, my heart! His servant! Can it be? *(Stammering)* Wh-wh-what brings you to me?" (4.12). And Tsingitang mocks her broken speech. Similarly, the restoration of speech marks Avsholem's return to Shulamis. Fearful of causing her too much trauma by appearing too suddenly, Avsholem echoes the last line of a song she sings outside her bedroom door. Her words regain meaning. And when they are reunited, Avsholem explains to Shulamis's father that he will cure his daughter "by speech alone" (4.13), at which point they both recite the oath that locked them together at the well. The oath, then, is only a symbol of the power of all words, which are necessarily heavy with signification.

Shulamis's authority derives from her disembodiedness. When Avsholem meets her, for instance, he does so as the prisoner of the dried well in the Judean desert. What could be more comfortable for Goldfaden than a disembodied female voice? On the other hand, Shulamis's female voice ("*Kol isha*") matters. Marginalized by Avsholem's marriage to Avigail, Shulamis claims centrality as

Figure 5.5. Micrograph of Goldfaden made up of the words of his operetta *Shulamis*. Courtesy of David Mazower.

a spiritual leader in the precincts of the synagogue, defined against the sensuality of Avigail. She is neither the object of desire as is Rachel in *La juive*, nor is she exactly like Miriam in *Doctor Almasada*, who expresses romantic desire for Alonso. She claims Avsholem as her own as she claims the Yiddish stage: through her claim to Jewish prayer, to the People of Israel, and the Yiddish language.

Conclusion: Bertha Kalich

While she was not among Goldfaden's earliest actors, Kalich (1874–1939) was the first woman on the Yiddish stage to write and publish her memoirs in 1925. This late date is when women begin to find a voice. Esther-Rachel Kaminska (1870–1925) follows with her memoirs a year later.[90] Kalich's memoirs banish the invocations of female Jewish modesty and prostitution that had previously dominated the description of actresses.[91] Kalich did not emerge professionally under Goldfaden though she worked with him early in her career. She appeared on the Yiddish stage for the first time in 1889 in her native Lemberg (now Lviv, Ukraine) at the age of sixteen. We cannot know how her story resembles and differs from those experiences of her precursors because we know so little about the latter. Born in 1874, Kalich (née Beylka Kalach) was raised by progressive parents. While they did not have a lot of money, they visited the theater and were open to secular culture. Kalich studied music and drama in private schools, attended the Lemberg Conservatory, and at age thirteen joined the chorus of the local Polish theater. As Kalich describes in her autobiography, in 1885 a fellow actor named Yankev Gimpel was able "to achieve the impossible" and secure a concession to produce Yiddish theater in Lemberg. Gimpel's theater was a modest venue with an indoor space and a larger outdoor space used during warmer months, but moneyed and seasoned theatergoers regularly sat in the first rows of his productions.[92] Moreover, celebrity actors, who traveled among European cities to find new audiences after the ban, appeared with regularity in Gimpel's theater. Urged to join, Bertha appeared first in small roles on Gimpel's stage. By 1890, she played the prima donna role of Shulamis opposite the actor Tobias (Tabachnikov), a former chorister of an Italian opera company who became a heartthrob on Goldfaden's stage in Russia and moved to Paris after the ban. According to Kalich, Gimpel marked Tobias's arrival in Lemberg with a banquet and champagne toast; it was the first time the young Kalich had seen the stage's splendor and glamor on display. Kalich's memoir exudes self-possession undetectable in the biographies of the first women. At the age of fifty (when they were first published), Kalich prefers to transmit an honest portrait of herself over one that abides by a set of Jewish or bourgeois conventions. As she writes,

> I have sat more than once and wondered if I should retell to my readers all of my secrets—even the most intimate of my life experience. . . . I don't know

> if it is right for me myself, for my family, for the sake of openness to divulge my romantic experiences of my young and later years. Not to mention those people about whom talk and gossip will arise if I do so. On the other side, I feel that I have no right to hide the most interesting episodes that, pulled together, comprise my life. I feel, for one thing, that my life story is based on the truth, and that the truth sometimes hurts, and therefore is always beautiful.[93]

Kalich openly discusses the sexual undertones of coed performances; she is not concerned by questions of propriety or modesty. Next to the uncertain biographical information we have of her precursors, Kalich's memoirs reflect an evolution in the culture of the Yiddish theater that ceded respectability and influence to its female participants.

Much like Yiddish theater was to Jacob Adler or Isaac Loewy, *Shulamis* was a revelation to Kalich. Even before Yiddish theater reached Lemberg, the song "Almonds and Raisins" ("*Rozhinkes mit mandlen*"), "from beyond the Russian border," circulated widely among the city's Jews. "How much heart and emotion was spent over [its] words, how much happiness and pride was felt by these souls, when a weaker voice on a Sabbath afternoon." Kalich recalls how she responded with visceral emotion on seeing the operetta for the first time: "I remember the tears that streamed from my eyes during the first performance of *Shulamis* and my single ambition became at that point to become Shulamis and to sing the song 'Sabbath, Festivals, and New Month' before a crowd of thankful people."[94] The aria not only showcased the vocal talents of the prima donna, but also the words of the songs signaled the shift of the Jewish woman to the center of the performance stage. According to Kalich, the role of Shulamis became the "*probeshteyn*," the standard audition role; it was the role Yiddish actresses most aspired to play.

That Goldfaden's actresses—the first females of theatrical Jewish performance—came into their own as performers on the Yiddish stage is substantiated with only bits of surviving evidence that attest to their lives. Perhaps the utter normalcy of Kalich's narrative alone lends support to the possibility that the pioneer actresses who came before her had already changed prevailing attitudes of Jewish purity and modesty. Even Goldfaden, through some of his characters, conceded more significance to women and his female actors. But the introduction of women to the stage was gradual and the incremental shifts in the culture of the theater reverberated not only in the lives of women, and not only in the way in which they were depicted, but also in the lives of their male counterparts. This chapter emphasized the reciprocal relationships among text, player, and playwright as well as illuminates these strands of culture with the thoughts of the actors where they are available. In the case of the female actors, they are not: a rigid template that emphasized the threat of prostitution and the fragility of female modesty stifled many of the nuances of their lives. At the same time, the delay in the rise of the female actor made the Yiddish stage hospitable to men who enjoyed playing female roles. Goldfaden wrote *Shulamis* under the influence of this specific cultural dynamic.

Notes

1. A. Goldfaden, "Goldfadens groyse oytobiografye: fun yassi nokh bukarest ba'al korkhekha ata molid," *Goldfaden Bukh*, ed. Jacob Shatzky (New York: Idisher Teater Muzey, 1926), 48–49.

2. "Teatr i muzika: evreiskie teatr," *Svetoch* 14 (1882): 4. This is a negative review of the show. *Svetoch* also ran announcements of the operetta in its newspapers daily throughout the operetta's run.

3. Quoted in Uri Finkel and Nokhem A. Oyslender, *Goldfadn: materyaln far a biografye* (Minsk: Institut far Vaysruslendisher Kultur, 1926), 60–61.

4. Apparently Goldfaden was embraced in Moscow where he played in the theater usually reserved for the resident German theater. See A. Gurshteyn, "A. Goldfaden in moskve (in 1880)," *Literarishe bleter* 95 (1926):138–140. See also Shmuel Tsitron's discussion of Goldfaden's success in Moscow, *Dray literarishe doyres: zikhroynes vegn yidishe shrifshteler* [Three Literary Generations] (Vilna: Sh. Shreberk, 1920), 26. Binevich's bibliography evidences Goldfaden's competitor, the Yiddish impresario Hartenshteyn, found an audience in Moscow.

5. "Moscow," in *YIVO Encyclopedia*, ed. Gershon David Hundert (New Haven: Yale University Press, 2008), 2: 1202–1205. See the numbers of residents that A. Gurshteyn provides in his thorough discussion of the Moscow press coverage on Goldfaden, "A. Goldfaden in Moskve," *Literarishe bleter* 95 (1926):138–140.

6. In August 1880, Goldfaden staged *The Sorceress* fourteen times in Moscow and there appears to have been a short stint in St. Petersburg the same year. Goldfaden returned for a five-week run in August of the same year. In 1881, Goldfaden's troupe claimed a summer stage in Krestovskii Park, the popular amusement park on the right bank of the Neva, the main resort destination for St. Petersburg's residents during this time. Al'bin M. Konechnyi, "Shows for the People: Public Amusement Parks in Nineteenth-Century. St. Petersburg," in *Cultures in Flux: Lower-Class Values, Practices, and Resistance in Late Nineteenth Century*, ed. Stephen Frank and Mark D. Steinberg (Princeton, NJ: Princeton University Press), 121–130.

7. For a list of all articles and announcements from this period, see E. Binevich, *Istoriia evreiskogo teatra v rossii, 1876–1883: Annoturoviannaia bibliografia* (Moscow: Obshestvo evreiskvoe naslednie, 1998).

8. Finkel and Oyslender's uneasiness with the artistic and commercial aspirations of Goldfaden's tours in St. Petersburg and Moscow may explain why they gave the sources from these places short shrift. Finkel and Oyslender's focus on Goldfaden's tour in St. Petersburg is devoted to their argument that there was an important shift in Goldfaden's mentality and artistic approach due to the pogroms that took place in the south following the assassination of Alexander II. They argue that Goldfaden moved away from the satirical character of his earlier work and identified with the growing Love of Zion (*Chibat Zion*) movement. (See *A. Goldfaden: Materialn*, 86–87.) This is not accurate. There is no evidence that Goldfaden reassessed his politics after the pogroms. See my article on this important question, "Ha-machaze Bar Kochba me-et Avrom Goldfaden," *Chulyot* 6 (2000): 79–90. Nyusinov does provide

analysis of the press coverage in Moscow but without speculating on the cultural ramifications of Goldfaden's tours.

9. *Odesskii listok ob"iavlenii*, no. 44 (February 23, 1880): 2.

10. "Retsenzia na operetty 'Sulamif' A. Gol'dfadena," *Mestnye Izvestiia* (July 12, 1880): 2.

11. H. Lenkin, "V Evreiskom Teatre," *Petersburgkaya Gazeta* C.3 (March 2, 1882): 3. "Predstavleniia truppy G. Gol'dfadena v zale gostinnitsy 'Demut,'" *Russkii Evrei*, no. 10 (1882): 387.

12. See the reviews of his early comedies in Finkel and Oyslender, *A. Goldfaden*, 43–73.

13. While *Shulamis* enjoyed great popularity and claimed an outsized emotional and symbolic place in the Yiddish theater's social life, it was representative of a stream of historical dramas that created a space for strong women on the Yiddish stage. The concentration of historical operettas in 1882 and 1883 attests to the growth of sophistication and stability experienced by existing professional troupes. Included in those works that reflect the rise of the female actor was Dina in *Bar Kokhba* and female roles in the following operettas: *Esther in Ein-Gedi, Deborah, Judah the Maccabee,* and *Uriel Acosta*. For their stage history during the first period of the Yiddish theater, see E. Binevich, especially, "Tovarishchestvo evreiskikh artistov pod O. Lernera, Odessa 1882–3," *Istoriia evreiskogo teatra v rossii, 1876–1883*, 35.

14. *Shulamis oder bas yerushalayim: muzikalishe-melodrama n raymen in 4 akten un 15 bilder* (Odessa: 1886). *Shulamis; or, the Daughter of Jerusalem*, first staged in 1880, was the most ambitious operetta ever performed in Yiddish and never surpassed in Yiddish musical theater. It is the only libretto that Goldfaden composed in rhyming couplets and, accordingly, it pulled the Yiddish operetta closest to the precincts of veritable opera. For a publication history of *Shulamis*, see Shmuel Rozhanski, *Oysgeklibene shriftn* (Buenos Aires: YIVO, 1963). For a fuller discussion of its cultural context including an analysis of its music, see Alyssa Quint and Ronald Robboy, eds., *Shulamis: A Critical Edition* (forthcoming from Dusseldorf University Press).

15. The operetta *Bontsye* dominated the repertory of the first two years of Goldfaden's theater and was played regularly by Grodner and his makeshift troupe even before Goldfaden emerged a year or two later. It was apparently serialized in Goldfaden's newspaper *Yisrolik* but does not appear in extant numbers of the newspaper. In 1882, it was the first Yiddish stage production in the United States when it was staged at Turn Hall in New York City by Thomashefsky and Golubok.

16. Faith Jones is the first to draw attention to this paradox. See Faith Jones, "Sex and Scandal in the *Encyclopedia of the Yiddish Theatre*" in *Inventing the Modern Yiddish Stage*, ed. Joel Berkowitz and Barbara Henry (Detroit, MI: Wayne State University Press, 2012), 251–274.

17. David Biale, *Eros and the Jews: From Biblical Israel to Contemporary America* (New York: Basic Books, 1992), 161.

18. A. R. Malachi, "Goldfadn-materialn," *A Centenary of Abraham Goldfaden*, ed. Jacob Shatzky (New York: YIVO, 1940), 7.

19. *Brayndele the Cossack* was never published. Goldfaden explains the evolution of the play and includes long excerpts in his autobiography. See Sholem Perlmutter, ed., "Der onfang fun yidishn teater," *Yidishe velt*, June 20, 1929, 3. YIVO has two incomplete manuscripts. Avraham Goldfaden Collection; RG 219; folder 3 and 4; YIVO Institute for Jewish Research.

20. Yitskhak Librescu, "Mayne memuarn," *Teater figurn* (Buenos Aires: Elisheva, 1936).

21. Ibid.

22. Her stage appearance is briefly recorded in the newspaper. See "Gorodskaia khronika," *Odesskii listok ob"iavlenii* (May 1, 1879): 3.

23. Zalmen Zylbercweig, *Leksikon fun yidishn teater* (New York: Farlag Elisheva, 1963), 4: 2583.

24. *Di kaprizne kale-moyd oder Kabtsenson et Hungerman: melodrama in 4 akten un 5 bilder* (Warsaw: Boymritter un Gonshor, 1887). See newspaper coverage of *Kaprizne-doch* in Binevich, "Zapreshchenie evreiskikh spektaklei," *Istoriia Evreiskogo teatra v rossii, 1876–1883*, 21.

25. I quote from the earliest version of the play that was simply titled *Di bobe mit dem eynikl* (Odessa: 1879). A later version containing significant changes is titled *Di bobe mit dem eynikl oder Bontsye di kneytlekhlegerin: melodrama in dray aktn mit gezang* (New York: J. Saphirstein, 1893). A review of the operetta appeared in *Donskaia pchela* (May, 8, 1880), n.p.

26. Chava Weissler, *Voices of the Matriarchs: Listening to the Prayers of Early Modern Jewish Women* (Boston: Beacon Press, 1998), 139.

27. This is especially stark in *Aunt Sosya* (*Di mume sosye*). Goldfaden published this play early in his career, in his second Yiddish-language anthology called *Di yidene: farsheydene geshikhte un teater in prost yudishn fun avrom goldfadn* (Odessa: 1869). Due to its large cast and absence of song (it is not an operetta like most of Goldfaden's works), it was not performed often. The Romanian maskil Abramsky (Avraham Hagershoni Abramsky) gave it a positive review in *Bamat yitskhak o gey chizayon* (1877). The literary scholar Leo Wiener also singled out *Aunt Sosya* as one of Goldfaden's finest works. See Leo Wiener, *History of Yiddish Literature* (New York: Charles Scribner's Sons, 1899), 237. For a close reading of *Aunt Sosya*, see my paper: A. Quint, "The Botched Kiss and the Beginnings of the Yiddish Stage," *Culture Front: Representing Jews in Eastern Europe*, ed. Benjamin Nathans and Gabriella Safran (Philadelphia: University of Pennsylvania Press, 2008), 79–102.

28. I quote from the earliest edition of this play that differs significantly from later editions. A. Goldfaden, *Di Bobe mit dem eynikl* (Odessa: 1879). This early edition, thirty-eight pages long, does not delineate scenes, only acts.

29. Quint, "The Botched Kiss," 79–102.

30. Here Goldfaden's references to the *tsena-urena* are taken almost directly from the text. The "hunger" refers primarily to the famine in Egypt but has a compelling double entendre in this context as a sexual hunger (Lublin: Feder Publishing, 1902). See page 14 for the reference to Adam and Eve and page 116 for the reference to Joseph.

31. On *Serkele*, see my article: A. Quint, "The Currency of Yiddish: Ettinger's *Serkele* and the Reinvention of Shylock," *Prooftexts* 24 (2004): 99–115.

32. Northrop Frye, *Anatomy of Criticism: Four Essays* (Princeton, NJ: Princeton University Press, 1957).

33. A celebrated performer named Sanye, the Bialystok Badkhn, for instance, is described as having a wardrobe of female clothes for the array of female characters he performed. Oyzer Marshalik, a wedding jester in Lemberg, "played the role of a women (*a yidene*) for which he would artfully hide his beard." See Y. Lifshits, "Badkhonim un leytsim bay yidn," *Arkhiv*, 73. On Oyzer Marshalik, see Zalmen Zylbercweig, *Leksikon fun Yidishn teater*, vol. I (New York: Elisheva, 1931), 143.

34. Zylbercweig, *Leksikon* I: 5240.

35. M. Zeifert, "Di geshikhte fun yudishn teater" in dray tsayt peryodn," *Di yidishe bine* yuvilyem oysgabe," (1897): n.p.

36. Ms. n.d.; Abraham Goldfaden Collection; RG 219, folder 5, YIVO Institute for Jewish Research.

37. Zylbercweig, *Leksikon*, I: 693–694.
38. Originally quoted in Shmuel Tsitron, *Dray literarishe doyres*, 45, and then referenced in Zylbercweig's entry on Goldfaden, *Leksikon*, I: 693.
39. Jacob Adler, "40 yor af der bine," *Varhayt*, October 29, 1916, 5.
40. Zylbercweig, *Leksikon*, I: 693.
41. Quoted in Zylbercweig, Zalmen, *Avrom Goldfaden un Zigmunt Mogulesko* (Buenos Aires: Elisheva, 1936), 152. The play was never published. Ms. n.d.; The Abraham Goldfaden Collection; RG 219; folder 7, The YIVO Institute of Jewish Research.
42. Zylbercweig, *Goldfadn un Mogulesko*, 34.
43. Jaco Adler, "40 yor af der bine," *Varhayt* (September 17, 1916): 5.
44. M. Teplitski, "Zikhroynes fun mayn lebn (fun der geshikhte–yidishn teater)," *Shikago* (September 1931): 45. See also Zylbercweig, *Leksikon*, II: 887–888.
45. Fishzon wrote his autobiography in Russian. It was translated into Yiddish in 1924 for serialization in *Morgn zhurnal* beginning October 10, 1924, 6.
46. Alter Fishzon, *Morgn zhurnal*, October 24, 1924, 6.
47. Ibid.
48. Ibid.
49. Ibid.
50. Ibid.
51. Literary scholar Marjorie Garber explains the cross-dresser as neither male nor female but as a third term that creates "a space of possibility." See Marjorie Garber, *Vested Interests: Cross-Dressing and Cultural Anxiety* (New York: Routledge, 1992), 10.
52. B. Gorin, *Geshikhte fun yidishn teater* I: 193. This is quoted by Michael Steinlauf, "Y.L. Peretz's Fear of Purim," *Jewish Social Studies* 1, no. 3 (Spring, 1995): 44–65.
53. Quoted in Zylbercweig, *Goldfadn un Mogulesko*, 329.
54. See also the work of David Mazower, who discusses the strong link between prostitution and the Yiddish theater in Buenos Aires. Michael Steinlauf's article, "Fear of Purim," suggests this connection existed in Warsaw's Yiddish theater. A review by the historian Y. Lifshits of the memoirs of the Russian Yiddish actor M. Midovonik makes mention of the actress Braginska as encouraging her choristers to make money as prostitutes in turn-of-the-century postban Russia. Braginska is discussed later in this chapter, though not in connection with prostitution. In "M. Midovonik mayne teater zikhroynes," *Arkhiv far der geshikhte fun yidishn teater un drama* (New York and Vilna: YIVO, 1930), 209.
55. Ester-Rokhl and Bertha Kalich did not act during this first period but began their careers after the 1883 ban. Abramovich's memoirs appear in *Forverts* from September 7, 1930, to December 28, 1930.
56. There is little evidence of resistance by tavern keepers or even by the religious establishment. See a rare condemnation of the Yiddish theater (but not its female actors) by Rabbi Kupfer in Bucharest dated to 1877, mostly in reaction to the participation of his choristers in the theater. Meyer Ben Avrom Halevi, "Di 'groyse shul' in bukaresht in der geshikhte funem yidishn teater," *Arkhiv*, 239–242. The Hebrew document is included in full, followed by a Yiddish translation. See also Zylbercweig, *Goldfadn un Mogulesko*, 33.
57. Nahma Sandrow makes this point. See Nahma Sandrow, *Vagabond Stars: A World History of Yiddish Theater* (Syracuse: Syracuse University Press, 1977, 1996), 55.
58. More information is required on the roles they took within troupes. In the case of Akselrod, for instance, she absorbed the power of her husband Avrom Akselrod (1858–1925) after

he died because of the power he held as well as the power she exerted as the troupe's prima donna. See Zylbercweig, *Leksikon*, 6.

59. See Freyda Freiman's two works, for instance, listed in the Marwick Bibliography, *Di opere zingerin: komedye-drama in fier akten*, m.s. Copyright March 3, 1920, and *Di aktrise: komedye drame in 4 akten*, m.s. Copyright March 31, 1920. The non-Yiddish actress Sarah Bernhardt and the French Jewish actress Rachel had an oversized impression on the Yiddish-language consciousness. The former was followed by the Jewish press in Russia and A. B. Cahan wrote a biography on the latter: *Rashel: A biografye* (New York: Forverts, 1938).

60. Important, too, is the career of Maria Lerner, the wife of Osip Lerner. Maria was the first woman to write for the Yiddish stage. Her play, *The Chained Widow* (*Di agune*), was staged in the Mariinsky Theater. Maria wrote in Russian for translation into Yiddish by her husband for the stage and for publication. According to a YIVO newsletter, for instance, Maria Lerner produced nine manuscripts in Russian for translation by her husband Osip. See *Yedies*, no. 24 (December 1927): 3.

61. See Carole B. Bailin, *To Reveal Our Hearts: Jewish Women Writers in Tsarist Russia* (Cincinnati, OH: Hebrew Union College Press, 2003).

62. See also a similar complaint earlier in an Odessa newspaper in 1879. Quoted in Y. Riminik, "Di ershte finf yor yidisher teater in odes," *Di royte velt* Kharkov 12(1926): 95.

63. These are my calculations based on Zylbercweig's biographies and memoirs. The theater scholar Faith Jones demonstrates that Zylbercweig's *Encyclopedia* is not exhaustive. From this first period, most actors—even minor ones—mentioned in memoirs have a biography in Zylbercweig's *Encyclopedia*. Almost none, of course, are mentioned by Goldfaden.

64. Khine Braginskaia-Fishzon, "My Memoirs," translated by Ri Turner, *Women on the Yiddish Stage*, forthcoming from Syracuse University Press. Originally published in *Der tog* in 1934 in serial form under changing titles.

65. "Miss Moshkovits," for instance, is mentioned in a short news item in *Russkii Evrei*: "Nam pishut iz Dinaburga," *Russkii Evrei* no. 8 (1881): 296–297. Zylbercweig's *Leksikon*. See Adler, "40 yor af der bine," *Di varhayt* (September 13, 1916): 5.

66. Zylbercweig, *Leksikon*, I: 58.

67. B. Vaynshteyn, "A kleyne meydele tret uf mit Avrom Goldfaden in Ades," *Forverts*, April 18, 1914, 3.

68. While we know of some manuscripts that were written by male players on the Yiddish stage and then lost, I have not come across a single reference to an unpublished memoir penned by a woman. Memoirs not published and no longer traceable include those by Joseph Lateiner and Cesar (Bezalel Grinberg), both of which are quoted by Zylbercweig and listed in the bibliographies of these men in his *Leksikon*.

69. Zylbercweig, *Leksikon*, I: 213.

70. Ibid., IV: 2951.

71. Binevich lists these advertisements in his bibliography with the following headings: "Anons benefisa Margarity Shvarts v Brayndele Kozak," *Khar'kovskie gubernskie vedomosti*, July 5, 1880, 2. "Zametka o debiute Aneti Grodner," *Vedomosti Odesskogo Gradonachal'stva*, August 28, 1879, 3. "Anons segodniashnego debuta aktrisy S. Natanson v tretiom predstavlenii Volka v ovechei shkure," *Listok obiavlenii. Rostov-na-Donu* (July 16, 1883): 1.

72. "Actors Own New Theatre: Culmination of Methods Which Have Been Followed in East Side Playhouses for Several Years Reached by Building of Grand Street House," *New York Times*, February 8, 1903. Found on a web-based archive; no page number.

73. Zylbercweig, *Leksikon*, II: 1008.
74. Jones, "Sex and Scandal," 251–274.
75. Ibid.
76. Ibid., 256.
77. Ibid., 257.
78. L. Elbe, "Vi azoy madam Liptzin iz gevorn an aktrise," *Der teater zhurnal*, October 1, 1901.
79. Jones, "Sex and Scandal." 259.
80. Alongside his operetta *Bar Kokhba*, it is the only libretto that Goldfaden composed in rhyming couplets. For a publication history of *Shulamis*, see Shmuel Rozhanski, *Oysgeklibene shriftn* (Buenos Aires: YIVO, 1963).
81. Seth Wolitz, "*Shulamis* and *Bar kokhba*: Renewed Jewish Role Models in Goldfaden and Halkin," *Yiddish Theatre: New Approaches*, ed. Joel Berkowitz (Oxford, Littman Library of Jewish Civilization, 2003), 88.
82. Mordechai Verbel, *Eydim neemanim o khulda ve-bor: maase nora ve-nifla yesodoto be-kodesh be-divrei khakhameynu z'l bemaskheet tanti, hushar be-arba shirim shulik ve-kharuzim* (Vilna: Rom, 1852); and "The Story of the Weasel and the Well in the Literature of the Enlightenment," *Criticism and Interpretation* 30 (August 1994): 121–155.
83. Naomi Seidman quotes Naomi Zohar's article, "The Story of the Weasel and the Pit in the Literature of the Haskalah," *Criticism and Interpretation* 30 (1994): 121–156. See Seidman's analysis of Mapu's *The Love of Zion* that relies, in part, on Zohar's work. Naomi Seidman, *The Marriage Plot: Or, How Jews Fell in Love with Love, and with Literature* (Stanford, CA: Stanford University Press, 2016), chap. 2.
84. Olga Litvak, *The Haskalah: the Romantic Movement in Judaism* (New Brunswick, NJ: Rutgers University Press, 2012).
85. See Shmuel Werses's fascinating study, *Yiddish Translations of* Ahavat Zion *by Abraham Mapu* [Hebrew] (Jerusalem: Akademon Press, 1989).
86. Seidman, *The Marriage Plot*. Seidman sees this as also associated with the form and content of the novel. Neither Verbel nor Goldfaden deploy the novel form (Verbel's story is told in metered rhyme) but both otherwise dovetail well with Seidman's observation.
87. All references to *Shulamis* are from Nahma Sandrow's translation included in Alyssa Quint and Ronald Robboy, eds. *Avrom Goldfaden's Shulamis: A Critical Edition*. Forthcoming from Dusseldorf University Press.
88. On *tkhines*, see Jean Baumgarten, *Introduction to Old Yiddish Literature*, trans. and ed. Jerold Frakes (Oxford: Oxford University Press, 2005), 260–285; and Chava Weissler, *Voices of the Matriarchs: Listening to the Voices of Early Modern Jewish Women* (Boston: Beacon Press, 1998).
89. The Mad Scene was a staple of the opera stage. It was epitomized in Donizetti's *Lucia di Lamermoor* (1835), from which Mogulesco drew to audition for Goldfaden but there were certainly other examples that Goldfaden likely knew, if only by reputation, from Bellini's *I Puritani* (also 1835) to Meyerbeer's *Dinorah* (1859). See Robboy's essay, "*Shulamis*, Its Music," in *Shulamis: A Critical Edition*, ed. A. Quint and R. Robboy, forthcoming from Dusseldorf University Press.
90. Kaminska's memoirs were serialized posthumously in *Der moment* in July of 1926. An English translation of Kaminska's memoirs by Michael Yashinsky appears in *Women on the Yiddish Stage*, forthcoming from Syracuse University Press.

91. Kalich's autobiography was serialized weekly. See Berta Kalich, "Mayn leben," *Der tog*, March 7, 1925–October 3, 1925. With Braginska's and Abramovitsh's memoirs, it is one of the only and earliest records of the eastern European Jewish experience by a woman. See bibliography for more on these sources.

92. For more on Gimpel's theater, see Zylbercweig, *Leksikon*, I: 479.

93. Kalich, "Mayn leben," *Der tog*, April 25, 1925.

94. Kalich, "Mayn leben," *Der Tog*, April 7, 1925, 7.

6 The Ban, Cultural Momentum, and the Modern Yiddish Theater

The Ban on Yiddish Theater in Russia

On August 17, 1883, Tsar Alexander III issued a secret circular prohibiting Yiddish theater.[1] It spelled the collapse of Yiddish theater in the Russian Empire, as well as the collapse of Goldfaden's career as a theater impresario. When the ban first circulated, Goldfaden and his colleagues figured it was a temporary or toothless gesture and its enforcement would be at the discrimination of local authorities that Goldfaden felt he could influence. First, he tried to reverse it. In his memoirs, he writes: "Like a worried father I rushed to St. Petersburg to plead before the minister for the life of my child."[2] When he could not throw around his influence in St. Petersburg, he sat tight in Odessa while other actors stayed in or close to Russia waiting for the government to soften its stance. Some sought out alternative sources of income, hoping that with time troupes would form again and return to their regular activity, much as what happened months after the assassination of Alexander II in March 1881. Spivakovski and his troupe, for instance, that had been playing a venue in Łódż when the ban was circulated moved westward beyond the Russian border to Königsberg and Berlin. Native Romanians like Lateiner and Mogulesco returned their troupe to Romania.[3] Those whose lives were most settled in Russia, men like Lerner and Shaikevitsh, remained there but pulled away from theater; the latter began cultivating his second career as a Yiddish novelist while the former also returned to writing, mostly in Russian.

Goldfaden lingered in Russia. He published a book of his poems, with the strong hope that the strict enforcement of the ban would slacken with time. He also sought but failed to secure government permission to edit and publish a Yiddish periodical.[4] The effort marks a kind of regression for Goldfaden back to his old ineffectual strategies that, nonetheless, indicate his devotion to Yiddish-language culture (albeit with commercial aspirations) and his commitment to his life in Russia. When Fishzon sought Goldfaden out after news of the ban circulated among performers, he found Goldfaden devastated: "The Yiddish theater was his life. But what, would he really up and leave Russia?" As Fishzon implies, Goldfaden harbored a profound sense of belonging to his native country.

The ban marginalized and robbed the Yiddish theater of cultural presence and prestige in the empire. That is not to say there was absolutely no Yiddish theater after 1883. Recently, the historian John Klier uncovered evidence of post-ban Yiddish theater performances (throughout the 1880s and 1890s) as well as requests to stage Yiddish theater, some of which were granted by the state. In Klier's eyes, these episodes are proof that the ban went unheeded and was only sporadically enforced. In fact, they prove the severe depletion and diminution of the Yiddish theater after 1883 evidenced by a comparison of the venues and participating actors. Overnight, Russia's Yiddish theater went from claiming important theaters in Odessa (under the direction of Goldfaden and Lerner), Rostov-on-Don (under Finkel), Kishinev (under Goldfaden and, separately, Shaikevitsh), Kharkov (now Kharkiv Ukraine, under Jacob Adler), and Moscow (under Gartenshtein) to a marginal and parochial cultural phenomenon.[5] In fact, the prohibition of 1883 reduced the scale of Yiddish-language performance close to its pre-Goldfaden dimension.

The post-ban productions of Fishzon figure among those whom Klier invokes in his study. Fishzon remained in Russia, and he succeeded in staging Yiddish theater over the ensuing decades, albeit sporadically, with hardship, and never in the big-city venues. By the time the ban was issued, Fishzon was a lightweight impresario whose troupe had played market towns and sometimes his native Berdichev.[6] Notwithstanding what Klier deems to be Fishzon's success in producing post-ban theater, Fishzon himself calls the effects of the 1883 ban catastrophic. He writes, "The decree was like a clap of thunder on a clear day. Imagine: we just started getting the hang of things, and it was cut down like a young sapling." His memory of the ban hardly resembles a mere pesky bureaucratic hurdle: "It was utter destruction for the actors. . . . We all felt as if we were in the middle of the ocean on a stormy day in a sinking ship. The ban broke me personally. I was left with a great wardrobe of costumes that had cost me a huge amount of money. It would be worth nothing now. My set designs were worth only their value in firewood and my actors were left to go hungry."[7] Fishzon's perspective illustrates how menacing the ban was even as it was intermittently enforced: without government authorization, there could be no investment in props, costumes, or, most importantly, talent. Fishzon, a relatively small fish in Yiddish theater during the Goldfaden era, became the most important purveyor of Yiddish theater in Russia after 1883, because the higher-profile Yiddish theater business had all but evaporated. Fishzon's rise in status was a result of the diminished landscape of Yiddish theater.[8]

The ban shut down the Yiddish theater as the urban and commercial force that Goldfaden had made of it, especially in Odessa. Odessa had become the Broadway of the Yiddish theater. While some Yiddish impresarios were later able to evade the 1883 ban at some moments in some cities and shtetls, it was strictly enforced in Odessa.[9] Whether or not the government meant to strike at the theater so strategically, the effects were close to fatal. For a period of over ten years, Yiddish theater existed neither in St. Petersburg nor in Moscow. The meaning of the post-ban theatrical episodes that Klier assembled must be assessed relative to pre-ban theatrical activity, and seen in this way they prove just how destructive the ban was. Even if one were to double the number of theater events (both actual and proposed) during the nearly twenty years that Klier examined from 1884 to 1903, it would not equal the number of shows that were typically produced by the professional Yiddish theater in any single year between 1879 and 1883. The Yiddish theater went from securing a position on the cultural landscape of the growing urban Russian and Russian Jewish middle class to a working-class, tavern-based affair from 1883 to 1905.[10]

Cultural Momentum Following the Ban of 1883

Goldfaden, Elite

The severe consequences of the ban work best to illuminate the cultural achievement of Goldfaden and his colleagues. Previous historians of the modern Yiddish theater have assembled evidence of what they have called "pre-Goldfaden" theater activity. They point out the many attempts at staging Yiddish-language productions as well as the substantial body of Yiddish-language dramatic literature penned throughout the nineteenth century. While all these precedents amounted to a good measure of inspiration, they did not generate the momentum necessary to create a sustainable cultural framework necessary to put on public theater. Goldfaden's efforts—part creative, part political, part commercial—did. Most of the approximately one hundred participants of the modern Yiddish theater working during this period would leave Russia—and most of them would eventually leave eastern Europe—in order to act on the Yiddish stage elsewhere.[11] They knew how to organize themselves and what repertoire to perform; they knew about set design and costumes and could duplicate their success elsewhere where there were no government restrictions. With this experience, socialized to a community of like-minded Jewish artists and driven by their passion to perform, they opted to remain actors rather than remain at home in Russia.

As I have underscored repeatedly by this point, in order to catch a glimpse of the most impressive moments achieved by Yiddish theater in the Russian Empire, one must ignore Goldfaden's deflated version of this period and, instead, consider events through the eyes of others and as they are captured by the contemporary press. In the realm of performance, for instance, Yiddish actors demonstrated great ability. Shaikevitsh explains that while many of the Yiddish actors were utter novices, they still took their craft seriously, seeking to impress their peers and fearing the sharp-eyed manager of Odessa's Mariinsky Theater who studied every detail of a production before opening night. Under the scrutiny of what the Russian press referred to as "the entrepreneur" Homer, every element was in place, from the choir and scenery to the actors in their roles on the stage. Even the flimsiest of dramatic works appeared professional on the stage, Shaikevitsh reports.[12] The actor Dovid Kessler recounts how a Yiddish show in Odessa would typically attract the actors of the city's competing Yiddish troupe to its performances.[13] They observed each other's acting styles and freely critiqued all aspects of a production. Friendships and collegiality also developed among actors of various troupes, of different languages, both Jewish and non-Jews. According to Odessa's official governmental newspaper, *The Odessa Civic Record* (*Vedomosti Odesskovo gradonachalstva*), the famous Italian tragic actor Tommaso Salvini (1829–1915) attended a performance of *The Sorceress*.[14] Salvini was an international celebrity whose acting in *Othello* inspired the Russian actor and theater practitioner Konstantin Stanislavski, who saw Salvini perform in Moscow in 1882. Stanislavski wrote that Salvini was the "finest representative" of his own approach to acting.[15] Around the same time, according to a local Odessa newspaper, Salvini praised the Yiddish performance publicly for its originality. The reviewer writes, "The famous artist watched the play extremely attentively. Apparently, he was captured by its originality. As usual, the theatre was full and applause was in abundance."[16] The Yiddish actor Avrom Fishkind's most prized possession when he emigrated to America was a letter of praise he had received from the editor of the St. Petersburg daily *New Times* (*Novoe Vremya*), Aleksey Suvorin (1834–1912), following his performance in *The Sorceress* in August 1881.[17] Before becoming an actor at nineteen years old, Fishkind, the son of a tailor, sang in a synagogue choir under the renowned cantor and composer Velvl Shostepoler in his native Kherson. He joined a troupe led by Adler and Rosenberg and then by Goldfaden. In his letter to Fishkind, Suvorin[18] wrote: "As the editor of *The New Times*, I must express my appreciation to you. You must be deemed an artist. I saw you in your performance of *The Sorceress* and I must tell you that there are few artists of your caliber. I thank you a thousand times over for your interpretation of this role."[19]

In his memoir, the chorus member, actor, and writer Hersh Amasya recalls a visit to the Yiddish theater by the celebrated Russian actor Mitrofan Ivanov-Kozel'skii (1850–1898), who was known for a number of his tragic roles including the title role of the German play *Uriel Acosta* in the Russian version by Karl Gutzkow.[20] A Yiddish-language production of the play, adapted and directed by Lerner (discussed in chap. 4) and produced by Lerner and Goldfaden, was put on the boards in Odessa after Ivanov-Kozel'skii's Russian performance.[21] Placards went up throughout Odessa announcing that the title role would be played by Abba Sheyngold, a former chorister from Romania and one of the first men to join Goldfaden's troupe. According to Amasya, Odessa's gymnasium students wondered who could be so brazen as to play the role after Ivanov-Kozel'skii, and they prepared an arsenal of tomatoes to throw at Sheyngold. Sheyngold, however, brought the house down and inspired a standing ovation that lasted ten minutes. Ivanov-Kozel'skii himself attended a performance and apparently climbed out of his loge and onto the stage to congratulate Sheyngold publicly. After the show, Ivanov-Kozel'skii rented a horse and carriage and rode around Odessa with Sheyngold, Goldfaden, and Lerner to celebrate their artistic achievement.[22]

The Yiddish theater drew so much attention to itself that a Russian entrepreneurial theater in Odessa sought out Jewish-themed works in order to compete with and emulate Goldfaden. The theater was run by Nikolay Miloslavsky (1811–1882), who was a pioneer of Russian-language, entrepreneurial theater and who had first tried to make inroads on the St. Petersburg theatrical scene before settling in Odessa.[23] The Soviet scholar Nyusinov explains that a series of newspaper articles in *Novorossiiskii Telegraf* and in Moscow's satirical journal *The Grasshopper* (*Strekoza*) chided Miloslavsky for his use of Jewish themes or, as one journalist put it using the slangy word for Yiddish, "*zhargonke*."[24] Nyusinov's prime objective is to reveal the anti-Semitism and harassment that Goldfaden suffered at the hands of both Jewish and non-Jewish journalists and reviewers. More relevant to this discussion, however, the episode demonstrates the significant impression Goldfaden had made in Russia, both commercially and artistically.

Of equal importance are the episodes of cross-linguistic collaboration, influence, and even admiration among the theater groups in which Yiddish troupes participated. The Yiddish actor M. L. Mayerson (1860–1928), for example, acted in Miloslavsky's Russian-language troupe under the name Mark Lazarovitsh Merison before joining Goldfaden and, from there, moved to a competing Yiddish troupe to act and direct alongside Finkel. Mayerson was active on the Yiddish stage until his activity in the Soviet-sponsored "Theater Corner" in Kiev.[25] His move might reflect the relative success that Yiddish theater achieved during this early period compared to an entrepreneurial Russian-language theatrical company. Would that sources were more forthcoming about these avenues of cultural influence and engagement.

Goldfaden's confidence in his cultural project—utterly absent in his record of his experience—is also reflected in his attempt to negotiate venues in Moscow. One of these venues was Gavrila Solodovnikov's Theater on Petrov Square in Moscow.[26] A sense of controversy, if not anti-Semitism, is evident in a short article in Russia's premier theater newspaper *The Prompter* (*Sufler*, St. Petersburg, 1878–1886) reflecting a kind of circling of the wagons in reaction to the idea of Yiddish theater in that venue: "The Jewish troupe will have no success among us in Moscow. Only Jews attend these shows. No Russian could be tricked into attending them even with sweets. The troupe has grown hateful to Moscow residents who try to imagine how to smoke [the Jewish troupe] out of its white-bricked capital city once and for all."[27] Still, Goldfaden attracted the attention of

Figure 6.1. Portrait of Goldfaden by Isaac Perkoff, London, c. 1900. Courtesy of the YIVO Institute for Jewish Research.

The Prompter repeatedly—and did so even before he introduced historical works that hewed more closely to the theatrical fare Russians were used to consuming.[28] Moscow's *Russian Record* (*Russki Vedomosti*) was more congenial in its report although its journalist still worried that Goldfaden might overstep the bounds of his troupe's quality. It reports a rumor circulating among Moscow audiences that those who lead Moscow's prestigious Artistic Circle (*Artisticheskiy kruzhok*) would like to invite "the Jewish troupe of A. Goldfaden" to produce a number of shows. The journalist continues: "Goldfaden's troupe isn't bad, it has its raison-d'être for a summer season and to perform in Lyudiker Theater of the German Club but in 'the Circle' that has its own troupe it is something that is unwanted and uncomfortable."[29] The press coverage of Goldfaden's theater points to his efforts to raise the profile of his theater in the empire. This is not meant as an assessment of the quality of his work. Rather, it is an attempt to shift the conversation about Goldfaden away from the socialist and folkist nomenclature of most twentieth-century historians who have told his story, and demonstrate not only that he was one of a small number of pioneers of entrepreneurial theater in the empire but also how significantly he identified with a class of Russia's elite cultural producers.

Goldfaden's Last Years (1883–1908)

By 1887 Goldfaden had given up on working around the ban. Russian officials were unrelenting in enforcing it. He had decamped to Warsaw in 1885 where he understood he could produce Yiddish theater under the guise of German-language performance. French and Italian opera had long been mainstays of the Warsaw theatrical scene, although the tsar sought to impose Russian culture on the empire's Polish subjects and therefore outlawed Polish theater while it allowed German theater there for consumption by its ethnic German population. By disguising his Yiddish theater as German, Goldfaden had hoped he could stage Yiddish theater in a venue authorized for use by a German theater troupe. But there were hurdles, including the question of approval by the censor: he needed to resubmit his operettas for approval in German by the Bureau of Censorship in St. Petersburg. In a brief collaboration with Goldfaden at the time, Fishzon found someone to translate some plays from Yiddish into abridged versions in German. With seven plays translated, Fishzon traveled to meet the censor in St. Petersburg who took three days to read them over. "For his work I timidly offered him 25 rubles," writes Fishzon in his memoirs. "He, on the other hand, was not so timid and grabbed the money before I had a chance to blink."[30]

Although his aura was still great, Goldfaden's successes in Yiddish theater in Warsaw were fleeting. Goldfaden earned accolades in Poland with a new operetta, *Ahasaverus*,[31] and then a staging of *Shulamis*.[32] The production was so successful, according to historian Yankev Shatzky, a Polish troupe became interested in it. A year later, *The Sorceress* was translated (*Czarownica*) and mounted on the Polish stage.[33] Judging from most sources, however, pseudo-Yiddish theater in Warsaw was a shadow of the best Yiddish theater of only a few years earlier. B. Gorin reports that such "concerts" consisted of bits and pieces of the former Yiddish theater repertory. And even so, whole scenes were eliminated when an unexpected policeman entered the theater to check if the performance was indeed in German.[34] Some historical sources portray Warsaw's Yiddish theater of this period as defiant of its Russian oppressors, but defiance could not make up for the meager scale of these productions and how they deprived the players and audience of the dignity that Goldfaden had doggedly pursued. Fishzon does not supply a date as to when Warsaw's local police chief shuttered these performances. At that point, Fishzon reports, "Goldfaden threw up his hands and said: Thank God I have been ejected from this special hell called Yiddish theater."[35]

While living in Warsaw, Goldfaden continued to circulate in exclusive social circles where his name attracted a blend of celebrity and notoriety. Tsitron reports tense discussion about Goldfaden's work in the Jewish salons he visited where members of the Jewish intelligentsia criticized his deployment of caricature on public stages. Goldfaden corresponded amiably and socialized with his fellow Jewish intellectuals, including such luminaries as Hebrew and Yiddish literary critic David Frishman (1859–1922), Yiddish author and editor Jacob Dineson (1856–1919), and Sholem Aleichem. The author and playwright Gershom Bader (1868–1953) also showed Goldfaden friendship in their letters. But Goldfaden knew of their ambivalence for his work.[36] The letters between Goldfaden and his peers demonstrate their willingness to collaborate with him but also their disapproval of his comic operettas. And they reveal the psychological toll such disapproval took. In a letter to Sholem Aleichem, Goldfaden lamented changes Dineson made to his operetta *Shmendrik* and compared them to "improvements" one might make to an ancient antiquity.[37] Instead of defending the quality of his work, Goldfaden desperately pleads that his work not be changed because of its significance to understanding the growth of the Yiddish theater.

While contending with such humiliations, Goldfaden mingled among prominent Warsaw glitterati and was treated as an equal member by many. He attended the debut of the rising international opera star Felicja Kaschowska (1872–1951) at the Grand Theater in Warsaw. Kaschowska was the daughter of a well-known cantor and would go on to a storied career on the international stage. At her performance of Meyerbeer's *Robert the Devil*, however, it was Goldfaden who signed her album with a small verse that playfully quotes a line from "Under the Sycamore Tree" by Polish composer Moniusko Stanisław (1819–1872): "When you possess a beautiful voice/And can sing/Sing the arias of Schubert, Mendelssohn, and Strauss/Their music is majestic/But—sing, as well, a little Yiddish./"*Tam na górze jawor stoi*"/Can be sung by every *goy*."[38] In 1889 a feuilletonist for the Hebrew-language *Ha-tsefira* wrote, "Since the Yiddish poet Goldfaden left our city for New York two years ago, the shine of the Jewish theatre has diminished and plays about Jewish life have been taken from the stage. No one mentions them and no one undertakes to produce Yiddish theatre."[39] Goldfaden's departure for America in 1888 signaled the end of the brief revival of Yiddish theater in Warsaw and the further diminishment of his celebrity.

The timing of Goldfaden's arrival in New York was unfortunate: his competitors as well as the members of his own troupe had, by 1886, beat him to New York and turned it into the center of Yiddish theater without him. As more and more actors had accepted the permanence of the ban over the preceding five years, they had moved farther and farther away from Russia and eventually to London and New York where the thirst for Yiddish theater was greatest. Furthermore, the memory of Goldfaden's abusive treatment and his general egomania lingered among many of his former actors.[40] Now in America, the same actors organized themselves anew and would eventually form the very first actors' union to be established in the United States, the Hebrew Actors' Union. Still, when Goldfaden's ship arrived in the harbor in New York—he traveled with his wife Paulina and his former competitor Spivakovski, according to Kessler's memoirs—Kessler and his entire company waited at the harbor to greet him.

> We immediately invited him and Spivakovski to our production of his *Bar Kokhba* that we wanted to put on that evening in his honor. We were sure Goldfaden would accept our invitation as a gesture of friendship. It was not meant to be. It did not suit Goldfaden to come to us as a mere guest. It was not like Goldfaden to throw away his native ancestral right (*heymishn yikhes*) and he would come to us on only one condition: on the condition that he would remain our director. I cannot forget his words, "for me to enter a theater, it must belong to me. In somebody else's theater I will not go."

Kessler does not mention here that he hoped for Goldfaden's permission to stage his works. Still, they could not submit to Goldfaden's will. When their old boss arrived and tried to take directorial control of New York City's Romanian Opera House, the city's most important Yiddish theater venue, they turned him away.[41] But for a small number of exceptions including an odd fundraiser for the aging impresario, no theater in New York played Goldfaden's work until after his death due to his refusal to allow troupes to perform his work under directors other than himself. Notwithstanding how much he dominated the repertoire of the Yiddish theater in Russia only a few years earlier with many of the same actors who likely knew all his works by heart, it was still a price that the actors were willing to pay in order not to work with him. Shut out of theater life by unionized actors who refused him any role, Goldfaden pursued other cultural projects. He established *The New Yorker Illustrated Newspaper* (*New yorker illustrirte tsaytung*), the first

Yiddish-language picture newspaper.[42] The paper folded a year later. Goldfaden then opened a drama school for working-class Jewish immigrants, one of the first of its kind.[43] A number of his students went on to have illustrious careers on the Yiddish stage, but Goldfaden tired of teaching and left for Europe, once again in the hopes of producing and directing theater.[44]

According to a letter that Goldfaden sent to Sholem Aleichem in 1889, the uprooted maestro was, at the time, nursing hopes of establishing a Yiddish theater in Paris. But soon he found that the city did not have a critical mass of Yiddish speakers with disposable income to sustain the level of theater he would hope to produce. As he remarked to Dineson about a Yiddish-speaking Parisian, "a franc dances in his pocket" for only a brief time. In 1890, the Galician metropolis of Lemberg afforded him the prospect of an audience. There he directed the young, rising star Bertha Kalich (chap. 5) at the theater run by Yankev Ber Gimpel (1840–1906), a veteran choral singer of the Polish municipal theater who secured a theater concession from the Austro-Hungarian government in gratitude for outstanding military service.[45] According to the memoir of Yiddish actor Kalmen Yuvelir, Goldfaden approached his role as director with great skill and thoughtfulness, especially in helping actors understand their characters and in creating sophisticated stage effects even under primitive circumstances.[46] Goldfaden produced new works including *The Righteous Advocate or Rabbi Yoselman and the Decrees from Alsace* (*Meylits yoysher oder rebbe yoselman un di gzeyres fun alsas*), *Rothschild*, and *Messianic Times* (*Mashiakhs tsaytn*) that depicted the movement of Jews from Russia to New York and Palestine and, indirectly, told Goldfaden's personal story of dislocation in New York.[47] From Lemberg, Goldfaden took the position of the director of Yiddish theater in Bucharest where he staged his play *The Tenth Commandment* (*Dos tsente gebot*) that starred Kalich, among others. As the theater historian B. Gorin remarks, it seems appropriate that Goldfaden's last days as a director would play out in Romania, the place of his first successes. Soon after it closed, Goldfaden again grew restless. As Kalich remarks, "Goldfaden decided that Bucharest was no longer where he wanted to be and prepared himself for another journey. Goldfaden could not stay in one place. He was pulled into the world and he knew very well that wherever he wished to go, an open door would welcome him."[48] In 1897 he returned to Paris. By this point, Yiddish theatrical performances had managed to claim some attention of critics in *Le Figaro* and *Revue d'Arts Dramatiques*, with Goldfaden's repertoire, but only at times with his direct involvement. Goldfaden felt he could not attract sufficient audiences to his shows in Paris though he tried on several occasions.

During this period, Goldfaden identified increasingly with the Zionist cause and circulated in Zionist circles. The pogroms of 1881 and 1882, which turned many of his intellectual peers away from the idea of a future for Jews in the empire, did not affect Goldfaden's loyalty to Russia. With each passing year after

1883 that the government did not reverse its action, Goldfaden's optimism for emancipation for Russian Jews waned and his commitment to Zionism grew. Still, he never visited Palestine. Goldfaden loved Paris, was fluent in French, and felt gratitude to the French for the years he lived there. During his Paris years, Goldfaden took in the World Fair and was a member of Paris's local Zionist group, *Mevaseret Zion* (see interviews he conducted with Zionist figures in *Yidishe Gazetn*).[49] He had close friendships with Naftali Herz Imber (1856–1909), the composer of what would become Israel's national anthem, and the legendary Hebraist Eliezer Ben Yehuda (1858–1922) who translated *The Two Kuni-Lemls* into Hebrew and published it in the form of a booklet that he included with his newspaper *Ha-Tsvi* in 1900.[50] In 1900, he was a Parisian delegate to the fourth Zionist Congress that took place in London,[51] and a photograph at the YIVO Institute for Jewish Research includes Goldfaden posing in what looks like the lobby of a theater, with Morris Rosenfeld, the most celebrated Yiddish poet of his time, known for his socialist and Zionist themes and the public recital of his work.[52]

Goldfaden continued to compose operettas. Among the works he produced during this period, the most successful was *The Sacrifice of Isaac or the Destruction of Sodom and Gomorrah: A Biblical Operetta in 4 Acts and 40 Scenes*, a work that hearkened back to his earlier operettas.[53] But the works could not halt his physical and artistic decline. By 1896, Goldfaden was fifty-six years old, being threatened with eviction by his Paris landlord, and suffering from what he described in his letters as severe asthma. On his sixtieth birthday, *The Advocate* (*Hamelits*) and *The Jew* (*Der yid*) closed their tributes to the founding father of the Yiddish theater with a call to help him in his time of need. In response, Boris Thomashefsky organized a benefit in his honor in 1901 that raised 3,500 francs for Goldfaden.

By the time he left Paris in 1903 and returned to New York City, he was physically and emotionally fragile. He continued to resent his outsider status. As he wrote to his brother Naftoli in 1902: "But to come to the city where my theater is, and my theater refuses to recognize me or take me in, is a tragedy in my eyes."[54] This time, however, when Goldfaden settled in New York, the Yiddish acting community was conciliatory, even pitying of their old boss. He was warmly welcomed by the young Zionists of the Theodor Herzl Club. In 1906, they put on his one-act Hebrew play, *David b'Milkhamah* (*David at War*), the first Hebrew-language play to be performed in America. Luminaries of the theater Adler, Thomashefsky, and the London-based Yiddish actress Dina Feinman performed some of his most popular works (*Bar Kokhba*, *Kuni-Leml*, *Brayndele the Cossack*, and *Shulamis*) in his honor. Around that time, Goldfaden penned a letter to his friend Isaac Perkoff, a British photographer with a strong interest in theater, in which he wrote, "I hear that in London you mean to build a permanent theatre. For my part, I am not interested; it is too late for me. It is for the younger

Figure 6.2. Mourners gathered at Goldfaden's tombstone, c. 1908. Courtesy of the YIVO Institute for Jewish Research.

generations."[55] Thomashefsky apparently staged his last play *Ben-Ami* only because of Goldfaden's failing health.[56] Goldfaden died in January 1908 during its run on the boards. News of his death attracted a sudden surge of people to Thomashefsky's production of *Ben-Ami*. But it was more Thomashefsky's production than Goldfaden's. The *New York Times* referred to him as "the Yiddish Shakespeare" as well as "a poet and a prophet." Between 75,000 and 100,000 people are said to have attended his funeral procession from the People's Theater in the Bowery to Washington Cemetery in Brooklyn.

Goldfaden Ubiquitous

While it took shape in the city, the modern Yiddish theater underwent a process of rapid popularization, even "vernacularization," that began soon after its creation. In a sense, the Yiddish theater demonstrates that there is no better way to generate "low" or "popular" culture than to produce high culture. Paradoxically, a contributing factor to this phenomenon was the ban of 1883: the Russian government's aggressive suppression of the Yiddish theater in the cities shifted the consumption of Goldfaden's operettas into market towns or shtetls and swept them under the auspices of modest theater troupes while the best talent emigrated westward to London and the United States.[57] After the ban of 1883, Goldfaden's theater reached "the masses" more so than it had under Goldfaden. His work shifted from "high" to "low," or from being characterized more by their city venues to being characterized by shtetl venues, from being associated with professional troupes to productions by semiprofessional and amateur groups during the years that followed the ban.

Such activity had already begun before the ban: Goldfaden had given permission to competitors to produce his works for a fee. Other troupes staged small, unauthorized productions. Fishzon mentions in his memoirs, for instance, that he tried but failed to negotiate permission to stage Goldfaden's works in his native city of Berdichev. Goldfaden wanted to charge him a flat fee of a thousand rubles, but Fishzon could not come up with this amount. In his memoirs, Shaikevitsh reports that he sought a similar deal with Goldfaden for Kishinev that also fell apart. Fishzon reports in his memoirs that instead of negotiating with Goldfaden, he bribed officials in the censor's office in St. Petersburg for authorized copies.[58] He "borrowed" the office's full supply of Goldfaden's plays, copied them over a period of one day, returned them, and got the censor's seal for his new copies. With these, he fearlessly mounted Goldfaden's operettas without paying the author a royalty.[59]

Unauthorized productions of Goldfaden's operettas and his unfair treatment of his actors account, in part, for the spread of his celebrity and the popularization of his operettas. In Goldfaden's eyes, there was nothing so cheap as theatrical talent; he readily absorbed willing entertainers into his troupe to replace those he had dismissed. With such a casual attitude toward his acting talent, however, Goldfaden unintentionally fortified the troupes of his competitors with well-trained actors who knew by heart most of his oeuvre. Almost all of Goldfaden's actors claimed he was exploitative and left him to join competing troupes. According to Zylbercweig's biography of the actor Leon Berger, for instance, actors knew to stay with Goldfaden long enough to memorize enough lines so as to be valuable to another troupe by the time they could no longer tolerate Goldfaden's abuse. The actor Bernard Vaynshteyn writes that Mogulescu[60] broke from Goldfaden and started another troupe with Joseph Lateiner[61] and his producer and troupe manager Librescu, whom Goldfaden had unceremoniously fired; their final season in 1883 consisted almost entirely of Goldfaden's works.[62] Not all playwrights had the same access to the Bureau of Censorship enjoyed by Goldfaden. For them, it was easier to stage Goldfaden's works, which were familiar to local authorities.[63]

While the press does not register all these performances, mention of them appears throughout Zylbercweig's biographical entries of the theater's first actors.

Cesar Grinberg (b. 1855), for instance, the son of a butcher in Iași, joined the chorus of a German operetta company as a teenager. After taking in a performance of Goldfaden's operetta *The Grandmother and the Granddaughter*, Grinberg pulled together a group of actors and traveled among Romanian shtetls. He likely worked off his own memory of the operettas. Tantsman (b. 1857), future actor and the son of a Warsaw-based manufacturer, pulled a group of friends together and put on a performance of Goldfaden's *Shmendrik*. His collaborator Shlifershteyn relates that these productions—put on by a few male factory workers—were so successful that they were encouraged to travel to different towns in the province. Eventually, this small group was absorbed into a professional group led by Grodner.

The oral proliferation of Goldfaden's works during the 1880s, 1890s, and beyond—modified, adapted, and abridged for smaller groups of entertainers—along with the publication of his most popular full-length operettas by 1887 fed the activity of shtetl-based amateur or mini-troupes.[64] In a tavern on Warsaw's Franciszkańska Street, for instance, Berish Bekerman (b. 1854) and his coplayers put on skits inspired by Goldfaden's repertoire on a makeshift stage. The other actors and singers would sing from "the wings (*hinter di kulisn*)."[65] The performances were so well attended that soon the original five-kopek ticket rose and the troupe staged and transferred to a proper theater on Muranowska Place.[66]

Amateur productions of this kind produced talent that nourished the few professional troupes that crystalized in the Russian Empire beginning as early as the 1890s. Yitskhak Viernik (b. 1886), the son of a petty trader who grew up going to *kheyder* and private tutors, began his theater career playing prima donna roles with other actors, all of whom would eventually have successful stage careers. They started their careers performing in private homes for various celebrations. The repertoire consisted of [Goldfaden's] *Kabtsenson et Hungerman* (also known as *The Picky Daughter*, discussed in chap. 5) and Shomer's [Shaikevitsh] *Der Treyfniak*.[67] Eventually Viernik went on to play with the theater troupe of the legendary Yiddish actress, Ester-Rokhl Kaminska (1870–1925), one of only a handful of other pioneers of literary Yiddish theater who relied on shtetl venues because of the obstacles in putting on Yiddish theater in cities. In much of eastern Europe, this state of affairs lasted until 1905 when new freedoms following the October Revolution represented a turning point for Yiddish theater in the empire.[68]

Such groups pushed the "Goldfaden brand" into shtetls that would never have seen a troupe of Goldfaden's caliber perform.[69] Others fashioned Goldfaden's work into cabaret sets. Herman Vaynberg (b. 1863), a seventeen-year-old entertainer in Lemberg, absorbed a version of Goldfaden's *Shmendrik* into his routine. Vaynberg was a descendant of the Vibranavker Tsadik but was born to a modern family and, as a child, sang in Cantor Bachman's choir in Lemberg's progressive synagogue, the Tempel. Over subsequent years, Vaynberg played pared down renditions of other Goldfaden works in taverns including the role of Shulamis in an all-male rendition of *Shulamis* in Adolf Lipshits's tavern.[70] Bernardo Vaysman, born in Bucharest in 1873, put on Yiddish theater in Siberia, Egypt, and Turkey before he settled in Argentina. Rosa Vaksman Kelnavits was born in 1874 to well-to-do parents in Galicia. After marrying Leon Mandeltort, they moved to America and opened a theater on Grand Street (in the Lower East Side) and reportedly put on Goldfaden repertoire for six years.

The rise of such semiprofessional and makeshift groups brings to light Goldfaden's oeuvre as it crystallized into the most enduring and popular examples of secular Yiddish culture. His operettas and songs developed a mass appeal, only after and also because of their beginnings in more rarefied cultural circles. His oeuvre had an irresistibility about it and a protean nature. Moving through communities orally, it underwent a folklorizing process—a more diffuse popularization via references and excerpts of Goldfaden's works—that has previously only been associated with his songs. But like his songs, the operettas in which so many of his songs were embedded were pliable enough to please a range of actors and audiences. The acts, songs, and idioms in Goldfaden's operettas nourished a cultural intimacy with consumers and became part of the language of the Jewish eastern European experience. As if corroborating his claims to reach masses of unenlightened Jews, his work shifted away from the bourgeois urban framework that prevailed from 1876 to 1883 toward the small-scale shtetl performances that popularized his works.

Goldfaden from Low to High

In 1933, Itsik Manger (1901–1969) reviewed the latest theatrical production of Michał Weichert (1890–1967), one of the most prominent participants in Poland's thriving avant-garde Yiddish theater scene, a world rich with intellectual and theatrical talent.[71] Weichert grew up in Stanislawów (Ivano-Frankivs'k, eastern Galicia) and began his education in *heder*, but as a child moved to the Polish school system. Eventually, he attended law and humanities programs at universities in Lwów, Vienna (receiving his JD in 1916) and Berlin. In Berlin, he studied theater with the preeminent German theater director, Max Reinhardt, before settling in Warsaw to establish his theater and dramatic studio. Among the works Weichert composed for the stage and to which he applied the full arsenal of his avant-garde theatrical techniques was *Trupe Tanentsap* (*Tanentsap Troupe*), a theatrical reimagining of Goldfaden's *The Two Kuni-Lemls*. Manger's review marked the fiftieth performance of the show that would play for 120 nights in Warsaw before Weichert went on tour in and beyond Poland.[72] The discovery of Goldfaden's work by the Yiddish avant-garde signaled a new chapter in his legacy.

While he was still alive, from around 1890 to his death in 1908, Goldfaden could only observe the successful cultivation of the institution he founded by composers and playwrights who shut him out or defined themselves against his work. In America, while Joseph Lateiner and Professor Hurvits dominated the commercial Yiddish theater with a steadfast commitment to musical pageantry, Y. L. Gordin and Sholem Aleichem composed dramas as opposed to operettas and achieved a new level of realism and psychological depth for the Yiddish stage. Y. L. Peretz also modeled a literary theater that he defined in contrast to what he saw as the light and self-denigrating fare of Goldfaden. He introduced symbolism to the Yiddish theater in works like *By Night at the Old Marketplace*, and Peretz and his protégés Dovid Pinski, Sholem Asch (with works like *God of Vengeance*), and S. Y. Ansky (with *The Dybbuk*) raised the artistic heights of the Yiddish theater during the first decades of the twentieth century. None of these men, reluctant heirs of Goldfaden's theater, might have predicted his work would enter the inner sanctum of literary theater that they shaped. As if in response to their contempt of Goldfaden, however, Manger wrote in his review of Weichert's play: "The return to [Goldfaden] has happened. The indication of a renaissance is a fact of history, this development of the Yiddish theater is so tangible one can reach out and touch it with one's hand."[73]

Weichert's 1933 *Tanentsap Troupe* was only one of a number of milestones that led to the canonization of Goldfaden's work as folk culture that began in the 1920s and was pursuant of the avant-garde's return to the primitive and folk culture. *The Sorceress* was the subject of a legendary avant-garde interpretation by the Moscow State Yiddish Theater (GOSET) and was staged in celebrated performances by Maurice Schwartz's (1889–1960) Art Theater in New York City with costumes designed by Zuni Maud and Yosl Kotler.[74] Manger himself authored a separate adaptation called *Hotsmakh shpil*.[75] This production based on Goldfaden's *The Sorceress* was staged in Cracow.[76] In Poland, Zygmunt Turkov (1896–1970) absorbed *The Two Kuni-Lemls* into the repertoire of the Warsaw Yiddish Art Theatre or VYKT (Varshever Yidisher Kunst Teater) in 1924 with the goal of reframing Goldfaden's parochial subject matter with contemporary European stagecraft.[77] He created a production that one reviewer approvingly called a "grotesque reconceptualization" of the play. In the same year, director of the New York Art Theater, Maurice Schwartz, modernized the operetta, as did the State Jewish Theater in Ukraine.[78]

In his reimagining of Goldfaden's *The Two Kuni-Lemls*, Weichert embeds the play in a play that depicts Rudolf Tanentsap, a small-time impresario of Yiddish theater, arriving in a small Galician shtetl with his troupe of actors and renting a barn for the use of his Yiddish spectacle. The play is meant to take place in the 1890s as it refers to the reign of Nicholas II. The audience of Weichert's play, then, watches the play from the point of view of the shtetl residents. As one reviewer wrote, "And everyone, everyone . . . sits alongside us, and watches together with us, . . . and together we react—each from his or her own point of view—to what takes place before our eyes." The reviewer praises the authenticity of the barn, the fiddle player, and "the wild primitivity (*primitivkayt*)" of the show that brings the early days of the theater to life.[79] The portrayal of a troupe staging a Goldfaden play amid authentic shtetl types dovetailed with Weichert's left-wing radical politics and the avant-garde's return to the primitive. It fortified the notion of Goldfaden as a vehicle of vernacular folk culture to emphasize its own avant-garde intervention. It returned Goldfaden's work—which had earlier shifted from city theaters into shtetls following the ban—back to the city.

Notes

1. Goldfaden dates it to September 14. See Klier's authoritative work on the ban. "'Exit, Pursued by a Bear': Russian Administrators and the Ban on Yiddish Theatre in Imperial Russia," *Yiddish Theatre: New Approaches* (Oxford: The Littman Library of Jewish Civilization, 2003), 159–174.

2. A. Goldfaden, "Goldfaden's kurtse oytobiografye," *Goldfaden-Bukh*, ed. Jacob Shatzky (New York: Idisher Teater Muzey, 1926), 42.

3. For positive reviews of their performances in Bucharest translated from the Romanian-language press (1885) into Yiddish, see Shas Roman, "Retsenzyes vegn yidishn teater in rumenye," *Hundert yor Goldfadn*, ed. Jacob Shatzky (New York: YIVO, 1940), 43–63.

4. A. Fishzon, "50 yor idish teater," *Morgn zhurnal*, April 24, 1925, 6.

5. E. Binevich, *Istoriia evreiskogo teatra v rossii, 1876–1883. Annoturoviannaia bibliografia* (Moscow: Obshchestvo evreiskoe nasledie, 1997).

6. His theatrical endeavors do not register in the press during the theater's first era. Even though he was involved in Yiddish performance for a long period, Fishzon could never cement a relationship with Goldfaden or command an important venue during this era. He does not figure among the ten impresarios and directors referenced by the press during this first period; most likely his company had a far lower profile and moved from shtetl to shtetl as opposed to bigger cities. See E. Binevich, *Istoriia evreiskogo teatra v rossii, 1876–1883*, n.p.

7. Fishzon, "50 yor idish teater," 6.

8. His and, even more so, the memoirs of his wife and fellow actor, Khina Braginskaia-Fishzon, document the many ways their Yiddish theater productions were regularly scuttled by antagonistic government officials. I recently discovered clippings of the published memoirs of Braginskaia-Fishzon's memoirs at YIVO in RG8. They were published in installments in pages of the New York newspaper *Der Tog* beginning in February 24, 1934, until March 29, 1934.

9. Klier does cite two later examples of Yiddish theater in Odessa, one in 1890 and another in 1899 where a "run" was halted by Odessa's police chief. How to reconcile Klier's claim that there were "a substantial number" of episodes of post-1883 Yiddish theater, on the one hand, and the bleak portrayal of the ban in Yiddish theater–related memoirs on the other? While Klier's research indicates brief runs (but mostly one-night spells) of Yiddish theater after 1883 in cities like Minsk, Vitebsk, Vilna, Grodno, and Kovno, almost none were produced in Odessa, Moscow, Rostov-on-Don, and Nikolaev.

10. This does not mean that the ban was anti-Semitic or political. In fact, Klier's characterization of the ban as "offhand" is persuasive, though the government's indifference to the

cultural efforts of its Jewish constituents was, arguably anti-Semitic—especially as it coincided with the freedom finally given to non-Yiddish theatrical entrepreneurs. Klier's research dismisses a couple of distracting and paranoid theories that circulated about the ban. There is no evidence that the ban, for instance, was the result of pressure by Goldfaden's enemies, as Finkel and Oyslender contend, by the moneyed aristocracy and the Orthodox Jewish establishment. Gorin advanced two theories: that the cutthroat competition among the Yiddish theater troupes precipitated the ban or that it was the work of Goldfaden's chief competitor, the apostate Lerner. For the full list of theories, see Zalmen Zylbercweig, *Avrom Goldfaden un Zigmunt Mogulesko* (Buenos Aires: Elisheva, 1936), 93–94.

11. This is my personal count based on Zylbercweig's lexicon biographies. I have included anyone who played in the Yiddish theater in the Russian Empire and left before the year 1888.

12. N. Shaikevitsh, "Dos teater," *Menshenfraynd*, no. 11 (1891): n.p.

13. Dovid Kessler, "Goldfaden, Lerner, Shaykevitsh," *Der Tog*, January 21, 1917.

14. "Soobscheniia Poseshchenií 'Koldunye' Tommaso Salvini, Chast neofitsialnaia," *Vedomosti Odesskogo Gradonachalstva*, January, 18, 1880, 3. Quoted in A. Gurshteyn's "Tsu der tsenisher geshikhte fun dem kishefmakherin," *Literarishe bleter* 95 (1926): 159.

15. In his autobiography, Salvini does not mention Yiddish actors per se but does refer to the "the festive greeting from [Odessa's] heterogeneous population." See Tommaso Salvini, *Leaves from the Autobiography of Tommaso Salvini* (London: T. Fisher, 1893), 195.

16. *Vedomosti Odesskogo Gradonachal'stva*, January 18, 1880.

17. In the last half of the nineteenth century, *Novoe Vremya* evolved from being an "influentially liberal orientated one to an officious one." See "Newspapers," *Saint Petersburg Encyclopedia*, April 15, 2015, http://www.encspb.ru.

18. For more on Suvorin, see Effie Ambler, *The Career of Aleksei S. Suvorin, Russian Journalism and Politics, 1861–1881* (Detroit: Wayne State University Press, 1972).

19. Quoted by Z. Zilbercweig, *Leksikon fun Yidishn teater* (New York: Elisheva, 1931). He includes a facsimile of the letter in *Leksikon*, VI: 5309.

20. While Kozel'skii eventually moved to St. Petersburg, it is remarkable that he was born in Zhitomir and apparently began his acting with the "N.N. Diukov Kharkov troupe" in 1873 and 1874 and began touring Russian cities in 1875.

21. "Anons zavtraschenie premyera 'Urielia Akosta' K. Gutzkova v per. O. Lernera," *Odesskii Listok Obiavlenie*, November 16, 1880, 2; "Zametke Urielia Akosta," reviews also appeared in *Vedomosti Odesskogo Gradonaschaltsva*, November 19, 1880, 2 and *Odesski Vestnik* November 21, 1880, 3.

22. H. Amasya, "Zikhroynes." *Yidish teater.* vol. 2. Warsaw: 1927, 204–205.

23. Miloslavsky's troupe played the Odessa Russian Theater, originally called Velikanov Theater after its initiator, the businessman A. C. Velikanov, who built the theater in 1874. On Miloslavsky, see Richard Stites, *Serfdom, Society, and the Arts in Imperial Russia* (New Haven, CT: Yale University Press, 2005), 254.

24. Ibid., 86, n. 2. Anecdotal evidence, perhaps, of the relative success Goldfaden was having compared to Miloslavsky. See Zylbercweig, *Leksikon*, II: 1302. Y. Nusyinov, "Di ershte bagegenishn fun der yidisher prese mitn teater," *Literarishe bleter* 95 (1926): 85–86, especially, 86, n. 2.

25. Zylbercweig barely mentions Mayerson in his encyclopedia and so even basic information on the actor and impresario's career awaits documentation. See the biographical information provided in a program for a jubilee celebration of his career produced in Kiev in 1926. RG 8; box 55; no folder; YIVO Institute for Jewish Research.

26. The theater mostly hosted touring opera companies at this time and was called the "Bouffe" at one point. Apparently it only became a legendary and prestigious theater when Solodovnikov opened a massive theater (with three thousand seats, by some reports) on the site of the much more modest theater after 1883. Advertisements for a number of Yiddish performances in *Sufler*, however, refer to them taking place in "Teatr Solodnikova." See, for instance, a performance of *Zhidovka* on May 8, 1883, in Binevich's bibliography. A similar discrepancy applies to a performance of *Rashi* that an advertisement in *Moskovskii Dnevnik Zrelishch i Obiavlenii* claims will take place in "Pushkinskii Teatr." Apparently, the original Pushkin Theater Company failed by 1882, although many of its actors formed a new troupe under Fyodor Adamovich Korsch, a pioneer of prerevolutionary theater, who might have occupied the same theater venue and who might have lent his venue to Gartenshteyn's troupe. See "Korsch" in Laurence Senelick, *Historical Dictionary of Russian Theater* (Lanham, MD: Scarecrow Press, 2007). See E. Binevich, "Evreiskaia Dramatuchskaia i Operetochnaia Truppa Y. Gartenshteyna. Moskva. 1883," n.p. On Gartenshteyn, see metion of him earlier in this chapter.

27. "Soobshcheniie ob uspeshni gastrolyakh truppie v moskve," *Sufler* 63/21 (1880): 3. Quoted in Y. Riminik, "Di ershte finf yor yidisher teater in odes, "*Di royte velt* 12 (1927): 33.

28. See *Sufler*, August 10, 1880; *The Prompter* also ran announcements and a review of the work of Yakov Gartenshteyn (n.d.) or Hartenshteyn. A discrepancy applies to a performance of *Rashi* that an advertisement in *Moskovskii Dnevnik Zrelishch i Obiavlenii* claims will take place in "Pushkinskii Teatr." See Binevich, "Evreiskaia Dramatuchskaia i Operetochnaia Truppa Y. Gartenshteyna. Moskva. 1883," n.p.

29. *Russki Vedomosti*, 1880, 213.

30. A. Fishzon, "50 yor idish teater," *Morgn zhurnal*, May 1, 1925, 6.

31. For a positive review, see J. Shatzky, "Goldfadn in varshe," *Hundert yor Goldfaden*, ed. Jacob Shatzky (New York: YIVO, 1940), 10.

32. Ibid., 9. A year later, *The Sorceress* was translated into Polish (*Czarownica*) and performed by Polish actors. See a positive review of the performance in A. R. Malachi, "Goldfadn-materialn," *Hundert yor Goldfaden*, 74–75.

33. See a positive review of the performance in A. R. Malachi, "Goldfadn-materialn," 74–75.

34. See B. Gorin, *Di geshikhte fun yidishn teater: tsvey toyznt yor yidish teater* [The History of the Yiddish Theater], 2 vols. (New York: Max N. Mayzel, 1923), 241 and J. Shatzky, "Goldfaden in Varshe," *Hundert yor Goldfaden*, 6–7.

35. A. Fishzon, "50 yor idish teater," *Morgn zhurnal*, May 1, 1925, 6.

36. See, for instance, Gershom Bader's edited volume, *Yidisher folks-kalendar: firter yorgang* (Lemberg: 1898/9), where Bader laments the paucity of published Yiddish literature during the previous decade. The only works that have been recently published are "Goldfaden's teater shtik. . . ." The ellipsis seems to imply that it is of dubious benefit to the growth of Yiddish culture. Bader published an article about his meeting with Goldfaden in 1900 and confesses how much he regrets criticizing his work. "Avrom Goldfaden's verk zaynen ufgefirt gevorn in opera heyzer ober er aleyn hot keyn notn nit gekent," n.p. n.d. in RG8 Box "Leon Kobrin."

37. An early publication of the play (one of the only works of Goldfaden published during this first period) shows significant changes between it and the one Dinezon edited and published in the late 1880s. See *Shmendrik, Shmendrik: komedye in dray aktn mit gezang in tentse farfast fun A. Goldfaden* (Odessa: 1879). The title page indicates Isaac Librescu (mentioned in

chap. 1) in Iaşi and Goldfaden's father-in-law Mordechai Verbel in Odessa as the publishers. It also has a cover drawn by Adolphe Verbel, Mordechai's son. The personae page announces that anyone who wishes to acquire the music may send a self-addressed envelope to Verbel at the cost of one ruble.

38. Shatzky, "Goldfadn in Varshe," 16.

39. Quoted in Malachi, "Goldfadn-materialn," 74.

40. See Nina Warnke, "The Child Who Wouldn't Grow Up" in *Yiddish Theatre: New Approaches*, ed. Joel Berkowitz (Oxford: Littman Library of Jewish Civilization, 2003), 205. For conflicting versions of what transpired between Goldfaden and the American Yiddish actors, see Zylbercweig, *Avrom Goldfadn un Zigmunt Mogulesco*, 101–108.

41. See Kessler's description of the pre-union "unions" or pacts the actors entered into with one another in order to freeze out Goldfaden from the Yiddish theater world. D. Kessler, "Goldfaden, Lerner, Shaykevitsh," *Der Tog*, February 4, 1917. Also see Zylbercweig, *Leksikon*, I: 314–315. For more on the Yiddish Actors Union, see the exhibition catalogue, E. Nahshon and K. Fisher, *Stars, Strikes and the Yiddish Stage* (New York: YIVO Institute for Jewish Research, 2009).

42. The first issue of the newspaper appeared October 22, 1887. Seventeen issues were published. Malachi, "Goldfadn-materialn," 75–77.

43. The poster announcing Goldfaden's dramatic school reads, "To learn mimic and declamations 3$/month or 4 ladies 1.50 per person per month. For every ten students one poor student will be included gratis." See "Goldfadens a statut far a yidisher dramatisher shul in nyu-york, in 1888," *Arkhiv far der geshikhte fun yidishn teater un drame* (Vilna/NY: YIVO, 1930), 287.

44. The school was taken over first by the well-known Yiddish actors Faynman and Karp and then by Jacob Gordin. For an announcement of the school's opening and a list of actors who graduated, see Zylbercweig, *Leksikon*, I: 318.

45. Berta Kalich, "Mayn lebn," *Der tog* (March 7–November 14, 1925).

46. L. Krishtol, "Avrom Goldfaden mit 35 yor tsurik: loyt a geshprekh mit dem shoyshpiler Kalmen Yoylvelir," *Goldfaden Bukh*, 34. Yoylvelir explains that while Goldfaden was shut out by the theater community in New York, he found audiences in European cities like Czernowitz.

47. For more on Goldfaden's works performed in Lemberg (not under Goldfaden's direction), see M. Balaban, "Reminiscences of Goldfaden and of the Jewish Theater in Lemberg" (Yiddish), in *Hundert yor Goldfaden*, 17–22. For a discussion of *Messianic Times*, see Donny Inbar, "A Closeted Jester: Abraham Goldfaden Between Haskalah Ideology and Jewish Show Business," PhD Diss. 2007, 183–187. Goldfaden also produced an operetta called "Rothschild" for which he collaborated on the music with Moritz Fall (father of the composer Leo Fall, 1848–1922).

48. Quoted in Zylbercweig, *Leksikon*, I: 323.

49. See the article by Yaakov Kirshenbaum in *Der Shpigl*, RG; box labeled "Leon Kobrin," no folder.

50. Ben Yehuda advertised it during subsequent Purim seasons. Later it was included among reading materials published for the Israel Defense Force from 1929 to 1950. The director Nakhmen Zibel staged another Hebrew translation of the operetta in Tel Aviv in 1927. After the establishment of the state, a Hebrew stage production of the operetta ran about four hundred times and was made into a musical motion picture in 1966 in Israel. It spawned two popular sequels: *Kuni-leml be-tel aviv* (*Kuni-Leml in Tel Aviv*, 1976) and *Kuni-Leml be kahir* (*Kuni-Leml in Cairo*, 1983). Donny Inbar, "No Raisins and Almonds in the Land of Israel," in

Inventing the Modern Yiddish Stage, ed. Joel Berkowitz and Barbara Henry (Detroit: Wayne State University Press, 2012), 296. About other productions mentioned here, see Zylbercweig, *Leksikon*, I: 304–305. The Israeli government also issued a postage stamp featuring an illustration of *The Two Kuni-Lemls*.

51. See Z. Shaykovski, "Goldfaden in Pariz," *Hundert yor Goldfaden*, 32–33. Goldfaden also befriended Austro-Hungarian architect Oscar Marmorek (1863–1909) who, along with Theodore Herzl and Max Nordau, was an organizer of the Fourth World Zionist Congress. Goldfaden went as a delegate via Bekhorey Zion (a breakaway Zionist group) and used it to raise money for himself and gain access to British Jewish high society. Goldfaden was not consistently taken seriously. For more on Goldfaden's Zionist activities, see *Hundert yor Goldfaden*, 33–35.

52. In a letter to his friend Dubinski, Goldfaden claims to have discovered Rosenfeld's talent before Rosenfeld earned his broader acclaim. See RG 219; folder 61, YIVO Institute of Jewish Research.

53. Goldfaden published this play in 1880.

54. J. Shatzky, "Briv fun Avrom Goldfaden mit a hakdome un derklerungn fun Dr. Yankev Shatzky," *Hundert yor Goldfaden*, 133.

55. Quoted in Zylbercweig, *Leksikon*, I: 332.

56. *Ben-Ami* was never published. "Ben Ami, oder der zun fun zany folk," ms. New York. 1906. Abraham Goldfaden Collection RG 219, folder 42. See two chapters devoted to this play in Bores Thomashefski, *Thomashefski's theater shriften* (New York: Lipshits Press, 1908); "Ben-Ami's shikzal" and "Ale lider fun Ben Ami," n.p. This work refers to another work in the following footnote in Thomashefski's book in English: "The words and music of Ben Ami for piano and violin for sale by J. Katznellenbogen, 66 Canal Street, N.Y."

57. Adler recounts that, for a time, his troupe traveled by wagon and played improvisational spaces in market towns: "After a short journey through the smaller shtetls we arrived in Kishinev. We played in Doctor Grossman's big theater, and the success there was indescribable." Adler also mentions by name the shtetl of Akkerman (now Belgorod-Dnestrovsky in Ukraine). J. Adler, "Mayn lebensbashraybung," *Der teater zhurnal*, October 1, 1901, 12. Another Goldfaden troupe is mentioned in a letter published in *The Russian Jew* penned by local Jewish resident of the Bessarabian town of Ataki (now Otaci) that attracted a steady stream of spectators from Mohilev-Podilski, across the Dniester, where Yiddish theater was prohibited by the local government. X. Shor, "Ataki Bes. Gub. Korrespondentstia Russkovo Evreia," *Russki Evrei*, no. 41 (1882): 1535. Fishzon and Shaikevitsh both tried negotiating permission to stage Goldfaden's works in his native city of Berdichev. Both attempts fell apart. Fishzon reports in his memoirs that, instead of negotiating with Goldfaden, he bribed officials in the censor's office in St. Petersburg for authorized copies. He "borrowed" the office's full supply of Goldfaden's plays, copied them over a period of one day, returned them, and got the censor's seal for his new copies. With these, he fearlessly mounted Goldfaden's operettas without paying the author a royalty.

58. See Barbara Henry, "Jewish Plays on the Russian Stage: St. Petersburg, 1905–1917," *Yidish Theatre: New Approaches* (Oxford: The Littman Library of Jewish Civilization, 2003), 61–76.

59. Lerner produced works by Goldfaden in Odessa from 1882 to 1883; Gartenshteyn staged his works in Moscow in 1883. See E. Binevich, "Tovarishestvo evreisix artistov O. Lernera. Odessa. 1882/3" and "Evreiskaia dramatechkaia operetochnaia truppa Y. Gartenshteina. Moskva. 1883," n.p.

60. Soon after this success, Mogulescu worked under Joseph Yehuda Lerner. He was a journalist who had connections and so he was able to get permission from the authorities

that allowed Mogulescu to play all of Goldfaden's work. In Goldfaden's works, Mogulescu made a huge impression on the Odessa public. Zylbercweig, *Leksikon*, II: 1183–1184. For press coverage of productions under Mogulesco, see Binevich's "Truppa evreiskikh akterov pod regisserstvom Z. Mogulesco. Odessa. 1880." n.p. Binevich's bibliography that covers Mogulesco's productions in Odessa in 1880 suggests that Mogulesco did not produce Goldfaden works there.

61. Lateiner contends that Goldfaden's operetta *The Two Kuni-Lemls* became a hit while its source—his own version of this play—was not censored by the government and languished. See Zylbercweig, *Leksikon*, II: 966. Binevich comes across one production of *Di tsvey Shmuel Shmuelkes.*

62. According to references in the press, Lateiner composed and mounted the following: *Di tsvey Shmuel Shmuelkes, Der Dibek* (unrelated to Ansky's *Der Dibek*); *Di Libe fun Yerushalayim (Poylisher Davener)*. A native of Romania (not Russia), Lateiner might have lacked the necessary connections or resources to navigate Russian government offices. He and his troupe left early although, according to Zylbercweig, it was after the ban was circulated. His early arrival in New York solidified his dominance and success there. See Zylbercweig, *Leksikon*, II: 966–967.

63. In February 1879, *Odesski Vestnik* reported that Russian authorities shut down Lateiner's operetta, *The Two Shmuel Shmuelkes* (*Di tsvey Shmuel Shmuelkes*) because the censor was not given enough time to evaluate its content: "Khronika," *Odesskii Vestnik*, February 16, 1879, 2. This is Binevich's summary of the article. Binevich's bibliography also includes an advertisement for this show that appeared in *Odesskii Vestnik*, February 10, 1879, 2.

64. Goldfaden published his works with Boymritter and Gonshor in Warsaw rather than by an Odessa publisher. Manuscript copies of Goldfaden's works consulted for this book can be found at YIVO, Columbia University, and the New York Public Library.

65. The troupe consisted of the actors Aharon Tager (the director), Kafka-Dubinski, Shmuelik, among others.

66. Zylbercwig, *Leksikon*, I: 196.

67. He performed with future actors such as Moyshe Zilberkastn, Menashe Skulnik, Dovid Kayzerovitsh, Sh. Z. Shidlover, Yablonski, and Dovid Greenshtayn. Zylbercweig, *Leksikon*, I: 727.

68. See Nina Warnke's important article on this period, "Going East: The Impact of American Yiddish Plays and Players on the Yiddish Stage in Czarist Russia, 1890–1914," *American Jewish History* no.1 (2004), 2–29.

69. The United States was also hospitable to renditions of Goldfaden's operettas, especially after his death in 1908. On the theater in New York City, see Judith Thissen, "Reconsidering the Decline of the New York Yiddish Theatre in the 1900s," *Theater Survey* 02 (November 2003): 173–197. Three theaters, together seating 9,000, sold over 2.5 million tickets during the 1900–1901 season when almost 300,000 eastern European Jews lived in New York. With time, Yiddish theatrical culture gave way to other places of entertainment, like nickelodeons and music halls, and Yiddish gave way to English.

70. Zylbercweig, *Leksikon*, I: 681.

71. "A propo a Goldfaden-shpil: tsu der 50-ter ufirung fun Trupe Tanentsap," *Der moment*, no. 263, November 17, 1933, n.p. *Trupe tansentsap* (Tel-Aviv: Menorah, 1966). For more on Weichert's fascinating life in the Yiddish theater, his experiences during the war in Warsaw, and his career as a critic, see Shmuel Niger and Jacob Shatzky. *Leksikon fun der nayer yidisher literatur, III.* 8 vols. (New York: Alveltlekhn yidishn kultur-kongres, faraynikt mit

Tsiko. Published by the World Congress for Jewish Culture, combined with CYCO [Central Yiddish Cultural Organization], 1856–1881), 344–345, and his memoirs, *Zikhroynes* (Tel-Aviv: Menorah, 1960–1970).

72. See an article entitled "Teater un Muzik," YIVO Institute for Jewish Research RG8. Box 58. Folder B. "Avrom goldfadn's teatrale misye," *Literarishe bleter* 95 (1926): 134–135.

73. "A Propo a Goldfaden-shpil," n.p.

74. Jeffrey Veidlinger, *The Moscow State Yiddish Theater: Jewish Culture on the Soviet Stage* (Bloomington: Indiana University Press, 2003).

75. For a discussion of Manger's production, see Mirosława Bułat, "Goldfaden and Cracow's Jewish Theatres," in *Yiddish Theatre: New Approaches* (Oxford: The Littman Library of Jewish Civilization, 2003), 147–149. For a program of the Maurice Schwartz performance, see the New York Public Library, *Di kishefmakherin* (*Koldunye*) program (New York: Yiddish Art Theater, 1925).

76. The stage history of *The Sorceress* is long and fascinating. The YIVO Institute for Jewish Research has photographs of an elaborate production of *The Sorceress* that was staged in 1942 by the Yiddish Art Union in Cairo, for instance, and in 1998 *The Sorceress* was put on in Italian translation at Trieste's Teatro Miela. Paolo Bertolone, "Goldfaden's *Kishefmakherin* and Operetta," in *Yiddish Theatre: New Approaches* (Oxford: The Littman Library of Jewish Civilization, 2003), 77–86. It was also produced in Israel in 1992. For a program and Hebrew version of the play, see "Ha-mekhashefa," *Yidishpil: teatron ha-yidish be-yisrael*, 1992, at the National Library of Israel.

77. See Mirosława M. Bułat, "'Cosmopolitan' or 'Purely Jewish,'" in *Inventing the Modern Yiddish Stage*, ed. J. Berkowitz and B. Henry (Detroit: Wayne State University Press, 2012), 117.

78. See N. Bukhvald, "Goldfadns a shpil modernizirt," *Di Frayhayt*, February 1, 1924, 5.

79. *On the Path* (*Ba-derekh*) RG8; Box 39; no folder. The YIVO Institute of Jewish Research.

Afterword

Modern Yiddish Theater and the Extravernacular

I OFFER A CONCLUSION by way of two thoughts that set my subject of Goldfaden and the modern Yiddish theater against a broader historical canvas. First, it occurs to me that the absence of both self-reckoning and crucial historical detail in Goldfaden's copious memoirs, coupled with (at times) his hysterical tenor, points us to a larger paradigm of the Jewish experience in the late-nineteenth-century Russian empire. As I describe in chapter 1, Goldfaden's resentment toward his fellow theater pioneers and his defensiveness about his comedies distorted his memory, so much so that he could not generate a coherent record of his triumphant experience in Russia. It is rather obvious to me now that another trauma clouded Goldfaden's backward glance of his achievements in Russia: Russia herself. For so long, Goldfaden had felt to be one of Russia's golden children: a beneficiary, first of an elite government-subsidized school and then of the government's decision to grant him the permission to stage his plays, something denied many theater entrepreneurs who had come before him. As he himself put it in one of his memoirs, all he needed to do was take a train to St. Petersburg to speak to the right official and his wish was granted. Even in 1881, as so many of his Jewish colleagues reformulated their political positions and opened themselves to political Zionism in the wake of the pogroms, Goldfaden remained wholly invested in the Russian-Jewish cultural project. The bounty Goldfaden had received made the ban against the Yiddish theater all the more devastating. Put in terms of Kenneth Moss's recent historiographical survey, the theater's rapid rise (1878–1883) bespeaks the freedom and positive cultural contact between Russian Jews and gentiles that is in accordance with the new wave of Russian Jewish historiography that deemphasizes Jewish cultural separateness. Its subsequent shuttering, however, bespeaks the muzzling of Jewish culture that we are familiar with from more traditional scholarship on the Russian-Jewish experience.[1] On the more personal psychological level of his memoirs, Goldfaden could not bring himself to write about Russia's temporary embrace of his theater because he could not stand to recall the government's unfeeling rejection of it.

Last, I offer a final lens I term the "extravernacular" to the question of Yiddish language that returns my discussion of the theater's rise to the greater picture of the emergence of modern Yiddish culture in the Russian Empire. This is distinct from vernacular culture that refers, for instance, to a Yiddish play intended for an audience that speaks only or mostly Yiddish. It is also distinct from the postvernacular. As scholar Jeffrey Shandler has shown, the postvernacular describes Yiddish language as it amassed symbolic meaning in the lives of people who learn to speak Yiddish as a second language.[2] Extravernacular describes the Yiddish operettas of Goldfaden's day, composed and produced by multilingual authors (fluent in Yiddish and other languages) and intended for a linguistically variegated audience. This audience included Yiddish-speakers alongside consumers who had a less-than-fluent grasp of Yiddish as well as Jews and non-Jews who knew no Yiddish at all. Extravernacular Yiddish operetta characterizes almost all of the Yiddish theater that played in the Russian Empire during this first period. The theater would not have survived without the constant support of the multilingual urban-based Jewish bourgeoisie that could afford relatively high ticket prices.

The category of the extravernacular puts in sharp relief an audience of modern Yiddish culture, including its literature, that we don't intuitively consider: those readers fluent in other language but who, nonetheless, sought out Yiddish culture no matter how much they knew the language. This applies, for instance, to Isaac Loewy (referred to in the introduction of this book) or Jacob Adler, both of whom knew Yiddish as their mother tongue alongside other languages they acquired in their youth. The category of extravernacular applies to those Jews and non-Jews who did not know any Yiddish, but whose presence in the theater raised the prestige of the shows and even changed their meaning (chap. 3). More so than many other languages, Yiddish was always embedded in the context of other languages, and its authors, composers, and actors always intended their work for the consumption of those beyond all-Yiddish communities. As Adler writes tellingly about his experience as a recognized celebrity on the street, "They pointed at us and called out '*Evreiski Aktyori*'" (Jewish actors). Many of Adler's fans spoke Russian on the street—that is, not Yiddish. Finally, it applies to Goldfaden, a native Yiddish speaker, to be sure, but one who prided himself on his fluency in a multitude of cultures and languages.

The profile of the Yiddish theater's audience changed significantly when it was reconstituted in the United States where it evolved to have a more vernacular sensibility. At the turn-of-the-century, American Yiddish theatergoers had less money and were less educated than Goldfaden's first audiences in Russia. New York's "enormous gallery-houses turned Yiddish theater into mass entertainment, accessible to a large percentage of poor, disenfranchised immigrants who previously were rarely able to attend a performance."[3] Many of them had come to the United States from shtetls while theater had been part of the cultural diet of Russia's first urban-bound theatergoers, Jewish or other. During its peak, few English-speaking Americans ever bothered to visit the Yiddish theater except to visit one of the city's exotic ethnic communities. In contrast, Yiddish theater claimed a place in Russian theatrical life under Goldfaden (1878–1883), episodically following the slackening of prohibitions against Yiddish theater in 1905, and, again, after the revolution with the establishment of state theaters like GOSET (1920–1949). The apex of its sophistication was felt most intensely in Poland between the two world wars, another moment in the life of the modern Yiddish theater that saw a surge in its extravernacular life.

Relatedly, the rise of the modern Yiddish theater suggests that the movement of culture between vernacular and extravernacular realms (as discussed in chap. 6) nourish a given culture's vitality. Notwithstanding the legal restrictions placed on it by governments and its ever-dwindling native-speaking audience base, the Yiddish theater continually found new footing as it traveled from middlebrow to low to high. Its lack of political borders required Yiddish to rely more heavily on the attention of audiences beyond its most immediate community of Yiddish speakers to sustain and cultivate its native riches. In his memoirs, Goldfaden lamented ushering a new cultural institution into the world only to see it take on new forms of expression beyond his control. And yet, by all accounts, the Yiddish theater's innate thirst for its given cultural landscape was its lifeblood.

Notes

1. Kenneth Moss, "At Home in Late Imperial Russian Modernity—Except When They Weren't: New Histories of Russian and East European Jews, 1881–1914," *The Journal of Modern History* 84 (June 2012): 401–452.
2. Jeffrey Shandler, *Adventures in Yiddishland: Postvernacular Language and Culture* (Berkeley: University of California Press, 2006).
3. Judith Thissen, "Reconsidering the Decline of the New York Yiddish Theatre in the Early 1900s," *Theatre Survey* 2 (November 2003): 189.

Appendix I
Synopses of Goldfaden's Operettas

The Sorceress

The Sorceress is kind of Jewish Cinderella story that features a villain named Grandma Yakhne, an invocation of the Russian folk villain, Bubbe Yaga. It opens at the home of the wealthy city merchant Avromtshe (diminutive of Avrom, from the biblical name Abraham), who is hosting a birthday celebration for his only daughter Mirele. Avromtshe has recently married a second wife, Basye, following the death of Mirele's beloved mother. Only interested in his money and in collusion with friends, Basye secretly frames Avromtshe, who is arrested by the end of the first act. As Avromtshe languishes in jail, Mirele is reduced to a servant in her stepmother's home. Impatient to get rid of Mirele for good, Basye enlists the help of the local sorceress, or fortune-teller, Bobe Yakhne, who kidnaps Mirele and sells her as an indentured servant to a Turkish merchant. A crook beneath her grandmotherly name and demeanor, Bobe Yakhne pretends to function as the spiritual leader of her community. Even Marcus, desperate to find his beloved Mirele after she has mysteriously disappeared, consults Bobe Yakhne, but to no avail. Hotsmakh, a poor traveling haberdasher and folk singer, also visits Bobe Yakhne, but only because he suspects (rightly) that she has put Mirele in danger. Hotsmakh, the only observant and visually identifiable Jew on the stage, is friends with Marcus, notwithstanding the difference of education and class between them. Marcus and Hotsmakh rescue Mirele and together they meet her father, who has been recently released from his unjust imprisonment. Bobe Yakhne, Basye, and the other villains are dead by the end of the operetta. (A complete translation of this libretto is in Appendix II.)

The Two Kuni-Lemls

The Fanatic or the Two Kuni-Lemls begins with two concurrent celebrations, both in the city of Odessa. At the home of the wealthy merchant Pinkhes, a new devotee to Hasidism, a spiritual Hasidic sing-along is attended by Hasidic friends. In a public park, young university students sing happily about the completion of their exams. Pinkhes's wife Rivka is happy when her husband's guests leave; she has little love for her husband's newfound Hasidic devotion. Recently, Pinkhes has fired Max, the tutor of his daughter Carolina, who instructed her in secular subjects. As he explains to his wife, he has made a plan with Kalmen the Matchmaker for Carolina to marry a young man named Kuni-Leml. Kuni-Leml has a stutter, has little intelligence, and limps, but he is of fine Hasidic lineage. Carolina overhears this plan and relays it to Max, whom she meets in the park. Max explains that he will disguise himself as Kuni-Leml and, so disguised, will convince Pinkhes that he should be Carolina's groom. While Max is executing his plan in Pinkhes's home, he encounters Kuni-Leml. Max manages to convince Kuni-Leml that he is not who he says he is . . . or plants enough doubt in his mind so as to force him to return to the matchmaker's house to get written confirmation of his identity. Meanwhile, Max goes on to convince Pinkhes that, as Kuni-Leml, he is also a "lamed-vavnik," a mythical figure in Hasidic lore who takes on the form of an ordinary person but who actually has magical powers. As such, Max "loses" his impediments and shows himself to be the perfect groom for Carolina: Hasidic and sound of body. In the end, when Kuni-Leml returns to the house and insists that he is the rightful Kuni-Leml, Sholem the prominent Hasidic sexton who is also stepfather to Kuni-Leml (and an uncle to Max) makes peace among the parties, convinces Pinkhes to allow Max to have Carolina for a bride, and negotiates the matchmaker's daughter as a bride for Kuni-Leml.

Bontsye the Wick-Layer or the Grandmother and the Granddaughter

This play portrays the pious Bontsye, a follower of the Sadegura rebbe, and her fraught relationship with her granddaughter Adele. Bontsye hired a tutor for Adele as a concession to modern times, but as Adele approaches marriageable age, she hires a matchmaker to find her a pious groom. Worried that Adele is losing her ties to Judaism, Bontsye tries to scare her with images of the hell visited on those who do not follow God's laws. Bontsye is a spiritual leader and, during the Days of Awe, she measures the graves for her community and makes candles from these wicks to be burned in repentance. Knowing that a match is imminent, Adele makes a plan with her tutor Ignats for them to run away together. Before they leave, Adele and Ignats read German poetry and confess their love to each other. When Bontsye asks them to translate the words, they invent a Jewish translation. In the last scene, Bontsye lies dying comforted by a final vision of the Land of Israel and a vision of her granddaughter.

Doctor Almasada

The story of *Doctor Almasada, or the Jews of Palermo* (*Doktor Almasada oder di yidn fun Palermo*) unfolds in the fourteenth-century Sicilian city of Palermo, under the Crown of Aragon. The story moves between two main camps of characters. The first camp includes the governor of Palermo, Don Pedro, and his wife, Isabella, whose daughter Elvira is dying of a mysterious illness. The second group is the elderly Jewish Dr. Almasada and his daughter. At the start of the play, Palermo's Jews have been driven out of the city by royal decree. Alonso, Dr. Almasada's Christian apprentice, recognizes that only Dr. Almasada can heal Elvira, but Jews are forbidden from treating Christian patients. Dr. Almasada and Alonso collaborate to convince the governor that he should be allowed to bring Almasada's Jewish medical genius to bear on Elvira's grave situation. Elvira is saved and her restoration convinces the governor to influence the ruling tsar to repeal the anti-Jewish laws. Among the other plotlines of the play are a false accusation of murder followed by a stint in jail for Dr. Almasada, the exploits of a band of Christian robbers, and what appears to be a forbidden romance between Alonso and the doctor's Jewish daughter Miriam. Alonso is the doctor to the royal family and loyal to his teacher, Dr. Almasada. Toward the end of the operetta, Alonso reveals himself to be Jewish. Alonso and Almasada cure Elvira and the exile of the Jews from the city is repealed.

Shulamis

Avsholem, a prince of Second Temple Jerusalem and descendant of the Maccabees, meets and falls in love with Shulamis. Shulamis is a shepherdess from Bethlehem whom he meets among the sand dunes of the Judean desert and rescues from a deep, dried-up well. They fall in love and pledge an oath to marry as soon as Avsholem can reach her home of Bethlehem following the festival he must attend in Jerusalem. Once he returns to his familiar patterns at home, however, Avsholem does not travel to Bethlehem but lingers in Jerusalem. And when a mating game is initiated among his friends, he pursues a beautiful local woman, Avigail, and takes her to be his wife. Avsholem's competitive nature and Avigail's beauty have conspired to pull him inextricably in this unexpected direction. A change of heart or, perhaps, the blunt force of human forgetfulness puts his oath to Shulamis out of Avsholem's mind. Avsholem's life now moves forward with Avigail and soon two children are born, cementing his new marriage, pushing the oath deeper below the surface. Shulamis, on the other hand, in Bethlehem, does not forget. When Avsholem fails to come for her, Shulamis pretends to go mad in order to ward off suitors and preserve the oath. In act 3, Avsholem's children die accidental deaths—one involving a well and the other a bobcat—causing Avsholem to remember his vow. He parts with Avigail and seeks out Shulamis in Bethlehem. Shulamis and Avsholem marry in the operetta's final scene.

Appendix II
The Sorceress

The Sorceress[1]

Avraham Goldfaden

Act I	*Bild I*
	The spoiled celebration
Act II	*Bild II*
	The Sorceress makes a plan
	Bild III
	The Market in Botoşani
Act III	*Bild IV*
	The stepmother
	Bild V
	The spell
Act IV	*Bild VI*
	The coffeehouse in Istanbul
Act V	*Bild VII*
	A return trip
	Bild VII
	The tavern burns

One who wishes to obtain the work *The Sorceress* should turn to Torshoy in the printing shop Boymritter and Gonshor 16 Bielinski Street.

The

Sorceress

(Witch)

Operetta in 5 Acts and 8 Entrances/Exits

Composed by

Avrom Goldfadn

(The music, costumes, and decorations of the play were also staged by the writer.)

Brought to the publishing house in the hands of the publishers A. Boymritter and his spouse, G. Gonshor, and his partner, Mr. Aharon Kalovski, who bought the rights from the writer.

Warsaw

Published by Boymritter and his spouse, Gonshor, 16 Bielinski Street

1887

Characters

MR. AVROMTSHE (ABRAHAM)

A respectable Jewish merchant, fifty years old, with a gray beard, short sidelocks, an old-fashioned top hat, a long, black linen frock, his pant legs over his boots.[2] He speaks slowly and measures his words.

MIRELE

His daughter from his first wife. A girl of sixteen. In Act I she wears a long colorful silk gown embroidered with flowers. Her shoes and her gloves match. On her head a wreath of flowers, in her hand a fan. She wears beautiful jewelry. In Acts II and II, a short and shabby dress with a dark apron and big floppy shoes. Her hair is matted and loose. In Act IV, she wears an elaborate short Turkish costume of various materials: silk, satin, velvet, embroidered with silver tinsel. A ribbon is plaited into her hair. In Act V, she wears a simple, beautiful travel costume, feminine, a hat with a veil.

BASYE

Avromtshe's second wife, of thirty-five years. In the first act, she wears a long black gown with a black jacket. Over her wig[3] a lace-trimmed bonnet. In the second and third acts she wears a simple woolen dress, a white, lace-trimmed jacket with a white apron, on her head a colorful, bright, silk headscarf. In the fifth act, the same costume with an overcoat.

LIZA

Basye's daughter from her first husband. A young girl of sixteen years, wears a hooped dress.

WITCH/BOBE YAKHNE

Basye's aunt. An older woman (over seventy). In the second and fifth acts, a dark dress with a calico jacket over her shoulders and red kerchief on her head. A shawl over her shoulders, a dark silk handkerchief on her head, glasses, in one hand a walking stick, in the other a little box of tobacco, on her left cheek a gray, hairy mole, her nose red—overgrown with a fuzz of hair, in the third act (second tableau) a black dress, a long black apron, woven with silver tinsel in various wild images, a long red shawl with wide fringes and sequins and buttoned together as a coat, on her head, an old Spanish-style turban.

ELYOKUM

Basye's uncle (around forty), a stout man, tall, has thick black sideburns and long mustache, on his head, a lambskin hat worn askew, velvet coat, two golden chains hang from his pocket watch, a wide red belt around his waist, plaid breeches, fingers laden with many rings.

MARCUS

Mirele's groom. A slim man of twenty-four years. In the first act, he wears a suit, vest, tie, white gloves. In all the other acts, an everyday handsome suit, with an overcoat, a fedora, and a travel bag on his shoulders.

HOTSMAKH

A man of thirty-eight years. A short, messy beard with two points. Two not-too-long sidelocks, a cap, a colorful kerchief around his neck, a long caftan, dark pants, with shoes. He wears his shabby box of haberdashery on his back as well as a bag of merchandise, wrapped in a linen. He walks stooped and on the side.

ZERAKH, CHAIMEVITZ

Tavern-keeper of forty-five years. Long and big boots, a short coat of fur with a red belt, on his head a large lambskin hat, askew over his eye, a red beard.

KHAYEMITSH

Zerakh's younger brother, eighteen years. He is dressed like Zerakh only without a beard but with long black sidelocks.

Butcher's boy; a twelve-year-old who sells hot beans; a commissar and soldier; buyers and sellers at the market; girls working for Sorceress; Turks, cafe-goers; a gymnast; a magician; a gypsy; an organ-grinder with his music box; guests, and an audience.

ACT I

Scene One

Entrance/Exit 1

(Mr. Avromtshe's garden, beautifully illuminated with a variety of colored lanterns that hang from a trellis among the trees. On either side of the stage, marble statues, and in the middle, an arc of flowers and green leaves over a stairwell. Stage left, a glimpse of the glass corridor that leads to Reb Avromtshe's home. On all sides, men and women stand around, guests with presents in their hands and bouquets that they brought for Mirele's birthday. Among them Reb Avromtshe, Basye, Liza, and Marcus. A curtain is raised to reveal Mirele crowned with a garland of flowers. She walks down the stairs to the stage and approaches the audience as the choir sings.)

CHOIR

FOR YOUR BIRTHDAY, FOR YOUR HOLIDAY TODAY
YOUR GOOD FRIENDS HAVE GATHERED
WE WISH YOU ALL THE BEST
MUCH PRIDE AND MUCH JOY.

MIRELE

WHAT GOOD IS THIS CELEBRATION TO ME
WHEN IT SERVES ONLY TO REMIND ME
OF THE ABSENCE OF MY MOTHER.

CHOIR

LET THEM GO
THE SAD JEWS

NOW WE MUST BE JOYOUS
WE BEG!
YOUR FATHER
MUST BELIEVE
THAT HE WILL BE VERY PROUD OF YOU.

MIRELE

I WAS HER ONLY CHILD
HER WHOLE LIFE WAS DEVOTED TO ME
HOW CAN I NOT BE SAD?
In my time of merriment
She is not here.

CHOIR

LET THEM GO . . .

MIRELE

SHE HAD ONLY ONE WISH: TO SURVIVE MY WEDDING CANOPY, WITH GOD'S HELP.
HOW CAN I NOT BE SAD?

CHOIR

LET THEM GO . . .

AVROMTSHE

(*To MIRELE*) Is this right, my daughter, after I have spent so much money on your birthday celebration to ruin it and to undo our merriment with such sad thoughts? True, your mother was taken from you too early. But that was God's will. And you yourself saw how much her illness cost me, proof that I did not want to see her die. I spent more and more money, and nothing helped. And anyway, we should not constantly remind ourselves of our losses—especially during a celebration. Besides, do you lack anything in your father's care? Do you not have every comfort? I am already an old man. My entire wealth, all of my labor, is for your sake. What are you lacking? Isn't your stepmother as loyal to you as if you were her own? (*MIRELE sighs.*) Why else would I have remarried after your mother's death if not for your sake? Did you not use to say yourself when Basye was living as a neighbor next door that she is as loyal to you as your own mother? For that reason alone I married her. I was looking neither for prestige nor for money, just so long as she was willing to care for you as if she were your own mother. Is this not true?

BASYE

(*She approaches MIRELE.*) Mirele, do you love me? Liven up a bit if only for my sake.

LIZA

(*Takes her by the hand*) Mirele, sweet Mirele. Give me a kiss and be happy.

AVROMTSHE

(*To MIRELE*) Isn't your beloved groom here, right beside you? (*MARCUS kisses her on her hand, and she leans her head on his shoulder.*) And how much longer do you think it will be until you marry? After the Sabbath I'll be making my way to the tailor to have wedding clothes sewn. When they are ready, we will have our wedding, in good time.

MARCUS

Enough. Enough of this sadness, Mirele. Let us begin the entertainment. (*To the people gathered*) Beloved guests: think of a game with which we can amuse ourselves that we can play now. (*At this moment, HOTSMAKH's voice is heard off-stage shouting, "Tselnik, tselnik, haberdashery, haberdashery."*) Oh, good, Hotsmakh is here; he will amuse us!

Scene Two

Entrance/Exit

HOTSMAKH

(Enters with a pack on his shoulders, in another hand a yardstick. He begins shouting from outside, "Haberdashery! Haberdashery! Buy it cheap! I'm not kidding around; whosoever wants to cheat a buyer will burn in fire! Garters, plastic spectacles, suspenders, leather needles, kosher soap, nonkosher purses, pareve[4] scissors, red envelopes, white tallow wax, brushes, buttons, shirt buttons. The devil take me!")

MARCUS

(*Pats him on the back*) What are you doing here, Hotsmakh?

HOTSMAKH

What is Hotsmakh doing here? *The devil take me?!* What do you mean? I do what I normally do? Go around to the coffeehouses, to the beer houses, until the end of days, *the devil take me!* I sell merchandise, for *parnose* for a living, my brother. I have a wife and many children. *The devil take me!* And I noticed the windows at Reb Avromtshe's laughing, so I thought to myself *the devil take me!* Why don't I go inside? And as I did, I see before a gathering of people, there should be no evil eye, *the devil take me!* You will, of course, buy something from me, I have a wife and many children. *The devil take me!* Buy something, trust me, whosoever wants to cheat a buyer, will burn in fire! Garters . . .

MARCUS

(*Pats him on the back*) Wait a minute, Hotsmakh! Now is not the time to be selling. Can't you see that we are celebrating here?

HOTSMAKH

A celebration, *the devil take me*? And Reb Avromtshe didn't invite me for schnapps? Are you celebrating Mirele's wedding, *the devil take me*?

BASYE

No, Hotsmakh. Today is Mirele's birthday.

HOTSMAKH

What is a *bathday*? You mean the day we go to the bathhouse? (*Everyone laughs.*)

AVROMTSHE

Quiet down now. Seventeen years earlier my Mirele, she should have a long life, was born. Therefore, today, it is a festival for us.

HOTSMAKH

A festival. Do I say a *tkhine*,[5] *the devil take me?* So you mean that when you remember the day you were born, you make a festival from it? I curse the day and year I was born into the world and this cursed life I lead! *The devil take me!* In any case, a holiday is a holiday, but perhaps I can interest you, Mirele, in something? Garters, for instance? Oh, generous Mirele, how often has she given me one of her old dresses to give to the missus at home or one of my many children? *The devil take me!* Your wife, Basye, on the other hand, still owes me a few kopeks from before the Shavuos Holiday[6] for the handkerchiefs she bought from me. No problem, of course, I trust her. I know she'll pay me (*He turns to BASYE.*), no, Basyenu?

BASYE

(*Angry*) Of course I'll give it to you, of course.

HOTSMAKH

Nu, buy it cheap, trust me, whosoever wants to cheat a buyer will burn in fire!

MARCUS

(*Cuts him off*) Wait, Hotsmakh, wait.

HOTSMAKH

Garters, suspenders . . .

MARCUS

Please, Hotsmakh. Leave your pack to the side . . .

HOTSMAKH

Elastics, eyeglasses, scissor-sharpening whetstone . . .

MARCUS

Now is not the time for selling. Now you are here as our guest . . .

HOTSMAKH

Red envelopes, white whetstone . . . (*MARCUS takes his pack away from him and places it in a corner.*) Mr. Mordkhe, you need to make sure that no one swipes any of my red garters . . .

MARCUS

(*To his audience*) *Nu*, my love, let's think up a game we can play to amuse ourselves. (He *thinks.*) Let's play blind man's bluff!

HOTSMAKH

Nah. Let's play buttons. Whoever can pull out a button gets a free drink, *the devil take me*!

MARCUS

There are plenty of drinks for everyone who wants, as today is a celebration. Hotsmakh, would you sing something for us, would you, Hotsmakh?

ALL

Yes, yes, Hotsmakh, sing for us. He has a beautiful voice.

HOTSMAKH

Even my voice I left at home today with my wife. But what's the difference? If everyone wants me to, I'll do it. What should I sing for you?

MARCUS

Sing what you can sing.

HOTSMAKH

Nu, I'll sing to you, "The Devil Take Me."

TODAY, PEOPLE ARE FALSE AND AFFECTED,
EVERYONE HAS HIS OWN OPINION.
THEY ARE ON TOP OF THE WORLD WHEN THEY SPEAK ALOUD,
BUT IN THEIR HEARTS THEY ARE DISPLEASED.
YOUR FRIEND MIGHT NOT BE SO ROTTEN
WHEN HE IS VISITING YOU AT HOME;
HE'LL BE FRIENDLY TO YOUR FACE,
BUT THEN HE'LL THINK TO HIMSELF, "THE HELL WITH HIM."

A GUY APPROACHES A LENDER
AND DEMANDS A RECEIPT FOR HIS LOAN.
THE LENDER SMILES PLEASANTLY
AND DISCUSSES,
"MY VISIT," SAYS THE CREDITOR, "DOES NOT PLEASE YOU.
BE HONEST, YOU NEED NOT BE ASHAMED."
"IT'S BEEN A PLEASURE," HE ANSWERS THE LENDER
AND THINKS TO HIMSELF, "THE DEVIL TAKE HIM."

A YOUNG WOMAN HAS AN OLD HUSBAND,
BUT A YOUNG MAN ALSO CIRCLES . . .
AT NOONTIME, SHE INVITES HIM IN,
AND HE IS A FREQUENT VISITOR.
THE OLD MAN MUST ALSO INVITE HIM IN CORDIALLY.
"BE HOSPITABLE," SHE SAYS, "THERE IS NO SHAME."
"COME AGAIN," SAYS THE OLD MAN ALOUD,
AND HE THINKS TO HIMSELF, "THE DEVIL TAKE HIM."

ON THE BOULEVARD, I WALK AMONG MANY GENTLEMEN,
AND I DO NOT SEE WELL WITH MY EYES.
UNINTENTIONALLY I BUMP INTO A MAN
WITH MY BAD EYESIGHT.
"PARDON," I APOLOGIZE WITH CIVILITY,
"ARE YOU HURT?" "NOT TO WORRY," HE SAYS,
"IT IS NO MATTER AT ALL," HE RESPONDS
BUT THINKS, "THE DEVIL TAKE HIM."

ONCE A CHARLATAN FELL FOR A GIRL;
HE HELD HER IN EMBRACE AND KISSED HER,
AND HE PROMISED TO MARRY HER
WITH A CANOPY AND RABBI.
"PREPARE THE WEDDING! DO NOT DRAG YOUR FEET!"
"I WILL CARE FOR YOU," HE SAYS FROM ONE SIDE OF HIS MOUTH,
AND THINKS TO HIMSELF, "THE DEVIL TAKE YOU!"

ALL

(*Applauding*) Bravo! Bravo, Hotsmakh!

HOTSMAKH

Bravo, *the devil take me*.

MARCUS

Now let us play blind man's bluff.'

HOTSMAKH

And become blind? May God protect us! I have a wife with many children!

MARCUS

No, this is a game that is popular among people in the world who are up on the latest fashions.

BASYE

Yeah, but on whom will befall the fate . . .

MARCUS

Let it be me. I'll be the first one to put the blindfold on. (*Someone puts the blindfold on him, and the crowd forms a circle around him. MARCUS, in the middle, sings, and the others respond.*)

ALL

(*Circling around him, singing*)
TRA-LA-LA! PLAYING AND SINGING!
TRA-LA-LA! THIS BULDS STRENGTH!

TRA-LA-LA! DANCING AND JUMPING!
TRA-LA-LA! GOOD! GOOD! GOOD!

MARCUS

(Gestures with his arms as if he is about to capture one of them, and they scatter in different directions).

MARCUS

I AM BLINDMAN!

ALL

(*Running toward Marcus*) WHAT A WONDER! *(Running away)*

MARCUS

DON'T RUN AWAY!

ALL

(*Running toward MARCUS*) HERE WE ARE! (*Running away*)

MARCUS

YOU ALL RUN AWAY!

ALL

(*Running toward*) COME ON, CATCH US! (*Running away*)

MARCUS

DON'T RUN AWAY!

ALL

(All the guests but MARCUS hold hands around him and sing the first verse again. MARCUS moves around with his hands before him reaching for people and capturing BASYE. There is laughter and shouts of "Bravo!" Someone takes the blindfold off of MARCUS and puts it on BASYE, and they resume singing the same verses with BASYE. BASYE, then she captures HOTSMAKH, and more laughter follows with a "Bravo!" HOTSMAKH is blindfolded, and they resume the song. In this case, the guests agree to sneak away to another room and leave HOTSMAKH feeling his way in the empty garden and saying, "Oh, so you are hiding. I will find you!")

Scene Three

(Until, finally, a COMMISSAR enters. During the game, the local COMMISSAR enters. Thinking he has captured one of the guests, HOTSMAKH takes hold of the COMMISSAR and does not let go.)

HOTSMAKH

I got you, Marcus! Now it's your turn to be the blind man! (*The COMMISSAR tries to loosen his grip, but HOTSMAKH does not let go*) No way, Mr. Marcus. (*HOTSMAKH takes the blinder off and, about it to put it on his captive, sees that it's the COMMISSAR and not MARCUS who he captured and falls to his knees in fear*). *Oyvavoy*! I have no tobacco, no, no. As I have a beard and sidelocks I have no Titan tobacco.[7] I only deal in kosher merchandise.

COMMISSAR

Who is the head of the household here?

HOTSMAKH

(Scared, not hearing his question) Oyvavoy! I have a proper weight![8]

COMMISSAR

(*Angry*) I haven't asked you about that. I am asking, who is the host of this party?

HOTSMAKH

(*Somewhat less scared but still misunderstanding the COMMISSAR, HOSTMAKH answers him incorrectly.*) I don't deal in spirits. We are celebrating here . . . maybe you want a drink.

COMMISSAR

(*Angry*) I am not asking about such things. I am asking about the head of the household.

HOTSMAKH

Who do you mean, Mr. Avromtshe? Not me? (*And he moves slowly toward the door in fear and shouts.)* Mr. Avromtshe! Mr. Avromtshe! Excuse me, but a particular sir would like to see you. [in Hebrew] *Un vayibrakh moshe. "And Moses fled!"*[9] (*HOTSMAKH flees the scene.*)

Scene Four

AVROMTSHE

(*To the COMMISAR*) What would you like, your honor? I am the head of the household.

COMMISSAR

In the name of the law, I have come to arrest you.

ALL

(*With fear*) What could this mean?

MARCUS

(To COMMISSAR) Can you tell us what crime this man committed? He is well known in this city as an upstanding citizen who has never brought a legal motion against anyone.

COMMISSAR

It is neither my nor your concern. Justice will clarify everything in good time.

MIRELE

(With a cry, she throws herself on her father.) Father! Father!

AVROMTSHE

Stay calm, my child, I have done nothing wrong, so there is nothing to fear. It must be a mistake, nothing more.

LIZA

(To BASYE) Oy, mother! Only yesterday the sorceress read cards and foretold this tragedy to the last detail.

BASYE

Be quiet!

ALL

Woe is us!

MIRELE

I don't feel so well . . . *Oy* . . . *(She falls to the ground. MARCUS and BASYE hold her up.)*

AVROMTSHE

Zay gezunt! Stay healthy! Farewell.

(Music plays. Everyone remains still with bowed heads; the COMMISSAR marches AVROMTSHE out slowly, and he slowly looks back to his guests. The curtain drops slowly.)

ACT II

Scene One (TWO MONTHS LATER)

(BASYE'S empty room. MIRELE enters dressed in rags, matted hair, with a bucket in her hand, worried, sad. Puts down the bucket and sings.)

AWAY FROM ALL OTHERS, IN THE DISTANCE
ON AN UNASSUMING HILL,
A LITTLE TREE GROWS
IN THE WILD FOREST, BUT ALL ALONE!

THE SUN BURNS THE TREE'S CROWN,
THE RAIN BEATS DOWN ON IT,
AND THE DROPS ON THE LEAVES
TRICKLE OFF LIKE TEARS.

NO SHADE PROTECTS IT;
IT IS TOSSED BY THE WIND.
I AM THIS TREE,
A LONELY ORPHAN . . .

MY FATHER IS NOT HERE, I DON'T HAVE A MOTHER . . .

A STEPMOTHER THAT TORTURES ME, OY!
AND NOT ONE PERSON
DEFENDS ME.

MIRELE

(She covers her face with her hands and cries.) Tears: flow, flow as far as you can. Maybe you will lighten my heavy and bitter heart! Like a heavy stone, my breast presses on me; my pain stifles my breathing. Oh, my heart is heavy, so heavy . . . Yes, you saw this, Sorceress, when you read my cards for me. Now I have come to believe you, you villainous woman! Why did you deal me such a bad hand, when you dealt others such good ones? Are you a better friend to my stepmother than you are to me? And if so, can you really manipulate how the cards fall? Oh, if it were really so. Tell me, Sorceress, you should be well; I have only the best wishes for you, but the nine of spades that fell close to the queen of clubs showed you only pain and tragedy! . . . Oh, the good woman [the sorceress] tried to console me, but it was impossible. Her words burrowed deeply into my heart, and each morning when I awoke from my sleep, my heart was heavy from the nightmares I suffered. They destroyed me . . . *(Pondering)* Wasn't the tragedy that my father would be suddenly sent away, or does an even greater tragedy lie before me? . . . Even when my father was still at home, my stepmother was already treating me badly. But I did not want to tell him because I did not want to cause him pain. He might now be thinking wherever he is that he left me in good hands, but no! Dear father! It is no longer the loyal Basye from earlier on, but it is the evil stepmother. I cannot take anymore of her! Her daughter is now the only child that matters, and she works me worse than she would a donkey. I must serve them, and throughout the nights they do not let me sleep. They send me out in the worst downpours, in frigid weather, and insult me, curse me, hit me, and pick on me to death, and I have no idea why. And here I have not one friend to whom I may share my bitter heart. My betrothed is away, trying to get my father released from jail. And so I have been left alone, a tragic orphan . . . Oh, flow tears, flow as far as you can. Maybe you will lighten my heavy and bitter heart!

Scene Two

BASYE

(Enters stage right—yelling) What are you doing still standing here, girl? Did I not send you to fetch a bucket of water and yet, you lazy nuisance, you haven't budged from this spot? *(She pushes MIRELE.)* You should be going to hell. Do you think you can behave with me as you behaved with your father? Not anymore! *(MIRELE cries.)* Stop that howling. If you keep on whining like that, I'll hit you over the head. Go already, you vile girl! I'll tear you up into little pieces! *(MIRELE retreats left, looking at her venomously.)* Watch: with the look she gives me, she should soon stop seeing altogether with those eyes! *(MIRELE exits.)*

Scene Three

BASYE

(To herself) That maid. I have to put an end to her completely. *(Pause)* One must really do something about her. I'll consult with Bobe Yakhne today; she'll give the best

advice. Hmmm. What can I do though, since she's not here? *(She looks left; to herself.)* Do I hear someone coming? Ha ha! I think it is Bobe Yakhne; look at how she drags herself around, the old witch. *(Out loud)* Come in, Bobe Yakhne, have no fear. No one else is at home.

Scene Four

BOBE YAKHNE

What else, Basye? Why have you called on me?

BASYE

I need you very badly, Bobe Yakhne. I need to ask of you to perform some magic on my behalf and get rid of that maid of mine [Mirele] once and for all.

BOBE YAKHNE

Still talking like a child? You are still convinced that I perform magic? You still believe that I stir cauldrons . . . that I spin a wheel in an oven, that I stick a pair of scissors in the earth and cause something that way? Those tricks I do only to swindle money out of fools who are idiots enough to believe in such things. Really, those things have no worth—what constitutes my magic? In the practical experience I gained in the world. Life experience and wisdom. The expertise to swindle, that is the whole of my magic; outside of that it's nothing . . . Didn't the people themselves say that you placed Abraham under a spell when you got him to marry you? And you yourself know how it played out. The whole thing was proof of my worldliness, and besides that nothing. The only thing I "divined" was that Abraham is a rich widower and has but one child, and you were a poor and deprived widow, so I ordered you to somehow become his neighbor and pretend to relate well to the child, smile, and smooth talk and serve her so she trusts you and Abraham would observe and take you as his wife.

BASYE

True, true. But what do we do with the maid to get rid of her?

BOBE YAKHNE

You want to get rid of her? That's nothing! *(She takes a pinch of snuff and thinks. All of sudden she slaps BASYE'S hand happily.)* Basye! I have thought up another bit of sorcery. You want to get rid of her completely? *(BASYE nods her head.)* Hear me out. Send her out to the market and give her some money—and put it in her pocket with your own hands. Without her looking, take it out of her pocket. I don't have to teach you how to do that; you have always been an expert. When she discovers she has lost your money, she'll be afraid to return home and she'll stay at the market. I'll approach her, and I'll figure out what I'll do with her. *(She takes a pinch of snuff and thinks some more, looks around, and gets closer to BASYE.)* And we can still make some money on her! Get a little closer; I want no one to overhear this—it could undermine the whole magic . . . You understand? . . . *Nu*, be well, and be smart! *(She leaves.)*

BASYE

Be well, and send Elyokum to me!

BOBE YAKHNE

Beautiful, beautiful. *(She takes a pinch of snuff, sneezes, and exits stage left.)*

Scene Five

BASYE

(Acting alone) Rarely, very rarely does one see women such as her: she has experienced so much, and even advanced in years she does not rest, doesn't even tire. *(Thinking)* No! This, it will turn out well for me, it will still be good with everyone, and I will certainly be able to take care of the solution myself. I can travel to an entirely different city. I need a place where no one knows me! *(She yells.)* Mirel! Mirel!

Scene Six

MIRELE

(Comes in from the right side) What is it, *mamenyu*?

BASYE

Quickly take this basket and go shopping in the market. *(MIRELE takes it out toward the right and turns it around. BASYE takes out a little pouch with gold, places it, and rattles it in her pocket, then takes it back.)* You see? I put some money in your pocket. Don't lose it, you unlucky one. Remember! A pox on you if you do! Go! *(Remains there and suddenly stands and looks at her.)* What is this? Why are you still here? Are you too sick to go?

MIRELE

It's really cold outside.

BASYE

You pampered creature, you're cold. The wind won't take you today. Hopefully it will tomorrow though. *(Rips off her shawl)* What? You put on my old shoes?

MIRELE

Mine are all tattered.

BASYE

(Loudly) Your stomach and innards should be tattered, living father! One needs immense wealth to support you. Not even two years ago did you get a pair of shoes made, but you've already ripped them. No, I don't have any more shoes for you. *(Rips the shoes off of her, gives her a shove)* Even so, I don't think you're too sick to go, so scram! *(Takes the shoes and shawl and exits right)*

Third Entrance/Exit

Scene Seven

(Marketplace in the winter. A row of wooden kiosks where bread, meat, cheese, are sold. On both sides Jewish women sit. Near the kiosks one sees many Jews with old

clothes and old boots walking around and calling out, one sells, another bartering, the women in the kiosk sing.)

YOUNG MEN. BUY, BUY, SHOPPERS,
COME, COME, HITHER!
IN THE MARKET
IT IS BUYER BEWARE!
BUY IF YOU ARE SKILLED,
BUY FOOD, DRINK, AND ALL ELSE.
BUY WHAT YOU DESIRE
VERY CHEAPLY.

SELLERS. FRESH FROM THE WATER, CARP AND TENCH.
BUYERS. NO, WE NEED FLOUR AND BRAN!–
WOMEN. YOU CAN FIND THAT WITH US!
BUYERS. MAKE SURE TO MEASURE IT FAIRLY!
CHOIR. BUY, BUY, SHOPPERS . . . ETC.

WOMEN. ONIONS, POTATOES, DILL, AND HORSERADISH!
BUYERS. WE WANT TO SEE EGGPLANTS!
WOMEN. YOU HAVE THEM HERE FRESH, A PAIR, A TRIPLE!
BUYERS. WE CAN'T BUY THAT; IT'S TOO EXPENSIVE!
CHOIR. BUY, BUY, SHOPPERS . . . ETC.

LITTLE BOYS. SOAP, BRUSHES, SPONGES!
BUYERS. NO, WE WANT DRIED PLUMS!
WOMEN. WITH US, WITH US YOU'LL FIND ALL YOU NEED!
BUYERS. WEIGH IT FOR US, ONLY A GOOD MEASURE!
CHOIR. BUY, BUY, SHOPPERS . . . ETC.

A BUTCHER *(Singing)*

FRESH, DRAINED, AND CLEAN
IT'S KOSHER
FROM A LITTLE LAMB.
ONLY ITS FEET REMAIN.
FEET, ONLY A FEW LEFT! . . .
OY! FRESH FEET, FRESH FEET.
YOU'LL SEE NO BETTER ELSEWHERE! . . .
FLESH AND FAT LIKE STRIPED SOCKS!

DON'T GO ELSEWHERE;
THEY'D SNATCH GOLD FROM WIND.
THEY HAVE NO MERCY.
GET A PIECE OF MEAT FOR THE WHOLE FAMILY,
AND ON TOP OF THAT IT'S ALSO CHEAP.

FRESH, FRESH FROM THE SLAUGHTER!
BUY WHAT YOU DESIRE:
GIZZARDS, LIVERS, OR EVEN BETTER,
A CHOICE PIECE OF KOSHER BREAST! . . .
OY! FRESH BREAST, FRESH BREAST,
BUT CAREFUL, I'VE SEEN IT ALL! . . .
THEY DISGUISE THE CUT,
WRAP UP IT—
DON'T GO ELSEWHERE, ETC.

FRESH, FRESH FROM THE SLAUGHTER,
THE RITUAL SLAUGHTERER OVERSEES IT:
A YOUNG HEIFER, A CHOICE ONE, A GOOD ONE.
ONLY DO BUISENESS WITH ME!
OY! FRESH HEIFERS, FRESH HEIFERS,
BUT CAREFUL, I'VE SEEN IT ALL! . . .

DON'T GO ELSEWHERE.
-

(When the BUTCHER finishes singing, all the others begin to yell, "Buy, buy, Jews; buy, women.")

LITTLE BOY

From the audience a small boy moves forward, with a small basket tied around his neck with hot beans. He sings.)

HOT BEANS, JEWS, HOT!

NOT ONE PERSON IN THE WORLD
THAT LIVES HIS YEARS,
ROCKING TO SLEEP WITH THE BIT OF MONEY HE EARNED—
A CRAFT IS A DISADVANTAGE!
HE FEELS TOO LAZY TO EARN WHAT HE EATS;
TOILING IS FOR HIM AN EMBARASSMENT!
HE LOOKS OUT ONLY TO FOOD AND SHELTER . . .
AND TO UNEARTHING A CHOICE INHERITANCE!
HE IS SICK (I AM TOO),
TO TOIL SO WITH SWEAT!
AND TO YELL LOUDLY,
HOT BEANS, JEWS, HOT!

HE MOVES THROUGH THE STREETS AND DOESN'T TIRE,
FOR HE ALREADY HAS HIS PIECE OF THE WORLD TO COME! . . .
HE IS THE GRANDSON OF A HASIDIC REBBE,
AND, IN GOOD TIME, HE'LL BE A SEXTON.

SOMES GIVE HIM ALMS, HE SAYS, TOO LITTLE,
AND HEAPS CURSES ON THEM
BECAUSE HIS GRANDFATHER WAS REBBE;
THEREFORE, HE IS OF ILLUSTRIOUS DESCENT.
HE IS SICK (I AM TOO),
ETC.

THERE WANDERS A SCOUNDREL IN THE STREET!
HE CAN'T LEARN ANYTHING!
HE WALKS AROUND VACANTLY
AND DOES NOTHING TO STRAIN A MUSCLE! . . .
HE TAKES A NAP IN THE THEATER LIKE A NOBLEMAN! . . .
HE HAS NOT A KOPEK TO HIS NAME—
AND YET HE HAS THE AUDACITY, THAT PHONY,
TO JEER AT THE POOR ACTORS.
HE IS SICK (I AM TOO),
ETC.

Scene Eight

(HOTSMAKH comes up in the market.)

HOTSMAKH

(Begins shouting from backstage) Haberdashery! Haberdashery! Buy it cheap! I'm not kidding around; whosoever wants to cheat a buyer will burn in fire! Garters, plastic spectacles, suspenders, leather needles, kosher soap, nonkosher purses, *pareve* scissors, red envelopes, white tallow wax, brushes, buttons, shirt buttons, *the devil take me!*

A GIRL

Hotsmakh, English needles—do you have any?

HOTSMAKH

So English they don't speak a word of French! How many do you need?

A GIRL

Twelve dozen needles.

HOTSMAKH

Twelve dozen will cost you less. *(He puts his pack down and opens it.)*

A GIRL

How much do twelve dozen cost?

HOTSMAKH

Not more than thirty kopeks.

A GIRL

Thirty kopeks, that much?

HOTSMAKH

I need to survive going home to a wife and many children. They cost me more to buy, but it's Sabbath Eve, and I'm prepared to give them away cheap.

A GIRL

It's too much. I'll give you only twenty kopeks.

HOTSMAKH

Such a young girl and already smart enough to bargain. For that, I'll give it to you for twenty-five kopeks, so hold out your little hand and let me count them. *(He takes his needles out and begins to count them)* One, two, three, four, five, six . . . How old are you that you can bargain so well?

A GIRL

I am thirteen.

HOTSMAKH

Fourteen, fifteen, sixteen, seventeen, eighteen, nineteen, twenty . . . And how old can that father of yours be, he should live a long life? You don't think I know him, that red-haired bandit. How old is he now?

A GIRL

My father is thirty-five.

HOTSMAKH

. . . I know your father to be at least forty, do you hear? Forty, forty-one, forty-two, forty-three, forty-four, forty-five, forty-six, forty-seven, forty-eight, forty-nine, fifty. Take a good look at me, young lady, and tell me how old you think I am with my little beard.

A GIRL

I know. About forty years old.

HOTSMAKH

Forty, she thinks. I am already approaching sixty, yes. Sixty-one, sixty-two, sixty-three, sixty-four, sixty-five, sixty-six, sixty-seven, sixty-eight . . . (He sighs.) *Oyvavoy.* We should both live as long as my grandfather lived. I had a grandfather that lived one hundred and twenty-five years. Yes, yes, one twenty-six, one twenty-seven, one twenty-eight, one twenty-nine . . . one forty-four. And there you have it, little girl. And only five needles remain. Listen, take them. I won't charge you for them. Honest. Now go home quickly and make sure you don't lose any so your mother doesn't accuse me of not counting right. (She gives him money and exits)

HOTSMAKH

Buy with confidence! I kid you not! Anyone who cheats a buyer will burn in fire! . . . .

A JEW

Hotsmakh! Linen, you have?

HOTSMAKH

And how! You'd never guess how much linen I have.

A JEW

So let me take a look.

HOTSMAKH

Right here, you see? (*He holds it in his hand, stretching it out, turning it over. When the customer takes it to hold in his own hands, Hotsmakh does not allow it but keeps turning it over and such.*) What questions are you asking me? You want to know the quality? You should only hope to live as long as this linen will last.

A JEW

Why aren't you letting me look at it?

HOTSMAKH

You don't need to look at it; let me know how much I should weigh for you . . .

A JEW

How much does an arshin[10] cost?

HOTSMAKH

A few coins more, a few coins less will also cost me my life. A quarter an arshin.

A JEW

What are you talking about, Hotsmakh?

HOTSMAKH

I only want to survive my coming home to my wife and children, the devil take me! It cost me a lot of money, this linen. Do you have any idea where its from? You never heard of the greatest manufacturer, "Seller and Swindlerson"? It's their linen, do you get it? If it wasn't so close to the Sabbath, I would never give it away for forty kopeks.

A JEW

That much? I can't afford it, Hotsmakh.

HOTSMAKH

How much do you need?

A JEW

I need thirty arshins.

HOTSMAKH

Not more than thirty arshin? If there are only a few arshin left over, you'll take them? It's useful to have it around the house to repair a child's shirt, patch up a pair of pants. I'll tell you what: seeing that it is soon the Sabbath, and I have to go to the bathhouse, I won't bargain with you too much. I'll take twenty kopeks off the price.

A JEW

Okay, Hotsmakh. Do you have a reliable arshin?[11]

HOTSMAKH

Of course. I have a spanking new arshin. I just bought it. (He weighs the linen and begins to count) One, two, three, four, five, six, seven, eight, nine … I've been dealing in these wares for over fourteen or fifteen years. sixteen, seventeen, eighteen, nineteen, twenty, twenty-one, twenty-two, twenty-three, twenty-four, twenty-five, twenty-six. These days the government doesn't leave us alone. Just the other day, I had to pay for tickets eighteen rubles, and thirty-six, thirty-seven, thirty-eight, thirty-nine, forty. There! Forty arshin and a half. I won't charge you for the last half. Look how much you're getting.

A JEW

So how much do I owe you?

HOTSMAKH

How much? It comes to eight rubles and ten kopeks. So here's the linens, and pay me as quick as possible—I need to get going.

A JEW

(He pays him and takes the linen.) Hotsmakh, why is the linen so light?

HOTSMAKH

It's the sign of high-quality linen. Take it in good health. *Vayivrakh moshe.* And Moses fled . . .

(He exits.)

Scene Nine

(MIRELE comes to the market and goes to a BUTCHER.)

MIRELE

Give me a good pound of meat. *(The BUTCHER weighs it for her. She reaches for the money in her pocket and can't find it, and wringing her hands, she begins to cry.)*

BUTCHER

What are you looking for, young lady?

MIRELE

Oy, I'm so depressed! This is just my luck! My stepmother gave me money to buy meat in the market, but someone stole it from me. What am I to do, Jewish children? What advice can one give? *(Cries harder. A crowd of people gather around her, who regard her with curiosity.)* Oh dear, woe is me! I'd rather be dead than return home to my stepmother without money or meat. Merciful Jews, give me advice! *(Singing)*

OH, MERCIFUL JEWS!
YOU HAVE A GOOD HEART!

YOU HAVE ENOUGH LAWS;
YOU DECIDE IF THIS IS FAIR.
WHY DO WE LET ONE RULE ANOTHER?
AND WHY DOES NO ONE CARE FOR AN ORPHAN?
OH, MERCIFUL JEWS!
YOU HAVE A GOOD HEART!

CHOIR

WHO IS THIS CHILD?
SHE IS CERTAINLY LOST!
HELP IS URGENT.
WHO KNOWS WHO SHE IS?

MIRELE

OH, MERCIFUL JEWS!
YOU HAVE A GOOD HEART!
LOOK AT THESE MARKS . . .
I HAVE SO MANY, SO MANY.
THEY ARE NOT FROM AN ANIMAL
BUT FROM A PERSON—FROM A WOMAN.
OH, MERCIFUL JEWS!
YOU HAVE A GOOD HEART!

CHOIR

WHO IS THIS CHILD? . . . ETC.

MIRELE

OH, MERCIFUL JEWS!
YOU HAVE A GOOD HEART!
TAKE ME IN; I'M ON MY HANDS AND KNEES.
GIVE ME A ROOF OVER MY HEAD! . . .
DON'T FORCE ME TO GO HOME;
THE MURDERESS WAITS TO KILL ME . . .
OH, MERCIFUL JEWS!
YOU HAVE A GOOD HEART!

CHOIR

WHO IS THIS CHILD? . . . ETC.

Scene Ten

(As MIRELE completes the last strophe, BOBE YAKHNE enters the scene, approaches MIRELE, and studies her.)

BOBE

Why are you crying, little girl?

MIRELE

No reason.

BOBE

Who do you belong to? What is your name?

MIRELE

My name is Mirele.

BOBE

Why do you sit here and cry? Do you have parents?

MIRELE

My father was arrested under false pretenses, and I have no mother; she died.

BOBE

What was your mother's name?

MIRELE

She was called Shifra the *nagidesta*, the rich woman.

BOBE

Are you Shifra Yokhanan's daughter? The city rabbi was your grandfather?

MIRELE

Yes.

BOBE

Woe is me! And you are her child? Woe is your aunt! *(She says the next words in a singsong way.)* What are you doing here? Naked and crying?

MIRELE

How are you my aunt?

BOBE

What do you mean? Your mother never told you about me? Your mother, may she rest in peace, and my father, may he rest in peace, were beloved cousins. I am so upset. What has happened to you, Mirele? And where is Avromtshe?

MIRELE

I already told you that they took my father away under false pretenses—

BOBE

No, no.

MIRELE

And I was left with my stepmother. She beats me, kills me, and harasses me to death. She just gave me some money to buy some meat at the market, and someone stole it. I am terrified to return home. She'll kill me. *(She cries.)*

BOBE

What kind of stepmother is that? Woe is me. Avromtshe, I suppose, couldn't do any better marrying a second time so late in life. I am terribly upset. You know, you can freeze dressed like that out here. Look, you're not wearing any shoes! Woe is me, your aunt. *(She takes a pair of slippers out from under her shawl and gives them to MIRELE.)* For the meantime, put on these slippers that I just bought here at the market, and come stay with me at my house . . . You'll warm up a bit. And then I'll bring you home and reckon with that shrew, your stepmother. *(She takes the shawl from her own shoulders and gives it to her.)* Put this shawl on so you don't freeze, and come with me to my home. And woe is me, your aunt. *(They exit together.)*

(The merchants begin to sing. As they sing it begins to snow, and they begin to rush around throughout the market to warm up. As they sing the final verse, the curtain falls.)

ACT III

Scene One

Fourth Entrance/Exit

(Basye's stark room. As the curtain rises, Basye is speaking with Elyokum.)

BASYE

So what do you say, Uncle Elyokum? Is it all ready?

ELYOKUM

Yes, Basye. All the seals are ready. I have all the papers in hand that testify that you are the sole titleholder of this money. And the house, too, is in your name alone. Everything is done.

BASYE

I thought that everything would be easier if we just sold everything and took off. If anyone were to find out, all would be lost!

ELYOKUM

I have no fear about that. Just let's get rid of the little Satan called Mirele.

BASYE

What is she doing? Where is she?

ELYOKUM

I have already taken care of her; she is imprisoned in a back room at Bobe Yakhne's. She knows no one is coming to rescue her. And I'm already planning to get in touch with a friend of mine from Istanbul to whom I can sell her so we can get rid of her. After that, all will be settled . . .

(There is a knock at the door on the left side.)

Basye

Go see who it is.

Elyokum

(He goes to the window and stands on his tiptoes, looking over) Basye, Marcus is coming.

BASYE

(Scared) Marcus?

ELYOKUM

Shhh. Do not be so surprised. You know the role you must play. I need to get out of here.

(ELYOKUM exits.)

Scene Two

(BASYE opens the door. MARCUS enters.)

BASYE

(With a fake smile) Marcus! What are you doing? How have you been?

MARCUS

(He takes off his hat and puts it on the table.) I haven't heard anything good. I hope, with God's help, that I influence the right people to release Avromtshe. It should all work out. Still, Basye, I hope my own will one day have the amount of money it has so far cost me to advocate for him.

BASYE

What do you mean? We shouldn't sleep until this is resolved. Well, we shall sell our last shirt to save Avromtshe. But this is really our affair. It should not be your problem any longer. Because you no longer belong to us.

MARCUS

(He remains frozen for a moment.) What do you mean by that? I no longer belong to you? *(He looks around the room.)* Where is Mirele? What happened?

BASYE

(She looks down, as she can no longer look at his face.) What happened? What do you mean "what happened?" You squander all your money on a child and you put your health on the line for her . . . and she just . . . just . . .

MARCUS

(Surprised) Woe is me. What happened here? Say it already! What do you mean "just . . . just . . . ?"

BASYE

(With a look of sympathy) Don't ask. But it's okay. We have already suffered enough. I'm already sick to my stomach with worry.

MARCUS

Answer me, Basye! Where is Mirele? What happened? Is she dead? Woe is me!

BASYE

It's even worse than if she were dead. That would not pain me as much as this does. A person dies, and it is not the biggest tragedy . . . Were I her real mother, it wouldn't bother me so much; of course, I'm her stepmother, and so what will the world say? That I am to blame, of course. That I did not protect her properly. Or that I mistreated her. And you know the truth better than that, don't you? You know how I protected her more than my own child. But did my protection of her do any good? If something will go bad, it will go bad.

MARCUS

(Impatiently) Oh no! You have robbed me of all my strength. Tell me already, what happened? God help me. Um got viln.

BASYE

What should have happened? You'll never believe it, but Mirele ran off with a lover. This is true.

MARCUS

(*Beside himself)* What? What are you talking about?

BASYE

(Cold-blooded) Exactly as you heard it. Suddenly, she simply vanished. I looked for her, Creator of the World. What happened? First, she is on her way to the marketplace to buy something or other and never came home. That was yesterday, in the morning. I quickly sent people out to find her. They searched every street. Finally someone returned with some information. She was seen leaving the city with a writer, that member of the municipal council. They say you must know him, that gentlemen who often comes to visit with us.

MARCUS

(Confused) What does this mean? I don't understand what you are telling me. Are you being serious with this? Mirele would do such a thing? It does not make sense to me. *(He pauses.)* Really, I am speechless.

BASYE

You think you are speechless? We all are; we walk around unable to speak. Do you think I have even closed an eye since the night she disappeared? I tell you as I am a Jewish daughter that it has taken all the strength I have for me not to lose my mind. I don't eat! I don't drink! Yet another tragedy has befallen us!

MARCUS

(He does not hear what she is saying. He stands still deep in thought.) What advice is there for a man like myself? I did not expect this.

BASYE

Advice? How can she do such a thing to us? My advice is to forget about her. Better the innocent be rescued. Come and sit down and rest. You have just come from a long journey . . .

MARCUS

(Interrupting her) What do you mean rest? You think I can rest at a time like this? What can I do?

BASYE

What can one do, indeed! Of course, her behavior is terrible. She murdered me and over nothing. I have no strength to drag myself around. I go around dumb. Soon, however, it is nighttime. What can you do at such a late hour? Rest here tonight. Tomorrow we will figure out what to do. Have something to eat; you must be starved. I'll go prepare something for you. Come to the kitchen soon. *(She leaves stage right.)*

Scene Three

MARCUS

(Alone, he stands deep in thought, watches BASYE with angry eyes as she leaves the room, and finally yells.) Yes, no, I'm not going! No, I am not trailing after her. I have no appetite now, anyway. I can't eat, nor can I drink, I can't even live! *(Somewhat calmer)* Where is one to go? Something is giving me a bad feeling. Would Mirele actually do such a thing? Who knows how much time must have passed? *(Pause)* Who can I ask for advice? Who can solve this mystery for me? *(Thinking further)* Should I? . . . I've never even believed in it . . . but with such unluckiness, it seems to me, one believes in even greater stupidities *(Stands thinking for a few seconds, then cries out with great determination)* Yes! It must go like so! I'll take the trouble to search for advice from the sorceress; she should lead me to where she is. Although I've never really believed in it, now I must carry this out. Yes, I must find her, even if it costs me my life! *(He makes as if to exit left but suddenly remains standing, turning toward the room, which BASYE entered, and speaks angrily)* Oh, you horrible woman, don't think that you've deceived me with your spiteful remarks, and your promises of great sufferings, ah! I see you. And understand exactly what you're doing! I am certain that this happened without your knowledge, that I am prepared to spend my entire fortune, my life, and must find her. I'm going . . . I'm going to the sorceress!

(Runs out slowly to the left)

Scene Four

Entrance/Exit Five

(The room changes—it transforms into the sorceress's secret room; a big, dark, arch, hanging off of the arch is a crocodile. On the right of the arch are stairs that lead up to a secret door! To the left there is a typical, small door. On a bright table lay many tongs and knives, and maps are tossed carelessly on the table. In the corner stands a hearth broom, and a large screen hangs—various items are seen in a small cupboard; books, rocks, tree bark, globes lay cluttered). On the top of the arch one can see out to another room, in which there is a magic mirror; under it a fire burns, and a large kettle cooks atop it. Around the kettle the girls are standing and sitting, wearing red, low-cut dresses, brushing their hair. They are holding little tin pots in their left hands and in their right, long tin spoons. Every minute they draw from the large kettle and mix it and tap the small pots in their hands. They sing while they work.)

GIRLS

FASTER, FASTER,
LIKE A WHIRLWIND,
WORK FLOWS THROUGH THE HAND!
DO IT FASTER,
COOK IT, BOIL IT;
IT MUST BE FINISHED TODAY.
MIX IN THE MAGIC ALSO!
IT MUST BE FINISHED FASTER!

(They sing it several times.)

Scene Five

(HOTSMAKH on the door to the left)

(One of the girls runs to the door) Who is knocking?

HOTSMAKH

(From outside) Hotsmakh, obviously! Take a look and cook up some dinner, *the devil take me!* Is Bobe Yakhne home?

GIRL

No, what do you want?

HOTSMAKH

First of all, I wanted her to do a magic trick to get my wife to stop screaming at me, *the devil take me!* What I mean to say is that she should give me an ointment so that when my wife opens her mouth to scream, I can *shmeer* it on her lips so she keeps silent, *the devil take me!* Secondly, I want her to perform a trick that would make this small piece of linen become an infinite amount, no matter how much I measure out, so I can keep on selling it and make more money.

GIRLS

Okay, that we can do. But first we have to blindfold you *(She calls out to another girl, who goes outside and helps blindfold him.)*

HOTSMAKH

(From outside) Can I bring my box of merchandise with me? I am nervous that you won't do any magic for me and none of my merchandise will be left, *the devil take me!*

GIRLS

Not to worry! Come in! *(They guide him inside blindfolded.)*

HOTSMAKH

(Takes some steps cautiously) Oyvavoy! Where are you taking me? You know, I'm starting to get a little scared. *The devil take me!* It feels to me like the earth is splitting beneath me. Stop leading me around. I have a wife and many children, *the devil take me!*

GIRLS

Wait, we will take the blindfold off, and you will see where you are. *(They take it off, and HOTSMAKH looks around and is scared.)*

HOTSMAKH

(With a scream) The devil take me! How have I come to fall in with snakes and *hekreshn*. (Looks at the picture of a snake) What a mouth! He can swallow me and my full box of merchandise whole. I regret having come in here. Get away from me with your magic. I don't need any magic! My wife is welcome to scream at me, *the devil take me!*

GIRL

No, we already started the brew; we must complete it. *(To another girl)* Give me a strand of hair.

HOTSMAKH

Why do you need a strand of hair?

GIRL

We need to pull out a few hairs.

HOTSMAKH

(Scared) From where? Perhaps from my beard, may God protect me?

GIRL

No, from your sidelock—

HOTSMAKH

Why not take it from your hair? *(He takes her braids and shows them to her.)*

GIRL

No it must be from your hair . . .

HOTSMAKH

Don't take more than three strands of hair, do you hear? Let me make this clear: three. Do not take more than three strands of hair. *(Joking)* A hair costs money. This is imported hair. *The devil take me! (The girls cut off the entire sidelock.)* So did you get them yet?

GIRL

Yes.

HOTSMAKH

But not more than three strands. Let me feel how much you took. *(He takes his hand to his left sidelock and jumps back with a mournful cry.)* Woe is me! Woe is me! What have you done . . . *(He stamps his feet on the ground.)* My sidelock. Take a look at me; do I have a Jewish face any longer? Have mercy on my second sidelock; she has become a widow. *(The girls laugh very hard.)* Oy vey! My heart told me not to come in here, but a spirit delivered me to see if Mirele might be here. Go, go away with your magic . . . Where is the door?

GIRL

Nu, and the garters in return for our magic.

HOTSMAKH

When my sidelock grows back, I'll give you the garters. *(He grabs his box and runs out. The girls accompany him with laughter.)*

Scene Six

GIRL

(To the other girls) Did you hear the children that—what kind of name did they call? "Mirele!" Did you already see the girl that Bobe brought here yesterday?

GIRL 2

No, she is locked in Bobe's secret room.

GIRL 1

Will we soon have a new friend?

GIRL 2

How so? If she's locked up, we definitely can't let her out into the street with her.

GIRL 1

I can bring you to I've been here much longer than you and I know the secret way to get into the room. If you want, come with me and I will open the door and we can bring her down. Come! *(Two girls go up the stairs to the right and return soon after with MIRELE.)*

Scene Seven

MIRELE

(Looking around nervously and scared. With a shaky voice) Who are you? How did I get here?

GIRLS

Don't be scared, my love. We are just like you. Tell us how you got here.

MIRELE

My aunt brought me here!

GIRLS

Yes, your aunt, Bobe Yakhne lives here.

MIRELE

And who are you?

GIRLS

We are your sisters.

MIRELE

(Looking at them nervously) No, no, you are not my sisters, and she is not my aunt. *(Wailing)* Oh, father! Dear, father, where are you?

GIRL

Just explain to us how you got here, my dear. Maybe we can help you.

MIRELE

(Bewildered) Help? . . . *(Sings)*

NO ONE CAN PRESUME TO HELP;
HUMAN HELP HAS MADE THIS WORSE.
NO, NO ONE CAN DO ME GOOD;
NO, ONLY GOD CAN HELP ME NOW.
WHAT ELSE CAN I TELL YOU?
BAD PEOPLE CAME
AND DUPED MY DEAR FATHER,
DROVE HIM AWAY, FAR FROM ME.
MY FINE SISTERS,
CHEER ME UP.

DON'T ASK ME WHAT HAS HAPPENED;
YOU CANNOT UNDERSTAND MY PAIN.
YOU CANNOT HELP MY SADNESS.

GIRLS

DON'T CRY; DON'T MAKE YOUR SITUATION WORSE.

TELL US MORE! TELL US! TELL US!

MIRELE

DO NOT AWAKE MY PAIN!
SO DEEP IN MY HEART,
IT LIES RIGHT THERE, THERE!

GIRLS

DON'T CRY; DON'T MAKE YOUR SITUATION WORSE . . . ETC.

MIRELE

DO NOT AWAKE MY PAIN! . . . ETC.

GIRL 1

Tell us more, dear child. What happened with you?

MIRELE

There is nothing more to say. I am unlucky! This I know . . . *(Suddenly a knock at the door is heard.)*

GIRL 1

Children! Did you hear that? Bobe Yakhne is here. Let's get her back up to the room. Bobe Yakhne cannot know. *(They lead her back up the stairs and return to their work and to their singing.)*

Scene Eight

GIRLS

FASTER, FASTER,
LIKE A WHIRLWIND,
WORK FLOWS THROUGH THE HAND! . . . ETC.

BOBE YAKHNE

(From the other side of the door) What are you doing? What's going on there?

GIRLS

(From inside) We're going to make you very happy.

BOBE YAKHNE

(From outside) What's taking so long?

GIRLS

(From inside) It needs to boil a little longer.

BOBE YAKHNE

Hurry up, children.

GIRLS

Soon, soon!

BOBE YAKHNE

Faster, faster!

GIRLS

Soon, soon!

FASTER, FASTER,
LIKE A WHIRLWIND,
WORK FLOWS THROUGH THE HAND! . . . ETC.

Scene Nine

(While the girls are singing, BOBE YAKHNE enters.)

BOBE YAKHNE

Children, go into the dark room and take your work with you. *(The girls disappear into the depth of the room. Once they are gone, she calls for ELYOKUM.)*

Scene Ten

ELYOKUM

(Runs inside from another room) What is it, BOBE?

BOBE

Have you securely trapped Mirele back there?

ELYOKUM

Ha ha! But good! She'll never escape.

BOBE

When are you taking her from here?

ELYOKUM

Tomorrow.

BOBE

That means you already have a buyer?

ELYOKUM

Yes, Bobenyu, a good and dear friend of mine from Istanbul. In fact, we already settled on a price.

BOBE

How much are you taking?

ELYOKUM

Fifty liras.

BOBE

That seems too little, but that's okay. As long as you get her out of here quickly; she can't be here for too long.

ELYOKUM

I know, I know, Bobenyu. Tomorrow I bring her to the ship and get the money and good day, gabardine! *(Suddenly, a knock is heard at the door.)*

BOBE

Elyokum, who do you think that could be? Take a look at who it is.

(He looks through the keyhole and jumps back.)

ELYOKUM

Bobe! Marcus! Mirele's fiancé is here!

BOBE

Marcus? Make yourself scarce; he shouldn't see you. *(She sits at her red table where her tarot cards are laid out.)*

ELYOKUM

Listen to me, Bob, I have some useful information for you. They say that Marcus always carries Mirele's picture with him in a golden locket with diamonds. Maybe you could work a little magic so the picture creeps out of his pocket and into your hand, if you know what I mean . . .

BOBE

Okay, okay, just get out of here already and lock the door behind you so no one can come in after you leave. If anyone comes calling, tell them I'm not in. Go!

Scene Eleven

MARCUS

(Stands just inside the witch's lair, amazed at the room he is in. After a while he takes a look around the room and approaches the BOBE.) So you are the sorceress?

BOBE

(Changing her voice so she sounds gentle, she answers him.) Yes, what would you like, sir?

MARCUS

I came to you so you can read my future in your cards. The truth is that I never believed in such things, but at this point I want to be convinced.

BOBE

You'll be convinced, but it will cost you.

MARCUS

Money is no object, as long as I find what I'm looking for.

BOBE

Take out a silver coin and spit on it three times, cut the deck and, when I say, take a card. That card will have an image that closely resembles the one you wish to meet and who you are constantly thinking about. *(MARCUS does as she says. BOBE shuffles the cards, places the deck on the table, and blows on them. Then, she looks hard at MARCUS, and then trains her eye on the deck of cards. She sighs.)* A sharp pain afflicts me in my chest. The cards reveal that you have a longing for someone whose picture you carry around in a golden medallion, but I don't know if this person is a loved one . . . perhaps, a bride . . .

MARCUS

(Looks at her in amazement) Yes, Bobe, she is my bride.

BOBE

A bride? *(With a smile)* You see that? I've already touched upon the truth. *(She takes the deck of cards, shuffles them again, and asks him to again cut the deck with a coin and lays them out again on the table.)* You see that, my good sir, the cards say that you must make a journey—or maybe you have already made one, I can't be sure—although I think you must make it in the future.

MARCUS

(Amazed) Yes, Bobe, that is correct.

BOBE

You need not be so amazed. We are not angels or seraphim; we only tell you what the verse means—nothing else. *(She takes a pinch of snuff.)*

MARCUS

Bobenyu, can you not perform some kind of magic that would transport the person here, to us? I'll pay anything you want, just so long as I might see her.

BOBE

That we can't do. That is not in our power. I can show you the person's name and her image in the magic mirror. Only if the image is similar to the one that you carry in your locket, then the locket is mine.

MARCUS

(Impatiently) Not just the locket may you have but all my possessions.

BOBE

Then follow me and sit down over here. *(She points with her cane to a pitcher, and Marcus sits down next to it.)*

IN THE DARKNESS OF THE NIGHT, A BIG FOREST.
I SEE BEFORE ME A FRIGHTENING FIGURE,

NOT FAT NOR THIN,
NOT TALL, SLIM;
SHOW YOURSELF, WITH MAGIC CUP,
AND ASHMADAI
FILL THE CUP ANEW.

(Mirele's name appears in large letters.)

MARCUS

Oy, Mirele!

BOBE

Oh, don't be so surprised. Come and put on this coat on. *(She gives him a long black coat.)* You need to cover your entire face with it. Just let your eyes look out to the mirror and dunk your pinky finger into this water *(gets him a pitcher with cloudy water)* and wash your eyes. *(He does all he is told.)* Now look into the mirror. But I must tell you beforehand: when you see what you see, you must stay silent. Don't say even a word, and make no movement until the magic is over. If you won't obey, it won't be my fault if something unlucky were to happen, like if you were to lose the use of your tongue, God forbid . . . Look straight ahead and be silent. *(Points again at the pitcher; he sits next to it. She approaches the mirror and recites the same chant. "IN THE DARKNESS OF THE NIGHT . . . ETC." She darkens the lights in the room so that MARCUS doesn't see her remove the mirror, and MIRELE's head appears. MARCUS begins to shake. The mirror is returned, and the image disappears. The lights of the room go on.)*

MARCUS

Oh! She was so lifelike, so natural. I don't know how to thank you, Bobenyu. Oh! Can you tell me, Bobe, where she is?

BOBE

No, that I cannot do. I have shown you too much already.

MARCUS

I thank you, Bobe. *(He takes out the locket and gives it to her.)* Now, I will journey into the world to search for Mirele. And God willing, I will find her. She should know that I would never forget her. Therefore, adieu. *(He runs out.)*

Scene Twelve

BOBE

Elyokum!

ELYOKUM

(Runs inside) Yes, Bobenyu. What happened with the locket?

BOBE

(Interrupting) Don't speak so much. Go and get Mirele out of here. She shouldn't be here for another second. Understand? He is beginning to search for her. See how much we can expedite her out of here. Things have gotten dangerous!

ELYOKUM

Yes, yes, you're right, Bobe. I am already on my way. *(On the stairs that lead to the secret room; Mirele's voice is heard from inside.)*

MIRELE

Where are you taking me?

ELYOKUM

Come, come. We'll tell you all that later.

Scene Thirteen

(ELYOKUM drags her out of the room.)

MIRELE

Where are you taking me?

ELYOKUM

(Shouting) Silence, you bitch!

MIRELE

(Crying and screaming) Auntie! Have mercy on me! Where are you taking me?

(The curtain drops.)

ACT IV

Scene One

Entrance/Exit Six

(A large coffeehouse in Constantinople. A large room with columns and curtains recede into the depths of the stage. Lamps and a large chandelier light up the room. To the left on a large cushion many Turks sit cross-legged, some smoke cigars, some sip from hookahs, others drink coffee and play dominos. There are many small tables in the coffeehouse. Around every table sit various men. Some are playing cards, some play chess. Others drink coffee or read the newspaper. Waiters run around the tables and serve them. To the right MARCUS sits at a table with a travel bag on his shoulders. A glass of beer on the table, he sits deep in thought and reads a newspaper. The Turks sing.)

WE THANK GOD!
FOR HE HAS

CHOSEN US ALONE FROM ALL THE NATIONS, ALLAH!
THE DEEP SEA
OUR SHIPS
TRAVERSE
ALLAH!
PROTECT THEM,
PROTECT THEM,
ONLY YOU ALONE—
OUR SWORD—
OH, THE SHARP SWORDS,
OUR SWORDS CANNOT BE RETURNED
TO THEIR SHEATHS WITHOUT BLOOD.

<u>*Scene Two*</u>

(A gymnast comes in and contorts himself on the ground. He finishes, takes back the saucer in which he was collecting money, and exits.)

<u>*Scene Three*</u>

(A magician enters. He sings.)

MY ART IS NOT A BLIND MAN'S BLUFF;
IT IS SLEIGHT OF HAND
ALL DONE BEFORE YOUR VERY EYES
OPEN, WITH NO COVER
ONLY WITH MY MAGIC WAND
I'LL SAY ONLY ONCE ONE, TWO, THREE.
THE THINGS SWITCH AROUND
AS IF BY THEMSELVES

I DON'T EVEN COME CLOSE
...
THEY HEAR MY WORD
FIRST THEY ARE HERE
THEN THEY ARE NOT

(Shows all kinds of items in gold, exits)

<u>*Scene Four*</u>

(A Romani performer comes in and dances.)

<u>*Scene Five*</u>

(In the middle of the performance, HOTSMAKH enters. He stands watching the dancer, dancing a little bit too, and when the performer finishes, he walks up to the tables and sings.)

HOTSMAKH

BUY, BUY LITTLE BUTTONS,
LITTLE KNICKNACKS, BEADS—
CHOOSE WHAT YOU WANT—
STEEL PENS,
HAND-PAINTED BOXES,
SEALING WAX—ONE OF A KIND!
NOTEBOOKS,
CIGARETTE HOLDERS,
YOURS TO LOVE FOR HALF THE PRICE!

CHORUS

(Laughing at him)
YOUR WORDS ARE HOLLOW!
YOUR CALLS ARE IN VAIN!
FUTILE IS YOUR DANCING AND RUNNING!
STOP DISTURBING US!
NO ONE NEEDS IT; NO ONE WANTS IT!
THERE'S NOTHING TO BUY FROM YOU!

HOTSMAKH

(Moves over to another table)
POCKETKNIVES, WALLETS—
CHOOSE WHAT YOU WANT—
EMBROIDERED SLIPPERS
AND EARRINGS, TEASPOONS,
TOOTHBRUSHES—ONE OF A KIND!
BUTTONS WITH DIAMONDS,
LEATHER BELTS,
YOURS TO LOVE FOR HALF THE PRICE!

CHORUS

YOUR WORDS ARE HOLLOW! . . . ETC.

HOTSMAKH

(At another table)
BUY, FOR GIRLS:
PINS, MAKEUP—
CHOOSE WHAT YOU WANT—
SOAPS, MUSHROOMS,
BRUSHES, COMBS,
ALMOND OIL—ONE OF A KIND!
ALSO ENTIRE BUNDLES,
BAGS, SACKS,
YOURS TO LOVE FOR HALF THE PRICE!

OYLEM

YOUR WORDS ARE HOLLOW! . . . ETC.

HOTSMAKH

(Looks at them angrily)
YOU INJURE ME ONLY WITHOUT VIOLENCE.
I'LL SOON LEAVE.
I HAVE A RIGHT TO RUN AWAY FROM HERE;
I RECOGNIZE IN THEIR FACES
THAT THEY ARE PENNILESS;
THEY HAVE NO REASON TO BUY!

I see that I won't have any luck with these "red yarmulkes." *(He goes to a table where men are sitting and playing cards.)* Would you like to hear about buying something? Pocketknives, fine necklaces—it comes in handy for playing cards—if one of you were to lose everything while playing, he would need something with which to hang or slaughter himself, no? Nobody's responding. *(He turns to the table where MARCUS sits and reads a newspaper.)* This one here who sits at the table seems like a fine young lad who will buy something from me. *(He bends over to open up his case and takes out a box of tobacco)* Good sir! I'll sell you this here tobacco box for very cheap, even though it cost me quite a lot, and I lost money for it. Don't forget that it is made of bone, and the bone is from an aurochs. Pay attention, sir. *(He notices MARCUS and talks further.)* See! How the toba— *(He looks him in the face.)* How the . . . ! It seems to me that this is Marcus, the devil take me, but I don't make mistakes. Is this Marcus?

MARCUS

(Watches, stunned) Hotsmakh?

HOTSMAKH

Yes, it's Hotmakh, and he cooks dinner, the devil take me.

MARCUS

What are you doing here?

HOTSMAKH

What do you mean what am I doing here? My merchandise takes me throughout the world. A comb, a brush, a pair of scissors are needed in every corner of the world. What are you doing here?

MARCUS

You obviously heard about the tragedy that befell me! I am looking for Mirele. They say she must be here.

HOTSMAKH

How do you know that she must be here?

MARCUS

I went around not knowing where to go. Basye said that she ran off, but I can't believe it. The sorceress said . . .

HOSTMAKH

(Interrupting, hops and yells) Oh, the sorceress! Do not even mention her name to me. Look what she did to me! *(He shows him his shorn sidelock.)* I've been left crippled, the devil take me!

MARCUS

(Not listening) I have been running around, and I never knew what to do first. Should I run to work for Avromtshe's freedom, or should I run to search for Mirele? But then some salvation came: the police brought the news that Avromtshe was freed and that the state has proven that he is an honest man.

HOTSMAKH

(With happiness) What, Reb Avromtshe is free? (He claps on the table.) Waiter, two beers, the devil take me!

MARCUS

Reb Avromtshe is free and has already arrived home safe and sound. His homecoming should have been a happy occasion, but he fell apart when he did not find Mirele in the house. His beloved and only child. *(The waiter comes to the table with the beers. HOTSMAKH gulps down his beer quickly and then moves closer to MARCUS. MARCUS does not notice, continues to narrate.)* I consoled him, though, and decided to journey throughout the world, and I promised him that as long as she lives I will look for her and will bring his only child, and my true love, to him. Its already been a few months, and as I already said, I met a man in the city who said he saw Mirele in Istanbul, and so I raced here to see if I could find her.

HOTSMAKH

(Takes the glass of beer in his hand) Nu, le-khayim, the devil take me. God will help. No person is overlooked. And anything is possible.

MARCUS

I just got a letter today from Avromtshe himself. Do you want to read it?

HOTSMAKH

Really? A letter from Avromtshe? *(He takes the letter and reads it. MARCUS becomes engrossed in a newspaper.)*

Scene Six

(MIRELE enters dressed in a traditional Turkish costume with a colorful hoop over her shoulders. In her hand is a drum. She drums and plays along to the tune of the organ-grinder who follows behind her. She begins to sing.)

MIRELE

I WAS MY FATHER'S ONLY DAUGHTER.
I'VE NEVER FELT GOOD THINGS.
OH, HOW MY MOTHER, THE WEALTHY WOMAN,
WOULD SHARE BREAD AND MONEY WITH THE POOR;
THESE DAYS, EVERY DAY IS A FAST FOR ME.
NOW I AM HUNGRY AND NAKED.
HAVE MERCY! HAVE MERCY!
A DONATION FOR A LONELY CHILD!
MY MOTHER DIED YOUNG,
MY FATHER IS ALSO GONE FAR AWAY.
I RECEIVED A STEPMOTHER,
BUT SHE QUICKLY CAME TO A CONCLUSION ABOUT ME;
SHE TORTURED ME TERRIBLY.
NOW SHE KICKED ME OUT.
HAVE MERCY! HAVE MERCY!
A DONATION FOR A LONELY CHILD!

MARCUS

Hotsmakh, do you hear a familiar voice? It reminds me of Mirele's voice.

HOTSMAKH

What would I know from a voice? Voice, shmoice. Let's start moving; let's get out of here. Soon that kid will come around with a tray and expect a bit of charity for her singing. The devil take me!

MARCUS

What's so bad about giving a little charity to a child?

HOTSMAKH

Heck, if its so easy to give charity, give it to me: I have a wife and a lot of children, the devil take me. And don't forget that you'll have to pay for the beer; I don't have a red cent on me.

MARCUS

No problem, I'll also pay for the beer.

(After MIRELE stops singing, she circulates among the tables collecting money. HOTSMAKH gets in between MIRELE and the table.)

HOTSMAKH

There is no money here for you. Go away in good health. There are enough beggars around without the likes of you, as I have a wife with many children, the devil take me.

(MIRELE pays no attention to him, and MARCUS looks in his pocket to give some money to her and finally looks up and is frozen. His hands begin to quake, so much so

that he is no longer able to take out the money. He wants to embrace her but cannot believe his eyes. MIRELE notices and takes a long look at MARCUS. She too begins to tremble, so much so that the tray drops from her hand.)

MARCUS

(Shouting, confused) Mirele!

MIRELE

Marcus? *(They embrace.)*

HOTSMAKH

The devil take me! *(As MARCUS and MIRELE embrace, HOTSMAKH falls to the ground and rakes together the fallen money.)*

MARCUS

(Looks MIRELE in the eyes) Dear Mirele! Is it really you? Is it you I behold? *(He embraces her.)*

HOTSMAKH

(On the ground) Dear gold! Is it really you? Is it you I behold?

MARCUS

How did you lose something? Did you not find it?

HOTSMAKH

(On the ground) Where did they get lost? I can't find them anywhere!

MARCUS

Look in the clothing.

HOTSMAKH

I looked, my children are already clothed.

MIRELE

Don't ask, I've already had enough tragedy. *(Embraces him.)*

HOTSMAKH

Come over here, my dear Mirele. God has helped us, as we've already seen. All will be right again. Soon I'll send a telegram home that we're coming. Your father is also free now.

MIRELE

(Happily) What, my father is freed? Oh, thank God! *(The organ-grinder goes to MIRELE and yanks her to him. She becomes scared and hides behind MARCUS.)*

ORGAN-GRINDER

Ha! What's this? Who are you? What did you do with my girl?

MARCUS

This isn't your girl? This is my bride, she got lost, but now I found her!

ORGAN-GRINDER

That doesn't matter to me. I'll have none of this nonsense. I bought her off the ship for fifty liras! Go home, slave! *(Starts to drag her home)*

MARCUS

(Angry) Stop! I'm telling you she's my bride, and I will give you as much money as you want for her, in good faith. I do not want to take her by force.

HOTSMAKH

We'll obviously give you money, the devil take me! Take the money! We'll give you everything, the devil should take you! This is Reb Avromtshe's daughter. She's walking around only in garters I sold to her—a sign that she is ours.

ORGAN-GRINDER

I want nothing of this unless you are willing to give me ten times the price she cost me. Otherwise, you don't take her.

HOTSMAKH

You want ten times the price? Just you see, I'll give you ten times! *(He makes to grab him by the beard.)* Were you to have a beard, I would rip it out!

MARCUS

Here, take your money. *(He takes out a wallet and pays him. The organ-grinder leaves.)*

HOTSMAKH

Now, children, I'm going to send a telegram that Reb Avromtshe should expect us by the red bridge, by the red tavern with the red innkeeper, where there is red wine! There we will stop, the devil take me! *(He picks up his things.)*

MARCUS

(Embraces MIRELE) Please, my dear, tell me what has happened to you in all this time you've been gone.

MIRELE

Believe me, dear Marcus. I am still in shock, I cannot say a single word now. During our travels I will tell you everything. *(They embrace and kiss.)* Marcus . . .

MARCUS

Mirele . . .

HOTSMAKH

The devil take me! Please, children. Enough with the kissing. Come, let us leave quickly.

MARCUS

Yes, yes. Mirele, come, let's go. *(He takes her by the hand, and they walk out together.)*

HOTSMAKH

(Follows after them) Have a good day! Farewell, peasants! The devil take me!

(After they leave, the Turks sing "We Thank God." When they reach the end, the curtains slowly begin to close.)

ACT V

Scene One

Entrance/Exit Seven

BASYE

Where is your magic with your creatures, with your tricks? Will they not do? I already told you to stick a scissors in the ground and draw blood out of the earth with it so Avraham will not be freed, but in the end he was freed and is already at home. I also told you to bewitch Marcus, and have him fall in love with my daughter and grow hateful of Mirele. But in the end he persisted in searching for her, and we recently received a telegram that he found her and they are on their way home. *(Shouting)* Where is your wisdom? We are all so terribly unlucky.

BOBE

Get a hold of yourself. Why are you shouting? Have I not told you dozens of times before that the reason I do such magic is only to dupe people out of their money, people stupid enough to believe such things? In reality, these tricks have no worth. You can't go up against God. Whatever the fate of a man is cannot be overturned.

BASYE

Now what are we going to do? We are lost! Imagine if they were to discover what we did with the false stamps, with the counterfeit banknotes, and with Mirele. At the very least, we will be sent to jail.

BOBE

(With a smile) What do you mean?

BASYE

(Angry) You still think there is reason to smile, even as we lose our blood? What has your wisdom done for us? If you're so smart, then think up a way to get us out of this mess, a way to prevent them from coming. Work some of your magic, because we will not survive their coming.

BOBE

No, it is much too late. They are already en route. Do you know when they are supposed to arrive?

BASYE

A telegram that they sent yesterday asked us to meet them at a halfway point tomorrow, a few versts from here at the red tavern.

BOBE

Is that so? *(She takes a pinch of snuff and considers this for a moment and then jumps up with glee.)* Basye! I have it! I have hatched another plan! You'll see what Bobe Yakhne is capable of.

BASYE

(Ironically) What are you capable of? Eating? I already know that you're capable of such things.

BOBE

(Angry) Don't get rid of me just yet. At least hear me out first. And then you can speak your piece. *(She takes a pinch of snuff.)* When will they arrive? Tomorrow?

BASYE

Yes, tomorrow, so?

BOBE

Ahh, very good. Listen carefully. I'm going home now, and I'll send you a flask of liquor with Elyokum that I'll mix myself in my own lab. When you arrive at the Red Tavern, you'll undoubtedly have a drink all together to celebrate. Put a little of this liquor in their glasses, and when they drink it they'll fall asleep. *(She takes a pinch of snuff and sneezes.)*

BASYE

(Impatiently) Nuu. Say once and for all, what do we do once they're asleep?

BOBE

(Coughing, angry) They will fall asleep. *(Sneezes.)*

BASYE

If they see me there, they'll no doubt want me dead. Mirele will tell her father everything. I should preempt her and get angry with her.

BOBE

Don't be a fool! At that point they'll be just where I want them. No matter what Mirele says, if she curses you, rats you out, don't answer. Just give them that liquor to drink. They will grow exhausted and then fall asleep. Then I'll arrive with Uncle Elyokum with all of the instruments we need, including a ladder, which I'll use to climb up into the attic. *(She takes a pinch of snuff.)* When you hear my signal, you should also climb up into the attic. *(She coughs.)*

BASYE

(Impatiently) Nuu, tell me what happens at the end! What will happen when we climb up to the attic?

BOBE

(Angry) At that point, you will be in the attic. What don't you understand? We will not fall asleep up there. Instead, we'll light the entire tavern on fire, after which we'll descend by ladder as all those asleep inside will burn. And that will bring an end to the whole story.

BASYE

(Happy) Now I am finally convinced that you are a witch; no normal person could devise such a plan.

BOBE

(With a smile) You should have a pain in your big mouth. Only now do you get what I'm capable of? What do you think, I speak in vain? Don't keep me any longer. I need to get going and prepare everything . . . We must see an end to this. A good day to you, and do not forget all I've told you.

(Leaves, stage left)

BASYE

(She accompanies her to the door.) Good day, and a good year. Go in good health. And prepare yourself well. *(She turns around.)* It is a magic trick that will hit hard. But what can be done? Everyone values their own life more than ten lives of others.

Scene Two

(AVRAHAM enters, stage right)

AVRAHAM

Basye, are you ready for the journey to meet up with the children? How God is great for allowing me to see my children again . . .

BASYE

(With a sympathetic face) Oy, I would also like for them to see one another. *(To herself) Oyvavoy.* I already told you the hardships that I lived through for you. Things were so bad in your absence, I barely survived. And you know my nature. I sacrificed everything. Still, when you speak to her. she'll tell you otherwise; that I was horrible and I treated her badly and I became the worst of what people say about stepmothers. But you know the truth: that there is nothing I wouldn't do for my children. That I feel toward her like her real mother, maybe even more. Oh, if only I can just see her . . .

AVRAHAM

(Impatiently) Why say such things? It's foolish. Lets just get going. Every minute we stay behind feels like a year.

BASYE

But, Avraham, I will not go with you unless you promise me that you won't believe the things they say about me.

AVRAHAM

Don't speak such foolishness! What am I? Just a child? I understand. I understand what takes place between a stepmother and a stepchild. There are always disagreements, foolishness; I guarantee nothing will happen to you. I won't listen to any bad thing they say, nor will I believe anything. How can I believe anything bad about you?

(They exit.)

Scene Three

Entrance/Exit Eight

(A large road that cuts through a forest and over a hill. In the forest there is a tavern with two stories. The top story is made of wood, the bottom from red brick. It is nighttime. One can hear the crickets chirping, through a window in the tavern is a burning candle. From offstage one hears the approach of a horse-drawn carriage. Enter HOTSMAKH, MARCUS, and MIRELE.)

HOTSMAKH

Stay! *(He crawls from beneath and approaches the tavern; behind him, MARCUS and MIRELE.)* Ahhh, the red brick, The Red Tavern: here lives the red leaser who sells red liquor! *(He knocks on the door.)* Hey, red one, open up!

ZERAKH

(From inside with a loud voice) Who's knocking? Go knock yourself in the head!

HOTSMAKH

It's Hotsmakh! It's Hotsmakh; take a look at me, cook me a meal, or let the spirit take both of us to the devil! Open up; I want to get my second sidelock drunk.

ZERAKH

(From inside) Who on earth did you bring to me?

HOTSMAKH

Open up and you'll see what refined guests I brought you. You can live until you're ninety-nine and you still wouldn't have such refined guests. Now open up!

ZERAKH

Wait a minute. I'll just get a light.

HOTSMAKH

(Approaches MIRELE and MARCUS, who are walking around arm-in-arm the whole time.) Ahh, finally he puts the lights on. Soon he'll let us in. *(The lease holder opens the door and HOTSMAKH goes to him and takes him by the nose)* Ah here comes the red heifer: take a look at what fine guests I brought you. *(The leaseholder moves the light close to MIRELE and MARCUS and looks them over.)* Have you any good liquor?

ZERAKH

I sent my brother Chayim into town to fetch some good liquor.

HOTSMAKH

(Hits him over the head) What is red isn't white. I can't believe it. As soon as I bring him some refined guests, he's out of liquor *(ZERAKH reenters the tavern, and one hears a carriage approaching. HOTSMAKH rushes to the side and looks to and fro, speaking to himself.)* If I am not mistaken, our people are arriving. *(He looks again, carefully, and then turns to MIRELE and MARCUS, happy.)* Reb Avromtshe is coming.

MIRELE AND MARCUS

Father is coming? (*They run to the side of the inn where HOSTMAKH is looking out at the road.*)

Scene Four

(AVRAHAM comes in with BASYE and everyone embraces and kisses everyone except for BASYE.)

MIRELE

My beloved father! *(She embraces him.)*

AVRAHAM

Oh, my beloved child! *(He embraces her and weeps.)*

HOTSMAKH

(Looks at them and begins to weep.)

MARCUS

So, Basye, you arranged a beautiful wedding for me and Mirele.

BASYE

(She looks down, not meeting his gaze.) What person human being can say he has never made mistakes in life?

MARCUS

You consider someone who deals the way you deal a human being?

HOTSMAKH

Nor does a human being buy scarves as far back as Shavuos and not pay for them until now.

MARCUS

(Looks at her angrily) Very nice! Very nice, Basye!

HOTSMAKH

Aha, you see? Marcus also says that you don't deal very nicely.

AVRAHAM

(Approaches MARCUS and embraces him.) Now, children. I beg you to be grateful that God has helped us and we are all healthy and whole. I must ask you not to fight; remember how terrible things were.

HOTSMAKH

No, no. I'll never give in before Basye pays me the money she owes me for the handkerchiefs.

AVRAHAM

(As HOTSMAKH speaks he pulls MARCUS toward him and speaks to him quietly.) Don't start complaining about her now. We'll sort things out when we get home. *(Aloud)* Now, children, to celebrate our being together, we'll all have a quick drink together.

HOTSMAKH

The tavern keeper has no liquor. The red heifer sent his brother into town for some liquor.

AVRAHAM

No liquor? Maybe there is someone who can get us some wine?

BASYE

Take a look. I know I am terrible person, but I did worry about everyone here. Look. *(She takes out a flask of wine.)*

(Everyone enters the tavern, and in a few minutes the voices of MARCUS and HOTSMAKH are heard: "To life!" *It is silent for a few seconds, there is a clang of glasses and drinking.)*

<u>*Scene Five*</u>

(BOBE YAKHNE and ELYOKUM, outside the tavern)

BOBE

(Quietly) Elyokum. Go, take a look. Is it working?

ELYOKUM

Look through the window. There are cries from inside. *(They run and hide behind trees.)*

BOBE

Elyokum, go take a look. Is it working?

ELYOKUM

(He goes to the window and looks inside again.) Bobe, its dark in there; they're sleeping.

BOBE

Go and bar the door so they can't get out. And bring me the ladder with everything else we need. *(Elyokum brings a ladder and leans it against the building beneath the window of the attic.)* Hold the ladder. I can kill myself climbing up this thing. (*She shouts into the building.)* Basye, Basye, are you there?

BASYE

(Whispering) Yes!

BOBE

Come up to the attic. Elyokum get up here as well, with everything else we need.

Scene Six

(Offstage a horse-drawn wagon is heard.)

CHAIMETZ

This damn horse can't make it down a road. I've been schlepping after him the entire night. I am exhausted. This nag is already half dead. *(He arrives at the tavern and knocks on the door.)* Zerakh! Zerakh! Open up! I brought you the liquor you wanted. *(Shouts louder)* What happened to you in there? Did you croak? *(He looks to the side of the tavern and spots the ladder.)* Who left the ladder here? It's in the perfect place for a thief to see our geese in the attic. I am going to put it in its rightful place. *(He moves it and returns and knocks on the window.)* Open up in there! (*He notices the barred door.)* Who barred the door? *(He unbars the door and knocks harder and louder. He sees smoke and flames seeping out from behind the door.)* Zerakh! Zerakh! Open up! (Breaks open the door) Zerakh, come out! The tavern is on fire! *(Everyone runs outside: AVRAHAM, MIRELE, MARCUS, ZERAKH.)*

(BASYE, BOBE YAKHNE, and ELYOKUM are on the second floor that is now engulfed in flames. They break a window and look down but do not see the ladder. They stretch their arms out and call for help. "Rescue us!" but they are engulfed by the flames.)

AVRAHAM

(He notices the sorceress.) Aha, if she had any involvement in this, it is for the better. This is the sorceress's handiwork? Let them burn!

HOTSMAKH

What a miracle! The devil take me! Another second in there, and my beard would have been singed together with my left sidelock . . . The devil take me! *(They all burn. The oylem sing, pointing with their fingers.)*

WHAT HORRIBLE PEOPLE THEY ARE!
WE WON'T SAVE THEM, EVEN IF WE CAN . . .
LET THEM REALLY BURN;
SO THERE WILL BE NO MORE MISFORTUNE.
BURN AS IF IN HELL!
THE PARABLE? EVERYONE KNOWS IT!
HE WHO DIGS A GRAVE FOR ANOTHER
FALLS IN IT HIMSELF, ALONE!
GOD HAS PUNISHED THEM VERY WELL,
AND WE ARE PROTECTED FROM HIS WRATH!

(The curtain falls.)

Notes

1. *The Sorceress* was first performed in Odessa in 1878, the first operetta Goldfaden mounted on his return to the Russian Empire. He only published it in 1887 after securing a contract with the Warsaw-based Yiddish publisher, Boymritter and Gonshor. This translation is based on this first edition. Few and unremarkable changes were introduced to later editions.
2. That he wears his pants over his boots indicates that he is not Hasidic.
3. Basye wears a *shaytl*, a wig that qualified as a proper head covering for a pious Jewish woman. Shaytls emerged as a new accessory in fulfilling the requirement for married women to cover their heads around the middle of the nineteenth-century. Initially, some rabbis resisted this innovation and rabbis issued many contradictory and passionate responsa. These are collected in an anthology, *Dat yehudit ke-hikhlata* [The Jewish Faith According to Its Laws] (Jerusalem: Vad mishemeret ha-tsniut, 1973). About the eventual acceptance of the shaytl, see Leila Leah Bronner's "From Veil to Wig: Jewish Women's Hair Covering," *Judaism: A Quarterly Journal* 42.4 (1993).
4. Neither a dairy nor a meat product; from the dietary law that prohibits milk products to be eaten with meat products. Pareve products may be eaten with either.
5. Although the word *tkhine* came to be associated with women's Yiddish-language prayers, the word referred to any supplementary prayer that might be added to the daily liturgy in honor, for instance, of a festival.

6. The festival of Shavuot (lit. Weeks) falls in the Hebrew month of Sivan, fifty days after the second day of Passover. Originally a harvest festival, Shavuot also commemorates the giving of the Law (the Torah).

7. The sale of tobacco was regulated by the government and one needed a license to sell it.

8. Using false weights was a common way to dupe buyers, and the state tried to curb this practice.

9. Some believed that Russians knew some Yiddish, which thwarted the Jews' reliance on it for reliably private communication, so they used Hebrew instead. "And Moses fled" is a phrase from the book of Exodus, which was code for "Take flight; someone is after you." It originally refers to Moses's escape from Egypt.

10. A denomination of weight.

11. Meaning a weight that he could weigh the fabric against.

Appendix III
Excerpt from the Memoirs of Avrom Fishzon

The following excerpt is from the memoirs of Yiddish theater actor Avrom Fishzon, who was a pioneer of modern Yiddish performance in the Russian Empire (a rival and collaborator of Avraham Goldfaden). Even before the modern Yiddish theater gained real traction in 1876 and 1877 in Romania, Fishzon and Yisrolik Grodner, actor and impresario, traveled among cities in southern Russia to put on singing and vaudeville shows. On a chance encounter with Goldfaden after he had attended one of their shows, he gave them an operetta that he had not yet published called The Grandmother and the Granddaughter. *The work lent itself to a modest production since it required only four actors: a matchmaker, a lover, and two female leads, a grandmother and a granddaughter. Fishzon and Grodner were very excited by it and felt that it would allow them to develop the artistic reach of their work while growing their troupe. The lack of female actors was an impediment that might have kept them from their creative goals but also forced them into an unexpected area of a performance when they both took on the female lead roles themselves. Fishzon wrote his memoirs in Russian and published them in 1912. They were translated into Yiddish for publication in 1924 and 1925 in the New York–based* Morgn zhurnal.

(The following section is from January 2, 1925, "Men greyt zikh tsu der *Bobe mitn eynikl.*" ["We prepare for the production of *The Grandmother and the Granddaughter.*"])

Days after the departure of my grandfather and father I was sunk in thought and somewhat depressed. Yisrolik [Grodner] buzzed around with new ideas and plans. He wanted to somehow include "The Grandmother and the Granddaughter" in our repertoire so that our shows can take on at least the semblance of real theater. But where would we get ourselves a grandmother? And what about a granddaughter? Yisrolik looked around for possible actresses to play these roles but in vain. Proper young ladies would not consider it even for a moment and Yisrolik did not want to consider the underclass—not so much for his own sake but for mine: he knew that I wasn't about to consort with *who-knows-who*. We had already attracted a good bunch of hangers-on who were so passionate about us they would follow us to the ends of the earth. They sprung from Ysrolik's good pals, and members of his guild—but what good were they to us? We were in need of girlfriends and not boyfriends. We were in need of a grandmother and a granddaughter.

Meanwhile—by the way—we would sit, the two us, learning and reciting the roles of the two female characters and in a short time we knew them by heart—by heart and with every flourish, like a Jew knows his *Ashrey*. We would put scenes on for our buddies, showing them our newest goods. Yisrolik talked just like a grandmother, an elderly woman, and everyone rolled with laughter watching him. I tried duplicating the manner of the granddaughter, talking and singing, and our buddies enjoyed my performance too. At one point they said we should put it on in a theater, just shave our beards; but for them such a thing as Jewish law was small potatoes and that wasn't the case for me and Yisrolik. We still tried to find girls for the roles. . . . Zhiotmir did not have a grandmother or granddaughter for us.

An actor for the role of Tuvye the Matchmaker came to us almost as if he fell from the sky. We were in our room at the Berdichev Inn, a place where a lot of journeying wagon-drivers would overnight. *Vayehi ha-yom*, And it came to pass, a wagon pulled up in the courtyard with a big band of beggars, *shnorrers*, cripples, music box players, who would be loosed upon the town each one with their thievish tricks and skits to collect money. Up in our room, we hear a sweet singing voice from the courtyard. We open the window and see a tall Jew encircled by curious onlookers: wagon-drivers but also men and women and children. The lanky Jew sang so sweetly he bewitched us too. He was singing something from *takhanun* (supplicatory daily prayer) and the audience sprayed him with kopeks and even one gilden. When he finished we immediately invited him up to our place and gave him a drink and asked him about himself. The long man began telling us such incredible tales I was barely able to conceive of the things he was saying.

Finally Yisrolik asked him how much he would need to leave the group of beggars and work on a steady income from us.

"I couldn't settle for less than 10 rubles," he said, "It's me and my wife."

"Listen," Yisrolik responded, "It's a shame for a young man like you to rely on beggars-income. If you promise me you will forget them I'll give you the 10 rubles a week, and sign a contract with you for a year."

He jumped up to chase down his wife and tell her the good news but he was unfamiliar with Zhitomir. Instead, he spent the afternoon with us drinking and eating and telling us terrifying tales of the *shnorisher velt*, the world of beggars, that had our hair standing on end and how he fell in with the band of beggars, until night fell and through the windows of the houses we saw residents lighting fires in their stoves.

"We can make a true gentleman out of this guy," said Yisrolik to me. Yisrolik went over to a shelf and took down the script, *The Grandmother and the Granddaughter*, and gave it to David the Long telling him he should learn the part of "Tuvye the Matchmaker." He glanced through the script for his lines and after a few minutes put the script down and spoke the words almost by heart just as the script called for (he was a Litvak by birth, but it seems he sought to suppress his Lithuanian accent). I saw on Yisrolik's face that he was very happy.

When we were alone, Yisrolik said to me, you'll soon see how well the Lithuanian will pull off the role of Tuvye. Tomorrow I will take him around and buy him some new clothes and he'll become a *mentsh*. . . . To this end, Yisrolik woke David early the next morning and brought him around town. By the time I was up and sitting down for my tea, the two men walked in and I was hardly able to recognize David: he was dressed in clean clothes with a white collar and a new hat—a different man utterly and completely. Yisrolik surveyed him with eyes shining with happiness.

But where to get a grandmother? We sat and thought one day, two days, a whole week. One night we sat with our pals and Yisrolik asked me to read the part of the granddaughter. . . . When it came time in the book for the granddaughter to sing I brought my voice up to the highest tenor I could manage and it was an off-the-charts performance. Yisrolik was bewitched by the combination of my voice with that song and said to me: "You know what Alter-Avraham son of Fishl Fishzon? You will play the role of the granddaughter."

I surged with happiness and my feet began to do a jig.

"But how?" asked the others. "How could he be the granddaughter if she (Adele) must be a girl?"

"So what?" Yisrolik answered. "The Grandmother Yakhne must also be Jewish woman and I will play that role—and I'll play it with my beard!"

Everyone began to laugh, myself among them. But Yisrolik's face registered only seriousness and I knew he was a man who did everything he said he would. I won't stretch this out: the next morning he showed up with a big bundle of goods as well as a tailor and pointed me out to him: "This is my bride, my mademoiselle; the clothes I told you about must be sewn for him."

The tailor smiled big but what is the saying: "a story is no song and a theater is no bathhouse." The tailor took to the job of measuring me with his tape measure for three different garments; that is, act I, a Chasidic Sabbath dress from real silk material; for act II, an aristocratic dress according to the fashion of the day with a crinoline (an under-dress that comprised four or five metal hoops so that when you wore it you felt like a wheel) and for act III, a dress of the most expensive satin. After taking the measurements he needed, the tailor took the merchandise and promised that in five days he would return with everything ready.

"Now brother Fishzon, come with me," said Yisrolik.

When Yisrolik calls, one obeys I thought to myself. He dragged me into a wig shop where he had me fitted with a female wig with two braids almost long enough to reach my knees and without batting an eyelash he paid right then and there the 25 rubles for it. I was stunned. . . . Then he escorted me to the best shoe store in all of Zhitomir and proceeded to buy three pairs of ladies' shoes, each one matching one of my dresses. And then he threw in a variety of additions and flourishes: gloves, hankies, combs, a parasol, etc. I looked on in silence. When he saw me loaded down with packages after we had reached home Yisrolik said to me, "Nu brother, we are now ready."

I couldn't contain myself any longer: "But we have spent so much money!"

He answered me coolly. "Just learn your lines well and about everything else I will worry." . . .

And so I thought to myself, he must know what he is doing. We were already worried about costumes of the granddaughter but the grandmother—I saw no trace of one. I had heard Yisrolik imitate an old grandmother—without teeth, sucking her gums and with a hoarse voice—yes, I heard—but a grandmother I did not see.

The day the tailor was meant to arrive came and went and instead of the fifth day, it took eleven days for him to finish all of the work on the dresses. The day he arrived, Yisrolik sent for the wig-maker. They sat me before the mirror. The wig-maker measured me for the wig, combed my hair, fondled it, and I sit trying to stifle my laughter. Once she had done what she needed to, the tailor applied his *chumash* (five books of Moses) to me, measured me with the first dress, it fits well, the second dress is even better . . . and for the grand finale, I was costumed extravagantly in the third—a wedding dress with the garland and all other bridal accessories. Everyone was overcome, even the tailor remarked: "If I myself did not know that I made this for a boy I might never have known." There were drinks ready for a "*Lekhayim*" on the table and, finishing off our work, we all ate and drank.

I stole a glance at myself in the mirror: "Ha-ha-ha . . . a girl with all the adornments. It is too bad that father had already departed, he might have also had a bit of a laugh. I studied my face and what had become of me—of me, the little study-house boy . . . and reader of Torah. . . . But what's the use? What is it my grandfather used to say? "*Tsurik is nisht keyn skhoyre,* Backwards isn't sellable goods." Or what is it that Queen Esther uttered, "If I perish, I perish [whatever will be will be]."

While everyone enjoyed themselves, Yisrolik disappeared but returned minutes later a creature utterly transformed: dressed like an old woman—but to the very last detail. If you weren't able to detect his beard, you would have thought it was an old woman—no one could have recognized him. What can I tell you? The entire hotel was overcome by laughter. And especially about me—don't ask—and I am laughing until this very day. Au contraire: how can one *not* laugh about [all this]? There is, I suppose, the obvious reason: you cannot see how you yourself appears. . . .

Why did Yisrolik not shave his beard? That you will come to learn later on. Meanwhile, we spent a little more time in Zhitomir and performed before our friends to get their feedback, how we came off in our female clothing, and in this way we rehearsed the play.

From December 5, 1924

Bibliography

Goldfaden's works and autobiographical writings are listed separately. So are the memoirs referred to throughout the book and the plays by contemporary playwrights.

Archival Collections

Columbia University Libraries: Rare Book and Manuscript Library
  Hebrew Manuscripts
Museum of the City of New York, New York, New York
  Collection of Yiddish Theater, 1883–2005
Princeton University Library: Rare Books and Special Collections, Princeton, New Jersey
  Leonard L. Millberg Collection of Jewish American Writers
YIVO Institute of Jewish Research, New York, New York
  RG 8: Esther Rachel Kaminska Theater Museum Collection
  RG 24: Rabbinical School and Teachers' Seminary
  RG 289: Papers of Sholem Perlmutter
  RG 219: Papers of Avrom Goldfaden
  RG 1843: Guide to the Records of the Hebrew Actors' Union 1874–1986
New York Public Library, New York, New York
  Thomashefsky Collection
  Yiddish Theater Collection

Newspapers and Journals

In Hebrew

Ba-derekh
Ha-melits
Ha-magid

In Russian

Donskaya Pchela
Khar'kovskie Gubernskie Vedomosti
Moskovskii Dnevnik Zrelishch i Obiavlenii
Nikolaevskaya Vestnik
Novoe Vremya
Odesskii listok obiavlenii
Odesski Vestnik
Peterburgskaya Gazeta
Pravda (1879–1880)
Rasszvet
Russkii Evrei

Russkie Vedomosti
Sufler
Strekoza
Svetoch
Vedomosti Odesskovo gradonachalstva
Voskhod

In Yiddish

Arbeter shtime
Emes
Forverts
Der Hamer
Kol Mevasser
Der Moment
Literarishe bleter
Der Tog
Di varhayt
Yidishe velt
Yisrolik

An Annotated List of Published and Unpublished Libretti by Goldfaden Cited

The picture of surviving works by Goldfaden is complex: while some Goldfaden plays and libretti have long publication histories, others survive only in manuscript form. Included here are only the works cited or mentioned in this book with (a) the earliest performance dates; (b) the earliest editions until and inclusive of 1887 when the libretti of many of Goldfaden's full-scale theatrical works were published for the first time by the Baumritter and Gonsior Publishing House in Warsaw; and (c) translations into English when applicable. Also included are notes regarding discrepant editions or other miscellaneous details. For broader discussions of these works, see reference to them throughout the book. For a complete list of Goldfaden's publications, see Jacob Shatzky's "Bibliografye" in *Goldfadn-Bukh* (pages 80–96). For works that are about or refer to Goldfaden, see Ephraim H. Jeshurin's "Avrom Goldfaden: bibliografye" (for full citation, see below). The plays are listed chronologically in order of their performance.

The Grandmother With the Granddaughter or Bontsye the Wick-Layer in 3 acts with song
Earliest full-scale operetta with regular performance history dates to as early as 1875.
Di bobe mit dem eynikl. Odessa, 1879.
Di bobe mitn eynikl oder bontsye di kneytlekhlegerin: melodramma in dray akten mit gezang farfast. Warsaw, 1887. There are significant discrepancies between these two versions of the play. I quote from the earlier one.

The Recruits
First performed throughout Romania in 1877
"Di rekrutn," m.s. n.d., Abraham Goldfaden Collection; RG 219; Series I; folders 1 and 2; YIVO Institute for Jewish Research.
Never published.

The Contractor or the Russo-Turkish War
Performed in Romania around 1878 and Odessa in 1881.
"Der podriachnik," m.s. n.d. Abraham Goldfaden Collection; RG 219; Series I; folder 9 and 10; YIVO Institute for Jewish Research.
Never published.

The Mute Bride
First performed in Romania in 1878.
"Di shtume kale," m.s. n.d., Abraham Goldfaden Collection; RG 219; Series I; folder 4 and 5.
Never published.

Shmendrik: A Comedy in 3 acts with Song and Dance
First performed first in Romania in 1877.
Shmendrik: komedye in dray aktn mit gezang in tentse farfast fun a. Goldfaden. Odessa, 1879.
Published again by Baumritter and Gonsior in 1887. Many discrepancies between the first and later published editions.

Breindele the Cossack: Dream Play in 4 acts
First performed in Romania in 1877.
Goldfaden's adaptation of *Bluebeard.*
"Breindele Kozak" ms., n.d. RG 219; Series I; folder 3 and 4; YIVO Institute for Jewish Research.
Never published.

The Picky Bride or Pauperman and Hungerman: Melodrama in 4 Acts
Performed first in 1880 in Russia.
"Di Kaprizne Tokhter, oder Kabzenzon un Hungerman," m.s. 1881 melodrama in 4 acts, 5 scenes, St. Petersburg, 46 pgs., 4 pgs. Censored copy. RG 219; Series I; folder 8; YIVO Institute for Jewish Research.
Di kaprizne kale-moyd oder Kabtsenson et Hungerman: melodramma in fir akten un in finf bilder. Warsaw: Baumritter and Gonsior, 1887.

Sambatyon
Performed by 1881.
Sambatyon," m.s. Abraham Goldfaden Collection; RG 219; Series I; folder 23; YIVO Institute for Jewish Research.
Never published.

Neither Beh, Nor Moo, Nor Cock-a-doodle-Doo Or the Struggle Between Education and Fanaticism
First performed in 1878.
Never published in Yiddish or English. Published in Russian.
Ni Me, Ni Be, Ni Kukuriku. [Russian] Odessa, St. Petersburg: 1880, 1881.

Aunt Sosya
Performed first in Russia by 1880, published earlier with poetry.
"Di mume sosye" in *Di yidene: farsheydene gedikhte un teater in prost yudishn fun Avrom Goldfaden.* Odessa, 1869.

The Fanatic or The Two Kuni-Lemls: An Operetta in 4 acts and 8 scenes

Performed as early as 1881.

"Der Fanatik, oder Tsvey Kuni Lemelekh: operetta in 4 akten, 9 tsenes." Censored in St. Petersburg, 8 April 1882, 49 pgs. m.s. RG 219 YIVO Institute for Jewish Research; folder 20.

Der fanatik oder di tsvey Kuni-Leml: opereta in 4 akten un 8 bilder. Warsaw, 1887.

See a complete translation of this libretto by Joel Berkowitz and Jeremy Dauber in *Landmark Yiddish Plays*. Complete reference provided in bibliography.

The Sorceress: An Operetta in 5 acts and 8 scenes

First performed in Russia in 1878.

Di kishefmakherin (tsoyberin): operete in 5 akten un in 8 bilder. Warsaw, 1887.

English translation in Appendix II of this book.

Shulamis or the Daughter of Jerusalem: A musical melodrama in rhyme in 4 acts and 15 scenes

First performed in 1880 in Russia.

Shulamis oder bas-yerushalayim: eyne muzikalishe melodrama in raymen in 4 aktn un 15 bilder. Warsaw, 1886.

There is a reference to an earlier edition of the play published in Odessa in 1884 but no known copy survives.

*Shulamis oder bas-yerushalayim: eyne muzikalishe melodramma in ferzen un in 4 akten un 15 bilder.*Warsaw: Baumritter and Gonsior, 1887.

English translation in *Shulamis: A Critical Edition*. See below for full reference.

Doctor Almasada or The Jews of Palermo: Historical Operetta in 4 acts and 11 scenes

Performed first in 1882 in Russia.

Doktor Almasada oder di yudn in palermo: historishe opereta in 5 akten un in 11 bilder. Barbet nokh a daytshn roman. Warsaw: Baumritter and Gonsior, 1887.

Judah the Maccabean

Performed first in 1882 and 1883 in Russia.

"Yehuda hamakabi," m.s. n.d. Abraham Goldfaden Collection; RG 219; folder 33 and 34; YIVO Institute for Jewish Research.

Never published.

Bar Kokhba, the Son of the Star or the Last Days of Jerusalem: a Muscial Melodrama in rhyme in 4 acts and 14 scenes

Performed first in 1882 in Russia.

Bar Kokhba, der zun fun dem shtern oder di letste teg fun yerushalayim: a muzikalishe melodrama in raymen in 4 akten mit a prolog in 14 bilder. Warsaw: Alapin, 1887.

Uriel Acosta

First performed in 1882 in Russia.

A satire of the German play *Uriel Acosta* that the playwright Osip Lerner translated and staged during this era.

"Uriel Akosta," m.s. n.d., Abraham Goldfaden Collection; RG 219; folder 46 and 47; YIVO Institute for Jewish Research.

The Sacrifice of Isaac or the Overturn of Sodom and Gomorrah: Biblical Operetta in 4 acts and 40 scenes
First performed in the 1890s.
Akeydes yitskhak oder mahapakhes sdom un amore: biblishe operetta in 4 akten un 40 tsenes. Cracow: Fisher, 1897.

Rabbi Yoselman or the Decrees from Alsace: Historical Operetta in 5 acts and 23 scenes
First performed in Lemberg in 1890s.
Rebbe Yoselman oder di gzeyres fun elzas: historishe operetta in 5 akten un 23 bilder. Lemberg: Nekheles, 1891.

King Ahasuerus or Queen Esther a Biblical Operetta in 5 acts and 15 scenes
First performed in 1890s.
Kenig Akhashverush oder kenigin Ester: biblishe operetta in 5 akten un 15 tsenes. Lemberg: Nekheles, 1890.

Ben-Ami, Or the Son of His People
Performed in 1907 to 1908 in New York City.
"Ben Ami, oder Der Zun fun Zayn Folk: national-patriotic musical drama in 4 acts with prologue and epilogue, originally created and specially written for my people," m.s. RG 219; folders 42–44; YIVO Institute for Jewish Research.
This libretto was never published but most of the songs with annotations appear in Boris Thomashefsky's *Teater shriftn.* For complete reference, see below.

Goldfaden's Published Poetry Cited (first editions when available)

Tsitsim u-ferahim: asefat shirim shonim. Zhitomir: Bi-defuso Yitskhak Mosheh Bakst, 1865.
Di yidene: farsheydene gedikhte un teater in prost yudishn fun Avrom Goldfaden. Odessa, 1869.
Dos yudele: yudishe lider oyf prost yudisher shprakh. Warsaw: Bernas and Yakobi, 1893.
Published originally in 1866 and eight times more by 1903.

Published and Unpublished Works by Playwrights Other Than Goldfaden Cited, listed alphabetically

Solomon Ettinger's *Serkele*
Written and circulated in manuscript as early as the 1840s and mounted by Lerner in 1881.
Ettinger, Solomon. *Serkele : oder di yortsayt nokh a bruder; gor a nay teater-shtik in finef oyftsyen.* Vilna: Kletskin, 1925.
Complete English translation in *Landmark Yiddish Plays* (see full citation below).

Nikolai Gogol's *The Inspector*
First performed in 1881 in Russia.
Der revizor. Translated by Nahum Shaikevitsh. Odessa, 1883.

Avrom Baer Gottlober's *The Veil*
Gottlober, Avrom Baer. "Dos dektukh: tsvey khasenes in eyn nakht," *A.B. Gotlobers Yidishe verk.* VilnA: B. Kletskin, 1927.
Not performed; a model of Goldfaden's *The Two Kuni-Lemls.*

Karl Gutzkov's *Uriel Acosta*

First performed in Yiddish in 1880 in Russia as adapted by Joseph Lerner.

Uriel akosta: a tragedye in finf akten. Translated by Joseph Lerner. Warsaw: Y. Lidski, 1903.

Y. Katznellenbogen's *Rashi*

First performed in Russia in 1881.

Never published, no extant copy.

Joseph Lateiner's *The Apostate*

No record of performance in the press.

"Der meshumed," m.s. RG 8; folder 170514, YIVO Institute for Jewish Research.

Joseph Lateiner's *The Destruction of Jerusalem*

No record of performance in the press.

Khurbn yerushalayim: historishe opereta in finf aktn. Warsaw: P. Kantarovitsh, 1908.

Joseph Lateiner's *The Dybbuk*

Performed first in Russia in 1881.

Lateiner, Joseph, "Dibik." m.s. RG 1843 Series II; Folder 2.The YIVO Institute of Jewish Research.

Never published.

Maria Lerner's *The Chained Widow*

First performed in Russia in 1881.

Lerner, Maria, *Di agune.* (Odessa, 1883.

For a complete translation of this play, see *Women on the Yiddish Stage*, eds. Alyssa Quint and Miryem-Khaye Segal. Forthcoming from Syracuse University Press.

Osip Lerner's *Judith*

Yehudis: a historishe drama in fir akten un finf bilder. Warsaw: Y. Alapun, 1888.

Osip Lerner's *Uncle Moses Mendelssohn*

Der fetṭer Moyshe Mendelsohn a dramatishes bild in eyn aḳt: nokh dem daytshen far der yudisher bihne. Warsaw: Boymritter un Gonshor, 1889.

Moses Lilienblum's *The Bigamist*

Performed in 1881 in Russia.

Never published and no extant manuscript copy.

Silvio Pellico's *Esther in Ein Gedi*

"Ester in ein-gedi." Translated by Ben-Tsiyon, Benedikt. M. S. Yiddish Theater Collection; New York Public Library.

Eugene Scribe's *La juive* adapted for the Yiddish stage by Joseph Lerner

First performed in 1881 in Russia.

Zhidovka di yudn: a tragedye in fifn akten. Translated by Joseph Lerner. Warsaw: Y. Lidski, 1903.

Nahum Shaikevitsh's *The Jewish Nobleman*
First performed in Russia in 1880.
Shaikevitsh, Nahum Meir. Der yidisher porets: drama in finf akten in tsen kartines. Vilna: 1897.

Goldfaden's Memoirs

Each of Goldfaden's autobiographical pieces covers a brief period: from childhood to his time in Romania with a few references to the height of his career in Russia that is covered in this book. See the full discussion of Goldfaden's autobiographical works in chapter 1.

"Goldfadens autobiografishe materialn," *Goldfaden-bukh*. New York: Teater Muzey, 1926. Three autobiographical treatments (originally published from 1887 to 1901) and republished.
"Fun Shmendrik biz Ben-Ami: draysikyeriker epokhn-gang der antvikling fun mayn yidish teater-kind," *Arkhiv far der geshikhte fun yidishn teater un drama* (New York and Vilna: YIVO, 1930), 265–272.
"Der onfang funem yidishn teater," ed. Sholem Perlmutter. *Yidishe velt*, Philadelphia (April 1929–June 1929).

Memoirs and Contemporary Accounts Cited

Arranged alphabetically by actor's last name, this list includes either autobiographical or biographical treatments as well as important bibliographical details. The first source to consult on actors is Zylbercweig's *Encyclopedia* (*Leksikon*).

Abramsky, Avraham Hagershoni. *Bamat yitskhak o gey chizayon*. Bucharest, 1877.
Adler, Tsili with Yakov Tikman. *Tsili Adler dertseylt*. 2 vols. New York: Tsili Adler Foundation un Bukh-Komitet, 1959.
Adler, Jacob. "40 yor af der bine: mayn lebn-geshikhte un di geshikhte fun yidishn teater." *Di varhayt* (April 30, 1916– February 22, 1919).
For a translation of most of this memoir, see Lulla Rosenfeld-Adler, *Bright Star of Exile: Jacob Adler and the Yiddish Theatre*. See full citation below.
———. "Mayn lebensbashraybung." *Di naye varhayt* (March 14, 1925–July 18, 1925).
Amasya, Hersh. "Zikhroynes." *Yidish teater*. vol. 2. Warsaw: 1927, 200–13.
Blank, Leon. "Memoyren vegn Hurvits, Kessler un Mogulesco," *Forverts* (October 5, 1928–January 29, 1929).
Braginskaia, China.[Memoirs], *Der tog* (February 24, 1934–March 11, 1934).
For a translation of excerpts of this memoir, see *Women on the Yiddish Stage*. Full citation below.
Dineson, Jacob. *Zikhroynes un bilder: shtetl, kinder, yorn, shreyber*. Warsaw: Ahisefer, 1928.
Fishzon, Avrom. "Fuftsik yor yidish teater." *Morgn zhurnal* (November 21, 1925). Originally, Biblioteka "Teatra i Iskusstva,"12 (1913). Besides the excerpt included in Appendix II of this volume, see Barbara Henry's translation of his Russian memoirs published online by *The Digital Yiddish Theater Project*.
Granofsky, Reuven. "Yitskhok Yoyel Linetski: Zikhroynes." In *Pinkes* I (1927–28), 152.
Kafka, Franz. *Dearest Father: Stories and Other Writings*, translated by Ernest Kaiser and Eithne Wilkins. New York: Schocken Books, 1954.

Kalich, Bertha. (Written with Tsvi-Hirsh Rubinshteyn). Serialized in *Der Tog* (March 7, 1925–November 14, 1925). A translation of most of her memoir will be included in *Women on the Yiddish Stage*. Full citation below.

Kaminska, Ester-Rokhl. "Zikhroynes." *Der Moment* (October 8, 1926). A translation of most her memoir will appear in *Women on the Yiddish Stage*. Full citation below.

Kessler, Dovid. "Erinerungen fun dem idishn teater," *Der Tog* (January 14, 1917).

———. "Goldfaden, Lerner, Shaykevitsh," *Der Tog* (February 4, 1917).

Kobrin, Leon. *Erinerungen fun a yidishn dramaturg: a fertl yorhundert yidish teater in amerike*. vol. I. New York: 1925.

Kovner, Yitshak. *Sefer ha-matstref: ketave mehaposa maskili mehaapos hatish'ah esreh*. Jerusalem: Mosad Bialik, 1998.

Krishtol, L. "Avrom Goldfaden mit 35 yor tsurik: loyt a geshprekh mit dem shoyshpiler Kalmen Yoylvelir," *Goldfaden-bukh*. New York: Yiddish Theater Museum, 1926.

Lateiner, Joseph. Lateiner wrote a memoir that was lost or published in a periodical (that I could not track down) after the first volume of *The Encyclopedia of Modern Yiddish Theater* was put out. It is quoted substantially by Zylbercweig, see "Yoysef Latayner" in *Leksikon*, II: 964. See full citation below.

Librescu, Isaac. "Di zikhroynes fun yitskhak libresko, der initsyator fun goldfadens teater." Hintern farhang, ed. Zalmen Zylbertsvayg. New York, 1926.

———. "Mayne memuarn." *Teater figurn*. Buenos Aires: Elisheva, 1936.

Lieber, B. "Zikhroynes vegn avrom goldfadn." *Yivo bleter* XXXV (1951): 246.

Maiadovnik, M. "Mayne teater zikhroynes, farshribn fun L. Dushman, Shtern." Minsk. (1926): no. 1: 59–63, no. 2–3: 29–35; no. 4: 32–36. Maiadovnik only surfaces after Goldfaden leaves Russia but he joins Fishzon and Braginska's troupe.

Margolis, M. "Iz moikh vospomonanii." *Voskhod* (September 1895).

Mogulesco, Sigmund. [Oytobiografye] *Forverts* (January 13–February 24).

"Vi Mogulesko is gevorn Mogulesko." *Di Varhayt* (February 4–15, 1914). Memories of Mogulesco following his sudden death in 1914 by J. Adler, Y. Entin, L. Miller, G. Zelikovitsh, inter alia.

Osherovits, M. "Dovid Kessler," *Arkhiv far der geshikhte fun yidishn teater*. Vilna: YIVO, 1930.

Paperna, Avraham. *Zikhroynes*. Warsaw: Tsentral Farlag, 1923.

———. "Di ershte yidishe drame" [The first Yiddish drama]. *Pinkes: a fertlyoriker zhurnal far yidisher literaturgeshikhte, shprakhforshung, folklor un bibliografye* 2 (1929).

Perkoff, Isaac. *Avrom Goldfaden: mayne memuaren un zayne briv*. London: Jouques Printing Works, 1908.

Shaikevitsh, Nahum. "Dos yidishe teater." *Der menshenfraynd: beletristishe vokhnshrift (farlag N/M/ shaykevitsh*, nos. 5–32 (1891). Additional biographical treatment of Shaikevitsh was penned by his daughters.

Shigarin, N. D. *Russkie evrei za granitsei*. Kiev: 1878.

Teplitski, M. "Zikhroynes fun mayn lebn (fun der geshikhte fun yidishn teater)." *Shikago* (August–September 1931): 45.

Thomashefsky, Bessie. *Mayn lebns-geshikhte* [My Life Story]. New York: Varhayt, 1916.

Thomashefsky, Boris. *Mayn lebns-geshikhte* [My Life Story]. New York: Trio Press, 1937.

Vaynshteyn, B. "Di ershte yorn fun yidishn teater in odes un in New York: zikhroynes." In *Arkhiv far der geshikhte fun yidishn teater* 243–254. See full citation below.

———. "A kleyne meydele tret uf mit Avrom Goldfaden in Ades." *Forverts* (April 18, 1914): 3.
Zeifert, Moshe, "Di geshikhte fun yidishn teater," *Di yidishe bine* (New York, 1897).
Zilberbush, David Yeshayahu, *Mipinkas Zikhronotai*. Tel Aviv: va'ad yovel ha-shemonim, 1935.
For an excerpt of this memoir, see Lucy Davidowicz's *The Golden Tradition: Jewish Life and Thought in Eastern Europe*. See full citation below.

Collections of Documents

Shatzky, Jacob. *Goldfaden Bukh, aroysgegebn funem teater muzey*. New York: 1926.
———. *Arkhiv far geshikhte fun yidishn teater un drama. ershter band*. Vilna and New York: YIVO, 1930.
———. *Hundert yor Goldfaden [A Centenary of Abraham Goldfaden]*. New York: YIVO, 1940.

Bibliographies

Binevich, Evgenii Mikhailovich. *Evreĭskiĭ teatr v Peterburge: opyt istoricheskogo ocherka*. vol. 1 of series "Evrei Petergurga: stranits y istorii." St. Petersburg: Evreĭskiĭ obshchinnyĭt entr e Sankt-Peterburga, 2003.
———. *Istoriia evreiskogo teatra v rossii. 1876–1883:Annoturoviannaia bibliografia*. Moscow: Obshestvo evreiskoe naslednie, 1997.
Jeshurin, H. Ephim. *Avrom Goldfaden: Bibliografye*. New York: YIVO, 1963.
Shatzky, Jacob. "Goldfaden bibliografye." In *Goldfaden-bukh*. New York: Idisher Teater Muzey, 1926.

Books Cited

Ansky, S. Y. *Narod i kniga: opyt kharakterstiki narodnago chitatelia*. Moscow: L. A. Stoliar, 1914.
Aptroot, Marion, Efrat Gal-Ed, Roland Gruschka, and Simon Neuberg. *Yiddish Studies Today*. Dusseldorf: Dusseldorf University Press, 2012.
Avrutin, Eugene. *Jews and the Imperial State: Identification Politics in Tsarist Russia*. Ithaca, NY: Cornell University Press, 2010.
Bailin, Carole B. *To Reveal Our Hearts: Jewish Women Writers in Czarist Russia*. Cincinnati: Hebrew Union College Press, 2003.
Baker, Michael. *The Rise of the Victorian Actor*. London: Rowman and Littlefield, 1978.
Barantchok, Shmuel, ed. *Ṿilna, yerushalayim de-liṭa: dorot aḥaronim, 1881–1939*. Tel Aviv: Ghetto Fighters' House, 1981.
Baumgarten, Jean. *Introduction to Old Yiddish Literature*, translated and edited by Jerold Frakes. Oxford: Oxford University Press, 2005.
Beck, Evelyn Torton. *Kafka and the Yiddish Theater: Its Impact on His Work*. Madison: University of Wisconsin, 1971.
Berkovitsh, Yisroel. *Hundert yor yidish teater in rumenye 1876–1956* [One Hundred Years of Yiddish Theatre in Romania 1876–1956]. Bucharest: Edition Kriterion, 1956.
Berkovitz, Joel. *Shakespeare on the American Yiddish Stage*. Iowa City: University of Iowa Press, 2002.
Berkowitz, Joel. *Yiddish Theatre: New Approaches*. Oxford: Littman Library of Jewish Civilization, 2003.

Berkowitz, Joel, and Jeremy Dauber. *Landmark Yiddish Plays: A Critical Anthology*. Albany: State University of New York, 2006.

Berkowitz, Joel, and Barbara Henry, eds. *Inventing the Modern Yiddish Stage: Essays in Drama, Performance, and Show Business*. Detroit: Wayne State University Press, 2012.

Biale, David. *Eros and the Jews: From Biblical Israel to Contemporary America*. New York: Basic Books, 1992.

———, ed. *Cultures of the Jews: A New History*. New York: Schocken Books, 2002.

Bilov, S., and A. Velednitsky. *Avrom Goldfaden, Geklibene dramatishe verk*. Kiev: Melukhe farlag, 1940.

Borovsky, Victor, and Robert Leach. *A History of Russian Theatre*. Cambridge, MA: Cambridge University Press, 1999.

Bristow, Edward. *Prostitution and Prejudice: The Jewish Fight against White Slavery 1870–1939*. New York: Schocken Books, 1983.

Brooks, Peter. *The Melodramatic Imagination: Balzac, Henry James, Melodrama, and the Mode of Excess*. New Haven, CT: Yale University Press, 1976.

Buzgan, Khevel. *Hantbukh far aktyorn* [Handbook for Actors]. Warsaw: M. Karpinovitsh, 1937.

Cammy, Justin, Dara Horn, Alyssa Quint, and Rachel Rubinstein, eds. *Arguing the Modern Jewish Canon*. Cambridge, MA: Harvard University Press, 2008.

Clowes, Edith W., Samuel D. Kassow, and J. L. West. *Between Tsar and People: Educated Society and the Quest for Public Identity in Late Imperial Russia*. Princeton, NJ: Princeton University Press, 1991.

Darnton, Robert. *The Great Cat Massacre and Other Episodes in French Cultural History*. New York: Vintage Books, 1985.

Davidowicz, Lucy, ed. *The Golden Tradition: Jewish Life and Thought in Eastern Europe*. New York: Schocken Books, 1967.

Denk, Dovid. *Hinter di kulisn* [Behind the Scenes]. New York: Farlag vokhnblat, 1959.

Dobrushin, Yekhezkel. *Di dramaturgye fun di klasiker* [The Dramaturgy of the Classic Writers]. Moscow: Emes, 1948.

Dohrn, Verena. *Jüdische Eliten im Russischen Reich: Aufklärung und Integration im 19. Jarhundert*. Cologne: Bohlau, 2008.

Du Quenoy, Paul. *Stage Fright: Politics and Performing Arts in Late Imperial Russia*. Philadelphia: Pennsylvania State University Press, 2009.

Dynner, Glenn. *Men of Silk: The Hasidic Conquest of Polish Jewish Society*. Oxford: Oxford University Press, 2008.

Dynner, Glenn, and Francois Guesnet, eds. *The Jewish Metropolis: Essays in Honor of the 75th Birthday Professor Antony Polonsky*. Leiden: Brill, 2015.

Endelman, Todd, ed. *Jewish Apostasy in the Modern World*. New York: Holmes and Meier, 1987.

Edlin, William. *Velt-barimte operas*. New York: Hebrew Publishing Co., 1907.

Etinger, Shloyme. *Ale ksovim*, ed. Max Weinreich. Vilna, 1925.

Eynes, Avrom. *Fun lublin biz rige: goles-oprikhtn fun yidishn aktyor* [From Lublin to Riga: Wanderings of a Yiddish Actor]. Riga: self-published, 1940.

Finkel, Uri, and Nokhem A. Oyslender. *Goldfadn: materyaln far a biografye*. Minsk: Institut far Vaysruslendisher Kultur, 1926.

Fishman, Dovid. *The Rise of Modern Yiddish Culture.* Pittsburgh: University of Pittsburgh Press, 2005.

Frame, Murray. *School for Citizens: Theatre and Civil Society in Imperial Russia.* New Haven, CT: Yale University Press, 2006.

Frank, Stephen, and Mark D. Steinberg, eds. *Cultures in Flux: Lower-Class Values, Practices, and Resistance in Late Nineteenth Century.* Princeton, NJ: Princeton University Press, 1994.

Frankel, Jonathan. *Prophecy and Politics: Socialism, Nationalism and the Russian Jews 1862–1917.* Cambridge, MA: Cambridge University Press, 1984.

Freeze, ChaeRan Y., and Jay M. Harris, eds. *Everyday Jewish Life in Imperial Russia: Select Documents 1772–1914.* Waltham, NH: Brandeis University Press, 2013.

Frye, Northrop. *Anatomy of Criticism.* Princeton, NJ: Princeton University Press, 1957.

Ginzburg, Shaul M. *Historishe Verk: Yidishe Layden in Tsarishn Rusland.* vol. 3. New York: S. M. Ginsburg Testimonial Committee, 1937.

Goffman, Erving. *The Presentation of Self in Everyday Life.* New York: Anchor Books, 1959.

Goren, Arthur A. *The Politics and Public Culture of American Jews.* Bloomington: Indiana University Press, 1999.

Gordon, Judah Leib. *For Whom Do I Toil: Judah Leib Gordon and the Crisis of Russian Jewry.* Oxford: Oxford University Press, 1988.

Gorin, B. *Di geshikhte fun yidishn teater: tsvey toyznt yor yidish teater* [The History of the Yiddish Theater], 2 vols. New York: Max N. Mayzel, 1923.

Greenblatt, Stephen. *Shakespearean Negotiations: The Circulation of Social Energy in Renaissance England.* Berkeley: University of California Press, 1988.

Henry, Barbara. *Rewriting Russia: Jacob Gordin's Yiddish Drama.* Seattle: University of Washington Press, 2011.

Herzog, Elizabeth, and Mark Zborowski. *Life Is with People: The Culture of the Shtetl.* "Introduction," Barbara Kirshenblatt-Gimblett. New York: Schocken Books, 1995.

Horowitz, Brian. *Empire Jews: Jewish Nationalism and Acculturation in 19th- and Early 20th-Century Russia.* Bloomington, IN: Slavica, 2009.

Howe, Irving. *World of Our Fathers.* New York: Harcourt Brace Jovanovich, 1976.

Inbar, Donny. "A Closeted Jester: Abraham Goldfaden between Haskalah Ideology and Jewish Show Business." Doctoral Dissertation, Graduate Theological Union. Ann Arbor, MI: ProQuest, UMI, June 2007.

Krasney, Ariela. *Habadkhan* [The Wedding Jester]. Ramat Gan: Bar Ilan University Press, 1998.

Lahad, Ezra. *Hamahazot beyidishbamakor uvertirgum: dramatisheverk af yidish, originele un iberzetste: a bibliografye* [Original and Translated Yiddish Plays]. Haifa: n.p., 2001.

Landis, Joseph, ed. *Memoirs of the Yiddish Stage.* New York: Queens College Press, 1984.

Lederhendler, Eli. *Jewish Responses to Modernity: New Voices in America and Eastern Europe.* New York: New York University Press, 1994.

———. *Jewish Immigrants and American Capitalism 1880–1920.* Cambridge, MA: Cambridge University Press, 2009.

Lentricchia, Frank, and Thomas McLaughlin. *Critical Terms for Literary Study.* 2nd ed. Chicago: University of Chicago Press, 1995.

Levine, Lawrence W. *Highbrow/Lowbrow: The Emergence of Cultural Hierarchy in America.* Cambridge, MA: Harvard University Press, 1988.

Litvak, Olga. *Conscription Literature and the Search for Modern Russian Jewry*. Bloomington: Indiana University Press, 2006.

———. *Haskalah: The Romantic Movement in Judaism*. New Brunswick, NJ: Rutgers University Press, 2012.

Loeffler, James. *The Most Musical Nation: Jews and Culture in the Late Russian Empire*. New Haven, CT: Yale University Press, 2010.

Mahler, Raphael. *Hasidism and the Jewish Enlightenment: Their Confrontation in Galicia and Poland in the First Half of the Nineteenth Century*, translated from the Yiddish by Eugene Orenstein and from the Hebrew by Aaron Klein and Jenny Machlowitz Klein. Philadelphia: Jewish Publication Society of America, 1985.

Mazower, David. *Yiddish Theatre in London*. 2nd ed. London: Jewish Museum, 1996.

Meir, Natan. *Kiev, Jewish Metropolis: A History, 1859–1914*. Bloomington: Indiana University Press, 2010.

Meisel, Nakhman. *Noente un eygene: fun Yankev Dinezon biz Hersh Glik* [Our Own: From Yankev Dinezon to Hersh Glik]. New York: IKUF, 1957.

Mintz, Alan. *Banished from Their Father's Table: Loss of Faith and Hebrew Autobiography*. Bloomington: Indiana University Press, 1989.

Miron, Dan. *A Traveler Disguised: The Rise of Modern Yiddish Fiction in the Nineteenth Century*. Syracuse, NY: Syracuse University Press, 1996. Originally published by Schocken Books, 1973.

Moseley, Marcus. *Being for Myself Alone: Origins of Jewish Autobiography*. Stanford, CA: Stanford University Press, 2006.

Moss, Kenneth. *Jewish Renaissance and the Russian Revolution*. Cambridge, MA: Harvard University Press, 2009.

Nakhimovsky, Alexander, and Alice Stone Nakhimovsky. *The Semiotics of Russian Cultural History: Essays by Iurii M. Lotman, Lidia la. Ginsburg, Boris A. Uspenskii*. Ithaca, NY: Cornell University Press, 1985.

Nathans, Benjamin. *Beyond the Pale: The Jewish Encounter with Late Imperial Russia*. Berkeley: University of California Press, 2002.

Nathans, Benjamin, and Gabriella Safran, eds. *Culture Front: Representing Jews in Eastern Europe*. Philadelphia: University of Pennsylvania Press, 2008.

Niger, Shmuel, and Jacob Shatzky. *Leksikon fun der nayer yidisher literatur*. 8 vols. New York: Alveltlekhn yidishn kultur-kongres, faraynikt mit Tsiko. Published by the World Congress for Jewish Culture, combined with CYCO (Central Yiddish Cultural Organization), 1856–1881.

Orchan, Nurit. *Staking a Claim: Women Writing in the Yiddish Press in Tsarist Russia* [Hebrew]. Jerusalem: Zalman Shazar Center, 2013.

Parush, Iris. *Reading Jewish Women: Marginality and Modernization in Nineteenth-Century Eastern European Jewish Society*, translated by Saadya Sternberg. Lebanon, NH: Brandeis University Press, 2004.

Pawel, Ernst. *The Nightmare of Reason: A Life of Franz Kafka*. New York: Farrar, Straus and Giroux, 1992.

Perlmutter, Sholem. *Yidishe dramaturgn un teater-kompozitors* [Yiddish Playwrights and Theater Composers]. New York: YKUF, 1952.

Plokh, Serhii. *Unmaking Imperial Russia*. Toronto: University of Toronto Press, 2005.

Quint, Alyssa. "The Botched Kiss: The Literary Origins of the Yiddish Theatre." PhD thesis. Harvard University, 2002.

Reyzen, Zalmen. *Leksikon fun der yidisher literatur, prese, un filologye*. 5 vols. Vilna: B. Kletskin, 1926–1929.

Rosenfeld, Lulla Adler. *Bright Star of Exile: Jacob Adler and the Yiddish Theatre*. New York: Thomas Y. Crowell, 1977.

Roskies, David. *The Jewish Search for a Usable Past*. Indiana: Indiana University Press, 1999.

Sandrow, Nahma. *Vagabond Stars: A World History of Yiddish Theater*. Syracuse, NY: Syracuse University Press, 1996. Originally published in New York: Harper and Row, 1977.

Seidman, Naomi. *The Marriage Plot: Or, How Jews Fell in Love with Love, and with Literature*. Stanford, CA: Stanford University Press, 2016.

Sedgewick, Eve Kosofsky. *Between Men: English Literature and Male Homosocial Desire*. New York: Columbia University Press, 1985.

Senelick, Laurence, ed. *National Theatre in Northern and Eastern Europe, 1746–1900*. Cambridge, MA: Cambridge University Press, 1991.

Shatzky, Jacob. *Geshikhte Fun Yidn in Varshe*. vol. 2. New York: YIVO, 1948.

Shigarin, N. D. *Russkie evrei za granitsei* [Russian Jews Abroad]. Kiev: 1878.

———. *Sholem Aleichem: madrikh le-khayav ve-leyetzirotav* [Sholem Aleichem: A Guide to His Life and Work]. Tel Aviv: Publication of the Porter Institute for Poetics and Semiotics, 1980.

———. *Sifrut yidish be-polin: mekhkarim ve-iyunim historiim*. Jerusalem: Magnes, 1981.

Shmeruk, Chone, and Tuniansky, Chava, eds. *Di yidishe literatur in nayntsenten yorhundert: zamlung fun yidisher literatur-forshung un kritik*. Jerusalem: Y. L. Magnes 1993.

Sholem Aleichem. *Wandering Stars*, translated by Aliza Shevrin. New York: Viking, 2009.

Slobin, Mark. *Tenement Songs: The Popular Music of the Jewish Immigrants*. Urbana: University of Illinois Press, 1982.

Stites, Richard. *Serfdom, Society, and the Arts in Imperial Russia: The Pleasure and the Power*. New Haven, CT: Yale University Press, 2005.

Tarnopol, Osip. *Opyt sovremennoi i osmotritel'noi reformy v oblasti iudaizma v Rossii: razmyshleniia o vnutrennem i vnieshnem bytiya russkikh evreev*. Odessa, 1868.

Taruskin, Richard. *Defining Russia Musically*. Princeton, NJ: Princeton University Press, 1997.

Todd, William Mills III. *Fiction and Society in the Age of Pushkin: Ideology, Institutions, and Narrative*. Cambridge, MA: Harvard University Press, 1986.

Tsitron, Sh. L. *Dray literarishe doyres: zikhroynes vegn yidishe shrifshteler* [Three Literary Generations]. Vilna: Sh. Shreberk, 1920.

Veidlinger, Jeffrey. *The Moscow State Yiddish Theater: Jewish Culture on the Soviet Stage*. Bloomington: Indiana University Press, 2003.

———. *Jewish Public Culture in the Late Russian Empire*. Bloomington: Indiana University Press, 2009.

Weissler, Chava. *Voices of the Matriarchs: Listening to the Prayers of Early Modern Jewish Women*. Boston: Beacon Press, 1998.

Weiskopf, Michael. *The Veil of Moses: Jewish Themes in Russian Literature of the Romantic Era*, translated by Lydia Wechsler. London: Brill, 2012.

Weitzner, Jacob. *Sholem Aleichem in the Theater*. Madison, NJ: Fairleigh Dickinson University Press, 1994.

Wengeroff, Pauline. *Rememberings: The World of a Russian-Jewish Woman in the Nineteenth Century*, translated by Henny Wenkar and edited with an afterword by Bernard D.

Cooperman. Studies and Texts in Jewish History and Culture 9. Potomac: University Press of Maryland, 2000.

Werses, Shmuel. *Yiddish Translations of Ahavat Zion by Abraham Mapu* [Hebrew]. Jerusalem: Akademon Press, 1989.

Zipperstein, Steve. *The Jews of Odessa: A Cultural History, 1794–1881*. Stanford, CA: Stanford University Press, 1986.

Zylbercweig, Zalmen ed. *Leksikon fun yidishn teater.* Volume I, New York, 1931; Volume II, Warsaw, 1934; Volume III, New York, 1959 (co-edited with Jacob Mestel). Volume IV, New York, 1963; Volume V, Mexico City, 1967; Volume VI, Mexico City, 1969.

———. *Avrom Goldfaden un Zigmunt Mogulesko*, Buenos Aires: Elisheva, 1936.

———. *Teater-mozaik*. New York: Itshe Biderman, 1941.

Index

Italicized page numbers indicate illustrations.

ALYSSA QUINT is Vilna Collections Scholar-in-Residence at YIVO Institute for Jewish Research. She is editor (with Justin Daniel Cammy, Dara Horn, and Rachel Rubinstein) of *Arguing the Modern Jewish Canon*. She is also a member of the Digital Yiddish Theatre Project.

www.ingramcontent.com/pod-product-compliance
Lightning Source LLC
LaVergne TN
LVHW010352080826
844660LV00004B/257
9780253038616